Costing

AN INSTRUCTIONAL MANUAL

T. LUCEY, M.Soc.Sc, F.C.M.A., F.C.C.A. J.Dip.M.A.
Head of the School of Business and Management at the
Polytechnic Wolverhampton.

Terry Lucey *has also written Quantitative Techniques
and Management Information Systems in this series.*

D.P. PUBLICATIONS
16 Bere Close
Winchester, Hants.
1981

ACKNOWLEDGEMENTS

Examination Questions

The author would like to express thanks to the following for giving permission to reproduce past examination questions:

Institute of Chartered Accountants in England and Wales (ICA)

Association of Certified Accountants (ACCA)

Institute of Cost and Management Accountants (ICMA)

Chartered Institute of Public Finance and Accountancy (CIPFA)

Each question used is cross referenced to the appropriate Institute or Association, the title of the paper and the date of the examination.

TERMINOLOGY

A major objective of the study of any technical subject, like accounting or costing, is to gain familiarity with the precise definitions of the technical terminology used. The terminology adopted in this manual is based on the 'Terminology of Management and Financial Accountancy' published by the ICMA. Appropriate definitions have been reproduced from the Terminology, by kind permission of the Institute of Cost and Management Accountants.

ISBN 0 905435 18 4
Copyright T. LUCEY © 1981

Reprinted 1982

Printed in Great Britain by
Spottiswoode Ballantyne Ltd.
Colchester, Essex.

Preface

AIMS OF THE MANUAL

1. This manual is designed to provide a thorough understanding of the theory and practice of cost accountancy. It is particularly relevant for;

a. Students preparing themselves for the examinations of the following bodies; Institute of Chartered Accountants, Association of Certified Accountants, Institute of Cost and Management Accountants, Chartered Institute of Public Finance and Accountancy and the Association of Technicians in Finance and Accounting.

b. Students on Foundation Courses in Accounting, Degree and Diploma Courses in Accounting and Business Studies and Students on Business Education Council (BEC) courses.

c. Managers and others in industry, commerce, local authorities and similar organisations who wish to gain a working knowledge of the principles and processes of cost accountancy.

SCOPE OF THE MANUAL

2. The manual covers in a comprehensive fashion the principles, techniques and methods involved in cost accountancy.

The manual does not cover all the more advanced topics found in some Management Accounting Syllabuses, which will be covered in a subsequent manual. However, because there are many overlaps between Cost and Management Accounting, topics common to both are included in this manual. Examples include; budgetary control, standard costing and marginal costing. Whatever the intended final level of study, thorough knowledge of the basics of cost accounting is an essential requirement. This point is stressed again and again in Examiner's Reports.

In the first part of the manual there is detailed coverage of the objectives, principles, techniques and methods of cost accountancy relating to the analysis and gathering of costs and of cost ascertainment. The second part of the manual concentrates upon the use of cost information for planning, control and decision making. At each stage, concepts are illustrated by practical examples and placed into context so that the reader is aware of the importance and relationships of the various aspects of costing.

TEACHING APPROACH

2. The manual has been written in a standardised format with numbered paragraphs, end of chapter summaries, with review questions and examination questions at the end of each chapter. This approach has been tested and found effective by thousands of students and the manual can be used for independent study or in conjunction with tuition at a college.

HOW TO USE THE MANUAL EFFECTIVELY

3. For ease of study the manual is divided into self contained chapters with numbered paragraphs. Each chapter is followed by *self review* questions, cross referenced to appropriate paragraph(s). You should attempt to answer the self review questions *unaided* then check your answer with the text.

In addition, each chapter has one or more *examination* type questions with a suggested solution, which includes notes on approach and on particular points of difficulty. Naturally examination questions are often wide ranging and include material covering more than one chapter. They are however placed at an appropriate point in the manual so that if the previous chapters have been studied all the necessary material will be available. The examination questions have mostly been drawn from past professional examinations and have been carefully selected not merely to repeat the material in the chapters but to extend knowledge and understanding. They should be considered an integral part of the manual. *Always* make some attempt at the question before reading the solution. It will be noted that some chapters have many more examination questions than others. This reflects the weighting given to the particular topic by the various professional bodies in their examinations.

In addition to the end of chapter questions, which have solutions, there is an Appendix to the manual which contains a further selection of professional examination questions, without answers. These can be used by lecturers for assignments and class work when the manual is being used as a course text or as extra revision when the manual is being used for independent study.

SEQUENCE OF STUDY

4. The manual should be studied in the sequence of the chapters. The sequence has been arranged so that there is a progressive accumulation of knowledge and any given chapter either includes all the principles necessary or draws upon a previous chapter(s).

NOTE TO REPRINTED EDITION 1982

5. Service department cost reallocation may well, in practice, be carried out with the aid of a computer. In view of this, and the widespread use of microcomputers/terminals in colleges and polytechnics, case material including a program is reproduced at the back of the book for teaching purposes i.e. to help student understanding by illustrating the subject matter in a realistic way.

The program, whilst written and tested on a Commodore Pet microcomputer, can easily be modified by computer departments/individuals to run on other microcomputers using cassette, or floppy disc, or a time sharing system.

Contents

1 What is Costing?

INTRODUCTION

1. This chapter provides some basic definitions, explains the purpose of cost accounting, its relationship to financial and management accountancy and provides an introduction to the whole manual.

COST ACCOUNTING – DEFINITION

2. "The application of accounting and costing principles, methods and techniques in the ascertainment of costs and the analysis of savings and/or excesses as compared with previous experience or with standards." *Terminology.*

Detailed explanation of the principles, methods and techniques used in cost accounting form the basis of subsequent chapters in this manual.

DEVELOPMENT OF COST ACCOUNTING

3. Ever since the use of money replaced barter, people have been concerned with costs. However, it was the concentration of manufacturing facilities into factories which gave impetus to the development of recognisable costing systems. Whilst the early developments were almost entirely related to manufacturing concerns, nowadays costing is used very widely indeed; in hospitals, transport undertakings, local authorities, offices, banks as well as in every manufacturing concern.

THE PURPOSE OF COSTING

4. The cost accounting system of any organisation is the foundation of the internal financial information system. Management need a variety of information to plan, to control and to make decisions. Information regarding the financial aspects of performance is provided by the costing system. Examples of the information provided by a typical costing system and how it is used are given in the following table.

Information provided by Costing System	Possible uses by Management
Cost per unit of production or for a process	As a factor in Pricing Decisions, Production Planning and Cost Control.
Cost of running a section, department, or factory	Organisational planning, cost control,
Wage costs for a unit of production or per period of production	Production planning, decisions on alternative methods, wages cost control.
Scrap/Rectification costs	Material cost control, production planning.
Cost behaviour with varying levels of activity	Profit planning, make or buy decisions, cost control.

•
•

•
•

EXAMPLES OF COSTING INFORMATION AND USES   Table 1

Note:

1. The examples given of uses are not mutually exclusive and it is common to find cost information being used for purposes other than those shown above.

2. The table provides a few examples only, in practice much more information is produced and used.

3. In most cases the usefulness of costing information is enhanced when the actual results and costs are compared to some target or standard figure.

COSTING MUST BE USEFUL

5. It cannot be emphasised too strongly that if the information produced by the costing system is not useful for managerial decision making, for control or for planning, then it has no value and should not be prepared. To ensure its usefulness the following factors should be considered:

a. Is the costing system appropriate to the organisation and the manufacturing process?

b. Do the reports, statements and analyses produced by the costing system contain the relevant information for the intended purpose?

c. Are the reports and statements produced at appropriate intervals and early enough to be effective?

d. Are they addressed to the person responsible for planning/decision making/ control?

e. Is the information produced in a relevant form and to a sufficient degree of accuracy for the intended purpose?

It follows from these factors that every costing system will, in certain respects, be unique, because it must be designed to suit the particular organisation, products and processes and personalities involved.

COSTING AND MANAGEMENT ACCOUNTING

6. The definition of management accounting is: "The application of professional knowledge and skill in the preparation and presentation of accounting information in such a way as to assist management in the formation of policies in the planning and control of the undertaking." *Terminology.*

It will be seen that there are similarities between the objectives of both management and cost accounting and indeed in practice there is no true dividing line. In general, management accounting is wider in scope and uses more advanced techniques. However, a fundamental requirement for management accounting is the existence of a sound costing system to provide basic data. Without this, sophisticated techniques will be useless. Both management accounting and cost accounting are in the main concerned with the provision of information (often in great detail) for internal planning, control and decision making purposes with considerable emphasis on the costs of functions, activities, processes, and products.

COSTING AND FINANCIAL ACCOUNTING

7. Financial accounting can be defined as: "The analysis, classification and recording of financial transactions, and the ascertainment of how such transactions affect the performance and financial position of a business." *Terminology.*

Financial accounting originated to fulfill the stewardship function of businesses and this is still an important feature. Most of the external financial aspects of the organisation, e.g. dealing with Accounts Payable and Receivable, preparation of final Accounts etc., are dealt with by the financial accounting system. Of course internal information is also prepared, but in general it can be said that financial accounting presents a broader, more overall view of the organisation with primary emphasis upon classification according to type of transaction (e.g. sales, purchases) and type of expense (e.g. salaries, materials) rather than the cost and management accounting emphasis on functions, activities, products and processes and on internal planning and control information.

SUMMARY OF RELATIONSHIPS BETWEEN COST AND MANAGEMENT AND FINANCIAL ACCOUNTING

8. The objectives of the various facets of accounting have been given above and the differences discussed. However, it must be realised that they all form part of the financial information system of an organisation and in many organisations the various facets are totally integrated with no artificial divisions between them.

OVERVIEW OF COSTING

9. Having defined cost, management and financial accounting and discussed the relationships between them, it is now possible to show more detail of cost accounting. The diagram (next page) summarises the major parts of the cost accounting process and shows in diagrammatic form how data is transformed into information. The rest of the manual provides detailed explanations for each of the elements in the diagram.

SUMMARY

10. a. Cost accounting is concerned with the ascertainment and control of costs.

b. The purpose of cost accounting is to provide detailed information for control, planning and decision making.

c. To be of use, costing information must be appropriate, relevant, timely, well presented and sufficiently accurate for the purpose intended.

d. Cost accounting and management accounting are closely related.

e. The emphasis of financial accounting is upon classification by type of transaction and type of expenditure rather than the functional analysis of cost accounting.

f. Cost, financial and management accounting all contribute to the financial information system of an organisation and increasingly in practice are totally integrated.

POINTS TO NOTE

11. a. Cost and financial information is not the only information required for management decision making, but it is usually an important if not a crucial factor.

b. Decision making is concerned with the future and with future costs and revenues. Cost accounting, which is based on historical data, can nevertheless provide some guide to future costs and is frequently a critical part of the information upon which a decision is made.

c. Because there is no real dividing line between cost and management accounting, many of the topics introduced in this manual, particularly in the latter part, are equally relevant to students studying costing or management accountancy.

3

OVERVIEW OF COSTING

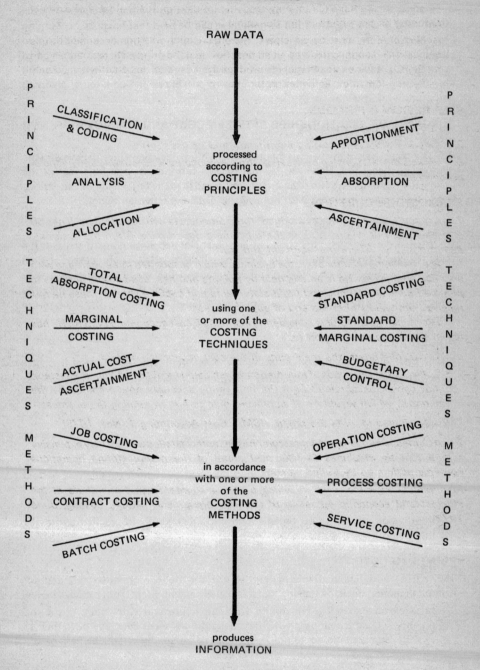

RAW DATA

P R I N C I P L E S

CLASSIFICATION & CODING

ANALYSIS

ALLOCATION

processed according to COSTING PRINCIPLES

APPORTIONMENT

ABSORPTION

ASCERTAINMENT

P R I N C I P L E S

T E C H N I Q U E S

TOTAL ABSORPTION COSTING

MARGINAL COSTING

ACTUAL COST ASCERTAINMENT

using one or more of the COSTING TECHNIQUES

STANDARD COSTING

STANDARD MARGINAL COSTING

BUDGETARY CONTROL

T E C H N I Q U E S

M E T H O D S

JOB COSTING

CONTRACT COSTING

BATCH COSTING

in accordance with one or more of the COSTING METHODS

OPERATION COSTING

PROCESS COSTING

SERVICE COSTING

M E T H O D S

produces INFORMATION

d. Cost and management accountancy is essentially for internal purposes. Financial accountancy is for stewardship purposes and is the basis of external reporting as prescribed in the Companies Act, 1980.

e. Not all of the costing principles, techniques and methods described in this manual will be applicable to a given firm. Some of the principles, techniques and methods are the basis of regularly produced information, whilst others may only be used in providing information for 'one off' decisions.

SELF REVIEW QUESTIONS

1. Define cost accounting. (2)

2. Give 6 examples of costing information and its uses. (4)

3. What is the relationship between costing, management accounting and financial accountancy? (6 & 7)

EXAMINATION QUESTIONS

1. A manufacturing company produces three products in two departments. It has 60 employees, 20 of whom work in the machining department, 30 in the assembly department and 10 are management and staff.

The managing director owns the business which he founded three years ago with only five employees. He is an engineer by training and has relied on the auditors to prepare half yearly trading and profit statements and balance sheets. These he has received ten weeks after the end of each half year.

The managing director is considering installing a cost accounting system. He has asked you to prepare a report to:

a. describe briefly the main aims of the cost accounting system;

b. list six specific types of information which could be obtained from the system, that cannot be obtained from the half yearly accounts now prepared by the auditors, which would be of significant help to him in running the business.

You are required to write the report. (ICMA, Cost Accounting 1, Nov. 1979)

2. A domestic appliance manufacturer has recently installed several very expensive semi-automatic machines to take over some of the manufacturing operations currently performed by skilled workers.

Required: Outline the ways in which a cost accountant could contribute to the efficient and economic operation of the new equipment. (ACCA, Costing, June 1979).

2 The Framework of Cost Accounting

INTRODUCTION

1. This chapter gives further basic definitions and explains the fundamentals of cost ascertainment.

A COST

2. This may be defined as:

> "The amount of expenditure (actual or notional) incurred on, or attributable to, a specified thing or activity."

Terminology.

It will be clear from a study of this definition that it relates to past costs which are the basis of cost ascertainment. At the simplest level, costs include two components, quantity used and price, i.e.

$$cost = quantity\ used \times price.$$

COST UNITS

3. Costs are always related to some object or function or service. For example, the cost of a car, a haircut, a ton of coal etc. Such units are known as cost units and can be formally defined as "A quantitative unit of product or service in relation to which costs are ascertained." *Terminology*

The cost unit to be used in any given situation is that which is most relevant to the purpose of the cost ascertainment exercise. This means that in any one organisation numerous cost units may be used for particular parts of the organisation or for differing purposes.

For example, in a factory manufacturing typewriters the following cost units might be used in the cost accounting system.

Cost Unit	Used for
a typewriter	production cost ascertainment
kilowatt-hours	electricity cost ascertainment
computer minutes of operation	computer running cost ascertainment
tonne-miles	transport cost ascertainment
canteen meals	catering cost ascertainment

Cost units may be *units of production*, e.g. tonnes of cement, typewriters, gallons of beer, or *units of service*, e.g. consulting hours, number of invoices processed, patient nights, kilowatt-hours, etc. They may be *identical* units as in the above examples, or they may be *dissimilar* as in a jobbing engineering factory where the cost unit will be the JOB or BATCH, each of which will be costed individually.

DIRECT COSTS

4. Costs may be classified in numerous ways, but a fundamental and important method of classification is into direct and indirect costs. Direct costs (comprising direct material costs, direct wages cost and direct expenses) are those costs which can be directly identified with a job, batch, product or service. Typical examples are

Direct materials	— the raw materials used in a product, bought in parts and assemblies incorporated into the finished product.
Direct wages or Direct labour cost	The remuneration paid to production workers for work directly related to production, the salaries directly attributable to a saleable service (audit clerk's salaries for example).
Direct expenses	— Expenses incurred specifically for a particular product, job, batch or service; royalties paid per unit for a copyright design, plant or tool hire charges for a particular job or batch.

It follows therefore that direct costs do not have to be spread between various categories because the whole cost can be attributed directly to a production unit or saleable service.

The total of direct costs is known as PRIME COST,

i.e. DIRECT MATERIAL + DIRECT LABOUR + DIRECT EXPENSES = PRIME COST

Note:

Invariably when direct costs are mentioned, the costing of production cost units is involved. Technically this need not be so, but unless the context of the question clearly points to some other conclusion, any reference to direct costs should be taken to refer to production cost units.

INDIRECT COSTS

5. All material, labour and expense costs which cannot be identified as direct costs are termed indirect costs. The three elements of indirect costs, indirect materials, indirect labour and indirect expenses are collectively known as OVERHEADS. Typical examples of indirect costs in the production area are the following:

INDIRECT MATERIALS	Lubricating oil, stationery, consumable materials, maintenance materials, spare parts for machinery, etc.
INDIRECT LABOUR	Factory supervision, maintenance wages, storemen's wages, etc.
INDIRECT EXPENSES	Rent and rates for the factory, plant insurance, etc.

INDIRECT MATERIAL + INDIRECT LABOUR + INDIRECT EXPENSES = OVERHEADS

Note:

In practice overheads are usually separated in categories such as Production overheads, Administration overheads, Selling overheads. The above are examples of Production overheads.

COST BUILD-UP

6. Having defined direct and indirect costs, the framework of cost build-up can be shown thus:–

DIRECT MATERIAL   INDIRECT MATERIAL

+   +

DIRECT LABOUR   =   PRIME COST   INDIRECT LABOUR = OVERHEADS

+   +

DIRECT EXPENSE   INDIRECT EXPENSES

PRIME COST + OVERHEADS = TOTAL COST

Note:

The above shows cost ascertainment at its most basic. Additional refinements are dealt with later in the manual.

CONVERSION COST

7. This is the term used to describe the costs of converting purchased materials into finished products.

It is thus total production cost minus material cost, i.e. the sum of direct wages, direct expenses and absorbed production overhead. The above is the definition given in *Terminology*, but students should be aware that alternative interpretations exist. For example, economists define conversion cost as total cost less material costs, i.e. all overheads are included, not just production overheads.

Alternatively, the term conversion cost is used to describe the cost of converting materials from one stage of manufacture to the next stage which need not be the finished state.

ADDED VALUE

8. This is the increase in market value of a product excluding the costs of bought out materials and services. It is thus equivalent to the economist's conversion cost plus profit. Added value is an important concept and considerable research has been undertaken into methods of incorporating added value concepts into internal and external accounting statements. Added value helps to highlight the relative efficiency of the firm without the analysis being obscured by external input costs which are largely uncontrollable.

THE BUILD-UP OF OVERHEADS

9. Overheads invariably include a large number of types of indirect costs so that the build-up of overheads is a more complicated process than the calculation of prime cost which merely consists of direct costs clearly related to the cost unit being produced. To understand this process, three further basic costing definitions are required, i.e. cost centre, cost allocation and cost apportionment.

COST CENTRE

10. 'A location, person or item of equipment (or group of these) in respect of which costs may be ascertained and related to cost units'. *Terminology.*

Typical examples of cost centres are: The Plating shop, The Works Office, The 1000 ton Power Press, The Milling Machines (consisting of 20 similar machines), Sales Representatives, Invoicing Section, Inspection, etc. In practice a cost centre is simply a method by which costs are gathered together, according to their incidence, usually by means of cost centre codes. Thus a purchase of carbon paper for use in the Invoicing Section would have a code representing say Office sundries – 457, and a code representing the Invoicing section as a cost centre, say 303, and would be coded —

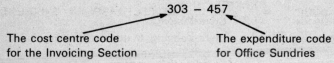

303 — 457

The cost centre code
for the Invoicing Section

The expenditure code
for Office Sundries

Similarly another purchase of carbon paper but for use in the Works Office (cost centre code 106) would be coded

106 — 457

Cost centre code
for Works Office

Expenditure code for
Office Sundries

COST ALLOCATION

11. 'The allotment of whole items of cost to cost centres or cost units'. *Terminology.*

The key part of this definition is 'whole items of cost'. Where the whole of a cost, without splitting or separation, can be clearly identified with a cost centre or cost unit, then it can be allocated (via the cost accounting coding system) to that cost centre or cost unit. It follows that direct costs can be allocated to particular cost units or groups of particular cost units, but cost allocation can, of course, apply equally to indirect costs. The examples shown in Para. 10 are examples of cost allocation of an indirect material cost.

COST APPORTIONMENT

12. Frequently it is not possible to identify the whole of cost with one cost centre and it is necessary to split a cost over several cost centres on some agreed basis. A classic example is that of Rates which are levied upon the premises as a whole, but which, for internal cost ascertainment purposes, need to be shared or apportioned between the cost centres. The basis normally used for Rates being the floor area occupied by the various cost centres. The formal definition of cost apportionment is:

'The allotment to two or more cost centres of proportions of common items of cost on the estimated basis of benefits received.' *Terminology.*

The basis upon which the apportionment is made varies from cost to cost. The basis chosen should produce, as far as possible, a fair and equitable share of the common cost for each of the receiving cost centres. The choice of an appropriate basis is a matter of judgement to suit the particular circumstances of the organisation and wherever possible there should be a cost/cause relationship.

Typical bases used are as follows:

Basis	Costs which may be apportioned on this basis
Floor Area	Rates, Rent, Heating, Cleaning, Lighting, Building Depreciation
Volume or Space Occupied	Heating, Lighting, Building Depreciation
Number of Employees in each Cost Centre	Canteen, Welfare, Personnel, General Administration, Industrial Relations, Safety

Book (or Replacement) Value
of Plant, Equipment, Premises,   Insurance, Depreciation
etc.

Stores Requisitions   Store-Keeping

Weight of Materials   Store-Keeping, Materials Handling

The process of apportionment is an essential part of the build-up of overheads, because many indirect costs apply to numerous cost centres rather than just to one.

Note:

Although cost apportionment is a normal part of the cost ascertainment process, it must be realised that it is a convention only and costs so apportioned are not verifiable.

OVERHEAD ABSORPTION

13. Direct costs, by definition, are readily identifiable to cost units, but overheads, which are often considerable, cannot be related directly to cost units, but nevertheless form part of the total cost of a product. Accordingly overheads must be shared out in some equitable fashion among all of the cost units produced. The process by which this is done is known as OVERHEAD ABSORPTION or OVERHEAD RECOVERY. Typically an overhead absorption rate, based on factors such as direct machine or labour hours is calculated and the overheads 'shared out' over the cost units or jobs according to the number of machine or labour hours involved. (Further details of overhead absorption are given in the following chapter).

THE BUILD-UP OF TOTAL COST

14. Having now defined the basic terminology of cost units, cost centres, cost allocation, cost apportionment and overhead absorption, the framework of cost ascertainment is shown on the following page.

SUMMARY

15. a. Costs must be considered in relation to cost units which may be units of production, a job or batch, or units of saleable service.

b. Direct costs are those which are readily identifiable to a cost unit. Direct Labour, Direct Materials and Direct Expenses form Prime Cost.

c. Conversion cost is the cost of converting materials into products. Added value is the increase in market value of a product less bought out materials and services, i.e. it includes profit unlike conversion cost.

d. All costs not identifiable as direct are termed Indirect Costs. Indirect Labour, Indirect Material and Indirect Expenses are collectively known as Overheads.

e. Cost centres may be physical locations, items of equipment, groups of personnel etc. They are a method of gathering indirect costs via the coding system of the firm.

f. Cost allocation is the allotment of *whole* items of cost. Cost apportionment is the *sharing* of a common cost amongst cost centres.

g. Overhead absorption (or recovery) is the process by which overheads are included in the cost of cost units, i.e. Prime Cost plus overheads absorbed = Total Cost.

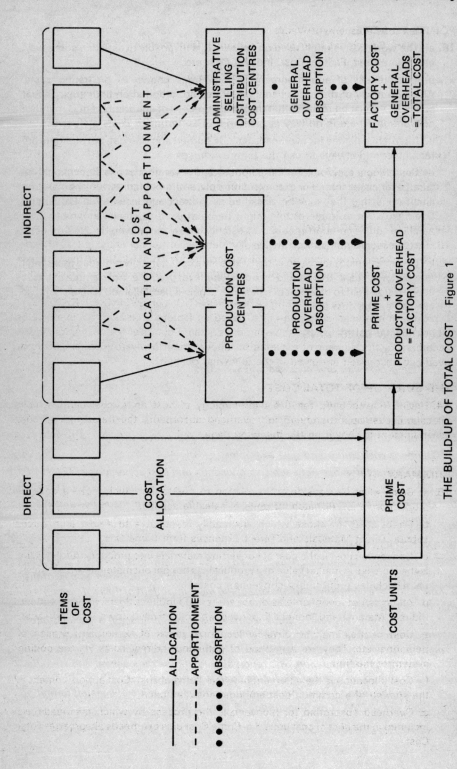

THE BUILD-UP OF TOTAL COST   Figure 1

POINTS TO NOTE:

16. a. The word cost is rarely used on its own. It is invariably qualified in some way, e.g. Prime Cost, Factory Cost, Indirect Cost etc.

b. The process of apportionment is sometimes known as pro rating costs. Although many of the bases used, e.g. Rates apportioned on floor area, appear sensible, it must be realised that the whole process of apportionment is merely a convention. There is no way of proving that apportioned costs are correct.

c. Alternative names for overheads include burden and on-cost, but students are recommended always to use the term overheads.

d. Costing is a tool for practical purposes and a commonsense view should be taken over each factor. For example, some costs, although direct, may be of such small value that they may be classified as indirect and included in Production Overheads. An example of this might be paint used to stencil a number on a machine tool. The effort required to establish how much paint is used on each machine would not be worthwhile.

e. On occasions it may be possible to classify a cost normally regarded as indirect as a direct cost and this should be done whenever possible. An example of this is commission paid to an agent or salesman to gain a particular job where the job is classed as the cost unit.

SELF REVIEW QUESTIONS

1. What is a cost? *(2)*
2. Define a cost unit and give examples. *(3)*
3. What is a direct cost? *(4)*
4. What is the make-up of prime cost? *(4)*
5. What are indirect costs? *(5)*
6. What is difference between conversion cost and added value? *(7 & 8)*
7. Define a cost centre and give examples. *(10)*
8. What is the difference between cost allocation and cost apportionment? *(11 & 12)*
9. Give examples of typical apportionment bases for: Heating, Insurance and Wage Administration costs. *(12)*

EXAMINATION QUESTION

1. The Corporate Report which was issued by the Accounting Standards Committee in 1975 suggested that a number of statements should be published as part of the annual report of a company; perhaps one of the most important of these statements is that of value added.

For a number of years, some companies have produced a value added statement and many more companies will follow this lead. The management of VAS Limited is interested in this development and has asked you, as management accountant, to prepare a report. The report should outline the concept and state the objectives and advantages of producing such a statement.

Prepare the report to your management and include in it a suggested format of the statement. (ICMA, Cost Accounting, 2 May, 1980).

3 Absorption of Overheads

INTRODUCTION

1. This chapter explains in detail the process of overhead absorption and the various bases used. The effect of under or over absorption of overheads is shown and also the way that under or over absorption is dealt with.

OVERHEAD ABSORPTION

2. This process was introduced in Chapter II from which it will be recalled that overhead absorption is the process by which overheads are included in the total cost of a product. The formal definition is:

'The allotment of overhead to cost units by means of rates separately calculated for each cost centre. In most cases the rates are predetermined'. *Terminology.*

Overhead absorption becomes of greater importance when dissimilar products are made which require different production processes or for jobs which, although using identical facilities, occupy the facilities for varying length of time. It is of importance in these circumstances because the overheads absorbed into the product or job should, as far as possible, reflect the load that the product or job places upon the production facilities. To be able to compute the overhead to be absorbed by a cost unit it is necessary to establish an overhead absorption rate (OAR) which is calculated by using two factors; the overheads attributable to a given cost centre and the number of units of the absorption base (labour hours, machine hours, etc.) that is deemed most suitable; thus

$$\text{OAR for cost centre} = \frac{\text{Total overheads of cost centre}}{\substack{\text{Total number of units of absorption} \\ \text{base applicable to cost centre}}}$$

The total overheads of a cost centre are established by the processes of cost allocation and cost apportionment described in the previous chapter. The various possible absorption bases are described below.

BASES OF ABSORPTION

3. The objective of the overhead absorption process is to include in the total cost of a product an appropriate share of the firm's total overheads. An appropriate share is generally taken to mean an amount which reflects the effort and/or loading and/or time taken to produce a unit or complete a job. In the unlikely event of identical products being produced by identical processes for the whole of a period, the total overheads could be shared equally amongst the products. Life is rarely so simple and to cope with practical situation various absorption bases have been developed. These bases are illustrated by the following example relating to Production Cost Centre 52.

Data relating to Cost Centre 52 for period 9:

Total Overhead for period	£6,000
Total Direct Labour hours for period	800
Total Direct Wages " "	£1,600
Total Direct Material used " "	£3,000
Total Machine Hours " "	1,200
Total Units produced " "	45

Using these data the following absorption rates could be calculated using the basic formula given in Para. 2 above.

$$\text{Direct Labour hour OAR} = \frac{£6,000}{800 \text{ hrs}} = £7.5 \text{ overheads per labour hour}$$

$$\text{Direct Wages OAR} = \frac{£6,000}{£1,600} = £3.75 \text{ overheads per £ of wages or } 375\% \text{ of wages}$$

$$\text{Direct Material OAR} = \frac{£6,000}{£3,000} = £2 \text{ overheads per £ of materials or } 200\% \text{ of materials}$$

$$\text{Prime Cost OAR} = \frac{£6,000}{£4,600} = £1.30 \text{ overheads per £ of Prime cost or } 130\% \text{ of prime cost}$$

$$\text{Machine Hour OAR} = \frac{£6,000}{1,200 \text{ hrs}} = £5 \text{ overheads per machine hour}$$

$$\text{Cost Unit OAR} = \frac{£6,000}{45 \text{ units}} = £133 \text{ overhead per unit produced}$$

USING THE CALCULATED OAR

4. When it has been decided what is the most appropriate rate to use for a given cost centre, the OAR is used to calculate the cost of a cost unit as in the following example.

A cost unit X has been produced in Cost Centre 52 and the following details recorded:

Cost Unit X

Direct Materials used	£23
„ Wages	£27.50
„ Labour Hours	12
Machine Hours	17

Assuming that it has been decided that the Direct Labour Rate is the most appropriate method to use, calculate the cost of the cost unit using the data given above.

Cost Unit X

	£
Direct Labour	27.50
„ Materials	23.00
= Prime Cost	50.50
+ Overheads (12 hrs @ Labour Hour OAR of £7.5/hr)	90.00
	£140.50

In practice, as in the above example, the most appropriate OAR for a given cost centre is decided upon and used for all the cost calculations of units passing through that cost centre. Different cost centres may well have different absorption bases and the factors influencing the choice of base are given later in this chapter. For comparative purposes the overheads which would be absorbed by cost unit X using each of the absorption bases is shown in the following table.

Cost Unit X Production Data

Direct Material	£23
,, Wages	£27.50
,, Labour hrs	12
Machine Hours	17

ABSORPTION BASE	DIRECT LABOUR HOUR	DIRECT WAGES	DIRECT MATERIAL	PRIME COST	MACHINE HOUR	COST UNIT
OAR (from Para 3)	£7.50 per hour	375% of Wages	200% of Materials	130% of Prime Cost	£5 per hour	£133 per Unit
COST UNIT X DATA	12 Labour Hours	£27.50 Wages	£23 Materials	£50.50 Prime Cost	17 Machine Hours	1 Unit
CALCULATION	12 x £7.5	3.75 x £27.50	2 x 23	1.3 x £50.50	17 x £5	1 x £133
OVERHEAD ABSORBED BY COST UNIT X	£90	£103.125	£46	£65.65	£85	£133

COSTS USING DIFFERENT ABSORPTION BASES   TABLE 1

Notes:
1. Although each of the bases have been used in the table, this is for illustration only. In practice one base only, that deemed most appropriate, would be used for cost calculations.
2. It will be noted that the various absorption bases produce substantially different amounts of overheads absorbed into the cost unit, ranging from £46 to £133.

CHOOSING THE APPROPRIATE ABSORPTION BASE
5. The factors involved in the choice of an appropriate base are given below, but it must be emphasised that the final choice is a matter of judgement and commonsense. There are no absolute rules or formulae involved. What is required is an absorption basis which realistically reflects the characteristics of a given cost centre and which avoids undue anomalies.

There is general acceptance that the time based methods (Labour hours, Machine hours and to a lesser extent Direct wages) are more likely to reflect the load on a cost centre and hence the incidence of overheads and so students are recommended to choose one of these methods unless there are special factors involved.

DIRECT LABOUR HOUR BASIS
Most appropriate in a labour intensive cost centre and, providing the time booking system is good, easy to use. However, most production nowadays involves substantial use of machinery so the Labour Hour method may become increasingly inappropriate.

MACHINE HOUR BASIS

Most appropriate in a mechanised cost centre. In such a cost centre many of the overheads are related to the machinery (power, repairs, depreciation etc.), so a machine hour rate should reflect fairly accurately the incidence of overheads.

DIRECT WAGES

This is a frequently used rate in practice and is easy to apply. Direct wages paid are related to time, but because of varying rates paid to different personnel, piecework and bonus systems, there is not an exact correlation between wages paid and time elapsed. If there was only one rate per hour paid throughout a cost centre and no form of incentive scheme, then the Direct Wages system would give identical results to the Labour Hour basis, but this is rarely the case.

DIRECT MATERIAL

This method has little to commend and if used could lead to absurd anomalies. For example, if an identical blanking process utilised either mild steel or stainless steel sheet and the stainless was five times the price of the ordinary steel, the Direct Material Absorption method would load the stainless product with five times the overhead, even though it was produced by an identical process taking identical time.

PRIME COST

Although part of Prime Cost is time related (direct wages), the inclusion of the direct material element would lead to possible anomalies as outlined above and accordingly its use is not recommended.

COST UNIT

Providing all the units produced in a period were identical with identical production processes and times, then this absorption method would give accurate results. However, such circumstances are unlikely, so the times when this method can be used are very rare.

PREDETERMINED ABSORPTION RATES

6. It will be recalled from the formal definition of overhead absorption given in Para. 2 that in most cases the rates are pre-determined. This simply means that the overhead absorption rate (OAR) is calculated prior to the accounting period, using estimated or budgeted figures for overheads and units of the absorption base chosen. Thus the general formula given in Para. 2 becomes

$$\text{Predetermined OAR for cost centre} = \frac{\text{Budgeted total overheads for cost centre}}{\text{Budgeted total number of units of absorption base}}$$

The major reason for this procedure is that the actual overheads and actual number of base units are not known in total until the end of the period and the actual OAR could not be calculated until then. This would mean that product costs could not be calculated until the end of a period and clearly this would frequently introduce unacceptable delays into such procedures as invoicing, estimating etc. This is such a major disadvantage that virtually all absorption rates used are predetermined.

UNDER OR OVER ABSORPTION

7. Using predetermined rates, overheads are absorbed into actual production throughout the accounting period. Because the predetermined rates are based on estimated production and estimated overheads, invariably the overheads absorbed by this process do not agree with the actual overheads incurred for the period. If the overheads absorbed are greater than actual overheads, this is known as OVER ABSORPTION. Conversely, if absorbed overheads are less than actual overheads, this is known as UNDER ABSORPTION. The following example shows a typical situation.

Assume that the data given in Para. 3 were budgeted figures and that the actual production, overheads etc. were as given below

Cost Centre 52 Data for Period 9

	Budgeted	Actual
Overheads	£6000	£6312
Direct Labour Hours	800	792
Direct Wages	£1600	£1705
Direct Materials	£3000	£2947
Machine Hours	1200	1172
Units produced	45	46

The predetermined overhead absorption rate for direct labour hours (which, it will be recalled, was judged the most appropriate for cost centre 52)

was £7.5 per hour

Total overheads absorbed by actual activity of 792 labour hours

= 792 x 7.5 = £5940 overheads

absorbed into production, but actual overheads were £6312.

∴ Under absorbed overheads = £6312 − 5940

= £372

Note:

It will be observed that under (or over) absorption can arise from either actual overheads differing from budget or a difference between the actual and budgeted amount of the absorption base or a combination of these two factors.

DEALING WITH UNDER AND OVER ABSORPTION

8. The budgeted figures used for calculating the predetermined OAR's are based on normal levels of production and overhead. There are many factors which cause actual results to differ from those expected and it must be realised that it is *actual* costs and overheads which determine the final profit. This means that the total of actual costs must appear in the final profit and loss account and not merely those calculated product costs which include actual prime cost plus overheads based on a predetermined OAR.

Accordingly, the amount of under absorbed overheads should be added to total costs before the profit is calculated and conversely the amount of over absorbed overheads should be subtracted from total cost.

This is now illustrated using the data from the previous paragraph relating to cost centre 52.

Actual Direct Material		Actual Direct Labour		Actual Prime Cost		Absorbed Overheads		Calculated Production Cost		Under Absorption		Total Production Cost
£2947	+	£1705	=	£4652	+	£5940	=	£10592	+	£372	=	£10964

P & L A/C

Notes:

a. The actual direct costs for each cost unit would of course be immediately available from the labour and material booking system for the job card.

b. The under (or over) absorption of overheads can only be established at the end of the period when actual activity or production and actual overheads are known.

c. Although eventually appearing in a Profit and Loss account or Operating Statement, the under or over absorption is sometimes put to a monthly suspense account as an intermediate stage and the net balance taken to P & L at the year end.

ABSORBING NON PRODUCTION OVERHEADS

9. The examples of absorption bases given in the preceding paragraphs relate to production overheads. However, a significant proportion of the overheads of a typical company are non-production overheads, e.g. Selling and Marketing Overheads, Research and Development Overheads, Distribution Overheads, Administrative Overheads etc. These overheads also form part of the total cost of a cost unit and have to be absorbed or charged to Profit and Loss account in some fashion. Although the absorption bases for production overheads appear to have some rationale, the methods in common use for non-production overheads unfortunately are somewhat arbitrary. The different methods used are given below, but it must be emphasised that provided a given method is used consistently by an organisation, the choice between the methods is probably not important except where costs are used as the basis of pricing. In such cases the choice of method may be very important.

TYPE OF OVERHEAD	ABSORPTION BASE(S) USED
SELLING + MARKETING	SALES VALUE or PRODUCTION COST
RESEARCH + DEVELOPMENT	PRODUCTION COST or CONVERSION COST or ADDED VALUE
DISTRIBUTION	PRODUCTION COST or SALES VALUE
ADMINISTRATION	PRODUCTION COST or CONVERSION COST or ADDED VALUE

TYPICAL ABSORPTION BASES FOR NON PRODUCTION OVERHEADS   TABLE 2

In each case, if an absorption rate is required, the calculation would follow the pattern for predetermined OAR's given in Para. 6. As an example assume that it is required to calculate an OAR for Selling and Marketing overheads and it is company policy to use Sales Value as an absorption base. The following estimated figures have been established for the period:—

Estimated Selling and Marketing overheads   £25,000
    „   total Sales Value   £280,000

$$\text{Selling and Marketing predetermined OAR} = \frac{\text{Estimated overheads}}{\text{Estimated Sales Value}}$$

$$= \frac{£25,000}{£280,000}$$

$$= 9\% \text{ of Sales Value}$$

Notes:

1. Conversion cost is Production cost less the cost of direct materials i.e. the cost of converting materials into products.

2. Added value is the sales value of a product less the cost of bought out materials and services. Unlike conversion cost added value includes profit.

3. Many variations exist in practice in dealing with non-production overheads and frequently firms charge particular categories of overheads directly to the P & L A/C and do not attempt the somewhat arbitrary process of absorption. A typical example is that of Research and Development overheads.

ABSORPTION COSTING

10. The process described in this chapter by which total overheads are absorbed into production naturally enough is known as absorption costing. The absorption of total overheads into product costs has implications for performance measurement, cost control, stock valuation etc. and students should be aware that the process described is subject to criticism by some managers and accountants. The criticism arises from the fact that overheads contain items, known as fixed costs – which do not change when the activity level changes and which would still have to be paid if there was no activity, e.g. rates – and items, known as variable costs, which vary more or less directly with activity, e.g. power consumption. To overcome some of the difficulties, an alternative method of costing has been developed, known as marginal costing, which, although using the process of absorption, excludes fixed costs from the absorption process. The explanation of fixed and variable costs and marginal costing is developed further in Chapter XIX.

SUMMARY

11. a. Overhead absorption is the process by which overheads are allotted to cost units.

b. Overhead absorption rates (OAR) are usually predetermined and are calculated by the general formula

$$\text{OAR} = \frac{\text{Budgeted overheads for cost centre}}{\text{Budgeted units of absorption base}}$$

c. The appropriate absorption basis to use is the one which most accurately reflects the incidence of overheads in a given cost centre.

d. Possible absorption bases include:

Direct Labour hours, Direct Wages, Machine hours, Prime Cost etc.

e. In general the most appropriate absorption bases are those based on time, particularly Direct Labour Hours and Machine Hours.

f. Because predetermined OAR's are based on estimates of overheads and activity, the amount of overhead absorbed into production is unlikely to agree with the actual overheads incurred.

g. When absorbed overheads are greater than actual overheads, there is OVER ABSORPTION; when they are less there is UNDER ABSORPTION.

h. The amount of under or over absorption is eventually charged to Profit and Loss account or Operating Statement.

i. Non-production overheads form part of total cost and sometimes are absorbed into product costs (usually by a percentage of Production Cost) or charged directly to Profit and Loss account.

j. Where all costs, including both fixed and variable, are included in production costs the process is termed absorption costing. Where only variable costs are included in production costs and fixed costs are charged to Profit and Loss account each period the system is known as Marginal Costing.

POINTS TO NOTE

12. a. Typically a product passes through several production cost centres, absorbing overheads from each one, often using a different absorption base in each cost centre, e.g. labour hours, machine hours as appropriate.

b. Any overheads under or over absorbed in a period must be dealt with in that period and should not be carried forward to a future period.

c. In some simple costing systems a single, factory wide OAR is calculated. This means that there is no need to accumulate overheads for various cost centres and overheads would be absorbed by the application of the one OAR for all types of work. Obviously this is easy to do but there is a loss of accuracy because the overheads absorbed do not necessarily reflect the loading or costs of the different cost centres.

SELF REVIEW QUESTIONS

1. *What is the objective of overhead absorption?* *(2)*
2. *How are overhead absorption rates calculated?* *(2)*
3. *Give six examples of absorption bases.* *(3)*
4. *What factors govern the choice of the absorption base?* *(5)*
5. *When is the Direct Labour Hour Basis – the Machine Hour Basis – most appropriate?* *(5)*
6. *Why are predetermined absorption rates invariably used?* *(6)*
7. *How does over/under absorption arise?* *(7)*
8. *How is under/over absorption dealt with?* *(7)*
9. *How are non-production overheads absorbed?* *(8)*
10. *What is the distinction between absorption costing and marginal costing?* *(9)*

EXAMINATION QUESTIONS

1. *From the data given you are required to:*

   a. prepare an 'overhead analysis sheet' showing the basis for apportionments made (calculated to the nearest £1);

   b. calculate (to two decimal places of £1) an overhead absorption rate based on direct labour hours for:
   i.   the assembly department;
   ii. the finishing department;

c. *state briefly, for each overhead item or group of items, why the basis of apportionment was chosen;*

d. *for purposes of apportioning costs, state what other information you would have preferred to have used for any of the items instead of the information given.*

Data:

The information given relates to a four-week accounting period. In addition to the cost centres listed there is an 'occupancy' cost centre which is charged with all the costs concerned with occupation of the building. The total of this cost centre should be apportioned before the stores costs are apportioned.

Department:	Machining	Assembly	Finishing	Stores
Area occupied, in sq. feet	24,000	36,000	16,000	4,000
Plant and equipment, at cost, in £000	1,400	200	60	10
Number of employees	400	800	200	20
Direct labour hours	16,000	32,000	4,000	–
Direct wages	£32,600	£67,200	£7,200	–
Number of requisitions on stores	400	1,212	200	–

Allocated costs:

	Total £	Machining £	Assembly £	Finishing £	Stores £
Indirect wages	34,000	9,000	15,000	4,000	6,000
Indirect materials	2,400	400	1,400	600	–
Maintenance	2,100	1,400	600	100	–
Power	2,200	1,600	400	200	–
Total	£40,700	£12,400	£17,400	£4,900	£6,000

Other costs:

	£
Rent	2,000
Rates	600
Insurance on building	200
Lighting and heating	400
Depreciation on plant and equpment	16,700
Wage related costs (holiday pay, graduated national insurance and company pension scheme)	28,200
Factory administration and personnel	7,100
Insurance on plant and equipment	1,670
Cleaning of factory premises by outside contract cleaners	800
	£57,670

(ICMA, Cost Accounting 1, May 1979)

2. a. *Explain why pre-determined overhead absorption rates are preferred to overhead absorption rates calculated from factual information after the end of a financial period.*

b. The production overhead absorption rates of factories X and Y are calculated using similar methods. However the rate used by factory X is lower than that used by factory Y. Both factories produce the same type of product. You are required to discuss whether,. or not, this can be taken to be a sign that factory X is more efficient than factory Y. (ICMA, Cost Accounting 1, Nov. 1979).

3. As cost accountant in a manufacturing company, you are faced with certain problems resulting from the need to prepare monthly management accounts:

a. The end of the month rarely coincides with the end of the working week. As a result, you often do not know exactly how much to accrue in the accounts for unpaid weekly wages.

Discuss how you would deal with this situation.

b. You use a method of overhead absorption costing and thus include overhead in your work-in-progress values.

At the end of the month there are some sub-assemblies that have been scrapped.

Discuss how you would deal with the overhead content of these scrapped sub-assemblies.

c. At the end of the month, goods have arrived from suppliers but the relevant invoices have either not yet been received or have not yet been processed for payment by the relevant accounting section.

Discuss how you would deal with this situation.

(ICMA, Cost Accounting 2, May 1977).

ELEMENTS OF COST

The preceding chapters of this manual have explained how the major elements of cost, materials, labour and overheads are used in cost ascertainment. Students should now be aware of the broad framework of basic costing and have a grasp of fundamental terminology.

The succeeding seven chapters explain in detail the make-up of the cost elements and explain the various costing problems associated with each element. Fundamental to accounting (and production control, inventory control, administration, data processing, etc.) are the processes of classification and coding. Accordingly the first chapter of this section deals with these processes.

4 Classification and Coding

INTRODUCTION

1. This chapter explains the importance of classification and gives examples of typical classifications found in firms. The principles of coding systems are explained and features of good coding systems are discussed.

CLASSIFICATION

2. Before any attempts can be made to collect, analyse and control costs, it is essential that all items (labour, material, overheads, etc.) can be precisely classified and also that their destination in the costing system (direct to cost units or indirectly to cost centres) can be identified. Classification is the process of arranging items into groups according to their degree of similarity and is formally defined as:—

"The arrangement of items in a logical sequence having regard to their nature (subjective classification) or the purpose to be fulfilled (objective classification)" *Terminology.*

The first part of this definition relates to the nature of expenditure, e.g. expenditure on raw materials, and the latter part indicates where the expenditure is to be charged, e.g. in the case of raw materials, direct to the cost unit.

CLASSIFICATION AND OBJECTIVES

3. The way items are classified must be related to the objectives of the systems using the classification. For example, the classification of materials must aid all the systems involved with materials and these would typically include: Purchasing, storage, stock control, production control, inspection, as well as the costing and accounting systems. Examples of the material classifications which would be found in a typical manufacturing company are the following:—

a. Raw materials, i.e. bought in material which is used in the manufacture of the product. According to the organisation, raw materials could be further classified into steel, timber, etc. etc.

b. Components and sub-assemblies, i.e. bought in components and sub-assemblies which are incorporated in the product.

c. Work-in-progress, i.e. partly completed assemblies and products incorporating raw materials and/or sub-assemblies.

d. Consumable materials, i.e. materials used in the operation of the factory and during production which do not appear in the product, e.g. cleaning rags, detergents, etc.

e. Maintenance materials, i.e. materials of all types used in maintaining machinery, buildings and vehicles, e.g. spare parts, lubricating oils and greases, cement, etc.

f. Office materials, i.e. materials used in the operation of offices, e.g. stationery, carbons, etc.

g. Tools, i.e. jigs, tools, fixtures, clamps, etc.

Note:

a. The above classifications are not exhaustive and others are frequently found.

b. Invariably there are sub-divisions within the above broad classifications. The extent of sub-division depends on the requirements of material control in all its facets.

CODING

4. A code is defined as, "A system of symbols designed to be applied to a classified set of items". *Terminology.*

It will be seen from the above definition that coding is the way that the classification system is applied, i.e. items are classified, then coded. The importance of well designed coding systems cannot be overemphasised. Coding is important with normal accounting systems, but becomes vital with mechanised and computerised systems. Accordingly an understanding of coding systems is vital to accountants. Coding is necessary:

a. To uniquely identify items, materials, etc. which cannot be done from descriptions.

b. To avoid ambiguity which would arise from using descriptions.

c. To aid processing, particularly important with computer based systems.

d. To reduce data storage. In the majority of cases a code is much shorter than a description.

FEATURES OF GOOD CODING SYSTEMS

5. a. Unique — each item should have one, and only one, code.

b. Clear symbolisation — codes should consist of either all numeric or all alphabetic characters. In general, particularly with computer based systems, numeric codes would be preferred. Also the use of numerous strokes, dashes, colons or brackets should be avoided. The following would be an example of bad notation,

$$56\text{-}503/291{:}8$$

c. Distinctiveness — codes which represent different items should, so far as practicable, look distinctive. Errors may occur if virtually identical codes describe different items. For example, if a code for raw materials was 9-3816 and a code for a bought in component was 7-3816, confusion may occur even though the codes are unique.

d. Brevity — codes should be as brief as possible consistent with meeting the requirements of the classification system. In general it has been found that seven digits is the maximum number of digits which can be reliably remembered.

e. Uniformity — codes should be of equal length and of the same structure. This makes it easy to see whether any characters are missing. Having fixed length codes also considerably facilitates processing.

f. Exhaustive — the coding structure should be exhaustive which means that it should encompass the full range of the classification as it exists and, of equal importance, be able to cope with new items as they arise. This latter point is a major practical problem when designing coding systems.

g. Ambiguity — the notation used for the coding system should avoid ambiguity. If there is a mixed alpha/numeric system, the letters I and O should not be used because of possible confusion with the numerals 1 and 0 (zero). In addition, when an all alphabetic system is used, the letters I, O, Q, S and G are most similar to other letters and numerals and should be avoided where possible.

h. Significant—Where possible the coding should be significant. This means that the actual code should signify something about the item being coded. For example, part of the code for vehicle tyres could indicate the actual size of the tyre. Thus a code for a 165 x 13 tyre would include 165.

i. Mnemonic—On occasions when an alphabetic system is used the actual code is derived from the item's description or name. Most people are probably familiar with the letter code used by airlines to denote various airports, for example

LHR   stands for London Heathrow
LGW   stands for London Gatwick

PRACTICAL ASPECTS OF CODING SYSTEMS

6. The previous paragraph has explained various features of coding systems. To implement coding systems which are useful and meaningful certain administrative considerations are necessary.

a. For most data processing purposes a "closed notation" is preferable, i.e. all codes should be of the same length. This effectively means sacrificing some of expansibility which is possible using an expansible notation such as the Universal Decimal Classification used for book classification in libraries. This system is capable of indefinite expansion, but each sub-division requires extra digit(s) and is less suitable for accounts purposes.

b. Because of the need to introduce new items from time to time, most coding systems used for costing purposes are forms of block coding. An example of this is the following:—

Item	Block assigned
Raw material	1000 – 2999
Work in progress	3000 – 3999
Indirect materials	4000 – 4999

This system allows, within limits, new items to be introduced into the correct block without destroying the coding structure.

c. Indexing – Ideally a code should be self indexing, as for example names in alphabetical order, but this is rarely possible. Accordingly a clear index or coding list should be readily available.

d. Centralised control – Depending on the particular circumstances new codes should only be issued centrally. It should not be possible for branches, junior staff, etc. to introduce a new code into the system.

e. Check digit verification – Because of the supreme importance of correct identification through the code number, particularly using computers, many important code numbers, account numbers, part numbers etc. have an extra digit suffixed which makes them self checking and guards against many of the common coding errors, e.g. transposition, incorrect character(s), character(s) missing, etc. The most common method used is termed Modulus 11 check digit verification.

f. Code layouts – Although there is the general need to keep codes as brief as possible, the requirements of particular systems often mean that codes are unavoidably lengthy. Experience would indicate that lengthy codes are better remembered and transcribed if they are grouped or subdivided into three's, i.e.

658 – 291 – 204   is better than   658291204

g. Preprinting — Wherever possible, codes should be preprinted on forms so that errors are reduced.

SUMMARY

7. a. Accurate classification of all items is a vital pre-requisite to any form of analysis and control.

b. Classification is the process of grouping together items which are similar.

c. The classification system must meet the objectives of all the systems which may use the classifications.

d. Coding is the way that the system is applied.

e. The features of good coding systems include; uniqueness, distinctiveness, exhaustiveness, unambiguousness, brevity and uniformity.

f. To ensure that coding systems actually work in practice, care should be taken over the need to allow space for expansion, indexing, central control, self-checking codes, code layouts and preprinting.

POINTS TO NOTE

8. a. Most coding systems used in accounting are composite systems. Typically they might contain two sections, the first section indicating the nature of the expenditure (termed subjective classification) and the second section indicating the cost centre or cost unit to be charged (termed objective classification).

   For example

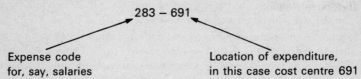

$$283 - 691$$

| Expense code | Location of expenditure, |
| for, say, salaries | in this case cost centre 691 |

b. The Financial Accounting System would be concerned with the subjective classification of an item and not the location of the expenditure, the objective classification.

SELF REVIEW QUESTIONS

1. *What is classification and why is the process of prime importance?* *(2)*
2. *What is coding and why is it necessary?* *(4)*
3. *What are the features of good coding systems?* *(5)*
4. *What is 'closed notation', 'block coding' and 'check digit verification'?* *(6)*
5. *What is subjective and objective classification and what is their importance in costing systems?* *(8)*

EXAMINATION QUESTIONS

1. *a. List the main groups of items you would expect to find in a functional classification of marketing costs.*

   b. How would you expect marketing costs to be analysed for management control purposes? What purposes are served by such analyses?

   (ACCA, Costing, December 1976).

2. *Y Limited has recently appointed a new stores controller, who has decided to introduce a new stores control system. He has asked you as Cost Accountant, to*

design for him a new Materials Code.

a. You are required to prepare a report to the Stores Controller, in which you should briefly:

  i. explain the principles to be observed in designing a Materials Classification Code;

  ii. state the advantages of such a coding system in a system of stores control.

b. Assume that the design of your coding system has been completed. Included in the range of Y Limited's products is a series of flat sections of varying dimensions and in four different raw materials, aluminium, brass, copper and stainless steel. Examples of coding of two of these are:

Material	Length	Dimensions Thickness	Width	Code Number
Stainless steel	4'	$\frac{7}{8}$''	3¾''	04081415
Brass	8½'	$1\frac{3}{8}$''	2''	02172208

  i. Determine the code for the following:

  Aluminium — 6'6'' x ¼'' x 3½''
  Copper   — 1' x ⅜'' x 4¼''

  ii. Describe the type of bar as defined by these codes:

  03112903
  01071721

(ICMA, Costing).

5 Materials — Purchasing, Reception and Storage

INTRODUCTION

1. This chapter explains the essentials of the material control process and shows the relationships between the major parts of the process. The objectives, activities and controls necessary in Purchasing, Goods Reception and Storage are discussed.

THE ESSENTIALS OF MATERIALS CONTROL

2. From the costing viewpoint the essentials of materials control prior to actual utilisation in production can be summarised as follows:

a. Materials of the appropriate quality and specification should be purchased only when required and appropriately authorised.

b. The suppliers chosen should represent an appropriate balance between quality, price and delivery.

c. Materials should be properly received and inspected.

d. Appropriate storage facilities should be provided and stock levels physically checked on a regular basis.

e. Direct materials used in production should be charged to production on an appropriate and consistent pricing basis.

f. Indirect materials used in production and non production departments should be appropriately charged to the correct cost centre and included in the overheads of that cost centre.

g. The documentation, accounting systems and controls at each stage should be well designed and effective.

h. Stock taking must be well organised to ensure that stock quantities on hand are available when required.

THE MATERIAL CONTROL PROCESS

3. The diagram at the top of the following page shows the elements of the material control process (prior to actual production material control).

The important features of purchasing, receipt, storage and issue are dealt with below whilst inventory control and materials costing are dealt with in subsequent chapters.

PURCHASING

4. Because such a large proportion of a firm's costs are represented by bought in materials and services, the purchasing function is of great importance and has become highly specialised. The responsibility of the purchasing function includes price, quality and delivery all of which are crucial factors. Late or non-delivery, poor and substandard materials, incorrect specifications etc. are all likely to have at least as great an impact on profitability as paying an unnecessarily high price. The avoidance of production delays, excessive scrap caused by incorrect materials and the avoidance of excessive stocks are among the aims of an efficient purchasing function. Frequently the purchasing function of a group or of a firm with numerous branches is centralised.

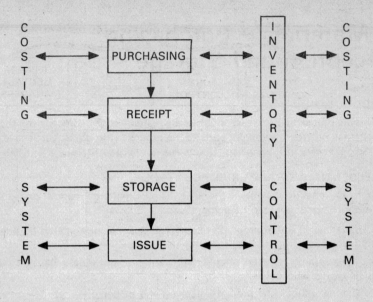

THE MATERIAL CONTROL PROCESS   FIGURE 1

This has many advantages including: larger quantity discounts, uniform standards, possibility of more continuous supplies in difficult times etc., but there may be disadvantages such as longer response times, some lack of flexibility in catering for specialised needs and general remoteness from the scene of operations.

PURCHASING PROCEDURES

5. Although the exact system obviously varies from firm to firm, the diagram on the following page shows a typical situation.

Notes to diagram:

a. Although the diagram shows each of the originating sources producing a Purchase Requisition, frequently Production and Inventory control may produce a schedule of requirements (often computer based) specifying delivery dates and call off rates.

b. The Purchase Order is the basis of the legal contract between the firm and the supplier and should unambiguously define the required goods or services. Virtually all organisations refuse to recognise an invoice from a supplier which is not covered by a purchase order. The issue of Purchase Orders must be closely controlled and signing restricted to a few senior people.

c. Progress chasing is shown as a purchasing procedure which it frequently is. However, it is sometimes the responsibility of Production Control and Works Administration.

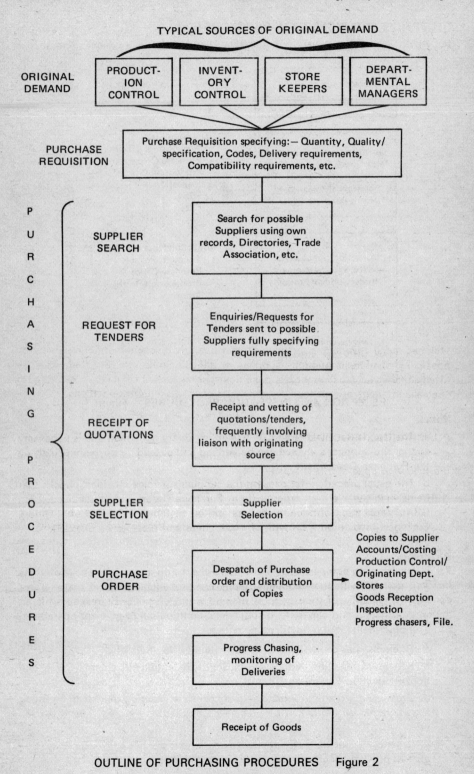

OUTLINE OF PURCHASING PROCEDURES   Figure 2

RECEPTION AND INSPECTION PROCEDURES

6. Again, whilst details vary, the following diagram shows a typical situation.

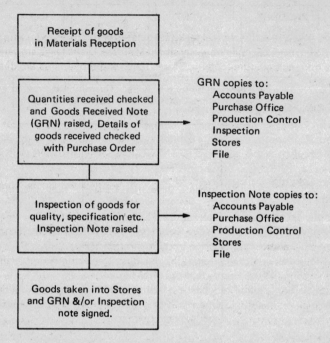

RECEPTION AND INSPECTION PROCEDURES   Figure 3

Notes:

a. The Goods Received Note (GRN) is an important document and is necessary so that the Supplier's invoice can be verified and passed for payment usually by the Purchase Department.

b. The usual procedure for passing the supplier's invoice includes: checks that items invoiced were as ordered (from Purchase Order) and as received (from GRN), Verification of price, discounts and credit terms (from Purchase Order), coding of invoice both for type of expenditure and place to be charged.

STORAGE

7. It is salutary to compare the controls and checks on a petty cash float of a few hundred pounds with the frequently haphazard procedures used in many stores containing hundreds of thousands of pounds worth of stock. Storekeeping is an important function and can make a substantial contribution to efficient operations. Storekeeping includes the following activities:

a. Efficient and speedy issue of required materials, tools etc.

b. Receipt of parts and materials from Goods Reception (i.e. external items) and from Production (i.e. internal items)

c. Organising storage in logical sequences, thus ensuring items can be found speedily, that all items can be precisely identified and storage space is used effectively.

d. Organising Stock Checks either on a continuous or a periodic basis so as to be able to provide accurate stock figures when required.

e. Protecting items in store from damage and deterioration.

f. Securing the stores from pilfering, theft and fire.

Notes:

a. It will be noted that the clerical tasks associated with stores recording are not mentioned above as, except in the very smallest stores, these tasks are carried out separately from actual storekeeping. Stores recording procedures are dealt with subsequently.

STORAGE – ISSUES AND RETURNS

8. The issue of materials must be appropriately authorised and the amount issued recorded so that the appropriate charge can be made to production or to the receiving cost centre. The usual way this is done is by a MATERIALS REQUISITION (MR). An MR would contain:

Quantity – Part No – Description – Job or Cost Centre to be charged – Authorisation

On presenting an MR to the storeman, it would be checked for correctness and authorisation and if satisfactory, the issue would be made. The MR would be retained by stores who would insert date of issue and forward the MR to Stores Records (for updating the Stock Records) and thence to the Cost Department (for pricing and charging). The storeman must ensure that the MR is amended when the issue cannot be made exactly as the original request, e.g. where only a part issue is made or an alternative material is acceptable when that originally requested is unavailable.

The procedure for goods returned to store is similar to that outlined above except that the document involved is termed a MATERIAL RETURN NOTE and, of course, the goods are taken into stores rather than issued.

STORAGE – STOCKTAKING

9. There are two approaches to the task of stocktaking – Periodic (Usually annual) and continuous.

Periodic Stocktaking

The objective of periodic stocktaking is to find out the physical quantities of materials of all types (raw materials, indirect materials, finished goods, W.I.P. etc.) at a given date. This is a substantial task even in a modest sized organisation and becomes a difficult if not impossible task in a large firm. The following factors need to be considered:

a. Adequate numbers of staff should be available who should receive clear and precise instructions on the procedures.

b. Ideally the stocktake should be done at a weekend or overnight so as not to interfere with production.

c. The stocktake should be organised into clearly defined physical areas and the checkers should count or estimate all materials in their area.

d. Adequate technical assistance should be available to identify materials, part no's etc. Far greater errors are possible because of wrong classification than wrong counting.

e. Great care should be taken to ensure that only valid stock items are included and that all valid items are checked.

f. The completed stock sheets should have random, independent checks to verify their correctness.

g. The quantities of each type of material should be checked against the stock record to expose any gross errors which may be due to stocktaking errors or faults or errors in the recording system. Small discrepancies are inevitable.

h. The pricing and extension of the Stock Sheets, where done manually, should be closely controlled. Frequently the pricing and value calculations are done by computer, the only action necessary being to input quantities in stock and part numbers.

Continuous stocktaking

To avoid some of the disruptions caused by periodic stocktaking and to be able to use better trained staff, many organisations operate a system whereby a proportion of stock is checked daily so that over the year all stock is checked at least once and many items, particularly the major value or fast moving items, would be checked several times. Where continuous stocktaking is adopted, it is invariably carried out by staff independent from the storekeepers.

Note:

Continuous stocktaking is absolutely essential where an organisation uses what is known as the Perpetual Inventory System. This is a stock recording system whereby the stock balance is shown on the record after every stock movement, either issue or receipt. With this system the balances on the stock record represent the stock on hand and the balances would be used in monthly and annual accounts as the closing stock. Continuous stocktaking is necessary to ensure that the perpetual inventory system is functioning correctly and that minor stock discrepancies are corrected.

STORAGE – CENTRALISATION vs. DECENTRALISATION

10. There is no conclusive answer as to whether there should be a centralised stores or several stores situated in branches or departments. Each system has its advantages and disadvantages which are given below.

Advantages of Centralisation

a. Lower stocks on average.

b. Less risk of duplication.

c. Higher quality staff may be usefully employed to specialise in various aspects of storekeeping.

d. Closer control is possible on a central site.

e. Possibly more security from pilferage.

f. Some aspects of paperwork may be reduced, e.g. purchase requisitions.

g. Stocktaking is facilitated.

h. Likelihood that more advanced equipment will be viable, e.g. materials handling, visual displays.

Disadvantages of Centralisation

a. Less convenient for outlying branches/departments.

b. Possible loss of local knowledge.

c. Longer delays possible in obtaining materials.

d. Greater internal/external transport costs in fetching and carrying materials.

SUMMARY

11. a. The material control process includes:
Purchasing, Receipt, Storage and Issue, Inventory Control, and associated costing procedures.

b. The purchasing function is very important and aims for an appropriate balance of price, quality and delivery.

c. The Purchase Requisition giving precise details of quantity required, specification, delivery etc. initiates the main purchasing procedures.

d. The main purchasing procedures are: supplier search supplier selection, ordering and progressing deliveries.

e. Goods must be properly received, inspected and a GOODS RECEIVED NOTE (GRN) raised.

f. The GRN is an important document which is used in the supplier invoice approval procedure.

g. Storekeeping involves issue and receipt of materials, storage space organisation, protection of materials from deterioration, stocktaking etc.

h. Items should not be issued from stores unless covered by a Materials Requisition (MR).

i. The MR is used for amending the stock records and for charging the issue direct to production or to a particular cost centre.

j. Stocktaking is carried out on a Periodic (usually annual) or Continuous basis. Continuous stocktaking is essential for Perpetual Inventory systems.

k. Centralised stores have the advantage of lower stocks, better facilities and staff and some administrative savings, but may cause inconvenience and delays.

POINTS TO NOTE

12. a. Many variations exist on the basic systems outlined in this chapter. In particular where there is continuous or assembly line operation, purchasing procedures are often integrated with production control and deliveries are received continuously, frequently directly to the production floor. Whatever the system, adequate, well designed controls are essential.

b. Because there is no clear advantage one way or the other, many organisations have a large central store supported by a number of smaller outlying stores.

c. The process of Continuous Stocktaking is sometimes known as Stock Audit.

d. Where a substantial quantity of items are required from stores say, for a particular job, the issue may be authorised by a Bill of Materials or Requirements Schedule, detailing all the items required rather than individual Material Requisitions. Frequently the Requirements Schedules are computer produced and the items required would be listed in the most economical sequence for the storemen, i.e. in location sequence or "Picking order".

SELF REVIEW QUESTIONS

1. What are the essentials of material control? (2)

2. Outline the main steps in the Purchasing Procedure. (5)

3. Where does the Goods Received Note (GRN) originate and what is its purpose? (6)

4. What are the major activities involved in storekeeping? (7)

5. What is Periodic and Continuous Stock taking? (9)

6. In what circumstances is it essential to use continuous stocktaking? (9)

7. What are the advantages and disadvantages of centralised storage? (10)

EXAMINATION QUESTIONS

1. A manufacturing company has a high growth record and is unable to satisfy the demand for its products. It is unable to expand its production facilities on its present site, so is planning to move to a development area where it can build a factory which will be much larger than its existing factory.

As cost accountant you have been asked to help in the planning stage and your particular responsibility is for the planning of a new store for raw materials and components.

You are required to state the factors to be considered in respect of the following:

a. centralised or de-centralised stores;

b. the use of a continuous stock-taking system;

c. the layout of stores.

(ICMA, Cost Accounting 1, Nov. 1974).

2. The manufacturing company by which you are employed has just taken a six monthly physical check of all its stocks. The valuations of this physical stock-taking differs considerably from balances at the stock-taking date shown in the stock accounts in the ledger.

You are required to state the steps you would take to investigate how the differences had arisen so that an accurate stock value may be obtained.

(ICMA, Financial Accounting 2, Nov 1979).

3. Outline the accountant's contribution to the process of material cost control in a manufacturing organisation where material is a significant element of total cost.

(ACCA, Costing, June 1980).

6 Materials – Stock Recording and Inventory Control

INTRODUCTION

1. This chapter shows typical stock recording procedures and how these relate to Inventory Control. The basic principles of Inventory Control are explained including the use and derivation of the Economic Ordering Quantity (EOQ).

STOCK RECORDING

2. However sophisticated the Inventory or Stock Control system is in the firm, a basic prerequisite is that stock movements (issue and receipt) are accurately recorded. In addition the stock record typically shows various control levels which relate to the Inventory Control system and which are explained later in this chapter. In some firms several stock records may be kept regarding a particular material, but this practice can introduce errors and discrepancies and has little to commend it.

The most frequently encountered records of stocks are Bin Cards and Stock Record Cards.

BIN CARDS

3. Where found, these are attached to or adjacent to the actual materials and the entries made at the time of issue either by the storeman or a stores clerk. They show only basic information relating to physical movements. A typical layout of a Bin Card is as follows

Bin Card

Part No .... Location ....

Date	Reference	Receipts	Issues	Balance

BIN CARD   Figure 1

Notes:

a. The reference column would be used for inserting the GRN or Material Requisition number.

b. The use of Bin cards is declining partly because of the difficulty of keeping them up to date and partly because of the increasing integration of stock recording and inventory control procedures, frequently using computers.

STOCK RECORD CARDS

4. To obtain a full picture of the stock position of an item it is necessary to know not only the physical stock balance, but also the Free Stock Balance. This is defined as

FREE STOCK
BALANCE $=$ Physical stock $+$ Outstanding replenishment orders
$-$ unfulfilled requirements or allocations

The free stock balance is a notional, not physical stock and is the key figure in Inventory Control. It is necessary to know physical stock for issue purposes, for stocktaking, and for controlling maximum and minimum stock levels and it is necessary to know the free stock position for replenishment ordering (these points are expanded below under Inventory Control). A typical Stock Record Card is shown below.

Stock Record Card

Control Quantities

| Material/Item Description . . . . | Maximum Level . . . . |

Material/Item Description . . . . Maximum Level . . . .

Material/Item Code . . . . Minimum Level . . . .

Stores Location Ref. . . . . Re-Order Level. . . . .

Special Requirements . . . . Re-order Quantity . . . .

Receipts				Issues				Physical Stock	Allocations			Orders			Free Stock Balance
Date	Ref	Qty	Price	Date	Ref	Qty	Price		Date	Ref	Qty	Date	Ref	Qty	

STOCK RECORD CARD   Figure 2

Notes:

    a. The entries in the Ref (Reference) columns would be Receipts (GRN No), Issues (Material Requisition No), Allocations (Job No or Customer's order No) and Orders (Purchase Order No)

    b. The above illustration shows a card for a manual or mechanised system, but even when the Stock Record is computerised, the same type of information is normally included in the computer file.

PERPETUAL INVENTORY SYSTEM

5. This system, mentioned in the previous chapter, simply means that after each issue or receipt the physical balance is calculated. The total of the balances represent the stock on hand and the system avoids the necessity for wholesale, periodic stocktaking. Instead, a continuous stocktaking system must be operated to ensure that the records accurately reflect actual stocks. If the records are to be relied upon at all times, stock discrepancies must be investigated immediately and appropriate corrections made either to the system or to the record or both. Typical causes of discrepancies between actual stocks and recorded stocks are the following:

    a. Errors caused by incorrect recording and calculation.

    b. Incorrect coding causing the wrong part to be issued and/or wrong card to be altered.

c. Under or over issues not noted.

d. Parts and materials returned to stores and not documented.

e. Shrinkage, pilferage, evaporation, losses due to breaking bulk etc.

f. Loss or non-use of GRN's, material requisitions and other appropriate documentation.

INVENTORY CONTROL*

6. This can be defined as the system used in a firm to control the firm's investment in stock. The system typically involves the recording and monitoring of stock levels, forecasting future demands and deciding when and how many to order. The overall objective of inventory control is to minimise, in total, the costs associated with stock. These costs can be categorised into three groups:—

Carrying costs:—

a. Interest on capital invested in stocks.

b. Storage charges (rent, lighting, heating, refrigeration and air conditioning.)

c. Stores staffing, equipment, maintenance and running costs.

d. Material handling costs.

e. Audit, stocktaking, stock recording costs.

f. Insurance and security.

g. Deterioration and obsolescence.

h. Pilferage, evaporation and vermin damage.

Costs of obtaining Stock:—

(Frequently known as ordering costs)

a. Clerical and administrative costs of Purchasing, Accounting and Goods Reception.

b. Transport Costs.

c. Where goods are manufactured internally, the set up and tooling costs associated with each production run plus the planning, production control costs associated with the internal order.

Costs of being without Stock (Stockout costs):

a. Lost contribution through the lost sale caused by the Stockout.

b. Loss of future sales because customers may go elsewhere.

c. Cost of production stoppages caused by Stockouts of W-I-P and raw materials.

d. Extra costs associated with urgent, often small quantity, replenishment orders.

* *This subject is covered in greater depth in 'Quantitative Techniques' T. Lucey, DP Publications.*

Note:

Some of the above items may be difficult to quantify, particularly Stockout costs, but nevertheless may be of considerable importance. The avoidance of Stockout costs is the basic reason why stocks are held in the first place.

INVENTORY CONTROL TERMINOLOGY

7. Some common inventory control items are now defined and illustrated in Figure 3.

a. Lead or procurement time. The period of time between ordering (externally or internally) and replenishment, i.e. when the goods are available for use.

b. Economic Ordering Quantity (EOQ) or Economic Batch Quantity (EBQ). This is a calculated reorder quantity which minimises the balance of cost between carrying costs and ordering costs.

c. Buffer Stock or Minimum Stock or Safety Stock. A stock allowance to cover errors in forecasting the lead time or the demand during the lead time.

d. Maximum Level. A stock level calculated as the maximum desirable which is used as an indicator to management to show when stocks have risen too high.

e. Reorder Level. The level of stock (usually free stock) at which a further replenishment order should be placed. The reorder level is dependent on the lead time and the rate of demand during the lead time.

f. Reorder Quantity. The quantity of the replenishment order frequently, but not always, the EOQ.

The following diagram shows a simple stock situation with the following assumptions and values:

Regular rate of demand of 100 units per week

Fixed lead time of 5 weeks

Reorder quantity 600 units

Maximum rate of demand 140 units per week

Safety stock 200 units

Reorder level 700 units

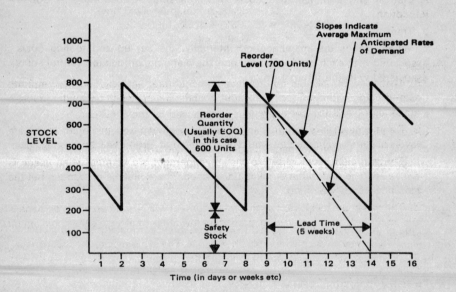

STOCK TERMINOLOGY ILLUSTRATED   Figure 3

Notes:

a. It will be seen that the 200 safety stock is necessary to cope with periods of maximum demand during the lead time.

b. With constant rates of demand, as shown, the average stock is the safety stock plus ½ reorder quantity i.e. in example above average stock = 200 + ½ (600)
= 500 units.

CALCULATING CONTROL LEVELS

8. Typical methods of calculating the major control levels: Reorder Level, Minimum Level, and Maximum Level, are illustrated below using the following data:

Average usage	100 units per day
Minimum usage	60 ,, ,, ,,
Maximum usage	130 ,, ,, ,,
Lead Time	20 – 26 days
EOQ (Previously calculated)	4000 units

Reorder level	=	Maximum usage x Maximum lead time
	=	130 x 26
	=	<u>3380 units</u>
Minimum level	=	Reorder level – Average usage in average lead time
	=	3380 – (100 x 23)
	=	3380 – 2300
	=	<u>1080 units</u>
Maximum level	=	Reorder level + EOQ – Minimum anticipated usage in minimum lead time
	=	3380 + 4000 – (60 x 20)
	=	<u>6180 units</u>

Notes:

a. These are the normal control levels encountered in basic inventory control systems. Each time an entry is made, a comparison would be made between actual stock and the control level.

b. Reorder level is a definite action level; maximum and minimum levels are levels at which management would be warned that a potential danger may occur.

c. The minimum level is set so that management are warned when usage is above average and buffer stock is being used. There may be no danger, but the situation needs watching.

d. The maximum level is set so that management will be warned when demand is the minimum anticipated and consequently stock may rise above maximum intended.

e. The calculation of control levels is done relatively infrequently in manual systems, but in a computer based system calculations would take place automatically to reflect current and forecast future conditions.

ECONOMIC ORDERING QUANTITY (EOQ)

9. It will be recalled from paragraph 7 that the EOQ is a calculated order quantity which minimises the balance of cost between ordering and carrying costs. To be able to calculate a basic EOQ certain assumptions are necessary.

a. That there is a known, constant stockholding cost.

b. That there is a known, constant ordering cost.

c. That rates of demand are known.

d. That there is a known, constant price per unit.

e. That replenishment is made instantaneously i.e. the whole batch is delivered at once.

The above assumptions are wide ranging and it is unlikely that all could be made in practice. Nevertheless the EOQ calculation is a useful starting point in establishing an appropriate reorder quantity.

The EOQ formula is given below and its derivation given in *'Quantitative Techniques', DP Publications.*

$$EOQ = \sqrt{\frac{2.Co.D}{Cc}}$$

where Co = Ordering cost per order

D = Demand per annum

Cc = Carrying cost per item per annum

Example:

Find the EOQ where the forecasted demand is 1000 units per month, the ordering cost is £350 per order, the units cost £8 each and it is estimated that carrying costs are 15% per annum.

$$Co = £350$$

$$D = 1000 \times 12$$
$$= 12,000 \text{ units per annum}$$
$$Cc = £8 \times 15\%$$
$$= £1.2 \text{ per item per annum}$$

$$EOQ = \sqrt{\frac{2.350.12000}{1.2}} = 2646 \text{ units}$$

Notes:

a. It will be seen that it is necessary to bring the factors involved to the correct time scale.

b. The EOQ formula given above is for replenishment in one batch. Where replenishment takes place gradually, for example where the items are manufactured internally and placed into stock as they are made, the formula changes slightly as follows

$$EOQ \text{ (with gradual replenishment)} = \sqrt{\frac{2.Co.D}{Cc(1 - \frac{D}{R})}}$$

where R = Replenishment rate per annum

SUMMARY

10. a. The two most common stock records are the BIN Card, or Stock Record Card (or its computer based equivalent).

b. The BIN card, where used, shows the basic issues, Receipts and Physical Balance.

c. As well as physical stock information the Stock Record Card shows the Free Stock Balance and the major control levels; Reorder level, Maximum level, and Minimum level.

d. The perpetual inventory system means that after each stock movement the balance on hand is calculated. To ensure that the records keep in line with actual stocks, continuous stocktaking is carried out.

e. Inventory control is the system used in a firm to control the investment in stocks and has the overall objective of minimising in total the three costs associated with stocks: carrying costs, ordering costs and stockout costs.

f. Reorder level is an action point, maximum and minimum levels are management indicators.

g. The EOQ is a calculated order quantity to minimise the balance of ordering and carrying costs and the basic formula is

$$EOQ = \sqrt{\frac{2.Co.D}{Cc}}$$

POINTS TO NOTE

11. a. Keeping stock records aligned with actual stocks is a major practical problem which is rarely solved completely successfully.

b. The inventory control system described in this chapter is the Reorder Level System, sometimes known as the TWO BIN System.

c. An alternative control system is known as the Periodic Review System where all stock levels are reviewed at fixed intervals and replenishment orders issued. These orders would be based on estimated usage, lead time etc. and would not be the EOQ used in the Reorder Level System.

SELF REVIEW QUESTIONS

1. *What is a Bin Card? (3)*
2. *What is the Free Stock Balance? Why is this figure of importance? (4)*
3. *What is the Perpetual Inventory System? (5)*
4. *What are the key elements in inventory control? (6)*
5. *What are the three categories of costs associated with stocks? (6)*
6. *Define:– Lead time, EOQ, Buffer Stock, Reorder level. (7)*
7. *How is the Minimum Stock level calculated? (8)*
8. *What are the assumptions necessary to use the basic EOQ formula? (9)*
9. *What is the EOQ formula? (9)*
10. *What is the EOQ formula with gradual replenishment? (9)*

EXAMINATION QUESTIONS

1. *B Limited, a young, fast-growing company, is planning to develop a new factory. The managing director of the company has discussed various aspects of the plan with functional heads and has now asked you, as management accountant, to provide him with a report on certain aspects of inventory control. He is interested particularly in the contribution which the following could make to a raw materials stock control system.*

    a. ABC inventory analysis;

    b. setting of stock levels;

    c. economic order quantity.

Prepare a report to your managing director, discussing briefly the important points of each of the above.

(ICMA, Cost Accounting 2, Nov. 1979).

2. a. Explain what is meant by the term 'economic order quantity'. Your explanation should be supported by a sketch or graph, which need not be on graph paper.

    b. Using the information stated below, you are required to prepare a schedule showing the associated costs if 1, 2, 3, 4, 5 or 6 orders were placed during a year for a single product.

From your schedule, state the number of orders to be placed each year and the economic order quantity.

Annual usage of product	600 units
Unit cost of product	£2.4
Cost of placing an order	£6.0
Stock holding cost as a percentage of average stock value	20%

    c. Comment briefly on three problems met in determining the economic order quantity.

(ICMA, Cost Accounting 1, Nov. 1978).

3. Companies in the U.S.A. and in the United Kingdom have taken part in surveys enabling data on inventories to be published. This data can be analysed in the way shown below. The actual figures in the table refer to your own company, but they are representative of the many companies included in a specific survey.

As management accountant of S Limited you are required to prepare a report to your managing director, in which you should present a Lorenz curve (as an appendix on graph paper), based on the data given. You should explain the relevance of the data, and with regard to inventory control, outline any conclusions which can be drawn from the data.

Category	Percentage of value	Percentage of quantity
High value	75	10
Medium value	20	30
Low value	5	60

(ICMA, Cost Accounting 1, Nov. 1974).

4. X Limited, a manufacturing company with several stores, has a materials control system which includes perpetual inventory records, re-order levels and continuous stocktaking.

    You are required for X Limited to:

    a. draw a diagram or flow chart to show how materials would be issued, replenished and paid for. The cycle should indicate the departments involved, the procedures used and documents raised.

    b. i.   draft a form for use by the stock checkers and include on it the following information of stock checks made in store Z on 15th May, 1978.

Item	Balances, in units		Physical stock, in units	Cost per unit £
	Stock card	Stores ledger		
A	200	200	180	20.00
B	170	170	172	5.00
C	740	760	700	0.60

    ii.   state action to be taken and documents to be raised to adjust discrepancies recorded in b. i. above;

    iii.   state a possible reason for the shortages and recommend a possible course of action by management to prevent future losses.

(ICMA, Cost Accounting 1, May 1978).

5.   *Replicars Ltd is seeking to improve stock control. The company manufactures a wide range of electrically driven model motor cars. The electric motors are imported and the management is trying to determine the physical stock level at which further supplies should be ordered and how many electric motors should be ordered on each occasion. The following information relates to one of the electric motors, stocked under the code reference L186, during the most recent production year:*

1.   *The supplier's list price is £800 per gross, i.e., per 144 motors, ex works. Normal freight charges are £20 per gross and normal delivery time is 20 working days. An express service is available by airfreight costing £52 per gross with a delivery time of 5 working days. L186 motors are supplied only in gross lots and Replicars receives a trade discount of 40 per cent of list price on purchases.*

2.   *Replicars has to purchase, in total, 36 gross in the production year to cover usage and damage during assembly. The maximum range of variation above and below recorded daily usage during the most recent production year is 8 motors.*

3.   *Replicars works for 250 days in each calendar year.*

4.   *Stockroom costs are approximately £12 per annum per gross stored. Insurance charges are estimated at 4 per cent per annum of the net delivered cost of average stock. Replicars expects an annual return of at least 20 per cent upon its average investment in stock, calculated in terms of net delivered cost.*

5.   *The cost of placing an order is £14 and the cost of receiving it in the stock room and testing the contents is £16.*

You are required to:

    a. compute the total annual cost of purchasing and stocking L186 motors for each of the following uniform order lot sizes — one, two, three, four, five and six gross. Indicate on your schedule the order lot size which you would recommend as being closest to the economic order quantity.

    b. compute the minimum stock reorder point for L186 motors, i.e., the point below which the stock should not be allowed to fall if out of stock occurrences are to be avoided and on the assumption that all stock is purchased from the normal supplier on a normal freight basis, and

    c. compare the costs of holding safety stock with the costs of replenishing through the express service over whatever range of out of stock occurrences per year you consider to be significant.

(ICA, Management Accounting, December 1977).

7 Materials – Pricing Issues and Stocks

INTRODUCTION

1. This chapter discusses the major costing problem relating to materials, that of pricing issues and material usage. The various pricing methods are described together with their advantages and disadvantages and the effect of the pricing system used on stock valuation and product costs. Examples are given to show the effects of using the various methods.

ACCURATE RECORDING

2. There is little point in detailed analysis of pricing systems for charging purposes unless the basic records are accurate and up to date. The system of issues, job recording, scrap records, material returns, material transfers, defective material returns, inspection records etc., etc. must be continually monitored to ensure its relevance and accuracy.

OBJECTIVES OF MATERIAL PRICING

3. There are two main objectives of material pricing:

a. To charge to production on a consistent and realistic basis the cost of materials used.

b. To provide a satisfactory basis of valuation for inventory on hand.

These objectives should be achieved by a materials pricing system which is the simplest effective one and which is administratively realistic.

PROBLEMS OF MATERIALS PRICING

4. In practice the problem of pricing material issues, which thus determine product costs, is complicated by several factors:

a. Rapidly changing prices for bought in materials and components.

b. The stock of any given material is usually made up of several deliveries which may have been made at different prices.

c. The frequent impossibility (and undesirability from a costing viewpoint) of identifying items with their delivery consignment.

d. The sensitivity of profit calculations to the pricing method adopted particularly where materials form a large part of total cost.

No one pricing method has all the advantages and it is necessary to use the most appropriate system to fulfill the requirements of a particular situation. The features of the various pricing systems are described below.

GENERAL FEATURES OF PRICING SYSTEMS

5. When an issue is made from Stores, the Materials Requisition would be passed to the Cost Department to be priced and extended so that the appropriate ledger entries can be made. At the simplest these entries would be

Debit	**Credit**
Work-in-Progress Control A/C	Stores Ledger Control A/C
(for direct material issues)	

OR

Overhead Control A/C
(for indirect material issues)

To be able to use some of the pricing systems described below (e.g. the FIFO and LIFO methods) the stock recording system has to be comprehensive enough not only to record overall quantities and prices, but also the number or quantity received in any one batch. This is so that issues can be nominally identified against batches which is necessary to establish the appropriate price to be charged.

FIRST IN FIRST OUT (FIFO)

6. Using this method issues are priced at the price of the oldest batch in stock until all units of that batch have been issued when the price of the next oldest is used and so on.

Characteristics

a. It is an actual cost system

b. It is a good representation of sound storekeeping practice whereby oldest items are issued first

c. Because it is actual cost system unrealised profits or losses do not arise.

d. The stock valuation is based on the more recently acquired materials and thus more nearly approaches current market values.

e. The FIFO system is acceptable to the Inland Revenue and is acceptable according to SSAP 9 (Stocks and Work-in-Progress).

f. Product costs, being based on the oldest material prices, lag behind current conditions.

In periods of rising prices (inflation) products costs are understated and profits overstated; in periods of falling prices (deflation) product costs are overstated and profits understated.

g. Because of the necessity to keep track of each batch the system is administratively clumsy.

h. Renders cost comparison between jobs difficult because the material issue price may vary from batch to batch even with issues made on the same day.

LAST IN – FIRST OUT (LIFO)

7. Using this method, issues are charged out at the price of the most recent batch received and continue to be charged thus until a new batch is received.

Characteristics

a. It is an actual cost system.

b. LIFO will frequently result in many batches being only partly charged to production where a subsequent batch is received.

c. Product costs will tend to be based fairly closely on current prices and will therefore be more realistic.

d. Stocks are valued at the oldest prices.

e. The LIFO system is generally not acceptable to the Inland Revenue and is not recommended by SSAP 9.

f. Administratively clumsy.

g. Renders cost comparison between jobs difficult.

h. In periods of rising prices LIFO, by keeping down disclosed profits, provides a hedge against inflation.

AVERAGE PRICE METHOD

8. The average price method is a perpetual weighted average system where the issue price is recalculated after each receipt taking into account both quantities and money value.

Characteristics

a. Although realistic, it is not an actual buying in price, except by coincidence.

b. The average price method is acceptable to the Inland Revenue and is one of the methods recommended by SSAP 9.

c. It is less complicated to administer than LIFO and FIFO.

d. It has an effect on product costs and stock valuation somewhere between the LIFO and FIFO systems.

e. The average price method makes cost comparison between jobs using similar materials somewhat easier.

f. With constantly fluctuating purchase prices, the average price method is likely to give more satisfactory results than LIFO or FIFO as it will tend to even out the price fluctuations.

g. Because it is based on actual costs, no unrealised stock profits and losses occur.

SPECIFIC OR UNIT PRICE

9. Where the item issued can be identified with the relevant invoice, the actual cost can be charged. This is usually only possible with special purpose items bought for a particular job.

STANDARD PRICE

10. This is defined as:

"A predetermined price fixed on the basis of a specification of all factors affecting that price". *Terminology.*

In effect a standard or planned price is an average price predicted for a future period and all issues and returns would be made at the standard price for the period concerned.

Characteristics

a. Not an actual cost, therefore stock profits and losses may arise.

b. Administratively simple. Only quantities issued and received need be recorded, not the money values as they are predetermined.

c. Very real practical difficulty in establishing an acceptable and meaningful standard price, particularly in volatile conditions.

d. If a realistic standard price can be established, some guidance to purchasing efficiency may be obtained.

e. Because material price variations are eliminated, manufacturing cost comparisons can be made more easily.

Note:

A standard issue price for materials may be used even where the firm does not use a full standard costing system — described in Chapter 23.

REPLACEMENT PRICE

11. A typical example of this method, sometimes known as the market price method, charges out issues at the buying in price on the day of issue. There are many variants to this system, for example, buying in prices may be established by means of a price index or actual prices updated on a monthly basis.

Characteristics

a. Not an actual cost price, therefore stock profits and losses may occur.

b. Issues would be priced at up to date values.

c. Major administrative problem in keeping replacement prices up to date.

d. Replacement pricing is more frequently used with estimating rather than normal stock issues.

e. Not acceptable to Inland Revenue.

f. Makes cost comparison between jobs difficult.

BASE STOCK METHOD

12. Although not strictly a method of valuing issues it is included in this section for completeness. The method assumes that initial purchases were to provide a buffer or base stock and that this base stock should appear in all subsequent stock valuations at its original value. Issues would be valued by one of the methods described earlier in this chapter. The base stock method would result in stock values which were totally unrealistic and its use is not recommended.

COMPARISON OF PRICING METHODS

13. Because of the effect on product costs and stock valuations, there is a need for an organisation to be consistent in its issue pricing methods. Apart from specific or unit prices all the methods are merely conventions, each with advantages and disadvantages. Provided that the system is used consistently and suits the operating conditions of the firm, any of the systems could be used. However, because of SSAP recommendations and the Inland Revenue, the use of the FIFO or the Average Price systems appear to be most common.

Based on the stores data below, issue prices using the FIFO, LIFO, Average Price and Standard Price systems are shown in Figure 1.

Stores data for part no 10x for October 198-
where the standard price is £4.50 per unit.

		Receipts	Purchase Price	Issues
Date	1/10	150 units @	£4.00	
	5/10	100 units @	£4.50	
	6/10			80 units
	12/10			100 units
	20/10	90 units @	£4.80	
	24/10			80 units

Stores Ledger Account using the FIFO Method

Receipt date	GRN No	Qty.	Price	£	Issue date	Mat'l Req.	Issue details	£	Balance (Memorandum only)	
			£						£	£
1/10/8-	5832	150	4.00	600					150 @ 4.00	600
5/10/8-	6291	100	4.50	450					150 @ 4.00) 100 @ 4.50)	1050
					6/10/8-	257	80 @ 4.00	320	70 @ 4.00) 100 @ 4.50)	730
					12/10/8-	492	70 @ 4.00) 30 @ 4.50)	415	70 @ 4.50	315
20/10/8-	7057	90	4.80	432					70 @ 4.50) 90 @ 4.80)	747
					24/10/8-	794	70 @ 4.50) 10 @ 4.80)	363	80 @ 4.80	384
					Bal C/F		80 @ 4.80	384		
		340	£1482				340	£1482		

Stores Ledger Account using the LIFO Method

Receipt date	GRN No	Qty.	Price	£	Issue date	Mat'l Req.	Issue details	£	Balance (Memorandum only)	
			£						£	£
1/10/8-	5832	150	4.00	600					150 @ 4.00	600
5/10/8-	6291	100	4.50	450					150 @ 4.00) 100 @ 4.50)	1050
					6/10/8-	257	80 @ 4.50	360	150 @ 4.00) 20 @ 4.50)	690
					12/10/8-	492	20 @ 4.50) 80 @ 4.00)	410	70 @ 4.00	280
20/10/8-	7057	90	4.80	432					70 @ 4.00) 90 @ 4.80)	712
					24/10/8-	794	80 @ 4.80	384	10 @ 4.80) 70 @ 4.00)	328
					Bal C/F		80	328		
		340	£1482				340	£1482		

Stores Ledger Account using the Average Price Method

Receipt date	GRN No	Qty.	Price	£	Issue date	Mat'l Req.	Issue details	£	Balance (Memorandum only)	
			£							£
1/10/8-	5832	150	4.00	600					150 @ 4.00	600
5/10/8-	6291	100	4.50	450					250 @ 4.20*	1050
					6/10/8-	257	80 @ 4.20	336	170 @ 4.20	714
					12/10/8-	492	100 @ 4.20	420	70 @ 4.20	294
20/10/8-	7057	90	4.80	432					160 @ 4.5375†	726
					24/10/8-	794	80 @ 4.5375	363	80 @ 4.5375	363
						Bal C/F	80	363		
		340		£1482			340	£1482		

Average Price calculations:

$$* \quad \begin{array}{lll} 150 \text{ units @ £4} & = & £600 \\ \text{plus} \quad \underline{100} \text{ units @ £4.5} & = & \underline{450} \\ = \quad 250 \text{ units} & = & £1050 \end{array} \qquad \therefore \text{ average price} = \frac{1050}{250} = £4.20$$

$$† \quad \begin{array}{lll} 70 \text{ units @ £4.2} & = & £294 \\ \text{plus} \quad \underline{90} \text{ units @ } 4.80 & = & \underline{432} \\ = \quad 160 \text{ units} & = & £726 \end{array} \qquad \therefore \text{ average price} = \frac{726}{160} = £4.5375$$

Stores Ledger Account using the Standard Price Method

Receipt date	GRN No	Qty.	Price	£	Issue date	Mat'l Req.	Issue details	£	Balance (Memorandum only)	
			£					£	£	£
1/10/8-	5832	150	4.50	675					150 @ 4.50	675
5/10/8-	6291	100	4.50	450					250 @ 4.50	1125
					6/10/8-	257	80 @ 4.50	360	170 @ 4.50	765
					12/10/8-	492	100 @ 4.50	450	70 @ 4.50	315
20/10/8-	7057	90	4.50	405					160 @ 4.50	720
					24/10/8-	794	80 @ 4.50	360	80 @ 4.50	360
						Bal C/F	80	360		
		340		£1530			340	£1530		

51

Notes:

a. The above account is shown fully completed for *illustration purposes only*. If the standard price method was to be used then quantities only need to be recorded thus saving some clerical work.

b. It will be noted that receipts, issues and balances are all at standard price. The gain/loss on purchasing would be written off elsewhere in the accounts, the stores ledger being entirely at standard price.

It will be seen that the various pricing systems produce issue prices ranging from £4 to £4.8 and closing stock valuations ranging from £328 to £384.

STOCK VALUATION

14. The application of any of the issue pricing methods automatically results in a closing stock valuation of the particular item in the stores ledger. The summation of the individual items i.e. the balance on the Stores Ledger Control Account, represents a valuation of closing stock. Invariably this valuation is used for operating statements and internal management accounts. In addition this valuation is frequently the basis of stock valuation for use in the financial accounts, but on occasion some adjustment to the figure is made. The general rule for stock valuation for financial accounting purposes is cost, net realisable value or replacement cost, whichever is the lowest.

SUMMARY

15. a. There must be a consistent, reasonably simple method of pricing issues so that production is charged a realistic figure for materials consumed.

b. The problems involved in pricing issues arise from changing purchase prices, the frequent impossibility of identifying materials with particular purchases and administrative problems.

c. The major pricing methods are First in First out (FIFO), Last in First out (LIFO), Average price and Standard price.

d. SSAP 9, Stocks and Work in Progress, recommend the use of either unit (or specific) price, FIFO, or Average price.

e. Many of the pricing systems are administratively clumsy, requiring either the monitoring of batches or frequent price calculations.

f. Some of the administrative problems can be overcome by the use of a Standard price system, but there is the very real practical problem of establishing a standard price. If conditions are such that frequent revisions of the standard price are necessary, many of the advantages of the system are lost.

POINTS TO NOTE

16. a. It will be apparent that there is no such thing as a 'true' issue price. It is a question of judgement which system is best suited to a particular organisation.

b. The stores ledger accounts shown in this chapter are examples of the perpetual inventory system described in Chapter 5, i.e. where a balance is shown after each receipt and issue.

c. Regardless of SSAP recommendations and Inland Revenue acceptability, *any* pricing or stock valuation system could be used for *internal* purposes. However, to avoid duplication of effort there is merit in using a system for internal purposes which will be acceptable as a basis of stock valuation for financial accounting purposes.

d. The issue pricing systems described in this Chapter are the most common. Other systems exist, an example of which is 'Next in First Out', (NIFO). In this system, issues are priced at the 'next' price i.e. the price of items which have been ordered but not received. This price would be close to current market prices. This system is complicated and rarely used.

SELF REVIEW QUESTIONS

1. What are the objectives of issue pricing systems? *(3)*
2. What are the basic ledger entries for material issues: to production? indirect materials? *(5)*
3. What is the FIFO System? *(6)*
4. What is the effect of the FIFO system in times of inflation? *(6)*
5. What are the characteristics of the LIFO system? *(7)*
6. Describe the average price method. *(8)*
7. What is a specific or unit price? *(9)*
8. Define a standard issue price. *(10)*
9. What is Replacement price? *(11)*
10. Using any of the issue pricing systems, how is the closing stock valuation established? *(14)*

EXAMINATION QUESTIONS

1. For the six months ended 31st October, an importer and distributor of one type of washing machine has the following transactions in his records. There was an opening balance of 100 units which had a value of £3,900.

Date	Bought Quantity in units	Cost per unit £
May	100	41
June	200	50
August	400	51.875

The price of £51.875 each for the August receipt was £6.125 per unit less than the normal price because of the large quantity ordered.

Date	Sold Quantity in units	Price each £
July	250	64
September	350	70
October	100	74

From the information given above and using weighted average, FIFO and LIFO methods for pricing issues, you are required for each method to:

a. show the stores ledger records including the closing stock balance and stock valuation;

b. prepare in columnar format, trading accounts for the period to show the gross profit using each of the three methods of pricing issues;

c. comment on which method, in the situation depicted, is regarded as the best measure of profit, and why.

(ICMA, Cost Accounting 1, November 1977).

2. a. Three students, K, L and M, are equal partners in a joint venture which involves them, on a part-time basis, in buying and selling sacks of product F. The transactions for the six months ended 30th September were as stated below. You are to assume that purchases at the unit costs given were made at the beginning of each month and that the sales were made at the end of each month at the fixed price of £1.50 per sack.

Month	Purchases		Sales
	Sacks	Unit cost £	Sacks
April	1,000	1.00	500
May	500	1.20	750
June	1,000	1.00	Nil
July	Nil	–	600
August	500	1.20	650
September	500	1.30	600

In October the student partners held a meeting to review their financial position and to share out the profits but there was disagreement because each partner had priced the issues on a different basis. K had used FIFO, L had used LIFO and M had used a weighted average, basing his weighted average on the whole of the six months' purchases. It was, however, agreed that the stock remaining at the end of September should be stored until next April.

You are required to:
i. show the records which each student kept of the transactions;
ii. show the amount each student ought to receive if the whole of the profit arising from each method of pricing the issues were distributed;
iii. comment briefly on the acceptability of the three different results arising from the transactions.

b. In the context of a manufacturing business, explain briefly what is meant by the last sentence of the following statement.

The Statement of Standard Accounting Practice No. 9 on Stocks and Work-in-Progress (SSAP 9) states in an explanatory note, paragraph 3 that 'In order to match costs and revenue, "costs" of stocks and work in progress should comprise that expenditure which has been incurred in the normal course of business in bringing the product or service to its present location and condition. Such costs will include all related production overheads, even though these may accrue on a time basis.'

(ICMA, Cost Accounting 1, Nov. 1979).

3. At the beginning of November the opening stock of a particular component was 440 units, total value £2,200.

During the month the following supplies were received:

8.11.1979   400 units, total value £1,800
15.11.1979   400 units, total value £2,200
22.11.1979   400 units, total value £2,400

There is a standard carriage charge included in the above amounts, of £100 per delivery, for transporting the components to the factory. The invoice for the goods received on 22 November had not been received by the end of the month.

Shown below are the issues from store during November:

2.11.1979	300 units,	16.11.1979	500 units
9.11.1979	50 units,	20.11.1979	20 units
13.11.1979	300 units,	28.11.1979	30 units

The components issued on 9 November were used in the general plant maintenance programme and those issued on 20 November were incorporated into plant and equipment being constructed by the company's engineers to mechanise part of the manufacturing process. All other issues were made direct to production for inclusion in the output of the company's products, the issue on 28 November being to replace components damaged by incorrect handling.

On 21 November 40 units were returned to store from production and, at the end of the month, the closing stock was 440 units.

Required:

a. Record the month's transactions in a stores account for this component indicating very clearly the account into which (or from which) the corresponding entry should be posted. You should assume the company operates an historic batch costing system, fully integrated with the financial accounts, and uses a first in, first out method of pricing material issues.

b. Briefly contrast the effects of using first in, first out with the last in, first out method of pricing material issues from store.

(ACCA, Costing, December 1979).

8 Labour − Remuneration Methods

INTRODUCTION

1. This chapter describes the basic methods of remuneration, those based on time and those which relate pay to output either directly or indirectly. Profit sharing schemes are also described.

TRENDS IN REMUNERATION

2. At present approximately half of manual workers are paid by some form of incentive scheme. This overall percentage masks extremely wide variations from industry to industry. For example, in general engineering around 80% of workers are paid wholly or partly by some form of incentive scheme, whereas in process industries the figure is as low as 15%. There is a general tendency (with, of course, exceptions) for larger firms to move away from direct incentive schemes to schemes such as measured day work. There is also a tendency for workers to become salaried employees which has clear costing implications as direct labour costs become more fixed in nature rather than varying with output.

REMUNERATION METHODS

3. The two main categories of remuneration are

    a. Time based

    b. Related in some way or another to output or performance.

Within these two categories there are innumerable variations some of which have general applicability whilst others are of a local and specialised nature. Remuneration systems are frequently complex and administratively cumbersome, but because the system is the result of negotiations, disputes and agreements over the years, attempts to rationalise and simplify are frequently met with hostility and suspicion. The two major categories of remuneration together with typical variations are dealt with below.

TIME BASED SYSTEMS

4.   a. **Basic System.**

At the simplest level workers would be paid for the number of hours worked at a basic rate per hour up to, say, 40 hours per week. Time worked in addition to 40 hours would be classed as overtime and is usually paid at a higher rate, for example, 'time and a quarter' (i.e. 1¼ x basic rate per hour), 'time and a half' (i.e. 1½ x basic rate per hour) or 'double time' (i.e. 2 x basic rate per hour) depending on the number of extra hours worked and when the overtime was worked. Although workers' pay is not related to output, this does not mean that output and performance is unimportant. On the contrary, it is normal practice to monitor output and performance closely by shop floor supervision and managerial control systems so that workers are paid for actually working and not merely attending.

    Advantages
    i. Simple to understand and administer
    ii. Simplifies wage negotiations in that only one rate needs to be determined unlike the continuous complex negotiations over individual rates usual in some incentive schemes.

Disadvantages
i. No real incentive to increase output.
ii. All employees in the grade paid the same rate regardless of performance.
iii. Constant supervision may be necessary.

Most appropriate for
i. Work where quality is all important e.g. jig and tool making.
ii. Work where incentive scheme would be difficult or impossible to install e.g. indirect labour, stores assistants, clerical work etc.
iii. Work where the output level is not under the employees' control e.g. power station workers.

b. **High day rate system**
This is a time based system which is designed to provide a strong incentive by paying rates well above normal basic time rates in exchange for above average output and performance. For its successful application it is necessary to ensure that the output levels are the result of detailed work studies and that there is agreement from the labour force and the unions involved on the required production level. A typical application of this system is on assembly line production in the car industry and in domestic appliance manufacture.

Advantages
i. It is claimed to attract higher grade workers.
ii. Provides a direct incentive without the complications of individual piecework rates.
iii. Simple to understand and administer.

Disadvantages
i. May cause other local employers to raise their rates to attract the better workers thus nullifying the original effect.
ii. Problems occur when the original target production figures are not met.

Most appropriate for:
Easily measurable output to which groups of workers contribute, e.g. car assembly.

Note:
The system is also called Measured Day Work and in practice such schemes may well have quite complex structures and rules.

c. **Common bonuses found in time based systems.**
In addition to the time rates explained above, bonuses or extra payments are frequently made. Some common examples are:
i. Shift bonus. Where a worker agrees to work shifts, particularly where rotating shifts are used, he receives an extra amount.
ii. Timekeeping bonus. Where a person's timekeeping has been good over the week a small bonus may be paid.
iii. Continuous working bonus. Where the plant has achieved continuous production without strikes, go slows or stoppages a weekly bonus is paid. This system appears to have had some success in one of the large car manufacturers.

Note:
Many variants exist, for example, many firms which operate a time based system

pay, in addition, some form of output bonus and conversely some of the above bonuses are found in firms where the main method of remuneration is by an incentive scheme.

GENERAL FEATURES OF INCENTIVE SCHEMES

5. All incentive schemes relate payment to output in some way or another. There are innumerable variations; some schemes apply to individuals whilst others apply to groups of workers, some have a direct and immediate relationship to output whilst others are more indirect. From a properly organised and well planned system both the firm and the employees can benefit. The employee from the extra income arising from increased production, and the firm from the reduced overheads per unit of the increased production. Unfortunately not all schemes achieve this ideal, but careful attention to the following factors will help to achieve this objective.

a. Remuneration should reflect workers' effort and performance and payment should be made without delay, preferably very soon after completion of the task.

b. The scheme should be reasonably simple to assist administration and to enable employees to calculate their own bonus.

c. Performance levels should be demonstrably fair i.e. they should be in reach of the average worker working reasonably hard.

d. There should be no artificial limit on earnings and earnings should be safeguarded when problems arise outside the employee's control.

e. The scheme should not be introduced until there has been full consultation and agreement with employees and unions.

f. The full implications of the scheme, performance levels, rates etc. must be considered, so that it will have a reasonable length of life. Rapid changes, particularly artificial ones to curtail earnings, destroy trust and cause problems.

ADVANTAGES AND DISADVANTAGES OF INCENTIVE SCHEMES

6. Advantages

a. Increases production thereby increasing wages but also reducing overheads per unit, particularly where there are substantial fixed overheads.

b. May enable firm to remain competitive in inflationary conditions.

c. May improve morale by ensuring that extra effort is rewarded.

d. More efficient workers may be attracted by the opportunity to earn higher wages.

Disadvantages

a. Frequently there are problems in establishing performance levels and rates with frequent and continuing disputes.

b. Some incentive schemes are complex and expensive to administer.

c. Some groups of workers, although relatively unskilled, may earn high wages through incentive schemes whilst others engaged on skilled work may become resentful when differentials are eroded.

INDIVIDUAL INCENTIVE SCHEMES

7. In general incentive schemes which relate to an individual worker seem to be the more usual and successful, probably because of the immediacy and direct relationship between effort and reward. The following are typical examples.

STRAIGHT PIECEWORK

8. At its most basic the worker would be paid an agreed rate per unit for the number of units produced. On occasions the number of operations would be the basis of payment or, where various types of articles are produced, a piecework time allowance per article would be set and the worker paid for the piecework hours produced. For example, assume the following data:

Week No. 37   Employee No. 58107   Clock hours 40

Output

      300 units of A, Piecework time allowance 1.8 mins/unit
      150 units of B, Piecework time allowance 1.5 mins/unit
      100 units of C, Piecework time allowance 2.2 mins/unit

Piecework rate   10p per minute produced.

Total production

$(300 \times 1.8) + (150 \times 1.5) + (100 \times 2.2)$ piecework minutes

   = 985 piecework minutes

$\therefore$ Gross wages = 985 × 10p

           = £98.50

Note:

It will be seen that the piecework time produced is not equivalent to actual clock hours. Piecework time allowances are merely a device for measuring the work content of dissimilar items.

Rarely, if ever, is piecework found on its own. Usually it is accompanied by certain safeguards, typical of which are: Guaranteed day rates and in lieu bonuses.

a. Piecework with guaranteed day rates. If earnings from piecework fall below normal day rates then there is a guarantee that day rates would be paid. This is to safeguard earnings when there are delays, shortages, tool breakages etc. which make it impossible for the employee to earn bonus pay.

b. In lieu bonuses. Where a worker is normally covered by an incentive scheme and is transferred to ordinary day work, frequently an in lieu bonus is paid on top of normal day rates. Such a bonus is often paid to support workers (fork lift truck drivers, labourers etc.) whose work is not amenable to the incentive scheme used for the rest of the factory.

DIFFERENTIAL PIECEWORK

9. One objection to straight piecework systems is that, because a flat rate per unit is paid, the incentive effect at higher production levels declines. Differential piecework seeks to overcome this by increasing the rate progressively at various production levels, e.g.

up to   100 units per day 10p/unit
           100-150 units per day 12p/unit
           150-200 units per day 15p/unit

Differential piecework would, of course, normally be accompanied by the usual safeguards of guaranteed day rates or in lieu bonuses.

Note:

On occasions in differential schemes the whole of the output is paid at the higher rate when the next production threshold is reached.

PREMIUM BONUS SYSTEMS

10. These systems, now mainly of historical interest, pay workers a normal day rate plus a bonus calculated upon the difference between the time actually taken for a job and a notional time known as the time allowed. There are several systems with variants, two of which, the Halsey and the Rowan, are illustrated using the following data:

> Normal day rate = £2 hour
>
> Part No. 52X
>
> Time allowed = 1 hour per 100 units
>
> Actual production in 8 hour day = 1500 units

The formula for the systems are

Halsey

$$\text{Bonus} = \tfrac{1}{2}T_s \times \text{day rate per hour}$$

Rowan

$$\text{Bonus} = \frac{T_t}{T_a} \times T_s \times \text{day rate per hour}$$

where

> T_a = Time allowed (in this example, 1 hour per 100 units)
>
> T_t = Time taken (in this example, 8 hours)
>
> T_s = Time saved (in this example, 15-8 = 7 hours)

It is clear that $T_s = T_a - T_t$

Wage calculations

Halsey system:

$$\begin{aligned}
\text{Bonus} &= \tfrac{1}{2}T_s \times \text{day rate per hour} \\
&= \tfrac{1}{2}(7) \times £2 \\
&= £7
\end{aligned}$$

$$\begin{aligned}
\text{Total wages for day} &= \text{Normal time earnings} + \text{Bonus} \\
&= £(8 \times 2) + £7 \\
&= \underline{£23}
\end{aligned}$$

Rowan

$$\begin{aligned}
\text{Bonus} &= \frac{T_t}{T_a} \times T_s \times \text{day rate per hour} \\
&= \frac{8}{15} \times 7 \times £2 \\
&= £7.47
\end{aligned}$$

$$\begin{aligned}
\text{Total wages per day} &= \text{Normal time earnings} + \text{Bonus} \\
&= £16 + 7.47 \\
&= \underline{£23.47}
\end{aligned}$$

Notes:

a. Bonuses involving various proportions of the time saved have been used in practice.

b. The two systems give differing results at different output levels, but give the same results when the job is completed in half of the time allowed.

c. A variant of the Halsey system is the Bedaux points system where the basic time unit is a minute and a minute of allowed time is known as a Bedaux point or B point.

GROUP INCENTIVE SCHEMES

11. Although individually based incentive schemes are common and frequently successful, on occasions they are inappropriate and some form of group scheme is used. These schemes are likely to be more appropriate

a. Where production is based on a group or gang basis, e.g. road surfacing, coal mining.

b. Where production is integrated and all efforts are directed toward the same end, e.g. all forms of production line manufacture, cars, domestic appliances etc.

c. Where the production methods or product makes it unfeasible to measure individual performance.

Any of the incentive methods (piecework, differential piecework, premium bonus systems etc.) can be used, with appropriate adaption, for a group scheme. In addition because of the wider scope of a group scheme, incentives based on cost savings, delivery dates, quality norms are also used.

Apart from the choice of the incentive scheme there is the problem of how to share the bonus amongst the group. Whatever method is used, it must have the full agreement of the group and unions involved.

ADVANTAGES AND DISADVANTAGES OF GROUP SCHEMES

12. Advantages

a. May engender closer cooperation in the group and a team spirit.

b. Administratively simpler with far less recording of labour times, production rates etc.

c. Support workers not directly associated with production can easily be included in the scheme.

d. Greatly reduces the number of rates to be negotiated.

e. May encourage more flexible working arrangements within the group.

Disadvantages

a. Less direct than individual schemes so may not provide the same incentive.

b. Less hardworking members of a group receive the same bonus and this may cause friction.

c. Not always easy to obtain agreement on the proportions of the bonus which group members will receive.

INCENTIVE SCHEMES IN PRACTICE

13. A significant proportion of production workers are paid under some form of incentive or bonus scheme and there is no doubt that some schemes are extremely effective. Many others are not and recognition of some of the following problems will help to ensure a workable and efficient scheme.

a. An incentive scheme will not solve the problems of badly managed, poorly organised, ill-equipped factories.

b. To ensure that only good production is paid for, sound quality control and inspection procedures are vital.

c. All incentive schemes should be based on efficient working methods following comprehensive work studies. Notwithstanding this, it should be recognised that rate fixing is a subjective process which will only be finalised after employer/employee/union negotiations.

d. Care should be taken not to enter into sham productivity deals i.e. where pay increases have been granted involving increased productivity which does not materialise.

PROFIT SHARING

14. Although this would not normally be classed as an incentive scheme, profit sharing is part of the package of benefits that an employee could receive. It can be defined as the payment to employees of a proportion of company profits. The amount received by individuals is usually related to their salary or wage level and the profit share may be given in cash or in shares of the company. In the latter case the system becomes a form of co-ownership. Profit sharing appears to be regarded as a welcome but minor bonus too remote from the workplace to have any real incentive effect.

SUMMARY

15. a. There is a trend away from direct incentive schemes to measured day work, particularly for the larger companies.

b. In addition to a basic time based system there are high day rate or measured day work systems which aim to attract good workers by paying above average rates for above average performance.

c. Incentive schemes seek to increase production and should be, as far as possible; simple, directly related to performance, paid promptly, installed after full consultation, reasonably permanent. *fair*

d. Straight piecework pays a fixed rate per unit, whereas differential piecework pays extra amounts per unit above certain quantities; the aim being to provide greater incentive to higher output.

e. Premium bonus systems pay day rates plus a bonus calculated upon the difference between actual time taken and a notional allowed time.

f. Group incentive schemes may use any of the incentive methods (piecework, premium bonus etc.) and are most suitable where a cooperative team effort is required.

g. Any form of incentive scheme must be based on proper work organisation, sound quality control and proper consultation.

h. Profit sharing may be by cash payout or share distribution. Frequently it is considered too remote to have any direct incentive effect.

POINTS TO NOTE

16. a. Incentive schemes may increase the labour cost per unit but as long as the reduction in overhead cost per unit is sufficient, the scheme should be worthwhile.

b. Some of the industrial relations problems of recent years have been caused by difficulties over incentive schemes where earnings were unchecked, and time related earnings which were subject to incomes policies.

SELF REVIEW QUESTIONS

1.   What are the two major categories of remuneration methods?   (3)
2.   What is 'time and a half'?   (4)
3.   In what circumstances is the use of the High Day Rate System appropriate?   (5)
4.   What bonuses are commonly encountered in conjunction with time based remuneration schemes?
5.   What factors should be considered when designing incentive schemes?   (7)
6.   What are the advantages and disadvantages of incentive schemes?   (8) 6
7.   What is straight piecework?   (10) 8
8.   What is an 'in lieu' bonus?   (10) 8
9.   What are the objectives of differential piecework systems?   (11) 9
10. What are Premium Bonus Systems?   (12) 10
11. In what circumstances are group incentive schemes most appropriate?   (13) 11
12. What is profit sharing?   (16) 14

EXAMINATION QUESTIONS

1.   A manufacturing company seeking to control its labour costs produces a labour cost report each month. The report for October is reproduced below.

Labour Cost Report

	October £	September £
Direct labour	28,100	24,400
Supervision	3,000	3,000
Material handlers	3,100	2,800
Inspectors	3,400	3,640
Repairs and maintenance labour	3,200	3,200
Administrative labour	2,400	2,400
Total labour costs	£43,200	£39,440
Sales value of production	160,000	136,000
Total labour costs as a percentage of sales value of production	27%	29%

You are required to comment on:

a. labour efficiency in October compared with that in September and state four possible factors which may have caused the percentage in October to be lower than in September;

b. the effectiveness of labour cost control by means of this report and suggest two better ways of controlling labour costs.

(ICMA, Cost Accounting 1, Nov. 1979).

2.   It is common cost accounting practice to treat direct wages as an item of variable cost. In certain circumstances however, such as when production plants are highly mechanised or automated, operators' wages are regarded as a fixed cost.

Discuss the factors which should be considered in the cost accounting treatment of operators' wages in different circumstances.

(ICMA, Cost Accounting 1, May 1978).

9 Labour – Recording, Costing and Allied Procedures

INTRODUCTION

1. This chapter describes typical time and output booking procedures and the process of wages calculation. The costing implications of wages, bonuses and overtime are described and an outline of wage rate determination, job evaluation, merit rating and personnel procedures is given.

THE NECESSARY RECORDS

2. Whatever the system of remuneration, records of attendance time for each worker are required. In addition, depending on the incentive scheme involved, records will be required for operations, processes, parts and products usually involving both times taken and quantities produced. These records form the basis of wage calculations and for such costing data as: direct and indirect labour costs, overhead buildup, labour cost control. The two types of records, those for attendance and for output, are described below.

ATTENDANCE RECORDS

3. In all but the very smallest concerns this is done by the use of clock cards, one for each worker, and a time recording clock usually based at the entrance to the factory. The clock card is the basis of time recording and whatever additional time records are kept, they must be reconciled with the total attendance time recorded on the clock card by the time recording clock.

OUTPUT RECORDS

4. The records necessary must be tailored to the requirements of incentive and labour cost control systems in operation. Unnecessary recording incurs extra clerical costs and may slow down production and should be avoided. The following are typical records: daily and weekly time sheets, job cards, operation cards.

DAILY AND WEEKLY TIME SHEETS

5. These are records, filled in by the worker and duly countersigned, which show how he spent his time during the day or week. The general objective is to reconcile all the time in attendance (recorded on the clock card) with time bookings either to jobs or operations i.e. direct wages, or to non-productive attendance such as a machine breakdown which would be analysed by the cost department as indirect wages.

Weekly time sheets tend to be more inaccurate but require less clerical effort. It really depends on whether the worker deals with numbers of small jobs, when daily time sheets would be preferred, or is employed on jobs which last a considerable time when weekly sheets may be adequate.

A typical time sheet is shown below.

| Time Sheet No. .... |
| Employee Name .... Clock Code .... Dept .... |
| Date .... Week No. .... |

Job No.	Start Time	Finish Time	Qty	Checker	Hrs	Rate	Extension

Analysis
Direct:
Job No(s)   £
_____   _____
_____   _____
_____   _____

Indirect:
Foreman's Signature   Codes No.   £
                                         _____   _____
                                         _____   _____
                                         _____   _____

Date ....

TIME SHEET   Figure 1

JOB CARDS

6. Unlike time sheets which relate to individual employees and may contain bookings relating to numerous jobs, a job card relates to a single job or batch and is likely to contain entries relating to numerous employees. On completion of the job it will contain a full record of the times and quantities involved in the job or batch. The use of job cards, particularly for jobs which stretch over several weeks, makes reconciliation of work time and attendance time a difficult task. These cards are difficult to incorporate directly into the wages calculation procedures.

OPERATION CARDS

7. These cards, sometimes known as piecework tickets, are provided for each operation or stage of manufacture so that each operation will have at least one card. In this way a job will have a number of operation cards and although this increases the paper work, it does enable the operation cards to be used directly in the wage calculation procedures. A typical operation card is now shown.

Operation Card				
Operators Name		Total Batch Quantity..........		
Clock No.		Start Time		
Pay Week No................	Date .... Stop Time			
Part No.		Works Order No.		
Operation		Special Instructions		
Quantity Produced	**No. Rejected**	**Good Production**	**Rate**	**£**
Inspector		Operative		
Foreman		Date		
PRODUCTION CANNOT BE CLAIMED WITHOUT A PROPERLY SIGNED CARD				

OPERATION CARD (or Piecework Ticket)   Figure 2

WAGES PROCEDURES

8. The flowchart (figure 3) shows in outline a typical wages procedure from the original clock card to basic cost accounting entries.

LABOUR COSTING

9. Using job cards and/or time sheets and/or output records and the payroll, the cost department carries out a detailed analysis of all wages paid to enable the labour costs involved in products, operations, jobs, cost centres and departments to be established. This is done for cost ascertainment and cost control purposes. Features of various aspects of labour costing are dealt with below.

    a. **Direct Wages.** That proportion of the wages of production employees directly attributable to production (i.e. as ascertained from job cards and/or time sheets) is charged to the job or operation in which engaged and the total of direct wages for the period is charged to a departmental Work-in-Progress control A/c. Direct wages would normally include earnings under piecework and bonus schemes, but would not normally include overtime and shift premiums. The reason for this is that such premiums, if classed as direct, would be charged only against the job(s) done during the overtime period which is unjust because it is fortuitous which jobs are done during ordinary or overtime.

    b. **Indirect wages.** The wages of such people as inspectors, stores assistants, clerks and labourers would be coded to the appropriate department to form part of the overheads of that department. In addition, the proportion of production workers' wages which cannot be classed as direct, e.g. idle time, overtime and shift premium would also be classified as indirect, included in overheads and subsequently absorbed into production costs via the appropriate overhead absorption rates as described in chapter 10.

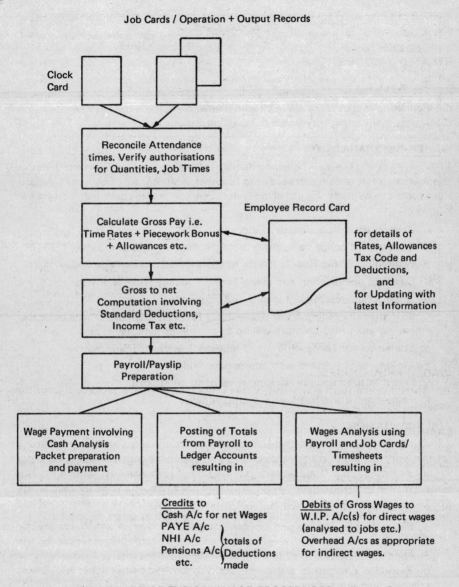

Job Cards / Operation + Output Records

Clock Card

Reconcile Attendance times. Verify authorisations for Quantities, Job Times

Calculate Gross Pay i.e. Time Rates + Piecework Bonus + Allowances etc.

Employee Record Card

for details of Rates, Allowances Tax Code and Deductions, and for Updating with latest Information

Gross to net Computation involving Standard Deductions, Income Tax etc.

Payroll/Payslip Preparation

Wage Payment involving Cash Analysis Packet preparation and payment

Posting of Totals from Payroll to Ledger Accounts resulting in

Wages Analysis using Payroll and Job Cards/ Timesheets resulting in

Credits to Cash A/c for net Wages PAYE A/c NHI A/c Pensions A/c etc. totals of Deductions made

Debits of Gross Wages to W.I.P. A/c(s) for direct wages (analysed to jobs etc.) Overhead A/cs as appropriate for indirect wages.

FLOWCHART OF TYPICAL WAGE PROCEDURES   Figure 3

c. **Labour cost control.** The cost department activities described above provide the raw data for cost ascertainment and also for cost control purposes. Cost control at its simplest will show various comparisons, for example, direct and indirect wages, suitably analysed, compared with the same classifications for the last period for each cost centre and department and will also show various ratios. The simplest of these would be the ratio of direct to indirect wages, compared period by period for each cost centre and department. In this way trends of labour costs will be shown and may give some guidance to management on cost control.

The above points are only a brief introduction to cost control and substantially more detail is given in chapters 22-25 on standard costing and budgetary control.

RELATED FACTORS

10. In addition to the recording and costing procedures described above, there are numerous other matters which have an impact on labour and labour costs. Some of the more important of these are dealt with below, namely — wage determination, job evaluation, merit rating, personnel policies and labour turnover.

WAGES DETERMINATION

11. This is a complex area where innumerable factors are involved. The factors vary in importance from one organisation to another and no simplistic, generalised statements can be made. Typical of the factors involved in wage determination are the following.

    a. General economic climate of industry.

    b. Government policy i.e. is there a wages norm or official incomes policy?

    c. Profitability of the firm. Is it able to pay higher than average wages?

    d. Extent of unionisation and union strength locally and nationally.

    e. Extent of unemployment locally and nationally.

    f. Cost structure of firm and industry e.g. a firm with high fixed costs of largely automatic plant may be more willing to accede to high pay claims.

    g. Strategic importance of firm and industry e.g. electricity industry.

    h. Availability of workers with appropriate skills.

    i. Extent of hazardous or dangerous working conditions.

    j. Wage rates prevailing locally and nationally.

JOB EVALUATION

12. This is a technique which seeks to show in a reasonably objective manner the relative worth of jobs. It attempts to do this by analysing the content of each job under various categories, e.g. Training required, Degree of responsibility, Working conditions, Types of decisions involved and so on, and giving a points score for each factor. The total of the points' scores for each job is then used to establish the ranking of one job to another and, by reference to pay scales, the normal salary for the job.

    Advantages

    a. Makes an attempt to be objective in ranking jobs.

    b. Reasonably effective within an organisation at ranking jobs, particularly relatively low level ones.

    Disadvantages

    a. Not suitable for ranking widely different jobs, particularly in different organisations.

    b. Gives a spurious air of objectivity to job comparison. The Job Evaluation process itself contains many subjective elements.

Notes:

    a. Job Evaluation studies the job, not the person doing the job.

    b. Job Evaluation is only one factor amongst many in determining the actual pay for the job.

MERIT RATING

13. Unlike job evaluation, merit rating is concerned with the individual employee. It seeks to rate an employee's performance to assist in determining whether a person should receive a merit award, promotion, demotion etc. It does this by considering the performance and attributes of an employee under various categories, for example, initiative, attendance, accuracy, willingness etc., etc. and giving a number of points for each factor. Merit rating under various guises is frequently encountered in staff appraisal schemes, particularly in larger firms, and is considered to be of value in providing a reasonably standardised basis to the difficult task of individual appraisal.

THE PERSONNEL FUNCTION

14. Most firms of any size have a Personnel department who have responsibility for numerous tasks involving labour. Typically these include:

    a. Advertising, recruiting and engaging labour.

    b. Discharge, transfer, administration of appraisal schemes.

    c. Industrial relations and union negotiations.

    d. Maintenance of personnel records and provision of statistical information to Government Departments, Trade Associations etc.

    e. Provision of information to management on such matters as absenteeism, lateness, labour turnover, normal and overtime worked etc.

    f. Staff development, training and educational schemes, including day release, apprenticeships and courses.

    g. Welfare, sports and social facilities.

    h. Safety and medical facilities.

    i. Manpower planning and forecasting.

In general terms the Personnel function has the responsibility to provide an efficient labour force which is cost effective and to keep labour turnover to a minimum.

LABOUR TURNOVER

15. This is usually expressed as a ratio, i.e.

$$\frac{\text{Number of employees replaced per period}}{\text{Average total number of employees in the period}}$$

Although some labour movement is of value, high labour turnover rates destroy morale, increase costs and reduce productivity. People leave jobs for a variety of reasons, some of which are avoidable, and it is normal to analyse the reasons for leaving so as to take corrective action where possible. Typical of the reasons for labour turnover are the following:

    a. Redundancy.

    b. Dissatisfaction over prospects, pay, hours, conditions.

    c. Lack of career structure.

    d. Lack of training or day release.

    e. Personal advancement.

    f. Marriage, pregnancy.

    g. Retirement.

    h. Discharge.

i. Move from locality.

j. Changes in domestic circumstances.

COSTS OF LABOUR TURNOVER

16. These costs can be substantial, yet to some extent are avoidable through enlightened personnel policies and good management. The costs arise in the following areas:

a. Leaving costs, i.e. interviews, preparation of documentation, disruption of output.

b. Replacement costs, i.e. advertising, selection, personnel department procedures.

c. Training costs, i.e. costs of required internal and external courses.

d. Learning costs, i.e. slower initial production, increased scrap, tool breakages, increased accident rate.

SUMMARY

17. a. Attendance records, usually in the form of clock cards, are always required.

b. Where incentive schemes are in operation, output records either by time sheets, job cards or piecework tickets are required.

c. The main elements in the wages procedure are: time reconciliation, gross pay calculation, gross to net calculation, payroll and payslip preparation, wage payment.

d. The total of gross wages is charged to Work-in-Progress A/cs for direct wages and Overhead A/cs for indirect.

e. Overtime and shift premiums are generally classed as indirect and form part of production overheads.

f. Numerous factors determine the level of wages paid including: national and local rates, cost of living, prosperity of industry, union strength and militancy, working conditions etc.

g. Job evaluation seeks to analyse the content of each job under various factors so as to establish the relative worth of one job to another.

h. Merit rating seeks to assess the efficiency of an individual for the purposes of bonuses, promotion etc.

i. The personnel function is wide ranging and important and includes: engaging and discharging labour, union negotiations, staff development and training, welfare and safety.

j. Labour turnover should be monitored closely and the reasons for each employee leaving ascertained.

k. The costs of labour turnover can be high and include: engaging new labour, learning costs, training costs, lower initial productivity.

POINTS TO NOTE

18. Every aspect of labour relations can be critical and affect costs. The old 'scientific management' approach to labour as merely an adjunct to machinery is outmoded in current conditions.

SELF REVIEW QUESTIONS

1. *What is a clock card? (3)*
2. *Why are job cards difficult to incorporate into wages procedures? (6)*
3. *What is an operation card? (7)*
4. *Describe the steps in a typical wage procedure. (8)*
5. *Are overtime and shift premiums normally included in direct wages? (9a)*
6. *Give some examples of reports which might assist labour cost control. (9c)*
7. *What are some of the factors involved in wage determination? (11)*
8. *What is the object of Job Evaluation? (12)*
9. *What is Merit Rating? (13)*
10. *Give six functions normally carried out by a Personnel department. (14)*
11. *What is the labour turnover ratio? (15)*

EXAMINATION QUESTION

1. a. *Based on the data shown below, you are required to calculate the remuneration of each employee, as determined by each of the following methods:*
    - i. *hourly rate;*
    - ii. *basic piece rate;*
    - iii. *individual bonus scheme, where the employee receives a bonus in proportion of the time saved to the time allowed:*

Data

Name of employee	Salmon	Roach	Pike
Units produced	270	200	220
Time allowed in minutes per unit	10	15	12
Time taken in hours	40	38	36
	£	£	£
Rate per hour	1.25	1.05	1.20
Rate per unit	0.20	0.25	0.24

   b. *Comment briefly on the effectiveness of method iii.*

(ICMA, Cost Accounting 1, May 1975).

10 Overheads

INTRODUCTION

1. This chapter revises the buildup and absorption of overheads (first covered in chapters 2 and 3) and discusses the problems of service department overheads. The various methods of depreciation are considered together with the impact on overheads of the method chosen. The treatment of special matters such as obsolescence, taxation, VAT and interest is also considered.

THE BUILDUP OF OVERHEADS

2. Figure 1 summarises the usual method of establishing production overheads and how these overheads are absorbed into production.

Stage 1. Cost elements

The raw data relating to Labour, Materials, Expenses are gathered from Invoices, Payroll, Goods Issued Notes and Requisitions.

Stage 2. Coding

All the raw cost data needs to be classified and then coded in respect of the type of expense and location. This process is fundamental to all the costing and management accounting procedures.

Stage 3. Cost analysis

Where costs can be allotted in their entirety to one cost centre this is termed allocation. Where the cost has to be spread over several cost centres this is known as apportionment. The bases of apportionment have been discussed in Chapter 2.

Stage 4. Service cost centres.

These are cost centres which provide a service to production cost centres. Examples are Maintenance, Stores and Boiler House. Their costs are built up by the usual process of allocation and primary apportionment and then their total costs are apportioned (secondary apportionment) over the production cost centres, thus forming part of production overheads which are absorbed into the cost units produced. The problems of service cost centres are dealt with in more detail below in Para. 3.

Stage 5. Production cost centres.

These are the cost centres involved directly in the production process. Typical examples are, the Assembly shop, Drilling machines, Centre lathes, Spray shop.

Stage 6. Overhead absorption

The overheads of each production cost centre are absorbed into the costs of the units produced, usually in proportion to the time involved i.e. by the Labour Hour or Machine Hour rate. This subject was dealt with in detail in Chapter 3.

SERVICE COST CENTRES

3. Because no production cost units pass through the service cost centres, it is necessary to apportion the service department costs to the production cost centres so that all production costs (including those for the servicing departments) are absorbed into production. Typical bases for secondary apportionment, i.e. the apportionment of service costs to production departments, follow Figure 1.

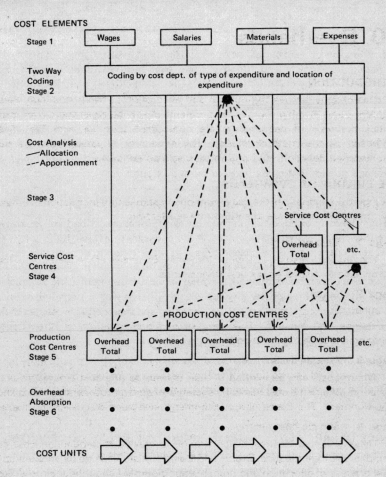

THE BUILD-UP OF OVERHEADS   Figure 1

Service Dept.	Possible bases of Apportionment to Production Cost Centres
Maintenance	Maintenance Labour Hours Maintenance Wages Plant values
Stores	No. of Requisitions Weight of Materials issued
Inspection	No. of Production Employees per cost centre No. of Inspection Tickets No. of Jobs
Production Control	No. of Production Employees per cost centre No. of Jobs
Power Generation	Metered Usage Notional Capacity Technical Estimate
Personnel Dept.	No. of Employees per Department

Notes:

   a. The basis chosen should be one that is judged to be the most equitable way of sharing the service department's costs over the departments which use the service. This may mean that a particular and unique basis of apportionment may have to be derived. It must reflect the use made of the services provided.

   b. Wherever possible, service department costs should be charged directly, i.e. allocated. An example of this would be maintenance wages and materials. When a maintenance job is done for a department, the wages and materials used would be charged directly to the department concerned. In this way only unallocated service department costs need to be apportioned.

ESTABLISHING SERVICE DEPARTMENTAL COSTS

4.   The necessity to apportion service costs has been described above. However, before this apportionment takes place, it is necessary to establish the total service department costs. This is discussed below in three differing circumstances: where service departments only do work for other departments and not each other; where some service departments do work for other service departments; and where service departments provide reciprocal services to each other as well as providing a service to production.

SERVICES TO NON-SERVICE DEPARTMENTS ONLY

5.   This is the simplest situation and is somewhat unlikely. It is the situation depicted in Figure 1 and total service department costs are easily arrived at by the usual process of allocation and primary apportionment from the raw data, i.e. Stages 1, 2 and 3 from Figure 1.

SERVICE DEPARTMENTS WORKING FOR OTHER SERVICE DEPARTMENTS

6.   Where a service department provides a service to another service department, for example maintenance to stores, it is necessary to apportion the *servicing* department's costs before that of the *serviced* department. In the example given, maintenance costs would be apportioned to stores (and appropriate production cost centres), then the stores' costs would be apportioned between the various production cost centres. The reason for this is, of course, that the total cost of the stores must include an appropriate charge for maintenance work done.

RECIPROCAL SERVICES

7.   A particular problem arises where two or more service departments work for each other as well as for production. For example, assume that Maintenance (M) do work for Stores (S) and Stores supply items to Maintenance. The total cost of M cannot be ascertained until the charge for S's service is known, and similarly the total cost of S cannot be found until the charge for M's work is known. Some way has to be found to break into this circular problem so as to be able to ascertain service department costs. This can be done by three methods: continuous allotment, elimination, and using simultaneous equations. These methods will be illustrated by using the following example:

Example

   A small factory has two service departments, Maintenance (M) and Stores (S) and three Production departments (P1, P2, and P3).

The service departments provide services for each other as well as for the Production departments and it has been agreed that the most appropriate bases of apportionment for service department costs are: Capital equipment values for Maintenance and number of requisitions for Stores.

The overheads applicable to each department following allocation and primary apportionment are:−

Department	Overheads £
M	6,800
S	2,700
P1	12,000
P2	19,500
P3	26,000

Total £67,000

Data for apportionment of Service Department overheads

	M	S	P1	P2	P3
Capital values	£15,000	£10,000	£50,000	£76,000	£64,000
Proportion	–	5%	25%	38%	32%
No. of Requisitions	900	–	2400	1620	1080
Proportion	15%	–	40%	27%	18%

The above data are used for each of the solution methods described below.

THE CONTINUOUS ALLOTMENT METHOD

8. The principle involved in this method is that the appropriate proportion of the costs of the first service department are allotted to the second (i.e. 5% of M to S), then the appropriate proportion of the second department is allotted back to the first department (i.e. 15% of S to M) and so on until the amounts allotted to and fro become insignificant. This is now shown.

Department M			**Department S**	
Amounts Allotted	**Workings**	**Direction and Amount of Allotment**	**Workings**	**Amounts Allotted**
£			£	£
6800 (original allotment)	(5% of £6800)	£340	2700 340	2700 (original allotment) 340
			3040	
		£456 ── (15% of 3040)		
456	£456			
	(5% of 456)	£23		
3		£23 (15% of £23)	23	
	£3	£3		
	5% of £3 insignificant			
£7259				£3063

The notional service department overheads, i.e. £7259 and £3063 are then used in the secondary apportionment thus:

	M	S	P₁	P₂	P₃
	Departments				
	£	£	£	£	£
Original Allotment	6800	2700	12000	19500	26000
Notional Overheads for M apportioned over serviced Depts.	−7259	363	1815	2758	2323
Notional Overheads for S apportioned over serviced Depts.	459	−3063	1225	827	552
	NIL	NIL	£15,040	£23,085	£28,875

Note:

Amounts rounded to nearest £.

The final apportioned overheads equal the original total allotments, i.e.

£15040 + 23085 + 28875 = £67,000

THE ELIMINATION METHOD

9. This is a simpler method which apportions in turn service department costs to users. Once a service department's costs have been apportioned the department is eliminated from further apportionments. This means that return charges from other service departments do not arise i.e. the cost effects of reciprocal servicing is ignored. The sequence in which departments are eliminated can be related to either the amounts involved or the number of departments serviced. The method is illustrated below using the data from Example 1.

	M	S	P₁	P₂	P₃
	Departments				
	£	£	£	£	£
Original Allotment	6800	2700	12000	19500	26000
Apportion Total of M (i.e. £6800) and eliminate M.	−6800	340	1700	2584	2176
Apportion Total of S (i.e. £2700 + 340)		−3040	1430	966	644
	NIL	NIL	£15,130	£23,050	£28,820

Notes:

1. In this case M was eliminated first as the largest amount was involved.

2. The apportionments of M are in the original proportions i.e. 5% - 25% - 38% - 32%.

3. The apportionments of S, because M is eliminated, are in the proportions of 40 : 27 : 18, i.e. the original percentages omitting the 15% relating to M.

4. It is claimed that the results produced by the elimination method are less 'accurate' than the results obtained by other methods. However, it must be emphasised that the procedures of absorption and apportionment are merely conventions so that the concepts of accuracy and inaccuracy in this context have doubtful validity. All that can be said is that the methods produce different results.

SIMULTANEOUS EQUATIONS (ALGEBRAIC METHOD)

10. This method utilises an equation for each service department, (in example 1, two equations) and solves these equations by the conventional methods, viz.

Let m = Total overheads for maintenance when the stores charges have been allotted.

s = Total overheads for stores when maintenance charges have been allotted.

m = 6800 + 0.15s

and s = 2700 + 0.05m

Rearranging these equations we obtain

m − 0.15s = 6800 . . . . Equation I

and s − 0.05m = 2700 . . . .   „   II

To solve Equations I and II it is necessary to eliminate one of the unknowns. This can be done in this example by multiplying Equation II by 20 and adding the result to Equation I thus

$$m - 0.15s = 6800 \quad \text{Equation I}$$
$$\underline{20s - m = 54000} \quad \text{20 x Equation II}$$
$$19.85s = 60800$$
$$s = \underline{£3063}$$

Substituting the value for s in one of the equations, the value for m can be obtained.

Substituting in Equation 1

m − 0.15 (3063) = 6800

m = £7259

Having thus obtained the values for m and s, the secondary apportionment can take place as shown in the last part of Para. 8 above.

Notes:

a. In this case the values obtained for m and s correspond exactly to the values obtained by the continuous allotment method. Sometimes there is a slight discrepancy.

b. Simultaneous equations can also be solved using matrix algebra. This method is dealt with in detail in 'Quantitative Techniques', T. Lucey, DP Publications.

DEPRECIATION

11. Most of the items which are classified as overheads, e.g. rent, rates, indirect labour and materials, office expenses, electricity and heating charges, have their values externally determined; e.g. the landlord fixes the rent, the local authority the rates and so on. However, a major item of overhead costs, that of depreciation, has its value determined internally and so consideration of the various depreciation methods is essential for accountants. Depreciation can be formally defined as,

"The diminution in the value of a fixed asset due to use or the lapse of time". *Terminology*.

Effectively, the conventions of depreciation accounting spread the cost of a fixed asset over its life and consequently over the production involved.

A further difference between depreciation and other overheads such as rates and salaries, is that it is a notional item of expense. For items such as rates, electricity and salaries an actual cash flow takes place. However, for notional items such as depreciation no cash flow occurs, the charge being merely a book-keeping entry. This does not mean that depreciation is unimportant. It would be unrealistic not to include the cost of expensive plant and buildings in the cost of a product and depreciation is the most practical way this can be done.

DEPRECIATION METHODS

12. There are numerous systems available each with particular characteristics, but they fall into two categories:

    a. Those that are time based.

    b. Those that are based on the volume produced or the level of activity.

Whatever method is used, it is necessary to establish the total amount that needs to be charged through depreciation. This amount, termed the 'net asset cost', is calculated as follows:

Net asset cost = Purchase price + Installation + delivery costs − Net scrap value

Notes:

    a. For registered organisations the purchase price is the Invoice value less VAT; for unregistered organisations it is the gross Invoice value.

    b. Net scrap value is the amount realised on disposal less disposal costs.
    The three most common methods of depreciation are, the Straight Line, Reducing Balance and the Production Unit (or Hour) methods.

STRAIGHT LINE DEPRECIATION

13. This method, sometimes known as the equal-instalment method, writes down the value of the asset by an equal amount each year. The charge per year is found by the formula:

$$\text{Depreciation charge per year} = \frac{\text{Net Asset cost}}{\text{Estimated life in years}}$$

Example:

The net asset cost of a power press is £38,000 and it is estimated to have a life of 10 years.

$$\text{Straight line depreciation p.a.} = \frac{£38,000}{10}$$

$$= \underline{\underline{£3800}}$$

Characteristics:

    a. Simple to understand and calculate.

    b. Charges an equal amount for depreciation over each year of the asset's life.

    c. Takes no account of the volume of activity during the year.

    d. Although an equal financial amount is charged each year, inflation causes this amount to have a declining impact on real values. In the example above, £3800 charged in year 10 has only approximately 25% of the real value of the £3800 charged in the first year, assuming a 15% inflation rate.

    e. A time based method.

REDUCING BALANCE METHOD (alternatively the Diminishing balance method)

14. Under this method a fixed percentage of the written down value of the asset is charged as depreciation each year. The effect of this is that decreasing amounts are charged each year in contrast with the straight line method which produces an equal charge each year. The fixed percentage to be used is the percentage which should be deducted from the written down value each year so that, over the life of the asset, the initial total installed cost is reduced to the net scrap value.

The percentage can be calculated by the following formula

$$\text{Percentage} = (1 - \sqrt[n]{\frac{s}{a}}) \times 100$$

where n = estimated life in years

s = net scrap value

a = total installed cost

Example:

If an asset has a total installed cost of £22500 and an estimated net scrap value of £2500 and is expected to last 10 years, what is the appropriate percentage to use for depreciation under the reducing balance method?

Solution n = 10

s = 2500

a = 22500

$$\text{Percentage} = (1 - \sqrt[10]{\frac{2500}{22500}}) \times 100$$

and solving by logs

$$\begin{array}{c} 3.3979 \\ \underline{4.3522} \\ 1.0457 \end{array} \quad \text{(i.e.} \quad \frac{2500}{22500})$$

$$10)\ \overline{1}.0457 \qquad \text{(i.e. finding 10th root)}$$

$$= 10)\ \overline{10} + 9.0457$$

$$= \quad 1.9046$$

antilog = $\underline{0.8029}$

∴ Percentage = (1 − 0.8029) x 100 ≃ 20%

This percentage would be deducted from the written down value thus

			Depreciation Charge	
		£	£	
Total installed cost	=	22500		
Depreciation = £22500 x 20%	=	− 4500	4500	Year 1
		18000		
Depreciation = £18000 x 20%	=	− 3600	3600	Year 2
		14400		
Depreciation £14400 x 20%	=	− 2880	2880	Year 3
		11520		
Depreciation = £11520 x 20%	=	2304	2304	Year 4

and so on.

Notes:

    a. In practice rates are not calculated for each asset as shown above. Invariably assets are classified into various categories e.g. motor vehicles, Plant and machinery etc., and a given percentage, usually determined by custom and practice, used for each category, e.g. Motor vehicles 30%, Plant 25% and so on.

    b. An approximation of the percentage rate can be found by the following simple formula: $\dfrac{200}{n}$ % where n is the life of the asset.

Characteristics of reducing balance method

    a. The depreciation charges are heavier in the earlier years and progressively decline. An argument for this is that as maintenance charges are likely to increase as the years go by, the combined depreciation/maintenance charge will even out. Unfortunately this degree of regularity is unlikely in practice.

    b. The method takes no account of the level of activity.

    c. Simple to understand and calculate. Within a category of assets with the same percentage, the calculation of the total depreciation charge is simply the given percentage of the total written down value regardless of the varying ages of the assets.

    d. A time based method.

PRODUCTION UNIT METHOD

15. Under this method the depreciation charge is based upon the estimated number of units to be produced by the machine over its life.

$$\text{Depreciation charge p.a.} = \frac{\text{Net asset cost}}{\substack{\text{Estimated life of machine}\\ \text{expressed in units}\\ \text{of production}}} \times \frac{\text{Units produced}}{\text{in the year}}$$

Example:

    A machine with a net asset cost of £30,000 is expected to produce 240,000 units over its working life. In a given year actual production was 27500 units. What is the depreciation charge for the year?

    Solution

$$\text{Depreciation/unit} = \frac{£30,000}{240,000}$$

$$= £0.125$$

$$\therefore \text{ Charge for year} = £0.125 \times 27,000$$

$$= \underline{£3375}$$

Note:

    An alternative form of this method uses production hours instead of production units.

Characteristics:

    a. Depreciation is directly related to activity thus becoming a variable cost.

    b. Only appropriate for a relatively narrow range of assets i.e. those directly involved in producing identifiable units.

c. Administratively cumbersome.

d. Ignores the depreciation effects of time.

OTHER DEPRECIATION METHODS

16. Alternative depreciation methods which are less frequently encountered are briefly described below.

a. Revaluation method

The depreciation charge is the difference between the value of the asset(s) at the beginning of the year and the assessed value at the year end. Used for items where normal depreciation methods are inappropriate, e.g. Livestock, Tools, Site Plant.

b. Sum of the digits

Somewhat similar in application to the reducing balance method in that decreasing amounts are charged each year.

Depreciation charge per year $= \dfrac{x}{n!}$ (Net asset cost)

where n $=$ estimated life of asset in years

n! $=$ Factorial n, i.e. the sum of the progression $1 + 2 + 3$ and so on up to n.

x $=$ n for year 1

n $-$ 1 for year 2

n $-$ 2 for year 3 and so on.

Example:

An asset has a net asset cost of £9000 and a life of 5 years. What is the first year's depreciation using the sum of the digits method?

Solution

$$n = 5 \quad \therefore \quad n! = 5 + 4 + 3 + 2 + 1$$
$$= 15$$

For Year 1 $\quad$ x $=$ n

$\therefore$ Year 1 depreciation $= \dfrac{5}{15}$ (9000)

$$= \underline{£3000}$$

b. Repair reserve method

In this method the annual charge comprises a normal straight line depreciation charge plus an estimated maintenance cost, i.e.

$$\text{charge per annum} = \frac{\text{Net asset cost} + \text{Estimated maintenance charge over life of asset}}{\text{Estimated life}}$$

c. Sinking fund

This method differs fundamentally from all the other methods described. The sinking fund method makes periodic investments external to the firm so that at the end of the life of the asset the realisation of the investment will produce cash equal to the cost of the asset. It will be remembered that other depreciation methods involve book-keeping entries only and no cash flow is involved. The formula is as follows:

$$\text{charge per annum} = \text{Net asset cost} \times \frac{1}{s_{\overline{n}|r}}$$

where n = estimated life in years

r = interest rate of sinking fund

and $\dfrac{1}{s_{\overline{n}|r}}$ is a value obtained from Sinking Fund Tables.

For example, an asset has a net asset cost of £18,000, is expected to last 5 years and investment opportunities exist at 8%. What is the charge per annum?

$$\text{Charge per annum} = £18,000 \times \frac{1}{s_{\overline{5}|8\%}}$$

$$= £18,000 \times .17046 \text{ (value from Sinking Fund Tables)}$$

$$= \underline{\underline{£3068}}$$

PLANT REGISTER

17. To be able to allocate and apportion depreciation charges (however calculated) an up to date record of all assets must be kept. This is termed a plant register. This may be on a card index system or, more frequently nowadays, on a computer file. Typically such a record would contain the following details:

    a. Plant description, serial number, supplier details including original cost.

    b. Technical data relating to speeds, capacities, fuel usage etc.

    c. Location.

    d. Depreciation method, estimated life and residual value, amounts written off, written down value.

    e. Details of capital allowances, balancing charges or allowances.

    f. Disposal details.

    g. Maintenance expenditure (usually reserved for major overhauls).

    h. Details of additions and enhancements.

OBSOLESCENCE

18. This may be defined as

"The diminution in the value of a fixed asset due to (a) its supersession by one which is technologically superior or (b) a cessation of the need of its use in consequence of a change in the production programme." *Terminology*.

There are some relationships between normal depreciation and the concept of obsolescence, but the main distinction is that obsolescence may be rapid and is usually difficult to forecast. Consequently it is not normal practice to make regular charges relating to obsolescence. Instead, when an asset is retired prematurely due to obsolescence, it is normal practice to charge the resulting loss directly to the general profit and loss account rather than to a particular product or department.

ASSETS IN USE AFTER BEING FULLY DEPRECIATED

19. When the useful life of an asset is underestimated, the situation may arise that an asset is fully depreciated, yet still in use. In such circumstances it is usual to continue to charge depreciation so as to maintain cost comparability with previous periods and so that current costs reflect all the costs of using the asset. The excess depreciation so charged can either be used to create a reserve against obsolescence or credited to the general profit and loss account. It is frequently possible to judge that the original life estimate is incorrect before the asset is fully written off. In such cases a new life estimate is made with a consequent change in the depreciation charge, so obviating the problem of having an asset in use which is fully written off.

REPLACEMENT VALUE AND HISTORIC COST

20. All the preceding paragraphs have assumed that depreciation is based on the original cost of the asset. Students should be aware that there are strong arguments for basing depreciation on current replacement values, not historical cost. The reason for this is that depreciation based on replacement values more nearly approximates to real economic values which are of greater importance to decision making management. However, the arguments for and against the use of replacement costs raise fundamental issues of accounting theory outside the scope of this manual.

SPECIAL OVERHEAD PROBLEMS

21. There are some items to which special consideration should be given as to whether they form part of overheads or not.

a. Taxation
Taxation is regarded as an appropriation of profit and is invariably omitted from routine costing systems. However, for many decision and planning purposes the effects of taxation can be crucial so that it should be included in special studies and reports where appropriate.

b. Value Added Tax
Because input VAT can be claimed back it does not represent a cost, so it is never included in the cost accounts.

c. Interest
Although there are some strong theoretical arguments for the inclusion of interest in the cost accounts, there are severe problems in devising a practical scheme. In general therefore interest payments or imputed interest is not included in the routine costing system. However, in a similar fashion to taxation, interest should be included in cost statements and investigation reports where it may have an effect on the decision to be taken. Typical examples include: the costs of alternative actions involving different capital investment, lease or buy decisions, financing decisions etc.

d. Notional costs
This is a hypothetical cost which is entered in the cost accounts so as to represent a benefit enjoyed by the organisation even though no actual cost is incurred. For example, the owner occupier of premises does not pay rent, yet some accountants would consider it correct to make a notional charge to overheads equivalent to the current rents for similar properties. In this way cost comparability with other organisations would be possible and the firm's costs would reflect a situation closer to current economic values. This could be vital if the firm was involved in any form of cost plus pricing. Obviously any notional charge into overheads and thence product costs would have to be counterbalanced by a credit to the general profit and loss account.

SUMMARY

22. a. Overheads are built up by a process of allocation and apportionment. They are 'shared out' over production by means of overhead absorption.

b. The overheads of service departments are built up by allocation and primary apportionment and are then spread over the production departments by secondary apportionment in proportion to usage.

c. The three methods of establishing service department overheads when reciprocal servicing occurs are: continuous allotment, elimination and the use of simultaneous equations.

d. Depreciation occurs through wear and tear and the passage of time. The accounting charge known as depreciation is a way of spreading the cost of an asset over its working life.

e. The most common methods of depreciation are: straight line, reducing balance, and production unit.

f. Other depreciation methods include: revaluation, sum of the digits, sinking fund and repair reserve.

g. Obsolescence is the loss in value due to supercession. It is not normal practice to make regular charges relating to obsolescence, but to write the loss off to the general profit and loss account when it occurs.

h. Taxation and interest are not included in routine costing. They may, however, be included as part of the special information regarding a particular decision.

POINTS TO NOTE

23. a. Non production overheads (administration, selling, research etc.) are an increasing proportion of the total costs of firms.

b. Because there are so many assumptions and conventions involved in establishing overheads, there is little point in pursuing minute accuracy over such matters as the bases of apportionment, depreciation and reciprocal service costs.

SELF REVIEW QUESTIONS

1. How are production overheads built up and eventually absorbed into production? (2)
2. What is a service cost centre? (3)
3. Give some possible bases of apportionment of service costs to production cost centres for: Maintenance, Inspection, Personnel Department. (3)
4. What are the three methods of establishing service department costs when reciprocal servicing takes place? (7)
5. Describe the continuous allotment method. (8)
6. What is the simultaneous equation method? (10)
7. Define depreciation. (11)
8. Why is depreciation a notional charge? (11)
9. What is the 'net asset cost'?
10. Describe straight line depreciation. (13)
11. Are equal amounts charged each year using the reducing balance method? (14)
12. What is the formula for the reducing balance method? (14)
13. What is the production unit method of depreciation? (15)

14. Give three other methods of depreciation. (16)

15. What is the major difference between the sinking fund method and all other methods? (16)

16. What are typical details kept in a Plant Register? (17)

17. Distinguish between depreciation and obsolescence. (18)

18. What is the costing treatment of an asset which is still in use after being fully depreciated? (19)

19. Is taxation a part of cost? (21)

20. Should imputed interest be included in routine costing statements and records? (21)

EXAMINATION QUESTIONS

1. Shown below is next year's budget for a small engineering factory manufacturing two different products in two production departments, namely a machine shop and an assembly department. A canteen is also operated as a separate department.

Product	A	B
Selling Price, per unit	£60	£70
Sales Volume	1,500 units	3,000 units
Increase (Decrease) in Finished Stocks	500 units	(500) units
Material Cost, per unit	£8	£5
Direct Labour:	hours per unit	hours per unit
Machine Shop (£3 per hour)	5	6
Assembly Department (£2 per hour)	4	4
Machining:		
Machine Shop	3	8
Assembly Department	1	–

	Machine Shop £	Assembly Dept. £	Canteen £	Total £
Production Overhead:				
Variable	26,000	9,000	–	35,000
Fixed	42,000	30,000	16,000	88,000
	£68,000	£39,000	£16,000	£123,000
Number of Employees	15	9	1	
Floor Area	4,000 sq. ft.	1,000 sq. ft.	1,000 sq. ft.	

Required:

a. Establish an appropriate overhead absorption rate for each production department and calculate the total budgeted cost per unit of each product. You must clearly state and briefly justify the methods of overhead absorption used.

b. Assuming the company operates a full absorption costing system calculate the impact on budgeted profit if, next year, the actual results are as predicted except that sales and production of product A are 300 units higher than budget.

(ACCA, Costing December 1979).

2. A light engineering company calculates its production overhead absorption rate at the end of each month by dividing the total actual overheads incurred by the total number of units produced in that month. This blanket absorption rate is then applied retrospectively to the month's production.

A variety of products are manufactured by the company and total demand is such that there are some unavoidable seasonal fluctuations in production activity. Production departments vary from light assembly work to semi-automatic machine shops and within each department the processing time for different products varies considerably, in some cases products do not pass through every department.

Required:

Critically examine the effect of the above system of overhead absorption on the company's product costs, pricing policy and consequent profitability.

(ACCA, Costing, June 1979).

3. The ABC Company has two production departments, viz. Machining and Finishing, and two service departments, viz. Maintenance and Materials Handling.

The overhead budgets per four week period are £9,000 for the Machining Department, and £7,500 for the Finishing Department. The Machining Department overhead is absorbed on a machine hour basis (300 per period) and Finishing Department overhead is absorbed on the basis of direct labour hours (3,000 per period).

In establishing the overhead budgets of the production departments, service department costs have been dealt with as follows:

Maintenance Dept.	60% to Machining Dept.,
	30% to Finishing Dept., and
	10% to Materials Handling.
Materials Handling:	30% to Machining Dept.,
	50% to Finishing Dept., and
	20% to Maintenance Dept.

During Period VI, the Machining Dept. was in operation for 292 hours and the number of direct labour hours worked by Finishing Dept. personnel was 3,100. Overhead incurred during Period VI was as follows:

	Machining	Finishing	Maintenance	Materials Handling
Materials	£2,000	£3,000	£1,000	£200
Labour	3,000	900	2,000	3,000
Other allocated costs	600	400	800	300

You are required to:

a. write up the overhead accounts for each of the production departments for Period VI showing the disposition of any under/over absorption,

b. state the factors which gave rise to the under/over absorption, and

c. analyse the under/over absorption under the headings you have stated in your answer to (b).

(ACCA, Costing, June 1975).

4. Shown below is next year's budget for the Forming and Finishing departments of Tooton Ltd. The departments manufacture three different types of component which

are incorporated into the output of the firm's finished products.

Component	A	B	C
Production	14,000 units	10,000 units	6,000 units
Prime Costs:	£ per unit	£ per unit	£ per unit
Direct Materials –			
Forming Dept.	8	7	9
Direct Labour –			
Forming Dept.	6	9	12
Finishing Dept.	10	15	8
	24	31	29

Manufacturing Times:

Machining –			
Forming Dept.	4 hrs per unit	3 hrs per unit	2 hrs per unit
Direct Labour –			
Forming Dept.	2 hrs per unit	3 hrs per unit	4 hrs per unit
Finishing Dept.	3 hrs per unit	10 hrs per unit	2 hrs per unit

	Forming Department £	Finishing Department £
Variable Overheads	200,900	115,500
Fixed Overheads	401,800	231,000
	£602,700	£346,500
Machine time required and available	98,000 hours	–
Labour hours required and available	82,000 hours	154,000 hours

The Forming department is mechanised and employs only one grade of labour, the Finishing department employs several grades of labour with differing hourly rates of pay.

Required:

a. Calculate suitable overhead absorption rates for the Forming and Finishing departments for next year and include a brief explanation for your choice of rates.

b. Another firm has offered to supply next year's budgeted quantities of the above components at the following prices:

Component A £30,   Component B £65,   Component C £60

Advise management whether it would be more economical to purchase any of the above components from the outside supplier. You must show your workings and, considering cost criteria only, clearly state any assumptions made or any aspects which may require further investigation.

c. Critically consider the purpose of calculating production overhead absorption rates.

(ACCA, Costing, June 1980).

5.   For a factory which has three production departments (2 machine shops and 1 assembly shop) and three service departments, one of which – Engineering Service Department – serves the machine shops only, you are required to:

   a. prepare an overhead analysis sheet, showing the bases of any apportionments of overhead to departments;

   b. calculate suitable overhead absorption rates for the production departments, ignoring the apportionment of service department costs amongst service departments;

   c. calculate the overheads to be absorbed by two products, Gamma and Delta, whose cost sheet shows the following times spent in different departments:

		Gamma	Delta
Machine shop:	A	5 machine hours	3 machine hours
	B	2 machine hours	7 machine hours
Assembly		7 direct labour hours	9 direct labour hours

The annual budgeted overhead costs for the year are:

		Indirect wages £	Consumable supplies £
Machine shop:	A	23,260	6,300
	B	20,670	9,100
Assembly		8,110	2,100
Stores		4,100	1,400
Engineering Service		2,670	2,100
General services		3,760	1,600
		£62,570	£22,600

	£	
Depreciation of machinery	22,000	
Insurance of machinery	4,000	
Insurance of building	1,800	(see note 1)
Power	3,600	
Light and Heat	3,000	
Rent and rates	7,050	(see note 2)

Notes:

1.   Because of special fire risks, machine shop A is responsible for a special loading of insurance on the building. This results in a total building insurance cost for machine shop A of one-third of the annual premium.

2.   The general services department is located in a building owned by the company. It is valued at £6,000 and is charged into costs at a notional value of 8% per annum. The cost is additional to the rent and rates shown above.

3.   The values of issues of materials to the production departments are in the same proportions as shown above for consumable supplies.

   The following data are also available:

Departments		Book value of machinery £	Area sq. feet	Effective H.P. hours %	Production Direct labour hrs.	Capacity Machine hrs.
Productive						
Machine shop	A	60,000	5,000	50	200,000	40,000
	B	45,000	6,000	33.1/3	150,000	50,000
Assembly		15,000	8,000	4.1/6	300,000	–
Service						
Stores		6,000	2,000	–		
Engineering service		18,000	2,500	12½		
General service		6,000	1,500	–		
		£150,000	25,000	100		

(ICMA, Costing)

6. The overhead allocated to the three production cost centres and two service cost centres of the manufacturing division of a company were:

Production cost centre:	1	£20,000
	2	24,000
	3	36,000
Service cost centre:	S	13,500
	T	9,500

After a study it is decided that the costs of the service cost centres should be apportioned as follows:

		Production cost centres			Service cost centres	
		1 %	2 %	3 %	S %	T %
Service cost centre:	S	Nil	55	35	–	10
	T	45	35	15	5	–

You are required to calculate the total overhead chargeable to each production cost centre by each of the following methods:

a. Ignoring the service that each of the two service cost centres gives to the other;

b. Using a 'two-step' method of apportionment whereby costs of the service that serves most cost centres is apportioned first, and the other service cost centre is then apportioned to the production cost centres;

c. Using the 'repeated distribution' or 'continuous allotment' method of apportioning the costs of service cost centres among the production and the two service cost centres.

(ICMA, Cost Accounting).

11 Costing Methods – Introduction

INTRODUCTION

1. This chapter gives a brief outline of the costing methods and discusses the relationship between them. It serves as an introduction to the following four chapters which describe the methods in detail.

WHAT IS A COSTING METHOD?

2. A costing method is a method of costing which is designed to suit the way goods are processed or manufactured or the way that services are provided. It follows therefore that each firm will have a costing method which has unique features. Nevertheless there will be recognisably common features of the costing systems of firms who are broadly in the same line of business. Conversely firms employing substantially different manufacturing methods, for example a food processors and a jobbing engineering factory, will have distinctly different costing methods. It must be clearly understood that whatever costing method is employed, the basic costing principles relating to analysis, allocation and apportionment will be used.

CATEGORIES OF COSTING METHODS

3. There are two broad categories of costing methods: specific order costing and operation costing with subdivisions within each category.

    a. Specific order costing
This can be defined as "The category of basic costing methods applicable where work consists of separate contracts jobs or batches, each of which is authorised by a specific order or contract." *Terminology*. In most cases the job or contract is identified as the cost unit and frequently, but not always, the jobs or contracts are different from each other. The main sub-divisions of specific order costing are

      i.   Job costing
      ii. Contract costing
      iii. Batch costing

    b. Operation costing (sometimes termed unit costing)
This can be defined as, "The category of basic costing methods applicable where standardised goods or services result from a sequence of repetitive and more or less continuous operations or processes to which costs are charged before being averaged over the units produced during the period." *Terminology*.

    The key feature of this rather lengthy definition is that operation (or unit) costing seeks to establish the average cost per unit during a period for a series of identical cost units. The main subdivisions of operation costing are:

      i.   Process costing, including Joint Product and By-Product costing.
      ii. Service costing.

These categories and sub-divisions are shown overleaf:

Note:

    The dotted line indicates an area of overlap between the two major categories. Although each batch is separate and identifiable and may be different from any other batch, within a given batch there will be a number of identical cost units over which the total batch costs will be averaged. Thus batch costing may have some of the characteristics of both specific order and process costing.

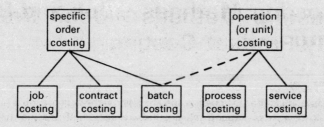

COSTING METHODS – CATEGORIES AND SUBDIVISIONS   Figure 1

COSTING METHODS AND COSTING PRINCIPLES

4. An important difference between the principles of costing in relation to specific order costing and Operation Costing is that, with Operation Costing, *all* costs i.e. labour, materials and overheads are allocated or apportioned to a *cost centre* from which these costs are shared out over the cost units produced. This differs from specific Order Costing where labour and materials may be able to be *directly* charged to a *cost unit* with only overheads having to be allocated or apportioned to a cost centre before sharing the costs over cost units.

COSTING METHODS AND COSTING TECHNIQUES

5. It must be emphasised that whatever costing method is used, it can be combined with any of the costing techniques if deemed appropriate. Thus, for example, a Process costing system could utilise the technique of either, Total Absorption costing or Marginal costing or Standard costing.

SUMMARY

5. a. Costing methods are designed to suit the method of manufacture or processing used by the firm.

b. Whatever method if used, it will employ basic costing principles relating to classification, analysis, allocation and apportionment.

c. The two main categories of costing methods are: specific order costing and operation (or unit) costing.

d. Specific order costing can be sub-divided into: Job Costing, Contract Costing, and Batch Costing.

e. Operation or Unit Costing can be sub-divided into: Service Costing, and Process Costing which includes Joint-Product and By-Product costing.

f. Whatever is deemed the most appropriate costing technique, e.g. Marginal Costing, Standard Costing etc. can be used with any of the costing methods.

POINT TO NOTE

6. Different parts of the same firm may require different costing methods. It is essential to relate the costing method to the particular activity being costed.

SELF REVIEW QUESTIONS

1. *What is a costing method?   (2)*
2. *What are the five main types of costing methods?   (3)*
3. *What is the relationship of a costing technique to a costing method?   (4)*

12 Costing Methods – Job and Batch Costing

INTRODUCTION
1. This chapter describes job costing and shows how the cost of a job is built up. The procedures necessary to support job costing are described and the main records illustrated. Batch costing is defined and its relationship with job costing is explained.

JOB COSTING – DEFINITION
2. The formal definition is given below and, although rather lengthy, provides an excellent description.

"That form of specific order costing which applies where work is undertaken to customers' special requirements. As distinct from contract costing, each job is of comparatively short duration. The work is usually carried out within a factory or workshop where each job moves through processes or operations as a continuously identifiable unit, although the term may be applied to such work as property repairs carried out on the customer's premises. The method may also be used in the costing of internal capital expenditure jobs." *Terminology*.

PREREQUISITES FOR JOB COSTING
3. The main purposes of job costing are to establish the profit or loss on each job and to provide a valuation of WIP. To do this a considerable amount of clerical work will be involved and to ensure an effective and workable system, the following factors are necessary:

  a. A sound system of production control.

  b. Comprehensive works documentation. Typically this includes: works order and/or operation tickets, bill of materials and/or materials requisitions, jig and tool requisitions, etc.

  c. An appropriate time booking system using either time sheets or piecework tickets.

  d. A well organised basis to the costing system with clearly defined cost centres, good labour analysis, appropriate overhead absorption rates and a relevant materials issue pricing system.

TYPICAL PROCEDURES IN A JOBBING CONCERN
4. Prior to examining the costing system it is necessary first to consider the typical flow of administrative procedures which ensure a job is manufactured correctly, delivered on time and charged for. An outline is shown in Figure 1 on the following page.

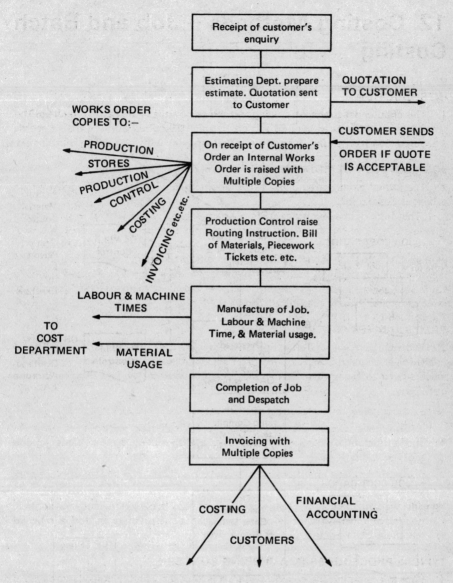

WORKS ORDER
COPIES TO:—

PRODUCTION

STORES

PRODUCTION
CONTROL

COSTING

INVOICING etc.etc.

QUOTATION
TO CUSTOMER

CUSTOMER SENDS

ORDER IF QUOTE
IS ACCEPTABLE

LABOUR & MACHINE
TIMES

TO
COST
DEPARTMENT

MATERIAL
USAGE

Receipt of customer's
enquiry

Estimating Dept. prepare
estimate. Quotation sent
to Customer

On receipt of Customer's
Order an Internal Works
Order is raised with
Multiple Copies

Production Control raise
Routing Instruction. Bill
of Materials, Piecework
Tickets etc. etc.

Manufacture of Job.
Labour & Machine
Time, & Material usage.

Completion of Job
and Despatch

Invoicing with
Multiple Copies

COSTING

FINANCIAL
ACCOUNTING

CUSTOMERS

TYPICAL NON-COSTING PROCEDURES IN A JOBBING CONCERN   Figure 1

JOB COSTING PROCEDURES

5. The main objective is to charge all costs incurred to the particular job. The usual means by which this is done is by creating a Job Cost Card (frequently just called the Job Card). The Job Cost Cards in total comprise the firm's work-in-progress and the detailed entries to the job cards would be debited in total to the work-in-progress account. The following diagram shows the major steps in a typical Job Costing process.

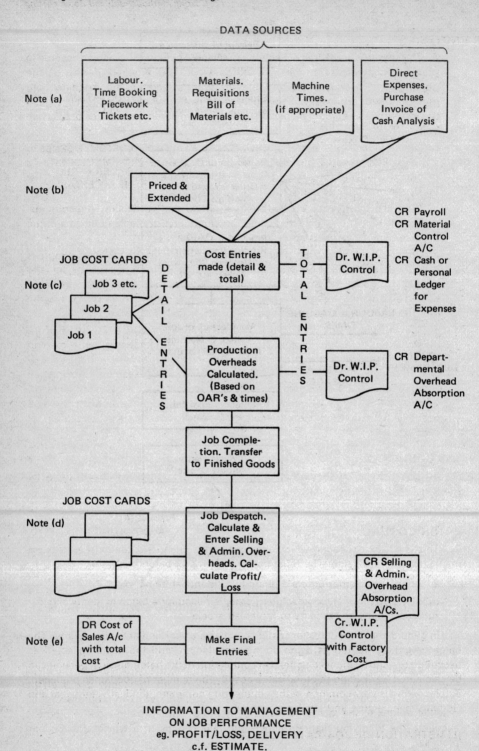

DATA SOURCES

Note (a)

| Labour. Time Booking Piecework Tickets etc. | Materials. Requisitions Bill of Materials etc. | Machine Times. (if appropriate) | Direct Expenses. Purchase Invoice of Cash Analysis |

Note (b) — Priced & Extended

Note (c)

JOB COST CARDS

Job 3 etc.
Job 2
Job 1

DETAIL ENTRIES

Cost Entries made (detail & total)

TOTAL ENTRIES — Dr. W.I.P. Control

CR Payroll
CR Material Control A/C
CR Cash or Personal Ledger for Expenses

Production Overheads Calculated. (Based on OAR's & times)

TOTAL ENTRIES — Dr. W.I.P. Control

CR Departmental Overhead Absorption A/C

Job Completion. Transfer to Finished Goods

JOB COST CARDS

Note (d)

Job Despatch. Calculate & Enter Selling & Admin. Overheads. Calculate Profit/Loss

CR Selling & Admin. Overhead Absorption A/Cs.

Note (e)

DR Cost of Sales A/c with total cost

Make Final Entries

Cr. W.I.P. Control with Factory Cost

INFORMATION TO MANAGEMENT
ON JOB PERFORMANCE
eg. PROFIT/LOSS, DELIVERY
c.f. ESTIMATE.

OUTLINE OF JOB COSTING   Figure 2

NOTES:

a. The contents and origin of Labour and Material bookings have been covered in previous chapters. The machine times would be required if any of the departmental overhead absorption rates were based on the machine hour method. Direct expenses e.g. royalties, tool hire etc., would be a direct charge to the job and details would be picked up either from purchase invoices or the cash book.

b. Labour time sheets and/or piecework tickets would be priced by reference to day and overtime rates, piecework and bonus rates. The materials issued would be priced using the stores record cards, employing one of the pricing systems, i.e. FIFO, average price etc.

c. After the prime costs had been entered, the production departments' overheads would be calculated using the labour and/or machine times and the predetermined overhead absorption rates (OAR's).

d. Until a job is despatched, it would normally be valued in the Work-in-Progress account at factory or works cost only. On despatch (or, in some systems, transfer to finished goods), the works cost would be loaded with an appropriate amount of selling and administration overheads. Any delivery costs can be charged to the job, the total cost established and the profit or loss calculated.

e. The individual Job Cost Cards will be retained and used as a basis for management information and future estimating. The closing book-keeping entries transfer the total cost of jobs despatched to cost of sales and the Factory cost is transferred from the W-I-P account (or in some systems the Finished Goods account). The amount of Selling and Administration overheads charged to jobs is credited to the overhead absorption account, so that eventually it will be possible to establish whether there has been under or over absorption of overheads.

JOB COST CARD

6. A typical job card is shown (Fig. 3). It is suitable for relatively small jobs or as the summary card for larger jobs which might have supporting schedules relating to Material, Labour and Overheads.

BATCH COSTING

7. This is a form of costing which applies where a quantity of identical articles are manufactured as a batch. The most common forms of batch are:

a. where a customer orders a quantity of identical items, or

b. where an internal manufacturing order is raised for a batch of identical parts, sub-assemblies or products to replenish stocks.

In general the procedures for costing batches are very similar to costing jobs. The batch would be treated as a job during manufacture and the costs collected as described previously in this chapter. On completion of the batch the cost per unit can be calculated by dividing the total batch cost by the number of good units produced. Batch costing is very common in the engineering component industry, footwear and clothing manufacture and similar industries.

ILLUSTRATION OF JOB/BATCH COSTING

8. The following example shows a typical cost buildup for batch of similar parts and

JOB COST CARD													Job No.			
Customer				Customers Order No.									Start Date			
Job Description													Delivery Date			
Estimate Ref.				Invoice No.									Despatch Note No.			
Quoted Price				Invoice Price												

Material					Labour									Overheads			
				Cost			Lab Anal Ref.	Cost Ctre			Bonus	Cost		M/c Hrs.	OAR	Cost	
Date	Req. No.	Qty.	Price	£	p	Date			Hrs.	Rate		£	p			£	p
Total C/F								Total C/F						Total C/F			

Expenses					Job Cost Summary	Actual		Estimate	
			Cost			£	p	£	p
Date	Ref.	Description	£	p					
					Direct Materials B/F				
					Direct Expenses B/F				
					Direct Labour B/F				
					= Prime Cost				
					Factory Overheads B/F				
					= Factory Cost				
					Selling & Admin. Overheads % on Factory Cost				
					= Total Cost				
					Invoice Price				
Total C/F					Job Profit/Loss				

Comments

Job Cost Card Completed by ....

TYPICAL JOB COST CARD   Figure 3

illustrates typical job costing procedures and the subsequent calculation of the unit cost and profit.

Example:

A company manufactures small assemblies to order and has the following budgeted overheads for the year, based on normal activity levels.

Department	Budgeted Overheads £	Overhead Absorption Base
Blanking	8000	1500 labour hours
Machining	23000	2500 machine hours
Welding	10000	1800 labour hours
Assembly	5000	1000 labour hours

Selling and Administrative overheads are 20% of Factory cost.

An order for 250 assemblies type X128, made as Batch 5931, incurred the following costs:

Materials	£3107
Labour	128 hours Blanking Shop at £2.25/hour
	452 hours Machining Shop at £2.50/hour
	90 hours Welding Shop at £2.25/hour
	175 hours Assembly Shop at £1.80/hour

£525 was paid for the hire of special X-ray equipment for testing the welds. The time booking in the machine shop was 643 machine hours.

Calculate the total cost of the batch, the unit cost and the profit per assembly if the selling price was £80/assembly.

Solution:

The first step is to calculate the overhead absorption rates for the production departments.

$$\text{Blanking} = \frac{£8000}{1500} = £5.33 \text{ O.A.R. per labour hour}$$

$$\text{Machining} = \frac{£23000}{2500} = £9.2 \text{ O.A.R. per machine hour}$$

$$\text{Welding} = \frac{£1000}{1800} = £5.55 \text{ O.A.R. per labour hour}$$

$$\text{Assembly} = \frac{£5000}{1000} = £5 \text{ O.A.R. per labour hour}$$

Total Cost – Batch No. 5931

	£	£
Direct Material		3107
Direct Expense		525
Direct Labour	128 x 2.25	
	452 x 2.50	
	90 x 2.25	
	175 x 1.80	1935.50
= PRIME COST		£5567.50

Production Overheads Absorption

$$£$$

= Blanking	128 x 5.33	
Machining	643 x 9.2	
Welding	90 x 5.55	
Assembly	175 x 5	7972.34
= FACTORY COST		£13539.84

+ Selling and Administrative overheads

20% of Factory Cost	=	2707.97
= Total Cost		£16247.81
Total Cost/unit	=	$\dfrac{£16247.81}{250}$ = £64.99
Profit/unit	=	£15.01

SUMMARY

9. a. Job costing is employed where work is done to customer's requirements, usually in a factory or workshop.

b. For job costing to be effective there must be a good system of production control, works documentation, material and labour booking.

c. All costs incurred must be charged to the job, usually on to a job cost card.

d. The job cost cards in total form the firm's work-in-progress.

e. The detail entries to the job cards would be debited in total to the Work-in-Progress account.

f. Prime costs are gathered from labour and material bookings on the shop floor and, in the case of expenses, from invoice or cash book analysis. Overheads are calculated based on predetermined overhead absorption rates and the time bookings.

g. Batch costing is very similar to job costing and is used where a batch of identical units are manufactured. Costs are gathered as for job costing and when the batch is completed, the total cost is divided by the number of good units made to establish the unit cost.

POINTS TO NOTE

10. a. Although job costing could be combined with any cost technique, for example standard costing or marginal costing, it is normally used with the total absorption technique. All the illustrations and narrative in this chapter have been based on the use of total absorption costing.

b. A realistic attitude must be taken to job costing. If there are numerous, small value jobs it is unlikely that the full process described in this chapter would be followed. Instead a General Jobbing account might be used which would be charged with the costs of small jobs and credited with the selling prices. Some loss of control and information are, however, inevitable consequences of this procedure.

SELF REVIEW QUESTIONS

1. *Define job costing.* (2)

2. What factors need to be present before a job costing system can operate efficiently? (3)

3. What is a job cost card? (5)

4. How is it completed? (5)

5. How does batch costing differ from job costing? (7)

EXAMINATION QUESTION

1. A factory with three departments uses a single production overhead absorption rate expressed as a percentage of direct wages cost. It has been suggested that departmental overhead absorption rates would result in more accurate job costs. Set out below are the budgeted and actual data for the previous period, together with information relating to job No. 657.

		Direct wages £000's	Direct labour	Machine	Production overhead £000's
			Hours in thousands		
Budget:					
Department:	A	25	10	40	120
	B	100	50	10	30
	C	25	25	–	75
Total:		150	85	50	225
Actual:					
Department:	A	30	12	45	130
	B	80	45	14	28
	C	30	30	–	80
Total:		140	87	59	238

During this period job No. 657 incurred the actual costs and actual times in the departments as shown below:

		Direct material £	Direct wages £	Direct labour hours	Machine hours
Department:	A	120	100	20	40
	B	60	60	40	10
	C	10	10	10	–

After adding production overhead to prime cost, one third is added to production cost for gross profit. This assumes that a reasonable profit is earned after deducting administration, selling and distribution costs.

You are required to:

a. calculate the current overhead absorption rate;

b. using the rate obtained in (a) above, calculate the production overhead charged to job No. 657 and state the production cost and expected gross profit on this job;

c. i. comment on the suggestion that departmental overhead absorption rates would result in more accurate job costs; and
   ii. compute such rates, briefly explaining your reason for each rate;

d. using the rates calculated in (c) (ii) above, show the overhead, by department and in total, that would apply to job No. 657;

e. show the over/under absorption, by department and in total, for the period using:

    i.   the current rate in your answer to (a) above, and

    ii. your suggested rates in your answer to (c) (ii) above.

(ICMA, Cost Accounting 1, Nov. 1977).

13 Costing Methods – Contract Costing

INTRODUCTION

1. This chapter defines contract costing and describes its characteristics. The procedures for progress payments and for calculating the profit on uncompleted contracts are explained and the costing procedures and book-keeping entries are shown and exemplified.

CONTRACT COSTING – DEFINITION

2. Contract costing has many similarities to job costing and is usually applied to work which is

   a. undertaken to customer's special requirements

   b. Relatively long duration

   c. Site based, sometimes overseas.

   d. Frequently of a constructional nature.

Because of the long time scale and size of many contracts, the necessity arises for intermediate valuations to be made of work done and for progress payments to be received from the client.

CHARACTERISTICS OF CONTRACT COSTING

3. Although details vary, certain characteristics are common to most contract costing systems:

   a. **Higher proportion of direct costs.** Because of the self-contained nature of most site operations, many items normally classified as indirect can be identified specifically with a contract and/or site and thus can be charged directly, e.g. telephones installed on site, site power usage, site vehicles, transportation, design and planning salaries.

   b. **Low indirect costs.** For most contracts, the only item of indirect cost would be a charge for Head Office expenses. This is usually only a small proportion of the contract cost and is absorbed normally on some overall basis, such as a percentage of total contract cost.

   c. **Difficulties of cost control.** Because of the scale of some contracts and the size of the site there are frequently major problems of cost control concerning: material usage and losses, pilferage, labour supervision and utilisation, damage to and loss of plant and tools, vandalism, etc.

   d. **Surplus materials.** All materials bought for a contract would be charged directly to the contract. At the end of the contract, the contract account would be credited with the cost of materials not used and, if they were transferred directly to another contract, the new contract account debited. If they were not required immediately, the materials would be stored and the cost debited to a stock account.

CONTRACT PLANT

4. A feature of most contract work is the amount of plant used. This includes cranes,

trucks, excavators, mixers and lorries. The usual ways in which plant costs are dealt with are as follows:

- a. **When plant is leased.** The leasing charges are charged directly to the contract.
- b. **When plant is purchased.** There are two methods in common use,
  - i. charge new plant at cost to the contract for which it was purchased. When the plant is no longer required and is transferred to another contract or to base, the original contract would be credited with the second hand value of the plant. In this way the contract bears the charge for the depreciation incurred. It will be appreciated that this is an example of the revaluation method of depreciation.
  - ii. where plant is moved frequently from contract to contract or where contracts are relatively short, a 'Plant Service Department' is created. This department organises the transfer of plant from contract to contract as required and each contract is charged a daily or weekly rental.

Note:

Whatever method is used for charging the capital costs of plant, the ordinary running costs; fuel, repairs and insurance would be charged direct to the contract.

PROGRESS PAYMENTS

5. The contract normally provides for the client to make progress payments either at specific stages of the work, e.g. when foundations are completed, first floor completion, or at particular agreed intervals. The basis for these interim payments is an architect's certificate of work satisfactorily completed. The architect's certificate shows the value of work done at selling prices and this certificate accompanies the invoice sent to the customer. The amount paid is normally the certified value less a percentage retention which is released when the contract is fully completed and accepted by the customer.

PROFIT ON UNCOMPLETED CONTRACTS

6. The objective of contract costing is to show the profit or loss on each contract. However, where a contract extends over more than one financial year, it is usually necessary to estimate the profit earned in a given financial year (that is, part of the total contract profit) so as to avoid excessive fluctuations in company results from year to year. Whilst anticipated losses would be allowed for, in full, as early as possible, the estimated profit in any period is conservatively estimated so as to allow for unforeseen difficulties and costs.

Normally, the profit to be taken in a period is restricted to a proportion (⅔ or ¾) of the difference between the *Value* and *Cost* of work certified, further reduced by the proportion which the money received to date bears to total value of work certified, i.e. the retention percentage.

Example:

Contract price	£500,000
Target length of contract	3 years
Work certified to date	£220,000
Cost of work certified	£187,500
Retentions 10%.	All monies due to date have been received.

Solution: £

value of work certified	220,000
less cost of work certified	187,500
	32,500
⅔ proportion =	21,667

Reduced by retentions = 90% x 21,667 = £19500

∴ Profit to be taken in period = £19500

Note:

SSAP 9 includes a section on the calculation of profit on contracts and students are advised to refer to this standard.

THE COSTING ENTRIES

7. A separate account will be kept for each contract with the general objective of establishing the overall contract profit or loss. To do this the following entries are required:

Contract Account

Typical Debit Entries	Typical Credit Entries
Debit Direct costs (Material, Labour)	Credit Plant, Materials transferred from Contract
Debit Direct expenses (Plant hire, Sub-contractors, Architects' fees, etc.)	Credit Valuation of Work certified
Debit Cost of Plant bought	
Debit any materials, plant etc. transferred to contract	
Debit Head Office Charges	
Debit Interim and Final Profit	

In addition there are, of course, contra entries within the contract account relating to carry forward/brought forward items, accruals and prepayments.

All of the above entries are shown in the following example.

EXAMPLE OF CONTRACT COSTING

8. The following information relates to Contract 87 on the Thornley site as at the 31st December 19-1.

Contract 87 – Thornley Site
Customer – Middlethorpe Corporation

	£
Wages	42,156
Materials delivered direct to site	54,203
Materials from Main Stores	657
Materials transferred to Riverview Site	1,590
Plant purchased (at cost)	12,500
Plant transferred to Thornley	5,250

	£
Sub-contractors charges	19,580
Site expenses (power etc.)	5,086
Materials on Site 31st December	18,300
Plant on Site 31st December	14,750
Prepayments at 31st December	507
Accrued wages at 31st December	921
Cost of work done but not certified (i.e. W-I-P) at 31st December	7,250
Head Office charges are 10% of wages	

Up to 31st December the value of work certified by the architect was £137,500 and Middlethorpe Corporation made progress payments of this amount less the agreed 15% retention.

From the above information prepare the Contract Account to 31st December 19-1 clearly showing the profit to be taken for the year and the opening entries for the year commencing 1st January 19-2.

Solution:

CONTRACT No. 87   CUSTOMER: Middlethorpe Corporation
SITE: Thornley

CONTRACT A/C

	£	£		£
Site Wages	42,156		Materials transferred out	1,590
+ accrued C/F	921	43,077	Prepayments C/D	507
Materials purchased	54,203			
Materials from Stores	657	54,860		
Plant purchased	12,500		Materials at site C/D	18,300
Plant transferred in	5,250	17,750	Plant at site C/D	14,750
Sub contractors		19,580	W-I-P C/D	7,250
Site expenses		5,086	Cost of Work	
Head office Charges		4,308	Certified C/D (Note (a))	102,264
		£144,661		£144,661
Cost of Work certified B/D		102,264	Value of work certified	137,500
Profit on Contract to date (Note (b))		19,967	(Note (d))	
Profit in suspense C/D (Note (c))		15,269		
		£137,500		£137,500
1st Jan. 19-2				
Prepayments B/D		507	Profit in suspense B/D	15,269
Materials B/D		18,300		
Plant B/D		14,750		
W-I-P B/D		7,250		

Notes:

a. The cost of work certified is the net balance of the first part of the contract account. The cost of *all* work done to date is £109,514 which includes the cost of work done, but not certified, i.e. the W-I-P, and the cost of work certified.

		£
Cost of all work to date	=	109,514
less Cost of work not certified	=	7,250
= Cost of work certified	=	£102,264

b. The profit to be taken on the contract to 31st December is calculated as follows:

		£
Value of work certified	=	137,500
less Cost of work certified	=	102,264
		35,236
⅔ proportion	=	23,490
Reduced by retentions = 85% x 23,490	=	£19,967

This latter figure is credited to the general P+L account of the company together with the interim profits taken on other contracts.

c. The profit in suspense is the difference between the total profit on the contract to date (£35,236) and the profit taken into account (£19,967), i.e.

£35,236 – 19,967

= £15,269

d. The value of work certified is credited to the contract account and debited to the customer's account. The personal account for Middlethorpe Corporation would be as follows

Middlethorpe Corporation

	£		£
Work certified, Contract 87	137,500	Cash progress payments (i.e. 85% of 137,500)	116,875

SUMMARY

9. a. Contract costing is akin to job costing and is used on relatively large scale, long term contracts which are frequently site based.

b. Because of the separate nature of most site work, more costs can be identified as direct, including many which are normally considered indirect.

c. If plant is purchased for use on a site, the contract account would be charged with the purchase price and credited with the second hand value of the plant on the contract completion or when the plant was transferred. In this way the plant depreciation would be charged to the appropriate contract.

d. Progress payments are made based on an architect's certificate of work done less an agreed retention percentage.

e. If a contract is uncompleted at the year end, a conservative estimate of the profit to date is taken. This is usually ⅔ or ¾ of the difference between the value and cost of work certified less the retention percentage.

POINTS TO NOTE

10. a. Some contracts are so large that an overall contract account as described would be of little use. In these cases the contract would be sub-divided into stages or areas and separate accounts opened.

b. Detailed cost records relating to many operational matters such as materials usage, labour costs, plant utilisation would be kept for day-to-day control purposes.

SELF REVIEW QUESTIONS

1. *What are typical characteristics of work for which contract costing is used?* *(2)*
2. *How are plant capital costs dealt with in contract accounts?* *(4)*
3. *What is a progress payment and how is it calculated?* *(5)*
4. *Why is it normal to calculate the profit on uncompleted contracts? How is this done?* *(6)*
5. *Give five typical debit, and two credit, entries in a contract account.* *(7)*
6. *What are the accounting entries for the value of work certified?* *(8)*

EXAMINATION QUESTION

1. *On 3rd January, 1978 B Construction Limited started work on the construction of an office block for a contracted price of £750,000 with completion promised by 31st March, 1979. Budgeted cost of the contract was £600,000. The construction company's financial year end was 31st October, 1978 and on that date the accounts appropriate to the contract contained the following balances.*

	£000
Materials issued to site	161
Materials returned from site	14
Wages paid	68
Own plant in use on site, at cost	96
Hire of plant and scaffolding	72
Supervisory staff: direct	11
indirect	12
Head office charges	63
Value of work certified to 31st October, 1978	400
Cost of work completed but not yet certified	40
Cash received related to work certified	330

Depreciation on own plant is to be provided at the rate of 12½% per annum on cost.

£2,000 is owing for wages.

Estimated value of materials on site is £24,000.

No difficulties are envisaged during the remaining time to complete the contract.

You are required to:

a. prepare the contract account for the period ended 31st October, 1978 showing the amount to be included in the construction company's profit and loss account;

106

b. explain the reason(s) for including the amount of profit to be shown in the profit and loss account;

c. show extracts from the construction company's balance sheet at 31st October, 1978 so far as the information provided will allow.

(ICMA, Cost Accounting 1, November 1978).

14 Costing Methods – Operation Costing

INTRODUCTION

1. This chapter defines operation costing and shows the sub-divisions normally found. The two simpler operation costing methods, output costing and service costing, are explained and examples given of where these would be used.

OPERATION COSTING – DEFINITION

2. This category of costing covers a wide range of manufacture and can be defined thus – "The category of basic costing methods applicable where standardised goods or services result from a sequence of repetitive and more or less continuous operations or processes to which costs are charged before being averaged over the units produced during the period." *Terminology*. The key features of this definition are:

continuous operations or processes – virtually identical units of output – total costs divided by number of units to give average cost per unit.

SCOPE OF OPERATION COSTING

3. It will be seen that operation costing is a generic term embracing a group of costing methods of varying complexity. These are shown in the following diagram:

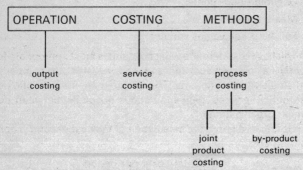

Output costing and service costing are relatively simple forms of costing and are described in this chapter. Process costing and its sub-divisions are dealt with in the next chapter.

OUTPUT COSTING

4. This is a costing method used where the organisation produces one product only. In consequence the whole production process is geared to the one product and is frequently highly mechanised. Typical examples of where output costing might be applied are: cement manufacture, certain dairies, mines, quarries etc. In such circumstances cost ascertainment is a simple process, i.e.

$$\text{Cost per unit (or tonne)} = \frac{\text{Total costs for period}}{\text{Number of units (or tonnage) produced in the period}}$$

Note:

Where output costing is used, partly completed units at the end of a period would normally be ignored. This is because of their relative insignificance and the fact that they would tend to even out from period to period.

SERVICE COSTING

5. This is defined as, "That form of operation costing which applies where standardised services are provided either by an undertaking or by a service cost centre within an undertaking . . . " *Terminology*.

Thus the services provided may be for sale, e.g. public transport, hotel accommodation, restaurants, power generation etc, or they may be provided within the organisation e.g. maintenance, library, stores.

A particular difficulty is to define a realistic cost unit that represents a suitable measure of the service provided. Frequently a composite cost unit is deemed the more relevant, for example, the hotel industry may use the 'occupied bed-night' as an appropriate unit for cost ascertainment and cost control. Typical cost units used in service costing are shown below.

Service	Possible Cost Units
Transport	Tonne-Mile, Passenger-Mile, Miles travelled
Hospitals	Patient-days, no. of operations
Electricity	Kilowatt-hours
Hotels	Occupied bed-nights
Restaurants	Meals served
Colleges	Full time equivalent student

Each organisation will have to determine what cost unit is most appropriate for its own purposes. Frequently if a common cost unit is agreed, valuable cost comparisons can be made between similar establishments. This is common, for example, over a wide range of local authority services, between various hospitals, between power stations and other similar organisations.

Whatever cost unit is decided upon, the calculation of the cost per unit is done in a similar fashion to output costing, i.e.

$$\text{Cost per service unit} = \frac{\text{Total costs per period}}{\text{No. of service units supplied in the period}}$$

OTHER COSTING PROBLEMS

6. Merely because the calculation of unit costs is a simple process in output costing and service costing, students should not be misled into thinking that no other costing problems exist in these industries. Many of the organisations involved are very substantial enterprises by any standard. Examples include power stations, large area hospitals, and city passenger transport undertakings. Such organisations have all the normal problems of large scale cost collection and analysis. They need to monitor and control their costs very closely and frequently employ sophisticated budgetary control systems. A particular problem in service organisations is caused by the high fixed cost of maintaining the total capacity which may be considerably underutilised at particular times. Examples include: electricity generation – where there is a substantial difference between peak and off peak demand, railways and bus services – where mid-day demand is substantially below rush hour periods, hotels – where there may be substantial differences between summer and winter or week day and weekend demand. The costing system should be comprehensive enough to show the effects of this type of demand on the costs of operation. Frequently this involves the analysis of costs into fixed and variable and the use of marginal costing techniques. These techniques are dealt with in detail later in the manual.

SUMMARY

7. a. Operation costing is applied where continuous operations or processes produce identical units of output. Total costs are averaged over all units produced.

b. Operation costing is a general term covering the particular methods of Output Costing, Service Costing and Process Costing.

c. Output costing is used where one product only is produced. Examples include, quarries and cement works.

d. Service costing is applied to organisations supplying a service or to cost centres providing internal services.

e. The cost unit to be used needs to be defined carefully. It is frequently a composite figure such as Tonne-mile or Patient-night.

f. Organisations employing output costing and service costing have all the normal problems of cost collection and analysis and frequently employ sophisticated costing techniques as part of the information service to management.

POINTS TO NOTE

8. a. Some service organisations do not supply identical or near identical service units to customers. Examples include: Architectural/Design/Accountancy services. In such cases a form of Job costing is used.

SELF REVIEW QUESTIONS

1. What are the key features of operation costing? (2)
2. What are the three major sub-divisions of operation costing? (3)
3. How is the cost per unit calculated using output costing? (4)
4. Define service costing. (5)
5. Give five examples of cost units found in service costing. (5)

15 Costing Methods – Process Costing

INTRODUCTION

1. This chapter explains the basis of all process costing systems and the ways in which normal and abnormal process losses are dealt with. The concept of equivalent units is explained together with how this concept is used to value finished units and work in progress at the beginning and end of a period.

PROCESS COSTING DEFINED

2. Process costing is a form of operation costing used where production follows a series of sequential processes. It is used in a variety of industries including: oil refining, food processing, paper making, chemical and drug manufacture, paint and varnish manufacture. Although details vary from one concern to another, there are common features in most process costing systems. These include:

a. Clearly defined process cost centres and the accumulation of all costs (material, labour and overheads) by the cost centres.

b. The maintenance of accurate records of units and part units produced and the cost incurred by each process.

c. The averaging of the total costs of each process over the total production of that process, including partly completed units.

d. The charging of the cost of the output of one process as the raw material input cost of the following process.

e. Clearly defined procedures for separating costs where the process produces two or more products (i.e. Joint Products) or where by-products arise during production. (Joint product and By product costing are dealt with in the next chapter).

CHOICE OF COST UNITS

3. As previously explained, the cost unit chosen should be relevant to the organisation and its product. In most cases the appropriate unit arises naturally having regard to the process and the way the product is sold and priced. Examples include:

Industry	Possible Cost Units
Brewing	Gallon, Barrel
Paint, Varnish	Litre, Gallon
Food processing	Can, Case, Kilogram, Tonne, Gallon, etc.
Oil refining	Gallon or multiples, Barrel

BASIS OF PROCESS COSTING

4. The basis of all process costing systems is shown in the diagram overleaf.

Thus it will be seen that material passes through the various processes gathering costs as it progresses. The above diagram shows the simplest possible situation. Typical complications which occur are the costing problems associated with process losses at various stages and the valuation of partly completed units at the end of an accounting period. These are dealt with below.

111

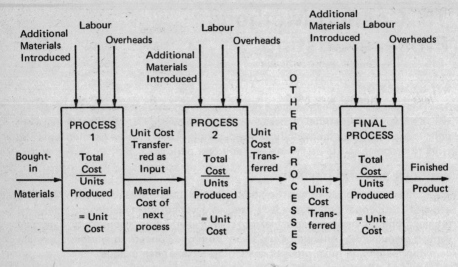

PROCESS COSTING OUTLINE   Figure 1

PROCESS LOSSES

5. With many forms of production the quantity, weight or volume of the process *output* will be less than the quantity, weight or volume of the materials *input*. This may be due to various reasons:

    a. evaporation, residuals, ash, swarf.

    b. unavoidable handling, breakage and spoilage losses.

    c. Withdrawal for testing and inspection.

    Because of increasing material costs, careful records must be maintained of losses occurring and the resulting cost implications. If losses are in accordance with normal practice, i.e. standard levels, they are termed <u>normal process losses</u>. If they are above expectation, they are known as <u>abnormal process losses.</u>

NORMAL PROCESS LOSSES

6. These are unavoidable losses arising from the nature of the production process and it is therefore logical and equitable that the cost of such losses is included as part of the cost of good production. If any value can be recouped from the sale of imperfect articles or materials then this would be credited to the process account thus reducing overall cost.

Example 1

    A food manufacturing process has a normal wastage of 5% which can be sold as animal feedstuff at £5 tonne. In a given period the following data were recorded:

    Input materials 160 tonnes at £23 per tonne

    Labour and overheads £2896

    Losses were at the normal level.

Compute the cost per tonne

Solution

		Tonnes	£
INPUT	Materials	160	3680
	Labour and overheads		2896
		160	6576
less	Normal loss 5%	8	40 cr
	Good production	152	6536

Cost per tonne of good production

$$= \frac{£6536}{152} = £43$$

Note:

The £40 credit to the Process account will be debited to a Scrap Sales account which will eventually be credited with the actual sale. Any balance on the Scrap Sales account will be taken to P+L account.

ABNORMAL PROCESS LOSSES

7.   Abnormal losses are those losses above the level deemed to be the normal loss rate for the process.

Abnormal losses cannot be foreseen and are due to such factors as; plant breakdown, industrial accidents, inefficient working or unexpected defects in materials. Conversely, unexpectedly favourable conditions might apply in a given period and actual losses may be lower than the calculated 'normal' loss. In such conditions abnormal gains would be made. The amount of abnormal loss or gain is calculated thus:

Abnormal loss (or gain) = Actual loss − Normal loss

It is an important costing principle, previously stated, that abnormal conditions should be excluded from routine reporting and only normal costs (which include normal process losses) charged to production. Accordingly the cost effects of abnormal losses or gains must be excluded from the Process Account. Abnormal losses or gains will be costed on the same basis as good production and therefore, like good production, will carry a share of the cost of normal losses. This is shown in the following example.

Example 2 – Abnormal loss

Assume the same data as in Example 1 except that actual production was 148 tonnes.

Compute the abnormal loss and show the relevant accounts.

Solution

Abnormal loss = Actual loss − Normal loss

= 12 − 8

= 4 tonnes

As the abnormal losses are valued at the same cost as good production (i.e. £43 tonne) the Process Account would be as follows.

Process A/C

	Tonnes	£		Tonnes	£
Material	160	3680	Good Production	148	6364
Labour and Overheads		2896	Normal losses	8	40
			Abnormal losses	4	172
	160	£6576		160	£6576

The other relevant accounts would be:

Abnormal losses A/C

	£		£
Process A/C	172	Scrap sales	20
		P + L	152
	£172		£172

Scrap Sales A/C

	£	
Process A/C	40	
Abnormal losses	20	

Note:
The sale of the 4 tonnes of abnormal losses at £5 tonne is credited to the Abnormal Losses A/c. This means that the net cost of £152 (£172–£20) is charged to the P+L A/c.

Example 3 – Abnormal Gain

Again assume the same data as Example 1 except that actual production was 155 tonnes.

Calculate the abnormal gain and show the relevant accounts.

Solution:

Abnormal gain = Actual loss – Normal loss
= 5 – 8
= 3 tonnes

These gains are valued at the same rate as good production. The relevant accounts are as follows:

Process account

	Tonnes	£		Tonnes	£
Material	160	3680	Good Production	155	6665
Labour + Overhead		2896	Normal loss	8	40
Abnormal gains	3	129			
	163	£6705		163	£6705

Abnormal Gains A/c

	£		£
Scrap Sales A/c	15	Process A/c	129
P + L	114		
	£129		£129

Scrap Sales A/c

	£		£
Process A/c	40	Abnormal gains	15

Note:

 a. Although an improvement in performance has been made, the Good Production is still valued at £43 per tonne.

 b. The credit to the Scrap Sales A/c of £15 is necessary so that the account only shows the effect of the 5 tonnes actually lost.

THE CONCEPT OF EQUIVALENT UNITS

8. At the end of any given period there are likely to be partly completed units. It is clear that some of the costs of the period are attributable to these units as well as those that are fully complete. To be able to spread costs equitably over part finished and fully complete units the concept of *equivalent units* is required. The number of equivalent units, for cost calculation purposes, is the number of equivalent fully complete units which the partly complete units (i.e. the WIP) represent. For example, assume that in a given period production was 2200 complete units and 600 partly complete. The partly complete units were deemed to be 75% complete.

$$\text{Total equivalent production} = \text{Completed units} + \text{Equivalent units in WIP}$$
$$= 2200 + \tfrac{3}{4}(600)$$
$$= 2200 + 450$$
$$= \underline{2650}$$

The total costs for the period would be spread over the total equivalent production.

$$\text{i.e. Cost per unit} = \frac{\text{Total Costs}}{\text{Total equivalent production (units)}}$$

EQUIVALENT UNITS AND COST ELEMENTS

9. The above illustration of effective units is the simplest possible. Frequently some overall estimate of completion is not possible or desirable and it becomes necessary to consider the percentage completion of each of the cost elements; material, labour and overheads. The same principles are used to calculate equivalent units, but each cost element must be treated separately and then the cost per unit of each element is added to give the cost of a complete unit. This is shown below.

Example 4

 In a given period production and cost data were as follows:

	Total Costs	Materials	5,115
		Labour	3,952
		Overheads	3,000
			£12,067

Production was 1400 fully complete units and 200 partly complete. The degree of completion of the 200 units WIP was as follows

Material	75% complete
Labour	60% ,,
Overheads	50% ,,

Calculate the total equivalent production, the cost per complete unit and the value of the WIP.

Solution:

Cost Element	Equivalent Units in WIP	+	Fully Complete Units	=	Total Effective Production	Total Costs Period £	Cost Per Unit £
Material	200 x 75% = 150	+	1400	=	1550	5115	3.3
Labour	200 x 60% = 120	+	1400	=	1520	3952	2.6
Overheads	200 x 50% = 100	+	1400	=	1500	3000	2.00
						£12067	£7.90

From the table it will be seen that the cost of a complete unit = £7.90

∴ Value of completed production = 1400 x £7.90 = £11,060

∴ Value of WIP = Total Costs − Value of completed production

= £12067 − 11060

= £1007

This can be verified by multiplying each element cost per unit by the number of equivalent units in the WIP of each cost element, thus:

Cost Element	No. of Equivalent Units in WIP	Cost per Unit £	Value of WIP £
Material	150	3.3	495
Labour	120	2.6	312
Overheads	100	2.00	200
			£1007

Note:

The way that the value of WIP can be cross checked by using the cost elements or the total values should be carefully studied. Remember −

Total cost for period = Value of completed units + Value of WIP

INPUT MATERIAL AND MATERIAL INTRODUCED

10. It will be recalled from Figure 1 that the output of one process forms the input material to the next process. The full cost of the completed units transferred forms the input material cost of the process and by its nature input material must be 100% complete.

Material introduced is extra material needed in the process and should always be shown separately from input material. Whenever there are partly completed units at the end of the period, they may contain two classifications of material, i.e.

INPUT MATERIAL (i.e. Previous process costs) always 100% complete.

MATERIAL INTRODUCED which may or may not be complete.

Note:

Input material may also be described as: Units transferred, Cost of Goods or units transferred or Previous process costs.

OPENING WORK-IN-PROGRESS

11. If, at the end of one period, there are partly completed units, it follows that there will be opening work in progress at the beginning of the next period. Usually the values of the cost elements of the brought forward WIP are known and, if so, the values are added to the costs incurred during the period. This is shown in the following example.

Example 5

Process Y

At the beginning of period 2 there were 800 units partly completed which had the following element values:

	Value £	%age complete
Input Material (from Process X)	8200	100
Material Introduced	5600	55
Labour	3200	60
Overheads	2400	45

During the period 4300 units were transferred from Process X at a value of £46,500 and other costs were:

	£
Material Introduced	24,000
Labour	19,500
Overheads	18,200

At the end of the period, the closing WIP was 600 units which were at the following stage of completion:

Input Material	100% complete	
Material Introduced	50%	,,
Labour	45%	,,
Overheads	40%	,,

The balance of 4500 units was transferred to Finished Goods.
Calculate the value of goods transferred to Finished Goods and the value of WIP.

Cost Elements	Equivalent units in Closing WIP	+	Fully Complete Units	=	(a) Total Effective Production	Opening WIP Values	+	Period Costs	=	(b) Total Cost	Cost per Unit $\left(\dfrac{b}{a}\right)$
						£		£		£	£
Input Material	600 x 100% = 600	+	4500	=	5100	8200	+	46500	=	54700	10.725
Material Intro.	600 x 50% = 300	+	4500	=	4800	5600	+	24000	=	29600	6.167
Labour	600 x 45% = 270	+	4500	=	4770	3200	+	19500	=	19500	4.759
Materials	600 x 40% = 240	+	4500	=	4740	2400	+	18200	=	20600	4.346
						£19400	+	£108200	=	£127600	£25.997

∴ Value of completed production

$$= 4500 \times £25.997$$
$$= £116,986.5$$

Value of closing WIP

$$= \text{Total Cost} - \text{Value of completed production}$$
$$= £127,600 - 116,986.5$$
$$= £10,613.5$$

This can be verified by calculating the elements of the WIP, i.e.
Equivalent units in each cost element x cost per unit

£

i.e. 600 x 10.725 = 6,435
    300 x 6.167 = 1,850.1
    270 x 4.759 = 1,284.93
    240 x 4.346 = 1,043.04

£10,613.07

(slight rounding error)

Note:

All that is necessary to deal with opening WIP is to add the values of each cost element brought forward to the period costs. The value of transfers out and closing WIP can then be calculated in the usual manner.

SUMMARY

12. a. Process costing is used where production follows a number of sequential processes frequently of an automatic nature.

b. The cost unit chosen should be relevant to the organisation and the product. Examples include; gallons, barrels, tonnes, kilograms.

c. Material passes through the various processes gathering costs as it progresses. The output of one process forming the input material into the next process.

d. Losses due to breakage, evaporation, machining, testing and other causes must be carefully recorded.

e. Normal process losses are unavoidable losses in production and form part of the cost of good production.

f. Abnormal losses are losses above the normal anticipated level and should be costed on the same basis as good production.

g. When partly complete units occur at the end of a period the number of equivalent units of complete production must be calculated.

h. The concept of equivalent units can also be applied to the cost elements in production; material, labour and overheads.

POINT TO NOTE

13. Although the calculation of the cost of W-I-P is a common examination question,

in practice where the W-I-P is a small fraction of throughput, period to period, it is likely to be ignored.

SELF REVIEW QUESTIONS

1. What are the characteristics of process costing systems? (2)
2. Give 6 examples of cost units found in process costing. (3)
3. What are the reasons for process losses? (5)
4. What are normal process losses and how are they dealt with in the costing system? (6)
5. What are abnormal process losses and how are they dealt with in the costing system? (6)
6. What is an equivalent unit? (8)
7. How is the value of W-I-P established in a process costing system? (9)
8. What is the distinction between 'Input Material' and 'Material Introduced'? (10)
9. How is opening balance of W-I-P dealt with? (11)

EXAMINATION QUESTIONS

1. a. Explain the fundamental differences between job costing and process costing and state three industries, other than the food industry, which use process costing.

b. A company within the food industry mixes powdered ingredients in two different processes to produce one product. The output of process 1 becomes the input of process 2 and the output of process 2 is transferred to the packing department.

From the information given below, you are required to open accounts for process 1, process 2, abnormal scrap and packing department and to record the transactions for the week ended 11th November, 1978.

Process 1

Input: Material A	6,000 kilograms at £0.50 per kilogram
Material B	4,000 kilograms at £1.00 per kilogram
Mixing labour	430 hours at £2 per hour
Normal scrap	5% of weight input
Scrap was sold for	£0.16 per kilogram
Output was	9,200 kilograms

There was no work in process at the beginning or end of the week.

Process 2

Input: Material C	6,600 kilograms at £1.25 per kilogram
Material D	4,200 kilograms at £0.75 per kilogram
Flavouring essence	£300
Mixing labour	370 hours at £2 per hour
Normal waste	5% of weight input
Output was	18,000 kilograms

There was no work in process at the beginning of the week but 1,000 kilograms were in process at the end of the week and were estimated to be only 50% complete so far as labour and overhead were concerned.

Overhead of £3,200 incurred by the two processes was absorbed on the basis of mixing labour hours.

Within process 1, abnormal scrap arose because some batches failed to pass the quality control check at the end of each mix. However, no loss in weight occurred and all scrap was sold for cash on the last day of the week. Any resultant balance on the abnormal scrap account was transferred to profit and loss account.

(ICMA, Cost Accounting 1, November 1978).

2. a. Outline the characteristics and purpose of:
    i.   Job Costing
    ii. Process Costing

   b. Explain carefully how material waste, or any other losses in production, should be treated in a process costing system, clearly indicating the reasons for your recommended treatment.

(ACCA, Costing, December 1979).

16 Costing Methods – Joint Product and By Product Costing

INTRODUCTION

1. Joint products and by products are described and exemplified and four accepted methods of by product costing are explained. The physical unit and sales value bases of apportioning joint costs, where joint products arise, are explained together with the notional sales value system necessary where subsequent processing after split-off point is required. The relationship of conventional product costing data and data for decision making is discussed.

DEFINITIONS

2. A joint product is the term used when two or more products arise simultaneously in the course of processing, each of which has a significant sales value in relation to each other. Examples of industries where joint products arise are as follows:

Oil Refining — The joint products include; diesel fuel, petrol, paraffin, lubricants.

Meat processing — The joint products include; the various grades of meat and hides.

Mining — The joint products frequently include the recovery of several metals from the same crushing.

On the other hand a By-Product is a product which arises incidentally in the production of the main product(s) and which has a relatively small sales value compared with the main product(s). Examples of by-products are;

Iron and steel manufacture — furnace slag is sold for use in cement and brick manufacture and for road construction.

Meat trade — bones, grease and certain offal are regarded as by-products.

Timber trade — sawdust, small offcuts, bark are usually regarded as by-products.

After the point of separation both joint products and by-products may need further processing before they are saleable.

Note:

It will be apparent from the foregoing that clear distinctions between by-products and joint products are not possible. The exact classification of a particular item is a matter of judgement depending on the particular circumstances. What is a by-product in one factory may be termed a joint product in another.

BY-PRODUCT COSTING

3. Because by-products, by definition, have a relatively small sales value, elaborate and expensive costing systems should be avoided. The most common methods of dealing with by-products are as follows:

   a. By-product net realisable value is deducted from the total cost of production.

b. Total costs (main product and by-product, if any) are deducted from Total Sales value of main and by-products.

c. By-product receipts are treated as incidental other income and transferred to general P+L account. This method is generally considered unsatisfactory except where the value is very small.

d. By-products treated as joint products. This method is most appropriate where the value of the by-product is relatively large. Details of joint product costing are dealt with in Para. 4 below.

None of the by-product costing methods is wholly satisfactory, but method (a) above probably has least disadvantages. This method is illustrated in the following example.

Example 1

During a period 2400 units of Large were produced and sold at £10 per unit. Total production costs were £17,500. Arising from the main production process 60 kgs. of Little were produced which were sold at £8 per kg.

Special packing and distribution costs of £2.20 per kg were incurred for Little. What were the net production costs and gross profit for the period?

Solution 1

		£	£
	Production Costs		17,500
less	Net Realisable Value of Little	480	
		− 132	348
=	Net Production Cost		17,152
	Gross Profit		£6,848
	Sales Value of Large		£24,000

JOINT-PRODUCT COSTING

4. Because joint products arise due to the inherent nature of the production process, it follows that none of the products can be produced separately. The various products become identifiable at a point known as 'split-off point'. Up to that stage all costs are joint costs, subsequent to the split-off point any costs incurred can be identified with specific products and they are known as 'subsequent' or 'additional processing costs'. This is shown diagrammatically on the following page.

It follows therefore that subsequent costs arising after the split-off point do not pose any particular costing problem because they are readily identifiable with a specific product and can be coded and charged accordingly. For product costing purposes the major problem in joint-product costing is to apportion the joint costs, i.e. those prior to the split-off point, on an acceptable basis.

APPORTIONING JOINT COSTS

5. The commonest methods of apportioning joint costs are:

a. The physical unit basis. The joint costs are apportioned over the joint products in proportion to the physical weight or volume of the products.

b. The sales value basis. Here the joint costs are apportioned in proportion to the relative sales value of the products.

The two methods are illustrated in Example 2.

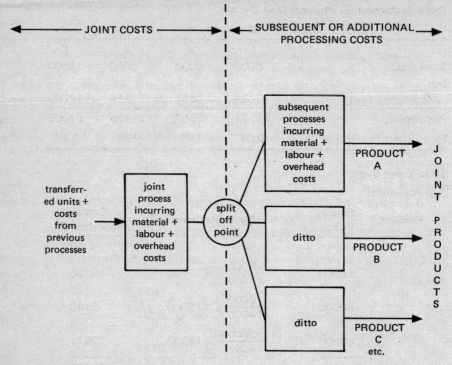

JOINT COSTS → ← SUBSEQUENT OR ADDITIONAL PROCESSING COSTS

Example 2

A process produces three products, X, Y and Z. Total joint costs were £12,000 and outputs, selling prices and sales values were:

X. 200 litres sold at £25 litre giving a sale value of £5000.

Y. 400 litres sold at £15 litre giving a sale value of £6000.

Z. 100 litres sold at £30 litre giving a sale value of £3000.

Apportion the joint costs and calculate the profit percentage on
  i.   the physical unit basis and
  ii. the sales value basis.

Solution 2

Physical unit basis

Cost Statement

Product	Output	Apportionment	Costs apportioned £
X	200	$\frac{200}{700}$ x £12,000	3,429
Y	400	$\frac{400}{700}$ x £12,000	6,857
Z	100	$\frac{100}{700}$ x £12,000	1,714
	700		£12,000

Profit Statement on Physical Unit Basis

	X	Y	Z	Total
	£	£	£	£
Sales Value	5000	6000	3000	14000
less				
Apportioned Costs	3429	6857	1714	12000
Profit/(Loss)	£1571	(£857)	£1286	£2000
Profit/(Loss) Percentage	31%	(14%)	43%	14%

Sales Value Basis

Cost Statement

Product	Sales Value	Apportionment	Costs apportioned
			£
X	£5000	$\frac{5000}{14000}$ x £12000	4286
Y	£6000	$\frac{6000}{14000}$ x £12000	5143
Z	£3000	$\frac{3000}{14000}$ x £12000	2571
	£14000		£12000

Profit Statement on Sales Value Basis

	X	Y	Z	Total
	£	£	£	£
Sales Value	5000	6000	3000	14000
less Apportioned Costs	4286	5143	2571	12000
Profit	£714	£857	£429	£2000
Profit Percentage	14%	14%	14%	14%

Notes:

a. It will be seen that the sales value basis produces the same profit percentage for each product. The method is widely used for this reason and for the assumption that the price obtained for an item is directly related to its cost.

b. The cost apportionment is made on the sales value of the products (i.e. Qty x price) and not the selling price per unit.

c. It must be emphasised that whatever method is used for apportioning costs, it is a convention only and its accuracy cannot be tested.

THE NOTIONAL SALES VALUE METHOD

6. On occasions the products which emerge from the split-off point are not saleable without further processing. It follows therefore that, at the split-off point, sales values are not known so that joint costs cannot be apportioned until some estimate is made

of a notional sales value at the split-off point. This is done by deducting subsequent processing costs from the final sales value to arrive at a notional sales value at split-off point. This is illustrated below.

Example 3

A process with joint costs of £5000 produces 2 products W and V, both of which need further processing before sale. The relevant data are as follows:

Product	Output	Subsequent Processing Costs	Final Selling Price	Final Sales Value
				£
W	2000 Kgs	£1500	£2 Kg	4000
V	4500 Kgs	£1250	£1.50 Kg	6750

Calculate the notional Sales Value at split-off point, the apportionment of joint costs, the profit on each product and the profit percentage.

Solution:

Cost Statement

Product	Final Sales Value	Subsequent Processing Costs	Notional Sales Value at Split-off	Apportionment	Apportioned Costs
	£	£	£		£
W	4,000	1,500	2,500	$\frac{2500}{8000} \times £5000$	1,563
V	6,750	1,250	5,500	$\frac{5500}{8000} \times 5000$	3,437
	£10,750	£2,750	£8,000		£5,000

Profit Statement

	W		V		Total	
	£	£	£	£	£	
Final Sales Value		4000		6750		10750
less						
Apportioned Costs	1563		3437		5000	
Subsequent Costs	1500	3063	1250	4687	2750	7750
Profit		£937		£2063		£3000
Profit Percentage		23%		31%		28%

COST APPORTIONMENT AND DECISION MAKING

7. The procedures outlined so far are acceptable for stock valuation and conventional profit calculation purposes, but may produce misleading information for particular types of decisions. A common type of decision is whether to sell a joint product at the split-off point or whether to incur further processing costs and sell at an enhanced price. In such circumstances, the amount of the joint costs and the method by which the joint costs are apportioned are *irrelevant*. All that matters is a comparison of the *increase* in *revenue* with the *increase* in *costs* necessary to achieve

that revenue. This is an example of the use of incremental costing which is important in decision making. To illustrate this approach assume the same data as in Example 2 except that the firm has the opportunity to process further Product Y at an additional cost of £3/litre in which case the product could be sold at £20/litre instead of £15/litre. Is this worthwhile?

		£
Incremental revenue possible	= £5 litre x 400 litres =	2000
Incremental costs necessary	= £3 litres x 400 litres =	1200
	Extra Profit =	£800

The conclusion from this is that it is worthwhile incurring additional costs on a product as long as the additional sales value gained exceeds the additional costs.

SUMMARY

8. a. When two or more products arise from a process and where each has a significant sales value, they are termed joint products. When a product of relatively small value arises incidentally it is termed a by-product.

b. The most common method of by-product costing is where the net realisable value of the by-product is deducted from the total production cost.

c. The point where joint-products are separately identifiable is the split-off point. Up to that point all costs are joint costs which, for product costing purposes, have to be spread over the products on a reasonable basis.

d. The main two methods of apportioning joint costs are the physical unit and the sales value bases.

e. The notional sales value basis is used where additional processing is necessary for the product to be saleable so that an actual sales value is not available at split-off point.

f. To decide whether additional processing is worthwhile to gain extra revenue, all that is necessary is to compare the incremental costs and incremental revenue. Joint costs and methods of apportionment are irrelevant.

POINT TO NOTE

9. Processing may produce Waste-Scrap-By-Products-Joint-Products in ascending order of value. The exact classification of any given item is a matter of judgement.

SELF REVIEW QUESTIONS

1. *What is a joint product? A by-product? (2)*
2. *What are three common methods of dealing with by-product costs? (3)*
3. *What is the 'split-off point'? (4)*
4. *What are the two most common methods of apportioning joint costs? (5)*
5. *Why are notional sales values at split-off point sometimes calculated? (6)*
6. *How is the decision made whether to sell at the split-off point or perform further processing? (7)*

EXAMINATION QUESTIONS

1. *XY Chemical Company Limited has three processing departments: 1, 2 and 3.*
    In department 1 batches of ingredients P, Q and R are mixed which, after processing, produce three products: QA, PA and PB.

QA requires no further processing and can be sold;

PA can either be sold or subjected to further processing in department 3;

PB requires further processing in department 2, having no saleable value in its present form.

In department 2, PB is mixed with ingredient S to produce PX, which is saleable.

In department 3, PA is mixed with ingredient S and, after processing produces PAS, which can be sold. It also produces a by-product AZ, which can be sold, but needs packing beforehand at a cost of £0.05 per lb.

Standard yields in each department are as follows:

Department 1 – a batch of 50 lbs P, 70 lbs Q, and 30 lbs R will yield 30 lbs PA, 20 lbs PB, and 50 lbs QA;

Department 2 – a batch of 20 lbs PB and 50 lbs S will yield 50 lbs PX;

Department 3 – a batch of 30 lbs PA and 20 lbs S will yield 10 lbs PAS and 40 lbs AZ.

Price and cost data are as follows:

Costs of ingredients:

Ingredient	Costs per lb. £
P	0.8
Q	0.6
R	0.2
S	0.3

Conversion cost per batch		£
Department:	1	32.00
	2	10.00
	3	24.00
Selling prices (per lb):	PA	2.00
	QA	3.00
	PX	1.10
	PAS	15.00
	AZ	0.40

During period 5, a total of 80 batches was produced in all three departments. At the end of the period, the following proportions of the period's production remained unsold:

QA 10% : PX 15% : AZ 20%

With the above exception, opening and closing stocks were equal.

Fixed overhead of £6,000 per period is incurred; the company's practice is to treat it as a period cost and not to apportion it to departments, or to absorb it into product costs.

You are required:

1. On the assumption that the company apportions costs on the basis of weight at the split-off point, to calculate:

a. the costs per batch of PA, PB, QA and PX;

b. the costs per lb of PAS on the basis that the net revenue from the sale of AZ is treated as:

i. income of the company as a whole;

ii. a reduction in the cost of the main product in the department in which it is produced;

c. the total profit that the company made during period 5.

(Assume for this purpose that closing stocks of by-product AZ have no value.)

2. If the company wished to apportion department 1 costs on the basis of the net sales value at the split-off point, to calculate:

a. the net sales value per lb of PB;

b. the costs per batch of PA, PB and QA, using the answer to 2 (a) above.

(ICMA, Cost Accounting 2, May 1977).

2. a. Polimur Ltd operates a process which produces three joint products, all in an unrefined condition. The operating results of this process, for October 1979, are shown below.

Output from Process:	Product A	100,000 kilos
	Product B	80,000 kilos
	Product C	80,000 kilos

The month's operating costs were £1,300,000. The closing stocks were 20,000 kilos of A, 15,000 kilos of B and 5,000 kilos of C. The value of the closing stock is calculated by apportioning costs according to weight of output. There were no opening stocks and the balance of the output was sold to a refining company at the following prices:

Product A £5 per kilo   Product C £9 per kilo
Product B £4 per kilo

Required:

Prepare an operating statement showing the relevant trading results for October 1979.

b. The management of Polimur Ltd have been considering a proposal to establish their own refining operations.

The current market prices of the refined products are:

Product A £17 per kilo   Product C £20.50 per kilo
Product B £14 per kilo

The estimated unit costs of the refining operation are:

Product	A	B	C
	£ per kilo	£ per kilo	£ per kilo
Direct Materials	0.50	0.75	2.50
Direct Labour	2.00	3.00	4.00
Variable Overheads	1.50	2.25	5.50

Prime costs would be variable. Fixed overheads, which would be £700,000 monthly, would be direct to the refining operation. Special equipment is required for refining Product B and this would be rented, at a cost not included in the above figures, of £360,000 per month.

It may be assumed that there would be no weight loss in the refining process and that the quantity refined each month would be similar to October's output shown in (a) above.

Required:

Prepare a statement which will assist management to evaluate the proposal to commence refining operations. Include any further comments or observations you consider relevant.

(ACCA, Costing, December 1979).

3. Papaver (Ruritania). Inc. operates a mill in which it processes wotsit roots, the basis of a staple Ruritanian dish. The roots are delivered in standard loads of 1,000 kilos by the Root Marketing Board. They are then washed, crushed, and cooked in three sequential processes.

The washing process washes out 50 kilos of valueless waste from each delivery, giving a standard yield of 950 kilos of washed roots. These are then put into the crushing process; this produces a standard yield of 400 litres of a nutritious juice (which is sold under a long-term contract to the Ruritanian State Healthcare Service), and 400 kilos of pulp. The process of cooking the pulp produces 400 kilos of rootmash, which is sold back to the Root Marketing Board in bulk containers.

The cooking is done in a detached cookhouse, near to the washing and crushing plant. No inventory is kept of roots, pulp, juice, or rootmash.

Each standard load of unwashed root costs $600.

The fixed costs per week, and the variable cost per load, of the processes are as follows:

Process	Variable cost of processing $	Weekly fixed cost $
Washing	1 per standard load	1,250
Crushing	10 per load of washed roots	5,000
Cooking	20 per load of pulp	3,750
Administration	nil	6,140

The juice is sold for $1.50 per litre, and the cooked rootmash for $1.00 per kilo. There is no corporation tax in Ruritania, but Papaver's gross sales revenues are subject to a 10% sales tax, which is deducted at source by the Root Marketing Board and the State Healthcare Service.

You are required to:

a. draft an income statement for Papaver for June 1978, a four-week accounting period during which 220 loads of uncleaned roots were processed, to show the total profit or loss and the amounts attributable to the production and sale of juice and rootmash respectively.

b. draft a statement showing how many loads of unwashed roots Papaver must process each week in order to break-even financially, and

c. draft a statement showing the effect on the break-even workload if Papaver accepted a Government offer to pay half the additional weekly fixed cost of $1,636 if Papaver will both revise the method of working the crushing process so that the standard yield is increased by 1%, and improve the cooking system so that no additional variable cost is incurred.

(ICA, Management Accounting, July 1978).

4. Product P63 is made by three sequential processes, I, II and III. In process III a by-product arises and after further processing in process BP, at a cost of £2 per unit, by-product BP9 is produced. Selling and distribution expenses of £1 per unit are incurred in marketing BP9 at a selling price of £9 per unit.

	Process I	Process II	Process III
Standards provide for:			
● normal loss in process, of input, of	10%	5%	10%
● loss in process, having a scrap value, per unit, of	£1	£3	£5

For the month of April 1978 the following data are given:

	Process I	Process II	Process III	Process BP
Output, in units	8,800	8,400	7,000 of P63	420 of BP9

Costs:				Total
Direct materials introduced	£	£	£	£
(10,000 units)	20,000			20,000
Direct materials added	6,000	12,640	23,200	41,840
Direct wages	5,000	6,000	10,000	21,000
Direct expenses	4,000	6,200	4,080	14,280

Budgeted production overhead for the month was £84,000. Absorption is based on a percentage of direct wages.

There were no stocks at the beginning or end of the month.

You are required, using the information given, to prepare accounts for:

a. each of processes I, II and III;

b. process BP;

c. i. abnormal losses;
   ii. abnormal gains;

showing the balances to be transferred to the profit and loss statement.

(ICMA, Cost Accounting 2, May 1978).

5. FPI Limited is in the food processing industry and in one of its processes, three joint products are manufactured. Traditionally, the company has apportioned work incurred up to the joint products pre-separation point on the basis of weight of output of the product.

You have recently been appointed cost accountant, and have been investigating process costs and accounting procedures.

You are required to prepare statements for management to show:

a. the profit or loss of each product as ascertained using the weight basis of apportioning pre-separation point costs;

b. the optimal contribution which could be obtained from the manufacture of these products.

The following process data for October are given:

Costs incurred up to separation point	£96,000		
	Product A £	Product B £	Product C £
Costs incurred after separation point	20,000	12,000	8,000
Selling price per tonne: Completed product	500	800	600
Estimated, if sold at separation point	250	700	450
	tonnes	tonnes	tonnes
Output	100	60	80

The cost of any unused capacity after the separation point should be ignored.
(ICMA, Cost Accounting 2, November 1979).

17 Planning, Control and Decision Making

INTRODUCTION

1. This chapter serves as an introduction to the rest of the manual. The emphasis of the manual now changes from basic costing principles to the provision of information for planning, control and decision making. A general outline of the elements of planning, control and decision making is given and the role and characteristics of information is described.

WIDER VIEW OF COSTING

2. The student who has conscientiously studied the manual so far will have a good knowledge of the language and procedures of basic costing. The material covered shows how data are gathered, classified, analysed and used for cost ascertainment. The rest of the manual is concerned with the wider use of costing information for planning, control and decision making purposes. It must be emphasised, however, that the existence of a sound, well organised basic costing system is fundamental to whatever use is made of the information, whether for routine cost ascertainment purposes or for a one-off decision. Before considering the various ways in which costing information can be of value to management, it is useful to examine some general considerations relating to planning, control and decision making.

PLANNING

3. Planning is a primary task of management. It is concerned with the future and relies upon information from many sources, both external and internal to the organisation, for it to be successful. Information for planning includes cost and financial data and also information relating to personnel, markets, competitors, production capacities and constraints, material supplies and so on. Because of its importance and the need for a systematic approach, particularly in larger organisations, a structured form of planning known as Corporate Planning has been developed and is increasingly being used.

THE STAGES OF PLANNING

4. Planning is the process prior to action. Good planning means taking correct decisions, having regard to all relevant factors, which will govern the organisation's future in accordance with some rational strategy. The planning process can be subdivided into five stages.

  a. **Setting Objectives**
  Objective setting is a difficult task, but it is one which should not be shirked. Typical of the headings under which objectives should be established are the following:

  Profitability
  Sales
  Market share
  Productivity
  Physical resources
  Financial resources
  Environmental and safety factors

When establishing objectives, frequently it is found that conflicts exist between them. It is a managerial task to resolve these conflicts so that clear objectives can be set.

b. Assessing the environment
This stage is concerned with a survey and analysis of the environment in which the organisation expects to operate. It will include forecasting, analysing trends, making surveys and investigations, in fact anything which will help to judge what will be the future external environment of the organisation.

c. Reviewing resources
Resources of all types (materials, labour, finance, capital equipment, premises etc) will be required to meet the organisation's objectives. The purpose of this stage is to consider the availability of all types of resource, from internal and external sources, over the planning period being considered.

d. Establishing feasible goals
Having set objectives, studied the environment and reviewed the resources available, various ways of achieving objectives are considered. Some of the alternatives will be found to be impractible and some of the objectives will be not be achievable within the planning period being studied. After reviewing the possibilities a set of feasible goals and ways to achieve those goals is established.

e. Implementing the plan
Finally a set of long term and short term plans will be developed containing sub-goals, operating budgets and targets.

CONTROL
5. The purpose of control is to help to ensure that operations and performance conform to the plans. There are two broad elements of the control process. Firstly, the comparison of actual and planned performance on a regular and continuing basis and secondly, the longer term process of reviewing the plan itself to see whether it needs modification in the light of the comparisons made or because of changes in the parameters on which the plan was based, for example, new government regulations, material shortages, new competition. It follows therefore that meaningful control is not possible without planning and planning without a complementary control system is pointless. In organisational systems control is exercised by the use of information, frequently of a financial nature.

Control and Feedback
The diagram on the next page shows the typical control process.

In general feedback gathers information on past performance from the output side of a process (a section, a department, a manufacturing process) which is used, after comparison, to initiate action to govern future performance by adjusting the Input Side of the process. Many systems have been developed to assist the control function. These include, budgetary control, stock control and production control.

DECISION MAKING
6. Management is involved with decision making at all levels;

at the strategic level – for example, the Board of Directors deciding to diversify the company's products or to acquire a subsidiary.

at the tactical level – for example, the Sales Manager deciding upon an

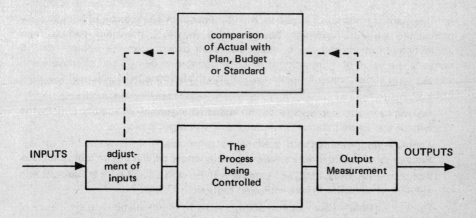

advertising campaign in a given region or the Production Controller deciding whether to sub-contract part of an order.

at the operational level – for example, the credit Supervisor deciding to suspend deliveries to a bad payer or a work's foreman deciding which men will deal with a particular job.

Decision making always involves a choice between alternatives. Decision makers need information on which to base their judgement; without information decisions are no more than inspired guesswork.

TYPES OF DECISIONS

7. Decisions range from those at the top level involving many external factors where a high degree of judgement is involved to more routine internal decisions with limited scope. H. A. Simon has classified decisions into programmed and non-programmed categories.

a. **Programmed decisions**. These are relatively structured decisions within a clearly defined area. The decision rules are known and frequently these types of decisions can be incorporated into computer based management information systems. A typical example is a reorder decision based on usage and reorder levels in an inventory control system.

b. **Non-programmed decisions**. These are decisions for which decision rules and procedures cannot be devised. Generally they are non-repetitive decisions, involving many external and internal factors, frequently with high levels of risk, and requiring information from a variety of sources.

INFORMATION FOR DECISION MAKING

8. It is important to understand that *all* decision making relates to the future. It follows therefore that the decision maker requires information regarding such things as future costs and revenues, future material supplies and prices, the likely state of the market in the future and so on. Information for decision making must therefore be orientated towards the future and invariably involves forecasting, estimating and extrapolation. Whilst it is self evident that we cannot foretell the future, it is found that past experience and records of performances, costs etc. frequently provide a sound basis for forecasting particular aspects of future operations. However, this is only correct if future conditions are expected to be broadly similar to those in the past. If not, then an organisation's experience and records are likely to be of substantially diminished value. Information has no value in itself; its value derives from improvements in the decisions which are taken based upon the information. To enhance the value of information it must be capable of being used effectively and surveys have shown that information which has the following characteristics is more likely to be used.

Relevance – i.e. appropriate to the manager's sphere of activity and to the decision in hand.

Timely – i.e. produced and available to the manager in time for him to use. Frequently an approximate answer speedily prepared will be the most valuable.

Accurate – i.e. sufficiently accurate for it to be relied upon by the manager and sufficiently accurate for the intended purpose.

Understandable – i.e. in a form readily usable by the manager. The avoidance of unexplained technical terms, the use of summaries, the use of graphical and other display methods are all ways to make information more understandable.

SUMMARY

9. a. Planning is concerned with the future and consists of five stages: Setting objectives, Assessing the environment, Reviewing resources, Establishing feasible goals, and Implementation.

b. Effective control must be preceded by planning, and planning without complementary control is pointless.

c. Control is exercised by feedback control loops whereby information regarding the output or performance is compared to the plan or standard and adjustments made (if necessary) to the inputs.

d. Management are involved with decision making at all levels, strategic, tactical and operational.

e. Decisions can be classified into programmed and non-programmed.

f. Future orientated information is necessary for decision making.

g. Information should be relevant, timely, accurate, and in an understandable form.

POINT TO NOTE

10. Cost and financial information is an important part of the total information requirements for planning, control and decision making, but it is not the only element. Sales, production, personnel and other information is frequently of supreme importance.

SELF REVIEW QUESTIONS

1. What are the stages in planning? (4)

2. What is the purpose of the control process? (5)

3. Draw a feedback control loop. (5)

4. Give examples of decision making at various management levels. (6)

5. What are programmed and non-programmed decisions? (7)

6. What are the characteristics of information which makes it most useful for decision making? (8)

18 Cost Behaviour

INTRODUCTION

1. This chapter explains why the study of cost behaviour is important, and discusses the behaviour of variable, fixed and semi-variable costs in both continuous and discontinuous forms. The assumptions normally made about cost behaviour are explained and analysed and the problems associated with cost behaviour predictions are detailed.

REASONS FOR THE STUDY OF COST BEHAVIOUR

2. If costs always remained unchanged and completely under control and if an organisation's activities and operations remained the same from period to period, then there would be little point in studying cost behaviour. Life is not as simple as that and an understanding of cost behaviour is vital for management and for accountants who advise them. A knowledge of cost behaviour is necessary across the whole range of cost and management accounting activities, particularly in the areas of cost control and planning and decision making. Typical problems which need detailed analysis of cost behaviour before they can be solved are the following:—

'What are the appropriate overhead costs if the throughput of the Assembly Department is increased by 15%?

'Is it worthwhile to introduce second shift working to cope with a special export order?'

'Should we accept a large contract at less than normal selling prices if it enables us to work at full capacity?'

COST BEHAVIOUR AND THE VOLUME OF ACTIVITY

3. Whilst other factors influence costs, a major influence is the level or volume of activity, and many of the reasons for studying cost behaviour relate to changes or proposed changes in the level of activity. The level of activity is expressed in many varied ways, e.g. tons produced, hours worked, standard hours produced, passenger/miles, invoices typed, sales, stores issues etc. etc. Students should also be aware that many alternative terms are used for the concept of 'level of activity', typical ones being capacity, output, volume, throughput. Activity level changes and the resulting cost changes form the basis of many practical decisions and many examination questions. The behaviour of cost in relation to changes in the level of activity is so important that it forms the basis of the accounting classifications of cost into fixed and variable costs.

COST BEHAVIOUR AND TIME

4. Normally the situations where cost behaviour is analysed for planning and decision making are 'short run' in nature. This means that the relationship between cost and activity and the classifications of the costs themselves are most appropriate over a relatively short time span only. What is a 'relatively short time span' depends on the particular circumstances, it may be three months, six months, one year; it is unlikely to be as long as five years. Over longer time periods unpredictable factors are bound to occur, methods will alter, technology will improve, so that predictions of cost behaviour are likely to be increasingly unreliable. In examination questions the time factor (in relation to cost behaviour!) is unlikely to be very significant, but in practice it can be a major problem.

PREDICTING COST BEHAVIOUR

5. Except in completely new situations where no previous experience exists, predictions about cost levels and cost behaviour in the future will be based on records of past costs and their associated levels of activity. Because of this, many of the statistical techniques of forecasting and extrapolation are of value when studying cost behaviour. Care however must be taken when using any form of forecasting technique that past conditions are indeed a guide to the future. It is the cost behaviour in the future that is being considered and if conditions in the future are likely to be significantly different from the past, then statistical forecasting techniques will be unable to produce valid predictions. Judgement will always play a part in cost prediction, but in many cases relatively simple statistical techniques can be of great assistance. Care must also be taken to base cost predictions on the facts of particular situations and not on arbitrary, general classifications. An example of this is the almost invariable rule, particularly in examination questions, of assuming that direct labour is a fully variable cost, whereas because of wage agreements, guaranteed daily and weekly rates, the growth of salaried works personnel, the impact of technology etc., direct labour in many situations increasingly assumes many of the characteristics of a fixed cost, i.e. it may, within limits, be relatively unchanged with varying levels of activity.

VARIABLE COST DEFINITION

6. "A cost which, in the aggregate, tends to vary in direct proportion to changes in the volume of output or turnover." *Terminology*.

It will be noted that the key feature of this definition is *variability* related to *activity*. Also the words 'in direct proportion' point to the typical assumption made in accounting that variable costs are, or can be, approximated by a linear function in relation to the level of activity. This is explained in more detail below.

VARIABLE COST BEHAVIOUR

7. The patterns of variable cost behaviour are many and varied, but two main divisions of continuous variable cost patterns can be made, i.e. LINEAR and NON-LINEAR or CURVILINEAR.

LINEAR VARIABLE COSTS

8. This is the simplest pattern and is where the relationship between variable cost and output can be shown as a straight line on a graph thus:—

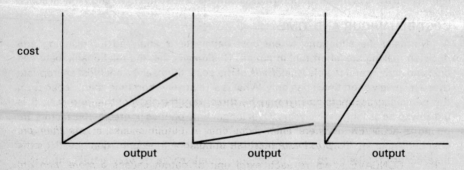

EXAMPLES OF LINEAR VARIABLE COST   Figure 1

For calculations and analysis it is usually more convenient to express the linear relationship algebraically thus

$COST = bx$

where x = volume of output in units

b = a constant representing the variable cost per unit.

Example 1

The materials contained in each assembly Z110 are

3	Brackets	@	£1.25 each
30	Screws	@	£0.02 each
6	Pulleys	@	£0.67 each

What is the expected variable cost of materials for producing 40 Assemblies?

Solution:–

Material	Cost/Assembly
£	£
3 x 1.25	= 3.75
30 x 0.02	= 0.60
6 x 0.67	= 4.02
	£8.37

$Cost = bx$

$= £8.37 \times 40$

$= £334.8$

NON-LINEAR OR CURVILINEAR VARIABLE COSTS

9. In general where the relationship between variable cost and output can be shown as a curved line on a graph, it would be said to be curvilinear. Many types of curves exist and two typical ones are shown below.

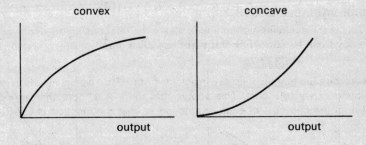

EXAMPLES OF CURVILINEAR VARIABLE COSTS   Figure 2

CONVEX — where each extra unit of output causes a *less than pro-portionate* increase in cost

CONCAVE — where each extra unit of output causes a *more than pro-portionate* increase in cost.

A simple example of a cost which could result in a curvi linear cost function is that of a piecework scheme for individual workers with differential rates. If the rates increased by small amounts at progressively higher output levels the graphing of wages for a number of workers would result in a concave cost function.

Whether the curves are convex or concave, if they have particular characteristics, they may be categorised as known statistical functions. One of the more common types is described below, which is known as PARABOLA, but many other types exist. The method by which a curve is identified is by the statistical technique of curve fitting.

Note:

Other statistical functions which may represent a cost function are:— simple exponential or compound interest curve, logarithmic, Gompertz etc.

CURVILINEAR VARIABLE COSTS – THE PARABOLA

10. Where the slope of the cost function changes uniformly with changes in output (as the Curves in Fig. 2) the curve is known as a Parabola and can be expressed algebraically thus:—

$$\text{Cost} = bx + cx^2 + dx^3 + \ldots px^n$$

Where x is as previously defined and b, c, d, . . . p are constants.

Example 2

Analysis of cost and activity records for a project show that the variable cost can be accurately represented by the function

$$\text{Cost} = £bx + cx^2 + dx^3$$

where b = 8   c = 0.5   and   d = 0.03,

calculate

    i.   Variable cost when production is 10 units
    ii. Variable cost when production is 15 units

Is the function convex or concave?

Solution:

    i. $\text{Cost} = £8 \times 10 + 0.5 \times 10^2 + 0.03 \times 10^3$

        $= £160$

    ii. $\text{Cost} = £8 \times 15 + 0.5 \times 15^2 + 0.03 \times 15^3$

        $= £333.75$

It will be seen that the increase in activity from 10 to 15 units results in more than a doubling of variable cost. This shows that there is a more than proportionate increase in the unit cost of extra production so that the function is CONCAVE.

Note:

It is the value of the constants which determine whether the function is convex or concave.

LINEAR APPROXIMATION

11. It is common practice in accounting, particularly under examination conditions, to make the assumption that variable costs are linear. This is often done even when the cost data are curvilinear. This is shown thus:

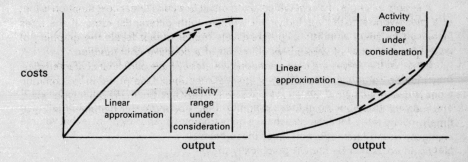

EXAMPLES OF LINEAR APPROXIMATIONS ON CURVILINEAR DATA   Figure 3

Features of linear approximation:–

a. Convenient and greatly simplifies calculations.

b. May be reasonably accurate representation in the short run over a limited range of activity variations.

c. May encourage too ready acceptance of the view that all variable costs are linear. All variable costs do not behave linearly and accurate cost prediction in practice must rely on analysis of cost and activity data, not upon overall blanket assumptions.

For examination purposes it can generally be assumed that, if a cost is identified as variable, it will be linear unless the context of the question clearly points to some other pattern.

RELATIONSHIP OF VARIABLE COST TO OTHER COSTS

12. Variable cost c.f. accounting concept of marginal cost.

Because of the assumption of linearity, variable cost equals accounting marginal cost i.e. the cost of an extra unit of output is the same as the average variable cost of all output.

Variable cost c.f. economic concept of marginal cost.

The economic concept of marginal cost, i.e. the cost of an additional unit, is based on curvilinear functions so that at certain activity levels marginal cost is falling and at other levels it is rising, whereas the accounting concept assumes a constant variable marginal cost. The above explanation covers a wide range of activity variations, but for limited activity variations, as in typical decision situations, the approaches are likely to give very similar results.

VARIABLE COST C.F. DIRECT COSTS

13. Direct costs are those costs directly identifiable with a product or saleable service, whereas variable costs are determined by their behaviour in relation to changes in activity levels. Thus it will be seen that variable costs and direct costs are determined by two quite distinct principles. Some variable costs, e.g. material and wages, can very often also be identified as direct costs.

EXAMPLES OF VARIABLE COSTS

14. Examples of costs that are frequently variable in behaviour are raw materials, sales commissions, royalties, production wages, carriage, packing costs etc. Care should be taken not to pigeon hole costs too readily. It is the behaviour of a cost in relation to activity that determines whether or not it is variable, not some general assumption.

FIXED COST – DEFINITION

15. "A cost which accrues in relation to the passage of time and which, within certain output or turnover limits, tends to be unaffected by fluctuations in volume of output or turnover." *Terminology*. The key parts of this definition are that fixed costs are time based and within limits, are unaffected by changes in activity. Because of this, they are sometimes called 'period costs'. Typical fixed costs are rates, salaries, insurance, rent etc. It is clear from looking at these examples that fixed costs do change from time to time; rent and rates, for example, change quite frequently. The key point is that volume changes, within limits, do not affect these costs.

Fixed costs can be shown graphically thus:–

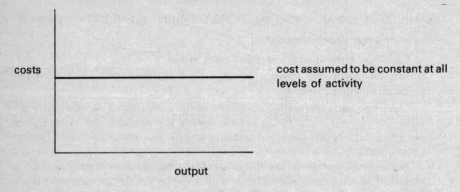

FIXED COST   Figure 4

The above graph is somewhat unrealistic in that it assumes that costs will be constant at all levels of activity from 0% to 100% which is not likely. More typically fixed costs could be graphed as follows:

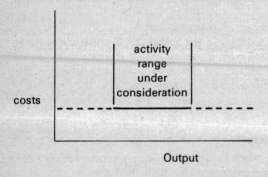

FIXED COST   Figure 5

Fixed costs can also be expressed algebraically:–

$$costs = a$$

where a is a constant. It will be noted that v, the volume of output, does not appear in this expression, so that changes in activity are deemed not to affect the fixed cost.

SEMI-VARIABLE COSTS

16. "A cost containing both fixed and variable elements which is therefore partly affected by fluctuations in the volume of output or turnover" *Terminology*.

Rarely is a cost purely fixed or purely variable, frequently there are elements of both classifications in a cost. A typical example would be electricity charges containing a fixed element, the standing charge, and a variable element, the cost per unit consumed.

Semi-variable costs can be shown graphically thus:–

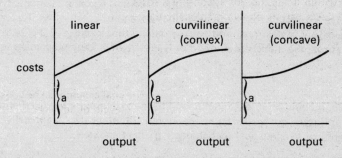

SEMI VARIABLE COST PATTERNS   Figure 6

In each case "a" represents the fixed element of the cost.

Semi-variable costs can also be expressed algebraically by combining the previous expressions for variable cost (Para. 8) and fixed cost (Para. 15) thus

LINEAR SEMI-VARIABLE COST

$$cost = a + bx$$

CURVILINEAR SEMI-VARIABLE COST

$$cost = a + bx + cx^2 + dx^3 + \ldots px^n$$

Example 3

Analysis of maintenance department costs shows that there is a fixed element of £500 per month and a variable element related to machine hours amounting to £2.25 per machine hour.

What is the expected cost for a month when the planned activity level is

    i.   1500 machine hours?

and ii. 1800 machine hours?

Solution:

    i.   Total cost $= a + bx$

$$= £500 + 2.25 \, (1500)$$
$$= \underline{£3875}$$

    ii. $= £500 + 2.25 \, (1800)$
$$= \underline{£4550}$$

(Alternatively, as only the variable costs will alter between 1500 and 1800 hours, the second answer could be calculated as follows:

$$£3875 + 300 \, (2.25) = \underline{£4550}.$$

The above example is for a clear cut linear cost, but, even when the underlying cost pattern is curvilinear, it is normal to make a linear approximation which greatly simplifies subsequent calculations.

Note:

Alternative terms for semi-variable costs are: semi-fixed costs and mixed costs.

ESTABLISHING THE APPROPRIATE COST CHARACTERISTICS

17. So far in the examples the value of the fixed and variable elements have been provided, but in practice these characteristics have to be established. Typically this is done by analysis of past cost and activity data, either visually by the 'scattergraph' technique or by the statistical method of least squares, known as linear regression analysis.

Note:

It is quite common in examinations to have to determine the fixed and variable elements of total costs. This can be done arithmetically, graphically (using a scattergraph) or by statistical techniques e.g. least squares.

SCATTERGRAPH TECHNIQUE

18. This is simple visual technique which can be employed with as few as two previous observations, but obviously there is some gain in accuracy if a number of previous cost and activity readings are available. Figure 7 shows the plotting of numerous costs recorded for activity levels between 40 and 100 units of output.

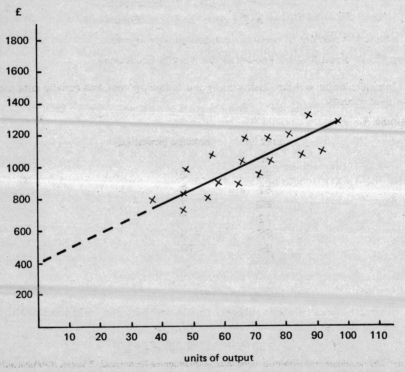

SCATTERGRAPH SHOWING VISUAL LINE OF BEST FIT   Figure 7

The solid line is drawn at an angle adjudged to be the best representation of the slope of the points. The dotted line is drawn to show the intersection with the vertical axis and thus gives an estimate of the fixed content of the cost being considered, in this case £400. The slope of the line, i.e. the variable element, is found as follows:

$$\text{cost @ zero activity} = £400$$
$$\text{cost @ 100 units activity} = £1250$$
$$\frac{1250 - 400}{100 - 0} = £8.5$$

.˙. the estimated cost function
$$= £400 + 8.5x \qquad \text{where } x = \text{units of output.}$$

The scattergraph technique is simple and convenient, but clearly no claims can be made for its accuracy.

LEAST SQUARES *

19. This is a statistical approach for establishing a line of best fit to data and has a variety of uses including the present one of establishing a cost function. The linear cost function can be represented by

$$y = a + bx,$$

where y equals cost and the other symbols are as previously defined.

To find the values of the constants, a and b, two simultaneous equations need to be solved. These are

$$\Sigma y = an + b\ \Sigma x \dots \text{Equation I}$$
$$\Sigma xy = a\ \Sigma x + b\ \Sigma x^2 \dots \text{Equation II}$$

where n = number of pairs of cost and activity figures.

(Note: These equations are known as the Normal Equations).

The calculation will be illustrated by the following cost and activity data taken from past records.

Example 4.

cost (y) £	activity (units) (x)
56	4
62	5
80	7
72	7
88	9
94	10

* **Note:** *This technique is dealt with in more detail in Quantitative Techniques, T. Lucey, D P Publications.*

Solution:

y	x	xy	x²
56	4	224	16
62	5	310	25
80	7	560	49
72	7	504	49
88	9	792	81
94	10	940	100
$\Sigma y = 452$	$\Sigma x = 42$	$\Sigma xy = 3330$	$\Sigma x^2 = 320$

and n = 6

Substituting in the equations given above we obtain

$$452 = 6a + 42b \ldots \text{I}$$
$$3330 = 42a + 320b \ldots \text{II}$$

Solving in the normal manner, i.e. eliminate one of the constants (in this case multiply Equation I by 7 and deduct from Equation II) we obtain

$$3330 = 42a + 320b \ldots \text{II}$$
$$\underline{3164 = 42a + 294b} \ldots 7 \times \text{I}$$
$$166 = \qquad 26b$$

∴ b = 6.385   and substituting in either equation the value of a is found to be   30.6

∴ the linear cost function is

$$\underline{y = 30.6 + 6.385x}$$

Notes:

a. The above is an outline of finding the constants a and b by the method of least squares which is sometimes known as REGRESSION ANALYSIS.

b. The least squares method should only be applied to cost and activity data which show evidence of real correlation. This can be tested, for example, by a 't' test of the basic data.

c. After the regression line has been calculated, its accuracy can be assessed by calculating its coefficient of determination (r^2).

PAST COSTS AND FUTURE COSTS

20. The analysis of past cost behaviour may be of help in predicting future cost behaviour, but care should be taken with *any* extrapolation into the future. The past will only be a guide to the future if conditions remain more or less the same. Conditions rarely remain the same, so judgement will always be required in cost prediction. Because many factors other than changes in activity levels influence costs, e.g. changes in organisation, technology, methods, climatic influences etc. etc., care should be taken not to adopt a too simplistic view of cost behaviour. On occasions no past data is available on which to base predictions. This is often the case with a new product and in such cases, or where significant changes in methods are anticipated for an existing product, cost estimates should be based on engineering and work study estimates.

ALTERNATIVE COST PATTERNS

21. So far, all of the cost patterns, whether linear or curvilinear, fixed, variable or semi-variable, have had regular, continuous characteristics. This is not always the case and various other patterns exist, examples of which follow.

STEP COSTS

22. These are costs which remain constant for a range of activity; then, when activity increases still further, the cost has to be increased by a significant amount. A typical example would be supervision costs. For a range of activities one supervisor will be sufficient, but there comes a point when an additional supervisor has to be appointed, so costs increase discretely. This can be shown graphically thus:

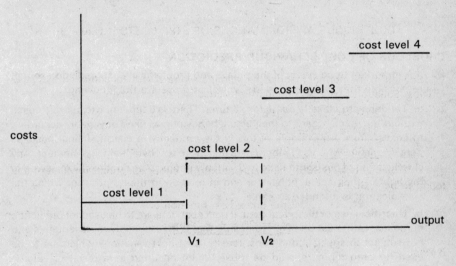

ILLUSTRATION OF STEP COSTS   Figure 8

There is not a simple algebraic expression which describes step costs as there is for continuous linear or curvilinear functions. Analysis involving step costs can be dealt with graphically or by either of the following methods.

i.   If the range of activities being considered lies within one step, e.g. between output levels v_1 and v_2 in Figure 8, then for analysis purposes the step cost can be treated as a fixed cost at cost level 2.

ii.   Continuous approximation of step costs.
      Many costs in the aggregate do increase by discrete amounts so that they are strictly step costs. In many cases the steps are frequent and relatively small so that approximation by continuous functions is reasonably accurate and facilitates subsequent analysis. This can be shown thus:

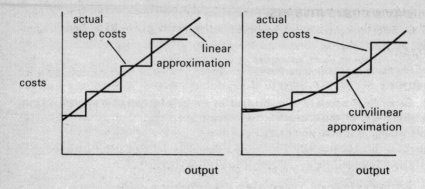

costs

output   output

CONTINUOUS APPROXIMATIONS OF STEP COSTS   Figure 9

PROBLEMS OF COST BEHAVIOUR PREDICTION

23. It is important to be aware of the pitfalls and problems in cost prediction so that where possible they can be avoided. Typical of these are the following:

a. **Tendency to classify costs for all time.** There is a tendency to classify costs, without too much regard to their actual behaviour, as fixed or variable according to conventions. An example of this is the tendency to classify labour costs as purely variable, whereas labour costs may have a substantial fixed element. Any classification of costs into fixed and variable needs to be continually reviewed in the light of their actual behaviour and in relation to the purpose for which the classification is intended to serve.

b. **Uncritical use of historical data.** If past cost data are to be used for prediction purposes, care must be taken to ensure that it is reasonably representative and not subject to special conditions. Ideally, past cost variations which are to be used for predictions, should be those which occurred as a result of volume changes only. Many factors other than changes in volume cause cost changes (e.g. technology changes, product mix changes, method and tooling changes, seasonal and climatic changes) and if past data are not adjusted to take account of non-volume factors there is the implicit assumption that the non-volume factors will act upon costs in the future in the same manner and proportions as in the past. This is a somewhat sweeping assumption.

c. **Linearity assumption.** Costs display a variety of forms and the too ready assumption of linearity for all variable costs may introduce unacceptable inaccuracies. Cost linearity makes for easy calculations, but easy calculations do not necessarily produce the best results.

d. **Use of statistical methods.** Providing that the base data are sound, a gain in accuracy can be obtained by the use of appropriate statistical methods. Where volume changes have been the major factor influencing cost levels then simple regression analysis, as described in the chapter, can be of value. Where several factors are known to have influenced costs, then more advanced statistical methods, such as multiple regression analysis may be required. Alternatively, where the data is curvilinear, statistical curve fitting should be employed to establish if the data fits one of the known statistical functions. However, no statistical method should be used uncritically, judgement will invariably be required in addition to the results of the statistical exercise.

In general it is probably fair to say that too much attention is paid to techniques of manipulating data and not enough to the quality of the base data.

SUMMARY

24. a. For many accounting purposes it is vital to be able to estimate accurately the behaviour of cost in relation to changes in the level of activity.

b. Generally the situations being studied are for a limited time period and for a limited range of activity variations i.e. short run.

c. Variable cost may be linear or curvilinear.

d. Linear approximations of curvilinear functions are frequently made.

e. Fixed or period costs are time, not activity related.

f. Semi-variable costs contain fixed and variable elements.

g. When past data are available, cost characteristics can be established visually by the scattergraph technique or by the method of regression analysis known as least squares.

h. Some cost patterns are not continuous, for example, step costs.

i. Many problems exist in accurately predicting cost behaviour and these include: inappropriate cost classifications, poor historical data, using linear approximation in inappropriate circumstances etc.

POINTS TO NOTE

25. a. Flexible budgeting, marginal costing, cost/volume/profit analysis have as their basis, predictions about cost behaviour.

b. It has been said with some truth that in the short run all costs are fixed and in the long run all costs are variable.

c. In practice costs do not behave in regular, predictable fashions. One example is that different types of variable costs vary with different activity indicators. One cost may vary with production, another with sales, another one with orders received. In examinations there is frequently the simplifying assumption that all variable costs are related to one indicator, say sales volume. This makes for simpler questions but it is not necessarily realistic.

d. On occasions it is necessary to resolve a total cost into its fixed and variable elements. This can be done, somewhat crudely, by using the scattergraph technique or by using regression analysis based on the least squares method.

SELF REVIEW QUESTIONS

1. What are the major reasons for the study of cost behaviour? (2)
2. What is normally assumed to be the major factor influencing the level of costs? (3)
3. Can statistical techniques be of value in predicting costs? (5)
4. Define a variable cost. (6)
5. What is a curvilinear variable cost? (9)
6. What is the formula for the cost function known as a Parabola? (10)
7. What is a linear approximation? (11)
8. Distinguish between variable cost and the economic concept of marginal cost. (12)

9. What is a direct cost? *(12)*

10. Define a fixed cost. *(15)*

11. What is a semi-variable cost? *(16)*

12. What is the formula for a linear semi-variable cost? *(16)*

13. What is the scattergraph technique? *(18)*

14. What are the least squares Normal Equations? *(19)*

15. Why is judgement required in cost prediction? *(20)*

16. What are step costs? *(22)*

EXAMINATION QUESTIONS

1. Albatross Pty, the Australian subsidiary of a British packaging company, is preparing its budget for the year to 30th June 1980. In respect of fuel oil consumption it is desired to estimate an equation of the form $y = a + bx$, where "y" is the total expense at an activity level "x", "a" is the fixed expense, and "b" is the rate of variable cost.

The following data relate to the year to 30th June 1979:

Year	Month	Machine Hours (000)	Fuel Oil Expense ($)	Year	Month	Machine Hours (000)	Fuel Oil Expense ($)
1978	July	34	640	1979	January	26	500
	August	30	620		February	26	500
	September	34	620		March	31	530
	October	39	590		April	35	550
	November	42	500		May	43	580
	December	32	530		June	48	680

The annual total and monthly average figures for 1978/79 were as follows:

	Machine Hours (000)	Fuel Oil Expense ($)
Annual total	420	6,840
Monthly average	35	570

You are required to:

a. estimate fixed and variable elements of fuel oil expense from the above data by both of the following methods:
   i. high and low points
   ii. "least squares" regression analysis

b. compare briefly the methods used in (a) above in relation to the task of estimating fixed and variable elements of a semi-variable cost.

c. accepting that the co-efficient of determination (r^2) arising from the data given in the question is approximately 0.25, interpret the significance of this fact.

(ICA, Management Accounting, July 1979).

2. a. 'Fixed costs are really variable: the more you produce the less they become'. Explain the above statement and state whether or not you agree with it.

b. You are required to sketch a separate graph for each of the items listed below in order to indicate the behaviour of the expense. Graph paper need not be used but your axes must be labelled.
   i. Supervisory labour;

   ii. *depreciation of plant on a machine hour basis;*
  iii. *planned preventive maintenance plus unexpected maintenance;*
  iv. *monthly pay of a salesman who receives a salary of £3,000 per annum plus a commission of 1% paid on his previous month's sales when they exceed £20,000; assume that his previous month's sales totalled £30,000.*

(ICMA, Cost Accounting 1, November 1977).

3. *The following graphs reflect the pattern of certain overhead cost items in a manufacturing company in a year. The vertical axes of the graphs represent the total cost incurred, whilst the horizontal axes represent the volume of production or activity. The zero point is at the intersection of the two axes.*
  You are required to:

  a. *identify which graph represents the overhead cost items shown below:*
(N.B. a graph may be used more than once.)

Ref.	Brief description	Details of cost behaviour
1	Depreciation of equipment	When charged on a straight line basis.
2	Cost of a service	£50 annual charge for subscription, £2 charge for each unit taken, with a maximum total charge of £350 per annum.
3	Royalty	£0.10 per unit produced, with a maximum charge of £5,000 per annum.
4	Supervision cost	When there is one charge hand for every eight men or less, and one foreman for every three charge hands, and when each man represents 40 hours of production, thus:
		Hours
		Under 320 one charge-hand
		321-640 two charge-hands
		641-960 three charge-hands,
		etc. plus one foreman.
5	Depreciation of equipment	When charged on a machine-hour rate.
6	Cost of a service	Flat charge of £400 to cover the first 5,000 units:
		Per unit
		£0.10 for the next 3,000 units
		£0.12 for the next 3,000 units
		£0.14 for all subsequent units
7	Storage/carriage service	Per ton
		£15 for the first 20 tons
		£30 for the next 20 tons
		£45 for the next 20 tons
		No extra charge until the service reaches 100 tons; then £45 per ton for all subsequent tonnage.
8	Outside finishing service	Per unit
		£0.75 for the first 2,000 units

£0.55 for the next 2,000 units
£0.35 for all subsequent units

b. *give an example of an overhead cost item that could represent those graphs to which you do not refer in your answer at (a) above;*

c. *draw one graph of a pattern of an overhead item not shown and give an example of an overhead cost item that it would represent.*

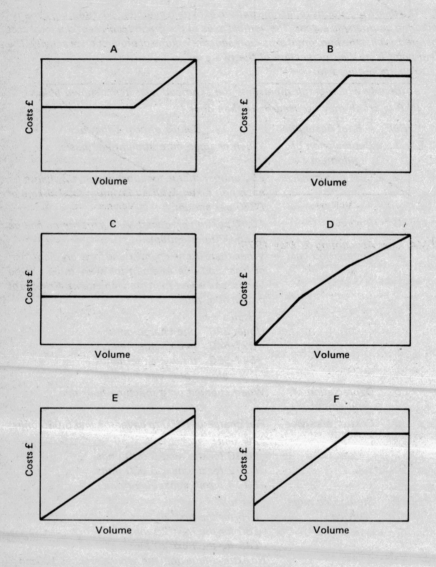

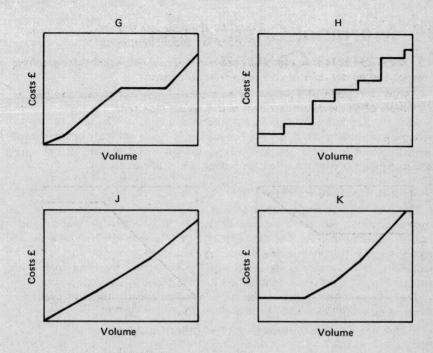

(ICMA, Cost Accounting 2, May 1975).

19 Marginal Costing and Absorption Costing

INTRODUCTION

1. This chapter defines marginal costing and contribution. The uses of marginal costing are discussed and a detailed comparison is made of its use compared with absorption costing. Stock valuation using marginal and absorption costing is explained together with the effect on profits of the different bases.

MARGINAL COSTING – DEFINITION

2. Marginal costing distinguishes between fixed costs and variable costs. The marginal cost of a product is its variable cost, i.e. it includes direct labour, direct materials, direct expenses and the variable part of overheads. It can be defined formally as, "a (costing) principle whereby marginal costs of cost units are ascertained. Only variable costs are charged to cost units, the fixed costs being written off in full against the contribution for that period". *Terminology.*

The term 'contribution' mentioned in the formal definition is the term given to the difference between Sales and Marginal Cost. Thus

MARGINAL COST = VARIABLE COST = DIRECT LABOUR
+
DIRECT MATERIAL
+
DIRECT EXPENSE
+
VARIABLE OVERHEADS

CONTRIBUTION = SALES – MARGINAL COST

The term marginal cost sometimes refers to the marginal cost per unit and sometimes to the total marginal costs of a department or batch or operation. The meaning is usually clear from the context.

Note:

Alternative names for marginal costing are the 'contribution approach' and 'direct costing'.

ALTERNATIVE CONCEPTS OF MARGINAL COST

3. To the economist, marginal cost is the additional cost incurred by the production of one extra unit. To the accountant, marginal cost is average variable cost which is presumed to act in a linear fashion, i.e. marginal cost per unit is assumed to be constant in the short run, over the activity range being considered.

These views can be contrasted in the following graphs:

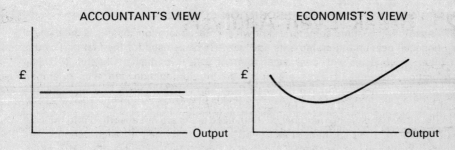

MARGINAL COST PER UNIT ` Figure 1

This difference of viewpoint regarding marginal cost per unit results in the following alternative views of a firm's total cost structure.

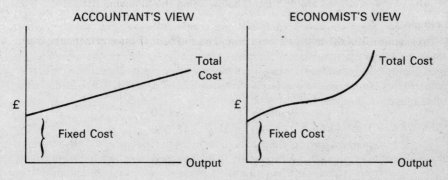

The economic model is an explanation of the cost behaviour of firms in general, whereas the accounting model is an attempt to provide a pragmatic basis for decision making in a particular firm. However, it is likely that differences between the two viewpoints are more apparent than real. A number of investigations have shown that marginal costs are virtually constant per unit over the range of activity changes studied. Accordingly for short run decision making purposes the marginal cost per unit should be assumed to be constant. Thus if the marginal cost per unit was £5 per unit, the total marginal cost for

> 100 units would be £500
> 150 units would be £750
> 200 units would be £1000
> and so on.

USES OF MARGINAL COSTING

4. There are two main uses for the concept of marginal costing:

a. As a basis for providing information to management for planning and decision making. It is particularly appropriate for short run decisions involving changes in volume or activity and the resulting cost changes. This is an important area of study for students and it is dealt with in detail in the following chapter.

b. It can also be used in the routine cost accounting system for the calculation of costs and the valuation of stocks. Used in this fashion, it is an alternative to total absorption costing. This facet of marginal costing is dealt with below.

MARGINAL COSTING AND ABSORPTION COSTING

5. Absorption costing, sometimes known as total absorption costing, is the basis of all financial accounting statements and was the basis used for the first part of this manual which dealt with cost ascertainment (see in particular Chapter 3). Using absorption costing, all costs are absorbed into production and thus operating statements do not distinguish between fixed and variable costs. Consequently the valuation of stocks and work-in-progress contains both fixed and variable elements. On the other hand, using marginal costing, fixed costs are not absorbed into the cost of production. They are treated as period costs and written off each period in the Costing Profit and Loss account. The effect of this is that finished goods and work-in-progress are valued at marginal cost only, i.e. the variable elements of cost, usually Prime cost plus variable overhead. At the end of a period the marginal cost of sales is deducted from sales revenue to show the contribution, from which fixed costs are deducted to show net profit.

The two approaches are illustrated below using the following data:

Example 1

In a period, 20,000 units of Z were produced and sold. Costs and revenues were:

		£
Sales		100,000
Production costs:		
	:– variable	35,000
	:– Fixed	15,000
Administrative + Selling		
overheads:– Fixed		25,000

Operating Statements

Absorption Costing Approach		Marginal Costing Approach		
	£			£
Sales	100,000	Sales		100,000
less Production Cost of Sales	50,000	*less* Marginal Cost		35,000
= Gross Profit	50,000	= Contribution		65,000
less Admin. + Selling				
Overheads	25,000	*less* Fixed Costs		
		Production	15,000	
		Admin. S + D	25,000	40,000
= Net Profit	£25,000	= Net Profit		£25,000

The above illustration, although simple, illustrates the general characteristics of both approaches.

The key figure arising in the Marginal statement is the contribution of £65,000. The total amount of contribution arising from Product Z (and other products, if any) forms a pool from which fixed costs are met. Any surplus arising after fixed costs are met becomes the Net Profit.

CHANGES IN THE LEVEL OF ACTIVITY

6. When changes occur in the level of activity, the absorption costing approach may cause some confusion. In Example 1 the activity level was 20,000 units and using the absorption approach, the profit per unit and cost per unit can be calculated as follows:

	£
Selling Price per unit	5
less Total cost per unit = $\dfrac{£75000}{20000}$	3.75
Profit per unit	£1.25

If these figures were used as guides to results at any activity level other than 20,000, they would be incorrect and may mislead. For example, if the level of activity of Example 1 changed to 25,000 units, it might be assumed that the total profits would be 25,000 x £1.25 = £31,250. However, the results are likely to be as follows:

Operating Statement (Absorption approach)

	£
Sales (25,000 x £5)	125,000
less Production Cost (£35,000 x 125% + 15,000)	58,750
= Gross Profit	66,250
less Admin + Selling overheads	25,000
= Net Profit	£41,250

The difference is, of course, caused by the incorrect treatment of the fixed cost. In such circumstances the use of the marginal approach presents a clearer picture. Based on the data in Example 1 the marginal cost per unit and the contribution per unit is calculated as follows:

$$\text{Marginal cost/unit} = \frac{\text{Marginal Cost}}{\text{Quantity}} = \frac{35,000}{20,000}$$

$$= \underline{£1.75}$$

$$\therefore \text{contribution/unit} = \text{Sales Price} - \text{Marginal cost/unit}$$

$$= £5 - £1.75$$

$$= \underline{£3.25}$$

If, once again, the activity is increased to 25,000 units, the expected profit would be:

(25,000 units x Contribution/unit) − Fixed costs

= (25,000 x £3.25) − £40,000

= £41,250 and the operating statement on marginal costing lines would be

	£
Sales	125,000
less Marginal cost (25,000 x 1.75)	43,750
= Contribution	£81,250
less Fixed costs	40,000
Net Profit	£41,250

Note:

Students will note that the marginal cost and contribution per unit are assumed to be constant and that the fixed costs remain unchanged.

STOCKS AND MARGINAL COSTING

7. Although the method of presentation was different, both marginal and absorption costing produced the same net profit for the data in Example 1. This was because there was no stock at the beginning or end of the period. Because the two methods differ in their valuation of stock, they produce different profit figures when stocks arise. This is illustrated below.

Example 2

Assume the same data as Example 1 except that only 18,000 of the 20,000 units produced were sold, 2000 units being carried forward as Stock to the next period.

Produce operating statements based upon marginal costing and absorption costing principles.

Operating Statements

Absorption Costing			Marginal Costing			
		£				£
Sales (18,000 x £5)		90,000	Sales			90,000
	£				£	
less Production			*less* Marginal cost	35,000		
Cost of Sales	50,000		– Closing Stock			
– Closing Stock			(2000 x £1.75)	3,500	31,500	
(2000 x £2.50)	5,000	45,000				
= Gross Profit		£45,000	= Contribution			£58,500
less Admin + Selling			*less* Fixed Costs			
overheads		25,000	Production	15,000		
			Admin S + D	25,000	40,000	
= Net Profit		£20,000	= Net Profit			£18,500

a. The closing stock valuations using the two approaches are:

Absorption Costing = Average Production Cost (including fixed costs)

$$= \frac{£50,000}{20,000} = \underline{£2.50}$$

Marginal Costing = Marginal cost i.e. variable costs only

$$= \frac{£35,000}{20,000} = \underline{£1.75}$$

b. By including fixed costs in stock valuation, absorption costing transfers some of this period's fixed costs into next period when they will be charged against the revenue derived from the stock carried forward (assuming it is sold). Marginal costing always writes off all fixed costs in the period they are incurred.

c. In a period with increasing stocks (as the one illustrated) absorption costing will show higher profits than marginal costing. Conversely in a period of decreasing stocks marginal costing will show the higher profits. The difference is, of course, entirely due to the different treatment of fixed costs in the stock valuation.

TYPICAL MARGINAL COSTING STATEMENTS

8. Wherever marginal costing is used in the routine accounting system, similar principles to those described above will apply. Some examples of marginal costing statements in typical situations are the following:

a. Where Multiple Products or Multiple departments exist

Marginal Costing Operating Statement

Product or Department 1	Product or Department 2	Product or Department 3	. . . . .	Total
Sales 1	Sales 2	Sales 3		Total Sales
less Marginal Cost 1 of Sales	Marginal Cost 2 of Sales	Marginal Cost 3 of Sales	. . . . .	Marginal Cost of Sales (Total)
= Contribut. 1	Contribut. 2	Contribut. 3	etc. =	Total Contribution
			less	Fixed Costs for whole organisation
				NET PROFIT

Notes:
   i.   No attempt is made to apportion fixed costs arbitrarily across products or departments.
   ii. With such a presentation the effects of eliminating a product or department or altering the level of activity can be shown more clearly. Care must be taken in assessing the effect of a product or department elimination to ensure that any effect on fixed costs is allowed for.

b. Process Costing
Where marginal costing is used in process cost accounting, the normal accounts and statements will be produced, as described in Chapter 15 except that:
   i.   Process accounts will contain variable costs only.
   ii. Transfers from one process to another will be at marginal cost.
   iii. Losses, abnormal and normal, will be valued at marginal cost only.
   iv. All fixed costs will be written off, each period, to costing profit and loss.

MARGINAL COSTING OR ABSORPTION COSTING

9. The arguments below relate to the use of these techniques in the *routine cost accounting system* of the organisation and not to their use for decision making or control.

Arguments for the use of marginal costing in routine costing:

a. Simple to operate.

b. No apportionments, which are frequently on an arbitrary basis, of fixed costs to products or departments. Many fixed costs are indivisible by their nature, e.g. Managing Director's Salary.

c. Where sales are constant, but production fluctuates (possibly an unlikely circumstance) marginal costing shows a constant net profit whereas absorption costing shows variable amounts of profit.

d. Under or over absorption of overheads is almost entirely avoided. The usual reason for under/over absorption is the inclusion of fixed costs into overhead absorption rates and the level of activity being different to that planned.

e. Fixed costs are incurred on a time basis, e.g. salaries, rent, rates etc., and do not relate to activity. Therefore it is logical to write them off in the period they are incurred and this is done using marginal costing.

f. Accounts prepared using marginal costing more nearly approach the actual cash flow position.

Arguments for the use of total absorption in routine costing.

a. Fixed costs are a substantial and increasing proportion of costs in modern industry. Production cannot be achieved without incurring fixed costs which thus form an inescapable part of the cost of production, so should be included in stock valuations. Marginal costing may give the impression that fixed costs are somehow divorced from production.

b. Where production is constant but sales fluctuate, net profit fluctuations are less with absorption costing than with marginal costing.

c. Where stock building is a necessary part of operations, e.g. timber seasoning, spirit maturing, firework manufacture, the inclusion of fixed costs in stock valuation is necessary and desirable. Otherwise a series of fictitious losses will be shown in earlier periods to be offset eventually by excessive profits when the goods are sold.

d. The calculation of marginal cost and the concentration upon contribution may lead to the firm setting prices which are below total cost although producing some contribution. Absorption cost makes this less likely because of the automatic inclusion of fixed charges.

e. SSAP 9 (Stocks and Work in Progress) recommends the use of absorption costing for financial accounts because costs and revenues must be matched in the period when the revenue arises, not when the costs are incurred. Also it recommends that stock valuations must include production overheads incurred in the normal course of business even if such overheads are time related, i.e. fixed. The production overheads must be based upon normal activity levels.

CONCLUSIONS REGARDING MARGINAL AND ABSORPTION COSTING

10. No generalised, all embracing answer can be given as to which technique should be used. Having regard to all the factors, the accountant should make a judgement as to which technique is more appropriate for the requirements of a particular organisation. Although any technique can be used for internal purposes, SSAP 9 is quite clear that absorption costing must be the basis of the financial accounts. It would appear that the use of a full marginal costing system in the routine cost ascertainment procedures of an organisation is relatively rare. This does not mean that marginal costing principles are unimportant. An understanding of the behaviour of costs and the implications of contribution is vital for accountants and managers. The use of marginal costing principles in planning and decision making, dealt with in the following chapter, is universal and is of considerable importance.

MULTI PERIOD EXAMPLE OF MARGINAL AND ABSORPTION COSTING

11. To bring together the various points covered in the chapter, a fully worked

example is shown below.

Example:

Stock, production and sales data for Industrial Detergents Ltd. are given below.

		Period 1	Period 2	Period 3	Period 4
Production	(litres)	60,000	70,000	55,000	65,000
Sales	"	60,000	55,000	65,000	70,000
Opening Stock	"	–	–	15,000	5,000
Closing Stock	"	–	15,000	5,000	–

The company has a single product, for which the financial data, based on an activity level of 60,000 litres/period, are as follows:

	Cost per litre
	£
Direct Material	2.50
Direct Labour	3.00
Production Overheads	
= 200% of direct labour	6.00
= Total cost/litre	£11.50
Selling price per litre	£18.00

Administrative overheads are fixed at £100,000 per period and half of the production overheads are fixed.

From the above information prepare operating statements on marginal costing and absorption costing principles.

Solution:

The first step is to establish the amount of fixed production overheads per period. The cost data shown above are based on 60,000 litres.

$$\text{Labour for 60,000 litres} = 60,000 \times £3 = £180,000$$
$$\text{Total production overheads} = 200\% \times £180,000 = £360,000$$
$$\therefore \text{Fixed production overheads} = \frac{£360,000}{2} = £180,000$$

The variable overhead recovery rate is accordingly 100% of direct wages so that marginal cost per litre can be established as follows:

	£
Material	2.50
Labour	3.00
Variable overhead	
100% of wages	3.00
	£8.50

Operating Statement using Marginal Costing

	Period 1 £		Period 2 £		Period 3 £		Period 4 £
Sales		1,080,000		990,000		1,170,000	1,260,000
Marginal cost of Production	510,000		595,000		467,500	552,500	
+ opening stock					127,500	42,500	
− closing stock			127,500		42,500		
= Marginal cost of Sales		510,000		467,500		552,500	595,000
Contribution		570,000		522,500		617,500	665,000
Fixed Costs (Admin + Prod'n)		280,000		280,000		280,000	280,000
NET PROFIT		£290,000		£242,500		£337,500	£385,000

Note:

Stocks are valued at marginal cost.

Operating Statement using Absorption Costing in Accordance with SSAP 9

	Period 1 £		Period 2 £		Period 3 £		Period 4 £
Sales		1,080,000		990,000		1,170,000	1,260,000
Total Cost of production	690,000		805,000		632,500	747,500	
+ opening stock					172,500	57,500	
− closing stock			172,500		57,500		
= Total Cost of Sales		690,000		632,500		747,500	805,000
GROSS PROFIT		390,000		357,500		422,500	455,000
Administration Costs		100,000		100,000		100,000	100,000
NET PROFIT		£290,000		£257,500		£322,500	£355,000
Planned Activity Level		60,000		60,000		60,000	60,000
Actual Activity Level		60,000		70,000		55,000	65,000
Difference		−		+ 10,000		− 5,000	+ 5,000
Overhead Over or (under) Absorption		−		+ £30,000		(£15,000)	+ £15,000

Notes:

a. Stocks valued at full production cost including fixed production overheads i.e. in this example £11.50 per litre. This represents the cost at normal activity levels in accordance with SSAP 9 recommendations.

b. The amount of over or under absorbed overhead represents the over or under recovery of fixed overheads caused when activity is above or below the planned activity level. In this example the fixed overheads are recovered at £3 per litre. . . in period 2 production was 70,000 litres as compared with 60,000 planned so the over absorption was 10,000 litres at £3 per litre = £30,000.

c. As explained in Chapter 3, the over/under absorption could be taken direct to P & L a/c or, more usually, taken to a suspense account from which the net balance at the end of the year would be written off to P & L.

d. The amount over absorbed would be deducted from total cost; the amount under absorbed would be added to total cost.

e. Because in this example, production and sales were equal over the periods concerned the profits using the two techniques can be reconciled thus:–

Profits using Marginal Costing

	£
Period 1	290,000
2	242,500
3	337,500
4	385,000
	£1,255,000

Profits using Absorption Costing

	£
Period 1	290,000
2	257,500
3	322,500
4	355,000
+ Net over absorption	30,000
	£1,255,000

SUMMARY

12. a. Marginal costing is a costing technique where fixed and variable costs are differentiated. Only variable costs are charged to cost units and fixed costs are written off in full each period.

b. Contribution is the difference between sales and variable cost. The pool of contribution is available to cover the fixed costs and, when the fixed costs have been covered, the balance remaining is profit.

c. Marginal costing can be used as the basis of the routine cost accounting system or for management decision making.

d. Total absorption costing incorporates both fixed and variable costs into production and consequently into stock valuation. Stocks under marginal costing are valued at marginal cost only.

e. Because of the different methods of stock valuation the two approaches produce differing profit figures when stocks exist at the beginning or end of a period.

f. When used as a basis of the routine cost accounting system marginal costing avoids the sometimes arbitrary apportionment of fixed overheads to products or departments, charges period costs when they are incurred, and is claimed to show a more realistic situation.

g. Absorption costing recognises that fixed costs are an inescapable part of production costs and consequently includes fixed elements in stock valuation. SSAP 9 recommends absorption costing principles for stock valuation.

POINT TO NOTE

13. Under examination conditions if the question emphasises the use of cost statements for planning or decision making purposes, it is likely that a marginal cost approach is required.

SELF REVIEW QUESTIONS

1. What is marginal costing? (2)
2. What is contribution and how is it calculated? (2)
3. Distinguish between the accountant's and economist's view of marginal cost. (3)
4. What are the main uses of marginal costing? (4)
5. What is the essential difference between marginal and absorption costing? (5)
6. How does the method of stock valuation differ between marginal and absorption costing? (7)
7. What arguments are there for the use of marginal costing principles in the routine costing system of an organisation? (9)
8. What are the arguments for absorption costing? (9)

EXAMINATION QUESTIONS

1. MS Limited manufactures one product only which is sold for £100 each. There is given below a budgeted profit and loss statement for one year based on sales and production at a normal level of activity.

Profit and Loss Statement

	£000	£000
Sales		1,000
Costs:		
Direct material	300	
Direct wages	200	
Production overhead: variable	50	
fixed	200	
Administration overhead: fixed	100	
Selling overhead: fixed	50	
		900
Net profit		£100

Budgets have been prepared for year ending 30th June, 1981 and year ending 30th June, 1982. In the budget to 30th June, 1981 sales have been shown as only 80% of the normal level of activity while production has been included at the normal level of activity. In the budget for year ending 30th June, 1982 sales have been shown as achieving the normal level of activity while production has been reduced to 80% of the normal level of activity to utilise stock made previously.

    a. You are required to prepare a budgeted profit and loss statement for each of the years ending 30th June, 1981 and 1982, based on a system of:
      i.   absorption costing;
      ii. marginal costing.
    b. Discuss briefly the effect on profit of these two different systems.

(ICMA, Cost Accounting 2, May 1980).

2. *Bittern Ltd manufactures and sells a single product at a unit selling price of £25. In constant price-level terms its cost structure is as follows:*

variable costs:	production materials	£10 per unit produced
	distribution	£1 per unit sold
semi-variable costs:	labour	£5,000 per annum, plus
		£2 per unit produced
fixed costs:	overheads	£5,000 per annum

For several years Bittern has operated a system of variable costing for management accounting purposes. It has been decided to review the system and to compare it for management accounting purposes with an absorption costing system.

As part of the review you have been asked to prepare estimates of Bittern's profits in constant price-level terms over a three-year period in three different hypothetical situations, and to compare the two types of system generally for management accounting purposes.

You are required:

a. in each of the following three sets of hypothetical circumstances, to calculate Bittern's profit in each of years t_1, t_2, and t_3, and also in total over the three-year period t_1 to t_3, using, first, a variable costing system, and then a full-cost absorption costing system with fixed cost recovery based on a normal production level of 1,000 units per annum:

i. stable unit levels of production, sales and inventory

	t_1	t_2	t_3
opening stock	100	100	100
production	1,000	1,000	1,000
sales	1,000	1,000	1,000
closing stock	100	100	100

ii. stable unit level of sales, but fluctuating unit levels of production and inventory

	t_1	t_2	t_3
opening stock	100	600	400
production	1,500	800	700
sales	1,000	1,000	1,000
closing stock	600	400	100

iii. stable unit level of production, but fluctuating unit levels of sales and inventory

	t_1	t_2	t_3
opening stock	100	600	400
production	1,000	1,000	1,000
sales	500	1,200	1,300
closing stock	600	400	100

(**Note:** All the data in i. – iii. above are volumes, not values)

b. to write a short comparative evaluation of variable and absorption costing systems for management accounting purposes, paying particular attention to profit measurement, and using your answer to part (a) to illustrate your arguments if you wish.

(ICA, Management Accounting, July 1979).

3. a. Comment briefly on the two most important features which you consider distinguish marginal costing from absorption costing.

b. For decision making purposes, a company uses the following figures relating to product B for a one-year period.

Activity:	50%	100%
Sales and production, in thousands of units	200	400
	£000	£000
Sales	1,000	2,000
Production costs:		
Variable	400	800
Fixed	200	200
Selling, distribution and administration expenses:		
Variable	200	400
Fixed	300	300

The normal level of activity for the current year is 400,000 units. The fixed costs are incurred evenly throughout the year and actual fixed costs are the same as budgeted.

There were no stocks of product B at the start of the quarter in which 110,000 units were produced and 80,000 units were sold.

From each of the questions (i) to (iv) below, you are required to select the appropriate answer. You must support each answer with an explanatory calculation.

i. The amount of fixed production costs absorbed by product B in the first quarter, using absorption costing, is:

£

1   80,000
2   40,000
3   110,000
4   55,000
5   None of these.

ii. The over/(under) absorption of fixed production costs in the first quarter is:

£

1   (5,000)
2   5,000
3   10,000
4   15,000
5   None of these.

iii. The net profit (or loss) for the first quarter using absorption costing, is:

£

1   (115,000)
2   50,000
3   (175,000)
4   125,000
5   None of these.

iv. The net profit (or loss) for the first quarter, using marginal costing, is:

£

1   35,000
2   (340,000)
3   65,000
4   (115,000)
5   None of these.

(ICMA, Cost Accounting 1, May 1979).

20 Marginal Costing and Decision Making

INTRODUCTION

1. This chapter explains what information is necessary for decision making and how marginal costing can provide suitable information. Limiting factors and their effects on the decision making process are described. Examples are given of marginal costing applied to a variety of decisions, including special price orders, product selection and make or buy decisions. The concept of differential costing is explained and illustrated and its relationship with marginal costing is described.

DECISION MAKING

2. Decision making is concerned with the future and involves a choice between alternatives. Many factors, both qualitative and quantitative, need to be considered and for many decisions financial information is a critical factor. It is therefore important that *relevant* information on costs and revenues is supplied. But what is relevant information? It is information about:

   a. Future costs and revenues. It is the expected future costs and revenues that are of importance to the decision maker. This means that past costs and revenues are only useful in so far as they provide a guide to the future. Sunk costs are irrelevant.

   b. Differential costs and revenues. Only those costs and revenues which alter as a result of a decision are relevant. Where factors are common to all the alternatives being considered they can be ignored; only the differences are relevant. In many situations the fixed costs remain constant for each of the alternatives being considered and thus the marginal costing approach showing sales, marginal cost and contribution is particularly appropriate.

SHORT RUN TACTICAL DECISIONS

3. These are decisions which seek to make the best use of existing facilities. Typically, in the short run, fixed costs remain unchanged so that the marginal cost, revenue and contribution of each alternative is relevant. In these circumstances the selection of the alternative which maximises contribution is the correct decision rule. In the long term (and sometimes in the short term) fixed costs *do* change and accordingly the differential costs must include any changes in the amount of fixed costs. Where there is a decision involving no changes in fixed costs normal marginal costing principles apply. Where the situation involves changes in fixed costs a more fundamental aid to decision making called differential costing is used. Marginal costing is covered first in this chapter and then differential costing.

KEY FACTOR

4. Sometimes known as a limiting factor or principal budget factor. This is a factor which is a binding constraint upon the organisation i.e. the factor which prevents indefinite expansion or unlimited profits. It may be sales, availability of finance, skilled labour, supplies of material or lack of space. Where a single binding constraint can be identified, then the general objective of maximising contribution can be achieved by selecting the alternative which *maximises the contribution per unit of the key factor*. It will be apparent that from time to time the key factor in an organisation will change.

For example, a firm may have a shortage of orders. It overcomes this by appointing more salesmen and then finds that there is a shortage of machine capacity. The expansion of the productive capacity may introduce a problem of lack of space and so on.

Note:

The 'maximising contribution per unit of the limiting factor' rule can be of value, but can only be used where there is a single binding constraint and where the constraint is continuously divisible i.e. it can be altered one unit at a time. Where several constraints apply simultaneously, the simple maximising rule given above cannot be applied. This is not usually a problem for examination purposes, but real life is rarely that simple.

EXAMPLE OF DECISIONS INVOLVING MARGINAL COSTING

5. Several typical situations in which marginal costing can provide useful information for decision making are given below. Once the general principles are understood, they can be applied in any other similar circumstances.

The steps involved in analysing such problems are as follows:

a. Check that fixed costs are expected to remain unchanged.

b. If necessary separate out fixed and variable costs.

c. Calculate the revenue, marginal costs and contribution of each of the alternatives.

d. Check to see if there is a limiting factor which will be a binding constraint and if so, calculate the contribution per unit of the limiting factor.

e. Finally, choose the alternative which maximises contribution.

The situations shown below are decisions involving acceptance of a special order, dropping a product, choice of product where a limiting factor exists, and make or buy.

ACCEPTANCE OF A SPECIAL ORDER

6. By this is meant the acceptance or rejection of an order which utilises spare capacity, but which is only available if a lower than normal price is quoted. The procedure is illustrated by the following example.

Example 1

Zerocal Ltd. manufacture and market a slimming drink which they sell for 20p per can. Current output is 400,000 cans per month which represents 80% of capacity. They have the opportunity to utilise their surplus capacity by selling their product at 13p per can to a supermarket chain who will sell it as an 'own label' product.

Total costs for the last month were £56,000 of which £16,000 were fixed costs. This represented a total cost of 14p per can.

Based on the above data should Zerocal accept the supermarket order?

What other factors should be considered?

Solution:

The present situation is as follows

		£	
Sales (400,000 x 20p)	=	80,000	
less Marginal cost		40,000	(= 10p/can)
= Contribution		40,000	
less Fixed Costs		16,000	
= NET PROFIT		£24,000	

On the assumption that fixed costs are unchanged, the special order will produce the following contribution

		£
Sales (100,000 x 13p)	=	13,000
less Marginal cost		
(100,000 x 10p)	=	10,000
= CONTRIBUTION		£3,000

. . . the new order brings in more contribution which, because fixed costs are already covered, results in increased net profit. Thus, purely on the cost figures, the order would be acceptable.

However, there are several other factors which would need to be considered before a final decision is taken.

a. Will the acceptance of one order at a lower price lead other customers to demand lower prices as well?

b. Is this special order the most profitable way of using the spare capacity?

c. Will the special order lock up capacity which could be used for future full price business?

d. Is it absolutely certain that fixed costs will not alter?

Notes:

a. Although the price of 13p is less than the total cost of 14p per can, it does provide some contribution, so may be worthwhile.

b. The process of marginal cost pricing to utilise spare capacity is widely used, e.g. hotels provide cheap weekend rates, railways and airlines have cheap fares for off peak periods, many manufacturers of proprietary goods produce own label products and so on.

c. The contribution from the special order can also be calculated by multiplying the quantity by the contribution per can i.e. 100,000 x 3p = £3,000.

DROPPING A PRODUCT

7. If a company has a range of products one of which is deemed to be unprofitable, it may consider dropping the item from its range.

Example 2

A company produces three products for which the following operating statement has been produced:

	Product X	Product Y	Product Z	Total
	£	£	£	£
Sales	32,000	50,000	45,000	127,000
Total costs	36,000	38,000	34,000	108,000
NET PROFIT (LOSS)	(£4,000)	£12,000	£11,000	£19,000

The total costs comprise ⅔ variable ⅓ fixed.

The directors consider that as Product X shows a loss it should be discontinued. Based on the above cost data should Product X be dropped? What other factors should be considered?

Solution:

First calculate the fixed costs, i.e.

⅓(36,000) + ⅓(38,000) + ⅓(34,000) = £36,000

Rearranging the operating statement in marginal costing form produces:

	Product X £	Product Y £	Product Z £	Total £
Sales	32,000	50,000	45,000	127,000
less				
Marginal Cost	24,000	25,333	22,667	72,000
= CONTRIBUTION	£8,000	£24,667	£22,333	£55,000
			less Fixed Costs	36,000
			= NET PROFIT	£19,000

From this it will be seen that Product X produces a contribution of £8,000. Should it be dropped the position would be:

	£
Contribution Product Y	24,667
Contribution Product Z	22,333
Total Contribution	47,000
less Fixed Costs	36,000
= NET PROFIT	£11,000

Thus dropping Product X with an apparent loss of £4000 *reduces* total profits by £8000 which is, of course, the amount of contribution lost from Product X.

Other factors which need to be considered:

a. Although Product X does provide some contribution, it is at a low rate and alternative, more profitable products or markets should be considered.

b. The assumption above was that the fixed costs were general fixed costs which would remain even if X was dropped. If dropping X resulted in the elimination of the fixed costs originally apportioned to X, then the elimination would be worthwhile. However, this is unlikely.

CHOICE OF PRODUCT WHERE A LIMITING FACTOR EXISTS

8. This is the situation where a firm has a choice between various types of products which it could manufacture and where there is a single, binding constraint.

Example 3

A company is able to produce four products and is planning its production mix for the next period. Estimated cost, sales, and production data are given below.

Product	W		X		Y		Z	
	£		£		£		£	
Selling Price/unit	20		30		40		36	
	£		£		£		£	
Labour (@ £2/hr)	6		4		14		10	
Materials (@ £1 kg.)	6	12	18	22	10	24	12	22
Contribution		£8		£8		£16		£14

Resources/Unit				
Labour (hours)	3	2	7	5
Materials (Kgs.)	6	18	10	12
Maximum Demand (Units)	5000	5000	5000	5000

Based on the above data, what is the most appropriate mix under the two following assumptions?

a. If labour hours are limited to 50,000 in a period *or*

b. If material is limited to 110,000 Kgs in a period.

Wherever products have a positive contribution and there are no constraints, there is a prima facie case for their production.

However, when, as in this example, constraints exist, the products must be ranked in order of contribution per unit of the constraint and the most profitable product mix established.

Accordingly, the contribution per unit of the inputs is calculated.

Product	W	X	Y	Z
	£	£	£	£
Contribution/Unit	8	8	16	14
Contribution/ Labour Hour	2.67	4	2.29	2.8
Contribution/Kg of Mat'l	1.33	0.44	1.6	1.17

Answer:

a. To make all the products up to the demand limit would require:

(5000 x 3) + (5000 x 2) + (5000 x 7) + (5000 x 5) = 85,000 labour hours

but as there is a limit of 50,000 hrs in a period, the products should be manufactured in order of attractiveness related to labour hours which is X, Z, W and finally Y.

Produce 5000 units X using 10,000 labour hours

   5000 units Z using 25,000 labour hours

   5000 units W using 15,000 labour hours

and no units of Y   —

which uses the total of   50,000 hours available

b. If the constraint is 110,000 kgs of material, then a similar process produces a ranking of Y, W, Z and finally X which will be noted is the opposite of the ranking produced if labour is the constraint.

When material is the constraint, the optimum production mix is:

5000 units of Y using 50,000 Kgs material

5000 units of W using 30,000 Kgs material

2500 units of Z using 30,000 Kgs material

and no units of X   —

which uses the total of   110,000 Kgs of material

Notes:

a. The above process of maximising contribution per unit of the limiting factor can only be used where there is a single binding constraint.

b. Most practical situations involve various constraints and many more factors than the example illustrated. In such circumstances, if linearity can be assumed, linear programming* will indicate the optimum solution. An outline of the graphical method of solving LP problems is given in the appendix to this chapter.

c. In general where no constraint is identified, a reasonable decision rule is to choose the alternative which maximises contribution per £ of sales value.

MAKE OR BUY

9. Frequently management are faced with the decision whether to make a particular product or component or whether to buy it in. Apart from overriding technical reasons, the decision is usually based on an analysis of the cost implications.

In general the relevant cost comparison is between the marginal cost of manufacture and the buying in price. However, when manufacturing the component displaces existing production, the lost contribution must be added to the marginal cost of production of the component before comparison with the buying in price. The two situations are illustrated below.

Example 4

A firm manufactures component BK 200 and the costs for the current production level of 50,000 units are:

COSTS/UNIT

	£
Materials	2.50
Labour	1.25
Variable overheads	1.75
Fixed overheads	3.50
TOTAL COST	£9.00

Component BK 200 could be bought in for £7.75 and, if so, the production capacity utilised at present would be unused.

Assuming that there are no overriding technical considerations, should BK 200 be bought in or manufactured?

* *Linear programming is fully described in Quantitative Techniques, T. Lucey, DP Publications.*

Solution

Comparison of the buying in price of £7.75 and the full cost of £9.00 suggest that the component should be bought in.

However, the correct comparison is between the MARGINAL COST of manufacture (i.e. £5.50) and the buying in price of £7.75. This indicates that the component should be manufactured, not bought in.

The reason for this is that the fixed costs of £175,000 (i.e. 50,000 units at £3.50) would presumably continue and, because the capacity would be unused, the fixed overheads would not be absorbed into production.

If BK 200 was bought in, overall profits would fall by £112,500, which is the difference between the buying in price and the marginal cost of manufacture, i.e. (£7.75 − 5.50) x 50,000.

Example 5

A firm is considering whether to manufacture or purchase a particular component 2543. This would be in batches of 10,000 and the buying in price would be £6.50. The marginal cost of manufacturing Component 2543 is £4.75 per unit and the component would have to be made on a machine which was currently working at full capacity. If the component was manufactured, it is estimated that the sales of finished product FP97 would be reduced by 1000 units. FP97 has a marginal cost of £60/unit and sells for £80/unit.

Should the firm manufacture or purchase component 2543?

Solution

A superficial view, based on the preceding example, is that because the marginal cost of manufacture is substantially below the buying in price, the component should not be bought in and thus further analysis is unnecessary. However, such an approach is insufficient in this more realistic situation and consideration must be given to the loss of contribution from the displaced product.

Cost analysis – Component 2543 in batches of 10,000

	£
Marginal Cost of manufacture	
= £4.75/unit x 10,000	47,500
+ Lost contribution for FP97	
= £20/unit x 1000	20,000
	67,500
Buying in price	
= £6.50/unit x 10,000	65,000

There is a saving of £2,500 per 10,000 batch by buying in rather than manufacture.

Note:

The lost contribution of £20,000 is an example of an OPPORTUNITY COST. This is defined as the value of a benefit sacrificed in favour of an alternative course of action. This is a highly important concept and examples frequently occur in practice and in examination questions. Whenever there are scarce resources, there are alternative uses which must be foregone and the benefit sacrificed is the opportunity lost. Where there is no alternative use for the resource, as in Example 4, the opportunity cost is zero and it can thus be ignored.

DIFFERENTIAL COSTING

10. Differential costing is a broader and more fundamental principle than marginal costing and therefore has a much wider application. Differential costing examines all the revenue and cost differences between alternatives so as to determine the most appropriate decision. Marginal costing assumes that the only differences between alternatives are changes in variable costs and revenues, i.e. that fixed costs do not alter. Because differential costing examines all differences, it is suitable for situations where fixed costs do alter and thus becomes appropriate for both short run and long run decisions. The process by which costs are divided into fixed and variable is still necessary so as to reflect more easily changes in activity levels.

APPROACH USING DIFFERENTIAL COSTING

11. The general approach to decision making outlined in the preceding chapter is still relevant with the proviso that even more care should be taken to identify all the cost changes, both fixed and variable, because there is no assumption that fixed costs will remain unchanged.

A useful way of presenting differential cost statements is as follows:

Alternative A	Alternative B	Difference A-B
–	–	–
–	–	–

The following illustration uses this approach.

DIFFERENTIAL COST EXAMPLE

12. A company, currently operating at full capacity, manufactures and sells saucepans at £2 each. Current volume is 100,000 pans per annum with the following cost structure.

Operating Statement for year

		£
Sales (100,000 at £2)		200,000
less Marginal Cost		
Labour	80,000	
Material	50,000	130,000
= Contribution		70,000
Fixed Costs		30,000
= NET PROFIT		£40,000

An opportunity has arisen to supply 30,000 pans per annum at £1.8.

Acceptance of this order would incur extra fixed costs of £8000 per annum for the hire for additional machinery and the payment of an overtime premium of 20% for the extra direct labour required.

Should this order be accepted? What other factors need to be considered?

Solution:

Differential Cost Statement

	Present Production Level		Projected Production Level		Difference	
	100,000 Pans		130,000 Pans		30,000 Pans	
	£		£		£	
Sales		200,000		254,000		54,000
less Marginal Cost	£		£		£	
Labour	80,000		108,800		28,800	
Materials	50,000	130,000	65,000	173,800	15,000	43,800
= CONTRIBUTION		70,000		80,200		10,200
less Fixed Costs		30,000		38,000		8,000
= NET PROFIT		£40,000		£42,200		£2,200

Thus purely on the cost figures the special order would appear to be worthwhile. Additional factors that would need to be considered include:

a. Will the special order disturb the existing full price market?

b. How accurate are the projected extra costs? The additional profit is small and could easily be wiped out by slight cost increases.

c. Can administration, despatch and other service departments cope with the 30% increase in throughput without extra costs?

IMPLICATIONS OF DIFFERENTIAL COST

13. The only relevant costs for decision making are those which will change as a result of the decision.

If costs are not expected to alter, then they are irrelevant to the decision. Particular examples of costs that are irrelevant are the following:

a. Sunk costs, i.e. costs which have already been incurred are irrelevant.

b. Book values of assets.

c. Cost of a fully utilised resource, i.e. if a limiting factor exists it will be used to the full and will therefore cost the same whatever alternative is considered. The differential cost between alternatives is therefore zero.

d. Conventionally prepared depreciation is not a differential cost and is therefore irrelevant.

e. Fixed costs. Any item which is genuinely fixed and will remain the same whichever alternative is chosen is not a differential cost and can be ignored in choosing alternatives.

OPPORTUNITY COST

14. Opportunity cost is an important concept for decision making purposes. It can be defined as the value of the best alternative foregone. Although often difficult to measure, the concept is of great importance because it emphasises that decisions are concerned with alternatives and that the cost of the chosen plan of action is the profit forgone from the best available alternative. An example will help to make the concept more concrete.

Example:

A firm rents a small workshop for £50 per week, but at present does not use it. They could sub-let the workshop for £80 per week, but they are considering using it themselves for a new project.

In assessing whether the new project is worthwhile, what is the appropriate cost to use for the workshop?

Solution:

The recorded historical cost of £50 is inappropriate for this purpose. If the project is initiated the firm will forgo the £80 rent they could obtain. This is the opportunity cost of the workshop and is the value to be included in the project appraisal.

SUMMARY

15. a. Decision making is concerned with the future and with the choice between alternatives.

b. Relevant information for decision making is concerned with future costs and revenues which will alter as a result of a decision.

c. Marginal costing is most appropriate for short run tactical decisions.

d. A key factor (or limiting factor or principal budget factor) is a binding constraint upon the organisation e.g. shortage of labour, machine time or space.

e. Where a single limiting factor exists which is binding, then the decision rule is to maximise contribution per unit of the limiting factor.

f. Evaluate the sales, marginal cost and contribution of the various alternatives and, if fixed costs remain unchanged, choose the alternative which maximises contribution.

g. Differential costing is a broader concept than marginal costing and examines all the revenue and cost differences between alternatives.

h. The only relevant costs for decision making are those which will change as a result of the decision, i.e. future costs. It follows that sunk costs are irrelevant.

i. Opportunity costs are the value of the best alternative forgone and are critical for decision making.

POINTS TO NOTE

16. a. In practice the classification of costs into fixed and variable is extremely difficult. Costs do not behave in simple, general fashions. Some costs, e.g. wages, are variable in nature when activity is rising, but may become fixed when activity reduces.

b. The concept of opportunity cost is all important for decision making. A relevant factor in choosing any alternative is the benefit sacrificed by not choosing some other alternative.

c. Past costs are not of themselves relevant for decision making. Their only value is that they may be of value in predicting future cost levels.

d. Always examine all the cost changes between alternatives. Do not be misled into assuming that because a cost is classified as fixed, it will always remain the same. So called 'fixed' costs can and do change quite frequently.

SELF REVIEW QUESTIONS

1. *What is relevant information for decision making?* *(2)*
2. *Distinguish between marginal costing and differential costing.*
3. *What is a key factor?* *(4)*
4. *What is the decision rule if there is a single binding constraint?* *(4)*

5.   What are the steps in analysing a problem in which the use of marginal costing is being considered?   (5)

6.   What are the general rules for dealing with an order at lower than normal prices?   (6)

7.   If a firm has a choice between various products and there is a single binding constraint how should it choose which products to manufacture?   (8)

8.   What is the general rule in 'make or buy' decisions?   (9)

9.   Is differential costing suitable for long run decisions?   (10)

10. Give examples of costs which are irrelevant for decision making.   (13)

11. What is opportunity cost?   (14)

Appendix

LINEAR PROGRAMMING (LP)*

1. LP is a mathematical technique concerned with the allocation of scarce resources. It is a procedure to optimise the value of some objective (for example, maximise contribution) when the factors involved are subject to constraints (for example, only 500 machine hours and 200 labour hours are available in a week).

LP can be used to solve problems which

a. can be stated in numeric terms,

b. all factors have linear relationships,

c. have one or more restrictions on the factors involved,

d. have a choice between alternatives.

STANDARD FORMULATION

2. Before attempting a solution, it is necessary to express the problem in a standard manner. This means determining the OBJECTIVE FUNCTION and the CONSTRAINTS. This is shown below using the following example:

A firm makes two products A and B which have a contribution of £15 and £10 per unit respectively. The production data are as follows:

	Per Unit		
	Machining Hours	**Labour Hours**	**Materials (Kgs)**
Product A	4	4	1
Product B	2	6	1
Availability per week	100	180	40

It is required to determine the production plan which maximises contribution.

This is a problem with 2 unknowns (i.e. number of units of A and B) with three constraints (i.e. availability of machine hours, labour hours and material).

The first stage is to express the problem in the standardised format,

i.e.

maximise 15A + 10B   (The objective function expressed
subject to: in contribution per unit)

4A + 2B	$\leqslant$ 100	(machining hours constraint)
4A + 6B	$\leqslant$ 180	(labour hours constraint)
A + B	$\leqslant$ 40	(materials constraint)

Because this is a problem with only 2 unknowns, a graphical solution is possible:

---

* This subject is dealt with in detail in "Quantitative Techniques" T. Lucey, DP Publications

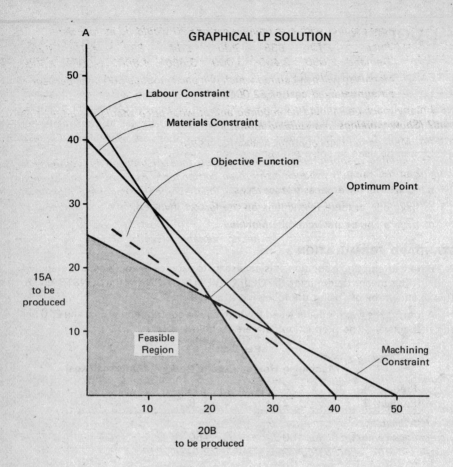

GRAPHICAL LP SOLUTION

Notes:

a. The solution is always obtained on the edge of the feasible region and in this case is 15 units of A and 20 units of B giving a contribution of

$$£(15 \times 15) + £(20 \times 10) = £425 \text{ TOTAL}$$

b. This solution uses the following quantities of the resources:

Machining hours	$(15 \times 4) + (20 \times 2) = 100$	(all utilised)
Labour hours	$(15 \times 4) + (20 \times 6) = 180$	(all utilised)
Material	$(15 \times 1) + (20 \times 1) = 35$	(5 Kgs spare)

c. The materials constraint is non binding, i.e. it is redundant. This can be seen from the graph as it does not touch the feasible region and also from the calculation in (b) which shows that there is 5 Kgs spare.

d. Where there are more than 2 unknowns, graphical solution is not possible and problems have to be solved using what is known as the SIMPLEX method.

EXAMINATION QUESTIONS

1. i. *'Maximise the contribution' has been said to be the golden rule of pricing. Explain and comment on this statement.*

    ii. *The marketing manager of your company has estimated that demand for a* new product with a marginal cost of £20 would be as follows:—

Price	£40	£38	£36	£34	£32	£30	£28
Demand	2,000	2,400	3,000	3,800	4,800	6,000	7,500

Machines will be acquired which will each produce 500 units per year at an annual fixed cost of £2,000.

How many machines should be acquired and at what price should the product be sold? (Show workings in a suitable format.)

(CIPFA, Management Accounting, November 1979).

2. Asp Limited manufactures a simple garden tool. At present the company is working at full capacity producing the three components A, B and C, one of each being required for the assembly of the tool. All the machines are capable of making all the components. Current cost data concerning one hundred tools are as follows:

	Machine hours	Variable £	Fixed £	Total £
Components — A	10	26	10	36
— B	16	32	12	44
— C	20	32	32	64
Assembly	—	52	22	74
	46	142	76	218
Selling price				250

The management is engaged in preparing next year's budget and an increase in sales is to be provided for. The factory is already having to work at full machine capacity to meet current demand and no increase in the present machine capacity can be effected for over twelve months, though facilities involving variable costs can be increased at very short notice. It is decided that one of the components will have to be bought out. The following quotations have been received:

Component		£
A	price per 100 tools	36
B	price per 100 tools	46
C	price per 100 tools	54

The sales manager feels sure that he can sell at least 50% more tools than at present and probably 75% more provided the factory capacity is available.

You are required:

a. to prepare a report for management giving your recommendations as to which component should be ordered from outside suppliers for the oncoming year if production is increased by 50% and 75% respectively, and

b. to explain the assumptions underlying your report.

(ICA, Management Accounting, December 1976).

3. Two decision making problems are faced by a company which produces a range of products and absorbs production overhead using a rate of 200% on direct wages. This rate was calculated from the following budgeted figures:

	£
Variable production costs	64,000
Fixed production costs	96,000
Direct labour costs	80,000

Problem 1

The normal selling price of product X is £22 and production cost for one unit is:

	£
Raw materials	8
Direct labour	4
Production overhead	8
	£20

There is a possibility of supplying a special order for 2,000 units of product X at £16 each. If the order were accepted the normal budgeted sales would not be affected and the company has the necessary capacity to produce the additional units.

Problem 2

The cost of making component Q, which forms part of product Y, is stated below:

	£
Raw material	4
Direct labour	8
Production overhead	16
	£28

Component Q could be brought from an outside supplier for £20.

You are required, assuming that fixed production costs will not change, to:

a. state whether the company should:
   i.   accept the special order in Problem 1;
   ii. continue making component Q or buy it from outside in Problem 2;
both your statements must be supported by details of costs;

b. comment on the principle you have followed in your cost analysis to arrive at your answers to the two problems.

(ICMA, Cost Accounting 1, May 1979).

4.   For LP Limited the following data are relevant to its products L and P:

	Product L	Product P
Per unit	£	£
Selling price	200.00	240.00
Costs:		
Direct materials	45.00	50.00
Direct wages:		
Department: 1	16.00	20.00
2	22.50	13.50
3	10.00	30.00
Variable overhead	6.50	11.50

Fixed overhead is budgeted at £275,000 per annum.

Relevant data for each department are:

	Numbers of employees	Hours per employee per week	Wage rate per hour £
Department: 1	20	40	2.00
2	15	40	2.25
3	18	40	2.50

In the present environment, it is not possible to engage any more employees. You are required to:

a. show mathematically the objective function and the constraints;

b. show on a graph the mix of products which will optimise the contribution of LP Limited;

c. state the production required to obtain the largest contribution and the amount of that contribution.

(ICMA, Cost Accounting 2, May 1978).

5. a. Identify the distinguishing characteristics of direct costs.

b. A research project, which to date has cost the company £150,000, is under review. It is anticipated that, should the project be allowed to proceed, it will be completed in approximately one year when the results would be sold to a government agency for £300,000.

Shown below are the additional expenses which the Managing Director estimates will be necessary to complete the work.

Materials – £60,000
This material, which has just been received, is extremely toxic and if not used on the project would have to be disposed of by special means, at a cost of £5,000.

Labour – £40,000
The men are highly skilled and very difficult to recruit. They were transferred to the project from a production department and, at a recent board meeting, the Works Director claimed that if the men were returned to him he could earn the company each year £150,000 extra sales. The accountant calculated that the prime cost of those sales would be £100,000 and the overhead absorbed (all fixed) would amount to £20,000.

Research Staff – £60,000
A decision has already been taken that this will be the last major piece of research undertaken, and consequently when work on the project ceases the staff involved will be made redundant. Redundancy and severance pay have been estimated at £25,000.

Share of General Building Services – £35,000
The Managing Director is not very sure what is included in this expense. He knows however that the accounts staff charge similar amounts every year to each department.

Required:
Assuming the estimates are accurate, advise the Managing Director whether the project should be allowed to proceed. You must carefully and clearly explain the reasons for your treatment of each expense item.

(ACCA, Costing, June 1979).

6. a. Explain and carefully distinguish between:
    i.   Opportunity Cost and Sunk Cost
    ii.   Fixed Cost and Controllable Cost
    iii. Direct and Indirect Cost

b. Briefly discuss the following statement:

'Historic costs are irrelevant, past events cannot be altered by analysis of expenditure previously incurred.'

(ACCA, Costing, June 1980).

7.   Shown below are the previous two years' summarised trading results for Soafit Ltd, a company manufacturing a single product.

		1978 £000's		1979 £000's
Sales		6,000		7,920
Cost of Sales:	£000's		£000's	
Direct Materials	2,000		3,000	
Direct Labour	1,000		1,150	
Overheads	2,000	5,000	2,420	6,570
Profit		£1,000		£1,350

Throughout 1978 the selling price of the product was £6 per unit and variable overheads, which vary with the number of units produced, amounted to £0.50 per unit.

At the beginning of 1979 the selling price increased by 10%, the purchase price of direct materials by 20%, and direct wage rates by 15%. During 1979 expenditure on overheads also increased, in the case of fixed overheads this amounted to £200,000.

The number of direct workers employed in the manufacturing process is constant, they remain unaffected by any change in the volume of output.

Stock levels remained unchanged throughout the above two year period.

Required:

a. Present a statement to management analysing the reasons for the increase in profit in 1979. All your workings and any assumptions must be shown.

b. Calculate the sales volume, in units, necessary to achieve a profit of £1,500,000 in 1980 if, at the beginning of the year the selling price had been reduced by £0.50 per unit, and the cost structure remains unchanged from 1979.

(ACCA, Costing, June 1980).

8.   Fleabane Ltd aims to maximise its profits. In one factory it manufactures two liquid products called Erigeron and Stachys. Each is a mix of readily-available ingredients which passes through three successive processes of heating, blending and cooling. The finished products are transferred at open market prices to an associated company, which bears all of the related storage and transport costs.

Fleabane's management accountant has prepared the following up-to-date cost statement for the two products, expressed in £s per gallon of final product:

		Erigeron		Stachys
Selling price		20		25
Materials and preparation		10		12
		10		13
Variable process costs:				
Heating process	4		1	
Blending process	1		5	
Cooling process	2		3	
		7		9
Contribution margin		3		4

Each process is costed at £1 per hour of process time per gallon. The processing facilities have no alternative use.

You are required, on Fleabane's receipt of an enquiry for the delivery of an extra one thousand gallons of each product during the coming month, to:

a. draft a statement showing how Fleabane should respond to this enquiry, assuming that the remaining unused capacity available in the coming month is four thousand hours for the cooling process and six thousand hours for each of the other two processes, and

b. draft a statement, showing how Fleabane should respond to this enquiry on the assumption instead that each process has only three thousand hours of unused capacity available in the coming month, showing the following:

i.   Fleabane's optimal production plan, and

ii. the range of contribution margins per product within which the optimal production plan will not alter.

Note:

Parts (a) and (b) of this requirement are entirely independent of each other.

(ICA, Management Accounting, July 1978).

9.   Rossington Ltd. manufactures three products A B & C. The sales director estimates that demand for these products in 1979 will be as follows:

	A	B	C
Units	12,000	20,000	16,000
Selling Price per unit	£45	£40	£35

The standard costs of production are estimated at:

	A	B	C
	£	£	£
Materials	19	12	18
Labour			
– Machinists			
(@ £2 per hour)	8	12	4
– Assembly			
(@ £1 per hour)	3	4	2

Fixed overheads are expected to be £200,000.

The works director states that the capacity of existing machines is 152,000 hours per annum though this will be increased to 200,000 hours in 1980 when new plant which is currently on order will be delivered. In the meanwhile a neighbouring firm has offered to manufacture any of the products on a sub-contract basis at the following prices:—

A £38
B £34
C £30

You are required to:—

a. Advise the managing director to what extent the services of the sub-contractor should be utilised in order to meet the expected demand for A, B and C.

b. Prepare a statement showing the profit you would expect if your advice is followed.

c. Explain briefly the reasoning you have applied in making your recommendation.

(CIPFA, Management Accounting, November 1978).

21 Break Even Analysis

INTRODUCTION

1. This chapter explains break-even analysis and shows how the behaviour of costs and profits can be predicted with varying levels of activity. Arithmetic and graphical methods are described and traditional and contribution break-even charts and profit-volume charts are illustrated. The assumptions underlying cost-volume-profit analysis and the limitations of the technique are explained. Finally, the accountant's and economist's approach to break-even analysis are compared.

BREAK-EVEN ANALYSIS

2. This is the term given to the study of the interrelationships between costs, volume and profit at various levels of activity. Frequently these relationships are depicted by graphs, but this is not essential.

The term break-even analysis is the one commonly used, but it is somewhat misleading as it implies that the only concern is with that level of activity which produces neither profit nor loss – the break even point – although the behaviour of costs and profits at other levels is usually of much greater significance. Because of this an alternative term, cost-volume-profit analysis or C-V-P analysis, is frequently used and is more descriptive.

USES OF C-V-P ANALYSIS

3. C-V-P analysis uses many of the principles of marginal costing and is an important tool in short-term planning. It explores the relationship which exists between costs, revenue, output levels and resulting profit and is more relevant where the proposed changes in the levels of activity are relatively small. In these cases the established cost patterns are likely to continue, so meaningful decisions can be taken. Over greater changes of activity and in the longer term existing cost structures, e.g. the amount of fixed costs and the marginal cost per unit, are likely to change, so C-V-P analysis becomes less appropriate.

Typical short run decisions where C-V-P analysis can be useful include; choice of sales mix, pricing policies, multi-shift working, and special order acceptance.

ASSUMPTIONS BEHIND C-V-P ANALYSIS

4. Before any formulae are given or graphs drawn, the major assumptions behind C-V-P analysis must be stated. These are:

a. All costs can be resolved into fixed and variable elements.

b. Fixed costs will remain constant and variable costs vary proportionately with activity.

c. Over the activity range being considered costs and revenues behave in a linear fashion.

d. That the only factor affecting costs and revenues is volume.

e. That technology, production methods and efficiency remain unchanged.

f. Particularly for graphical methods that the analysis relates to one product only or to a constant product mix.

g. There are no stock level changes or that stocks are valued at marginal cost only.

It will be apparent that these are over simplifying assumptions for many practical situations. It is because of this that C-V-P analysis can only be an approximate guide for decision making. Nevertheless, by highlighting the interaction of costs, volume, revenue and profit useful guidance can be provided for managers making short run, tactical decisions.

C-V-P ANALYSIS BY FORMULA

5.   C-V-P analysis can be undertaken by graphical means which are dealt with later in this chapter, or by simple formulae which are listed below and illustrated by examples

a. Break-even-point (in units) $= \dfrac{\text{Fixed Costs}}{\text{Contribution/unit}}$

b. Break-even point (£ sales) $= \dfrac{\text{Fixed Costs}}{\text{Contribution/unit}} \times \text{Sales Price/unit}$

or Fixed Costs $\times \dfrac{1}{\text{P/V ratio}}$

c. P/V ratio $= \dfrac{\text{Contribution/unit}}{\text{Sales Price per unit}} \times 100$

d. Level of Sales to result in target profit (in units) $= \dfrac{\text{Fixed Cost} + \text{Target Profit}}{\text{Contribution/unit}}$

e. Level of Sales to result in Target profit (£ sales) $= \dfrac{(\text{Fixed Cost} + \text{Target Profit}) \times \text{Sales price/unit}}{\text{Contribution/unit}}$

Note:

The above formulae relate to a single product firm or one with an unvarying mix of sales. With a multi product firm it is possible to calculate the break even point as follows:

Break-even-point (£ sales) $= \dfrac{\text{Fixed Costs} \times \text{Sales Value}}{\text{Contribution}}$

Example 1

A company makes a single product with a sales price of £10 and a marginal cost of £6. Fixed costs are £60,000 p.a.

Calculate

a. Number of units to break even

b. Sales at break-even point

c. P/V ratio

d. What number of units will need to be sold to achieve a profit of £20,000 p.a.?

e. What level of sales will achieve a profit of £20,000 p.a.?

f.   Because of increasing costs the marginal cost is expected to rise to £6.50 per unit and fixed costs to £70,000 p.a. If the selling price cannot be increased what will be the number of units required to maintain a profit of £20,000 p.a?

Solution:

Contribution = Selling price − marginal cost

$= £10 - 6$

$= \underline{£4}$

a. $\quad \begin{array}{l} \text{Break-even point} \\ \text{(units)} \end{array} = \dfrac{£60,000}{£4}$

$\qquad\qquad\qquad = \underline{15,000}$

b. Break-even point

$\quad$ (£ sales) $\quad = 15,000 \times £10$

$\qquad\qquad\qquad = \underline{£150,000}$

c. P/V ratio $\qquad = \dfrac{£4}{£10} \times 100$

$\qquad\qquad\qquad = \underline{40\%}$

d. $\quad \begin{array}{l} \text{Number of units} \\ \text{for target profit} \end{array} = \dfrac{£60,000 + 20,000}{£4}$

$\qquad\qquad\qquad = \underline{20,000}$

e. Sales for target

$\quad$ profit $\qquad\quad = 20,000 \times £10$

$\qquad\qquad\qquad = \underline{£200,000}$

(Alternatively, this figure can be deduced by the following reasoning. After break-even point the *contribution* per unit becomes *net profit* per unit, so that as 15,000 units were required at break-even point, 5000 extra units would be required to make £20,000 profit,

$\quad \therefore$ total units = 15,000 + 5000 = 20,000 x £10 = £200,000)

f. Note that the fixed costs, marginal cost and contribution have changed

No. of units for target profit $= \dfrac{£70,000 + 20,000}{£3.50}$

$\qquad\qquad\qquad\qquad = \underline{25,714}$ units

Note:

The P/V ratio stands for the Profit/Volume ratio. As such it is a complete misnomer. A more accurate term would be the Contribution to Sales ratio. In spite of this, the term P/V ratio is widely used.

GRAPHICAL APPROACH

6. This may be preferred

a. Where a simple overview is sufficient.

b. Where there is a need to avoid a detailed, numerical approach when, for example, the recipients of the information have no accounting background.

The basic chart is known as a Break Even Chart which can be drawn in two ways. The first is known as the traditional approach and the second as the contribution approach. Whatever approach is adopted, all costs must be capable of separation into fixed and variable elements, i.e. semi-fixed or semi-variable costs must be analysed into their components.

THE TRADITIONAL BREAK-EVEN CHART

7. Assuming that fixed and variable costs have been resolved, the chart is drawn in the following way:

a. **Draw the axes**

– Horizontal showing levels of activity expresses as units of output or as percentages of total capacity.

– Vertical showing values in £'s or £000s as appropriate for costs and revenues.

b. **Draw the cost lines**

Fixed cost. This will be a straight line parallel to the horizontal axis at the level of the fixed costs.

– Total cost. This will start where the fixed cost line intersects the vertical axis and will be a straight line sloping upward at an angle depending on the proportion of variable cost in total costs.

c. **Draw the revenue line**

This will be a straight line from the point of origin sloping upwards at an angle determined by the selling price.

Example 2

A company makes a single product with a total capacity of 400,000 litres p.a. Cost and sales data are as follows:

Selling price   £1 per litre
Marginal cost   £0.50 per litre
Fixed costs   £100,000

Draw a traditional break-even chart showing the likely profit at the expected production level of 300,000 litres.

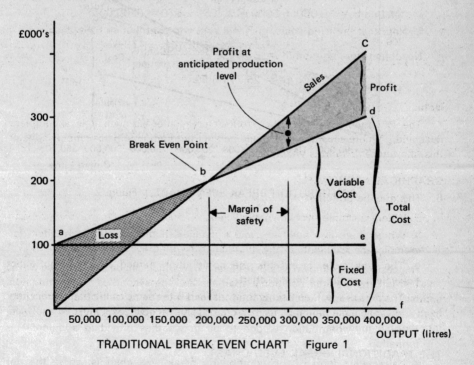

TRADITIONAL BREAK EVEN CHART   Figure 1

From the graph it will be seen that break-even point is at an output level of 200,000 litres and that the width of the profit wedge indicates the profit at a production level of 300,000. The profit is £50,000.

Notes:

   a. The 'margin of safety' indicated on the chart is the term given to the difference between the activity level selected and break-even point. In this case the margin of safety is 100,000 litres.

THE CONTRIBUTION BREAK-EVEN CHART

8. This uses the same axes and data as the traditional chart. The only difference being that variable costs are drawn on the chart before fixed costs resulting in the contribution being shown as a wedge.

Example 3

   Repeat Example 2 except that a contribution break-even chart should be drawn.

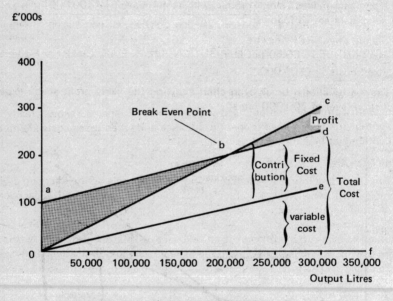

CONTRIBUTION BREAK EVEN CHART   Figure 2

Notes:

   a. The area c.o.e. represents the contribution earned. There is no direct equivalent on the traditional chart.

   b. The area d, a, o, f represents total cost and is the same as the traditional chart.

   c. It will be seen from the chart that the reversal of fixed costs and variable costs enables the contribution wedge to be drawn thus providing additional information.

   An alternative form of the contribution break-even chart is where the net difference between sales and variable cost, i.e. total contribution, is plotted against fixed costs. This is shown below once again using the same data from Example 2.

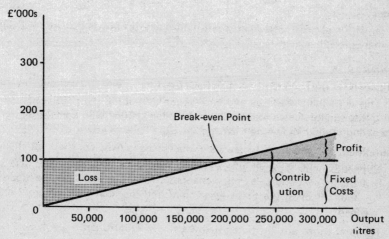

ALTERNATIVE FORM OF CONTRIBUTION BREAK EVEN CHART   Figure 3

Notes:

 a. Sales and variable costs are not shown directly.

 b. Both forms of contribution chart, Figures 2 and 3, show clearly that contribution is first used to meet fixed costs and when these costs are met the contribution becomes profit.

PROFIT CHART

9. This is another form of presentation with the emphasis on the effect on profit of varying levels of activity. It is a simpler form of chart to those illustrated so far because only a profit line is drawn.

 The horizontal axis is identical to the previous charts, but the vertical axis is continued below the point of origin to show losses. A profit line is drawn from the loss at zero activity, which is equivalent to the fixed costs, through the break-even point.

 This type of chart is illustrated below using, once again, the data from Example 2.

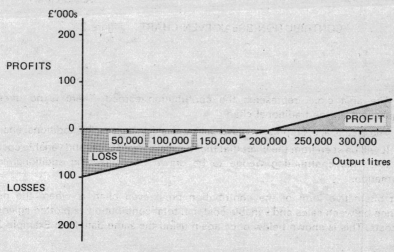

PROFIT CHART   Figure 4

191

Note:

Lines for variable and fixed costs and sales do not appear, merely the one summary profit line.

CHANGES IN COSTS AND REVENUES

10. Several of the main types of chart have been described and it should be apparent that they are all able to show cost/revenue/volume/profit relationships in a simple, effective form. It is also possible to show the effect of changes in costs and revenues by drawing additional lines on the charts. The changes are of two types:

a. Fixed cost changes. Increases or decreases in fixed costs do not change the slope of the line, but alter the point of intersection and thus the break-even point.

b. Variable cost and sales price changes. These changes alter the slope of the line thus affecting the break-even point and the shape of the profit and loss 'wedges'.

These changes are illustrated below using a Profit-Chart.

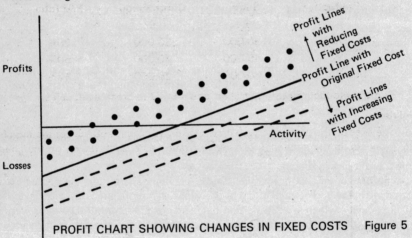

PROFIT CHART SHOWING CHANGES IN FIXED COSTS   Figure 5

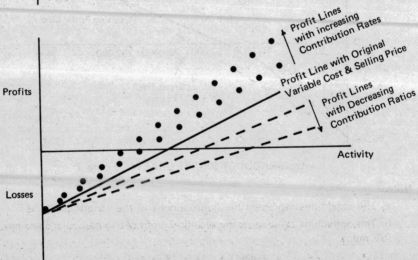

PROFIT CHART SHOWING CHANGES IN CONTRIBUTION RATIO   Figure 6

Note:

The above chart shows the effect of variable cost and/or sales price changes which alter the contribution. If, say, an increase in variable costs was exactly counterbalanced by an increase in sales price, the contribution would be the same and the original profit line would still be correct.

A MULTI-PRODUCT CHART

11. All of the charts illustrated so far have assumed a single product. Equally they could have illustrated a given sales mix resulting in an average contribution rate equivalent to a single product. An alternative method is to plot the individual products each with their individual P/V characteristics and then show the resulting overall profit line. This is shown below:

Example

A firm has fixed costs of £50,000 p.a. and has three products, the sales and contribution of which are shown below.

Product	Sales	Contribution	P/V ratio
	£	£	
X	150,000	30,000	20%
Y	40,000	20,000	50%
Z	60,000	25,000	42%

Plot the products on a profit chart and show the break-even sales.

Solution:

The axes on the profit chart are drawn in the usual way and the contribution from the products, in the sequence of their P/V ratio i.e. Y, Z, X, drawn on the chart.

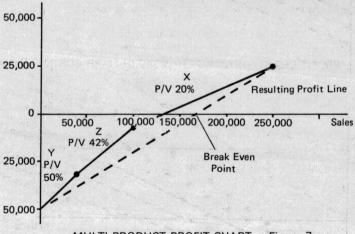

MULTI-PRODUCT PROFIT CHART   Figure 7

Notes:

a. The solid lines represent the contributions of the various products.

b. The dotted line represents the resulting profit of this particular sales mix and P/V ratios.

c. Reading from the graph the break-even point is approximately £170,000. The exact figure can be calculated as follows:

Product	Sales	Contribution
	£	£
X	150,000	30,000
Y	40,000	20,000
Z	60,000	25,000
TOTALS	£250,000	£75,000

$$\text{overall P/V ratio} = \frac{£75,000}{£250,000} = 30\%$$

$$\therefore \text{Break-even point} = \frac{\text{Fixed Costs}}{\text{P/V ratio}}$$

$$= \frac{£50,000}{.3}$$

$$= \underline{£166,667}$$

LIMITATIONS OF BREAK-EVEN AND PROFIT CHARTS

12. The various charts depicted show cost, volume and profit relationships in a simplified and approximate manner. They can be useful aids, but whenever they are used the following limitations should not be forgotten.

a. The charts are reasonable pointers to performance within normal activity ranges, say 70% - 120% of average production. Outside this relevant range the relationship depicted almost certainly will not be correct. Although it is conventional to draw the lines starting from zero activity, as they have been drawn in this chapter, relationships at the extremes of activity cannot be relied upon. A typical relevant range of activity could be shown as follows.

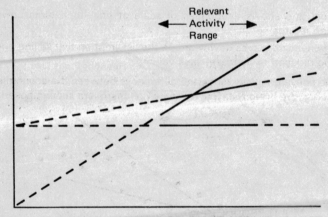

BREAK-EVEN CHART SHOWING RELEVANT ACTIVITY RANGE   Figure 8

b. Fixed costs are likely to change at different activity levels. A stepped fixed cost line is probably the most accurate representation.

c. Variable costs and sales are unlikely to be linear. Extra discounts, overtime payments, special delivery charges etc. make it likely that variable cost and revenue lines are some form of a curve rather than a straight line.

d. The charts depict relationships which are essentially short term. This makes them inappropriate for planning purposes where the time scale stretches over several years.

THE ACCOUNTANTS' AND ECONOMISTS' VIEW OF BREAK-EVEN CHARTS

13. The break-even chart used by accountants has been dealt with earlier in the chapter, Figure 1. The chart drawn by economists is shown below.

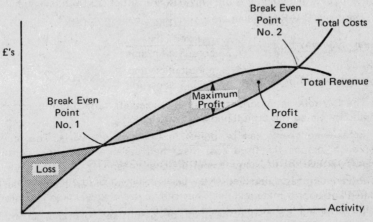

ECONOMISTS BREAK-EVEN CHART   Figure 9

Notes:

a. More correctly this is a chart showing the point of profit maximisation.

b. BEP No. 1 is equivalent to the single BEP shown on accountants' charts. BEP No. 2 is at the point where declining aggregate revenues equal increasing aggregate costs.

c. The cost line shows economies of scale at first, then turns upwards as diminishing returns set in.

d. The revenue line curves downward on the assumption that selling prices will have to be reduced to increase sales volume.

Within the relevant activity range the differences between the economist's and accountant's chart are not great. The two types of charts are superimposed below.

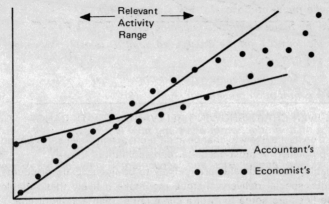

ACCOUNTANT'S AND ECONOMIST'S CHARTS COMPARED   Figure 10

SUMMARY

14. a. Break-even analysis or more descriptively cost-volume-profit analysis studies the relationship between costs, volume, sales and profit.

b. C-V-P analysis is most appropriate for short run tactical decisions.

c. The major assumptions behind C-V-P analysis are that all costs are resolvable into fixed and variable, linearity is assumed, technology and efficiency remain constant and that volume is the only determinant of cost and revenue changes.

d. The main C-V-P formulae are

$$\text{Break-even point} = \frac{\text{Fixed costs}}{\text{contribution/unit}}$$

$$\text{P/V or C/S ratio} = \frac{\text{contribution/unit}}{\text{Selling price/unit}} \times 100\%$$

e. The P/V ratio is important, but is an inaccurate term. More descriptively it should be called the Contribution to Sales ratio.

f. Break-even charts can be drawn in two different ways. The 'traditional approach' graphs the fixed cost first, then variable costs, the 'contribution approach' reverses the sequence of the cost lines.

g. Profit charts plot profit against the level of activity and are simpler than Break-even charts.

h. All of the charts can show the effects of varying fixed costs and/or contribution ratios.

i. Profit charts showing the contributions of various products can be drawn.

j. Break-even charts may provide a useful overview, but they have several limitations including: non-linear and stepped cost functions, difficulties of extrapolation outside normal activity levels and inappropriateness for long term planning purposes.

k. The economist's break-even chart employs non-linear relationships and shows two break even points.

l. Over the relevant activity range the accountant's and economist's charts are likely to show a similar picture.

SELF REVIEW QUESTIONS

1. What is an alternative term to break even analysis? (2)
2. What is the major purpose of C-V-P analysis? (3)
3. What are the major assumptions behind C-V-P analysis?
4. What is the formula for: the Break even point (£ sales)? P/V ratio? (5)
5. What is the C/S ratio? (5)
6. How is the traditional break-even chart drawn? (7)
7. What is a contribution break-even chart? (8)
8. How is a Profit chart drawn? (9)
9. What is a multi-product profit chart and how is it drawn? (11)
10. What are the major limitations of break-even and profit charts? (12)
11. How does the economist's and accountant's view of break-even charts differ? (13)

EXAMINATION QUESTIONS

1. a. From the data given below you are required to present on graph paper a profit-volume (P/V) graph to show the expected company performance based on the budget for one year.

	£000's
Sales	600
Marginal cost	350
Fixed cost	150

Determine the breakeven point and the margin of safety.

b. Discuss briefly the limitations of a profit-volume graph.

(ICMA, Cost Accounting 2, November 1977).

2. A company has decided that its profit on turnover is insufficient and after investigation, has concluded that it must attempt to change its mix of sales.

You are required to:

a. present on graph paper a profit-volume (P/V) graph to show:
   i.   the results of the budgeted sales mix for the year; and
   ii. the expected results if the sales mix were changed to that recommended by the sales director;

b. comment on the results shown on your graph.

Budgeted data for the year:

	£000
Total budgeted sales value	5,000
Total fixed overhead	800

Sales of individual products

Product	Mix %	Total variable costs £000
W	40	1,500
X	10	600
Y	30	1,200
Z	20	600

Proposed budget for the year:

The sales director is faced with severe competition in his market, so does not believe that he can increase total sales. However, he believes that if he discontinues product X, he can increase sales of the remaining products, so that the original total budgeted sales value would be unchanged. His recommendation is based on an estimate that the sales mix should be:

		%
product:	W	40
	Y	20
	Z	40

(ICMA, Cost Accounting 2, November 1978).

3. a. MC Limited manufactures one product only, and for the last accounting period has produced the simplified profit and loss statement shown below:

Profit and Loss Statement

	£	£
Sales		300,000
Costs:		
Direct materials	60,000	
Direct wages	40,000	
Prime cost	100,000	
Variable production overhead	10,000	
Fixed production overhead	40,000	
Fixed administration overhead	60,000	
Variable selling overhead	40,000	
Fixed selling overhead	20,000	
		270,000
Net profit		£30,000

You are required to construct a profit-volume graph from which you should state the break-even point and the margin of safety.

b. Based on the above, draw separate profit-volume graphs to indicate the effect on profit of each of the following:
  i. an increase in fixed cost;
  ii. a decrease in variable cost;
  iii. an increase in sales price;
  iv. a decrease in sales volume.

(ICMA, Cost Accounting 2, November 1979).

4. A market gardener is planning his production for next season and he asked you, as a cost accountant, to recommend the optimal mix of vegetable production for the coming year. He has given you the following data relating to the current year:

	Potatoes	Turnips	Parsnips	Carrots
Area occupied, in acres	25	20	30	25
Yield per acre, in tonnes	10	8	9	12
	£	£	£	£
Selling price per tonne	100	125	150	135
Variable costs per acre:				
fertilisers	30	25	45	40
seeds	15	20	30	25
pesticides	25	15	20	25
direct wages	400	450	500	570

Fixed overhead,
  per annum £54,000

The land which is being used for the production of carrots and parsnips can be used for either crop, but not for potatoes or turnips. The land being used for potatoes and turnips can be used for either crop, but not for carrots or parsnips. In order to provide an adequate market service, the gardener must produce each year at least 40 tonnes each of potatoes and turnips and 36 tonnes each of parsnips and carrots.

a. You are required to present a statement to show:

   i.   *the profit for the current year;*

   ii.   *the profit for the production mix which you would recommend.*

b. *Assuming that the land could be cultivated in such a way that any of the above crops could be produced and there was no market commitment, you are required to:*

   i.   *advise the market gardener on which crop he should concentrate his production;*

   ii.   *calculate the profit if he were to do so; and*

   iii. *calculate in sterling the break-even point of sales.*

(ICMA, Cost Accounting 2, May 1980).

5.   *MC Limited operates four departments, in which three products are manufactured. The company is currently experiencing a critical shortage of labour in department 3 and there are no immediate prospects of an improvement in this situation.*

   You are required to:

a. *show the contribution which each product can make towards company profit;*

b. *suggest the product on which the company should concentrate its resources, giving brief reasons;*

c. *indicate the steps necessary to achieve the production you have recommended in answer to (b) above;*

d. *calculate the amount of profit per annum that could be expected if the company were to adopt your suggestion.*

Standard data, per unit of product:		*X*	*Y*	*Z*
Product:	*Price per unit*	*units*	*units*	*units*
	£			
Costs:				
Direct material: A	*3.00*	*3*	*5*	*3*
B	*5.00*	*4*	*6*	*7*
	Rate per hour	*hours*	*hours*	*hours*
	£			
Direct wages:				
department: 1	*1.50*	*4*	*8*	*10*
2	*1.75*	*12*	*4*	*8*
3	*2.00*	*3*	*2*	*4*
4	*2.25*	*8*	*12*	*4*
		£	*£*	*£*
Variable overhead		*20*	*25*	*35*
Selling price		*136*	*140*	*165*

Budgeted data, for the year:

		£
Direct wages, department:	1	495,000
	2	1,225,000
	3	360,000
	4	1,175,000
Fixed overhead		1,000,000

(ICMA, Cost Accounting 2, May 1979).

6. The variable cost of the power drill manufactured by Hometools Limited is £4 and the selling price £10. The company expects its net profit for the year just ending to be £275,000 after charging fixed costs amounting to £85,000.

The company's production capacity is not fully utilised and market research suggests three alternative strategies for the forthcoming year, viz.:

Strategy	Reduce selling price by	Sales volume expected to increase by
1	5%	10%
2	7%	20%
3	10%	25%

a. Assuming the same cost structure as the current year, evaluate the alternative strategies available to the company and state which is the most profitable.

b. Suggest other considerations which management would probably have in mind in making its decision.

(ACCA, Costing, June 1978).

22 Budgets

INTRODUCTION

1. This chapter defines budgeting and describes the benefits that can be derived from a budgetary system. The budget process is explained and the steps in budgetary planning and control are detailed. The relationship of the various individual budgets is shown and the way they contribute to the Master Budget. Fixed and flexible budgets are explained and the all important behavioural aspects of budgeting are analysed.

WHAT IS A BUDGET?

2. A budget is a quantitative expression of a plan of action prepared in advance of the period to which it relates. Budgets may be prepared for the business as a whole, for departments, for functions such as sales and production, or for financial and resource items such as cash, capital expenditure, manpower, purchases etc. The process of preparing and agreeing budgets is a means of translating the overall objectives of the organisation into detailed, feasible plans of action.

PLANNING AND CONTROL

3. The budgetary process is an integral part of both planning and control. Too often budgets are associated with negative, penny-pinching control activities whereas the full process is much broader and more positive than that. Budgeting is about making plans for the future, implementing those plans and monitoring activities to see whether they conform to the plan. To do this successfully requires full top management support, cooperative and motivated middle managers and staff, and well organised reporting systems.

THE BENEFITS OF BUDGETING

4. The following benefits are those that can be derived from the full budgetary process. They do not accrue automatically, they have to be worked for. Indeed some organisations have systems of budgeting which are narrowly conceived and consequently they do not obtain the range of advantages which are possible. The benefits are dealt with under the following headings: planning and coordination, clarification of authority and responsibility, communication, control, motivation.

PLANNING AND COORDINATION

5. The formal process of budgeting works within the framework of long term, overall objectives to produce detailed operational plans for different sectors and facets of the organisation. Planning is the key to success in business and budgeting forces planning to take place. The budgeting process provides for the coordination of the activities and departments of the organisation so that each facet of the operation contributes towards the overall plan. This is expressed in the form of a Master Budget which summarises all the supporting budgets. The budget process forces managers to think of the relationship of their function or department with others and how they contribute to the achievement of organisational objectives.

CLARIFICATION OF AUTHORITY AND RESPONSIBILITY

6. The process of budgeting makes it necessary to clarify the responsibilities of each manager who has a budget. The adoption of a budget authorises the plans contained within it so that management by exception can be practised, i.e. a subordinate is given a clearly defined role with the authority to carry out the tasks assigned to him and when activities are not proceeding to plan, the variations are reported to a higher level. Thus the full budgetary process is an excellent example of management by exception in action.

COMMUNICATION

7. The budgetary process involves all levels of management. Accordingly it is an important avenue of communication between top and middle management regarding the firm's objectives and the practical problems of implementing these objectives and, when the budget is finalised, it communicates the agreed plans to all the staff involved. As well as vertical communication, the budgetary process requires communication between functions to ensure that coordination is achieved, for example, there must be full communication between the sales and production functions to ensure that coordinated budgets are developed.

CONTROL

8. This aspect of budgeting is the most well known and is the aspect most frequently encountered by the ordinary staff member. The process of comparing actual results with planned results and reporting on the variations, which is the principle of budgetary control, sets a control framework which helps expenditure to be kept within agreed limits. Deviations are noted so that corrective action can be taken.

MOTIVATION

9. The involvement of lower and middle management with the preparation of budgets and the establishment of clear targets against which performance can be judged have been found to be motivating factors. However, there are many factors to be considered in relation to the human aspects of budgeting and these are dealt with in greater detail later in this chapter.

THE BUDGET PERIOD

10. Planning and therefore budgeting must be related to a specific period of time. The general process of budgeting breaks down long range plans and objectives prepared for, say, the next five years into shorter, operational periods invariably of one year. Typically these are subdivided into monthly periods for the purpose of monitoring and control. Budgets can be prepared for any length of time and longer periods may be appropriate for particular types of budget. For example, a research and development budget may be prepared for the next three years because the long term nature of the activity makes yearly budgets less appropriate. Because of rapidly changing conditions many organisations review and modify their budgets on a rolling basis. Typically, each quarter or half year, budgets are reviewed for the following twelve months. This process is known as continuous budgeting.

LIMITING FACTOR OR KEY FACTOR OR PRINCIPAL BUDGET FACTOR

11. It will be recalled from chapter 9 that the limiting factor is that factor which, at any given time, effectively limits the activities of an organisation. It may be customer demand, production capacity, shortage of labour, materials, space or finance. Because such a constraint will have a pervasive effect on all plans and budgets, the limiting factor must be identified and its effect on each of the budgets carefully considered during the budget preparation process. Frequently the principal budget factor is customer demand i.e. the company is unable to sell all the output it can produce. The limiting factor can and does change – when one constraint is removed some other limitation will occur – otherwise, of course, the organisation could expand to infinity.

THE BUDGET PROCESS

12. The diagram, shown on the following two pages, is a simplified outline of the budget preparation process. For ease of illustration, it is shown as a sequential series of steps, but in practice the procedure is less straightforward. There is considerable discussion and consultation, additional information is requested, revisions are made, steps repeated and so on.

THE INTERRELATIONSHIP OF BUDGETS

13. The diagram on page 206 shows the major budgets and their interrelationships for a typical manufacturing concern. In practice there would be more budgets than those shown, there would in fact be a budget for each budget centre.

Notes:

a. There are many more relationships than depicted; for example, the capital expenditure budget depends on various factors such as the level and type of sales, the usage of machinery, the overall long term objectives of the organisation etc.

b. Only the main functional budgets are shown. Invariably these are broken down into departmental budgets for day-to-day control purposes.

c. Because of the importance of liquidity and cash flow the cash budget frequently receives special attention. It is usually subdivided into months and has the following form:

Cash Budget

	Month 1	Month 2	Month 3	etc
Opening Cash Balance B/F				
+ Receipts from Debtors				
+ any Sales of Capital Items				
+ any other Cash Receipts				
= TOTAL CASH AVAILABLE				
– Purchases				
– Wages and Salaries				
– any other Cash Disbursement				
– Capital Expenditure				
– Tax Payments				
= CLOSING CASH BALANCE				
C/F to Month 2				

FIXED AND FLEXIBLE BUDGETS

14. A fixed budget is defined as: 'A budget which is designed to remain unchanged irrespective of the volume of output or turnover attained'. *Terminology*. i.e. it is a single budget with no analysis of cost. On the other hand a flexible budget is a budget which is designed to adjust the permitted cost levels to suit the level of activity actually

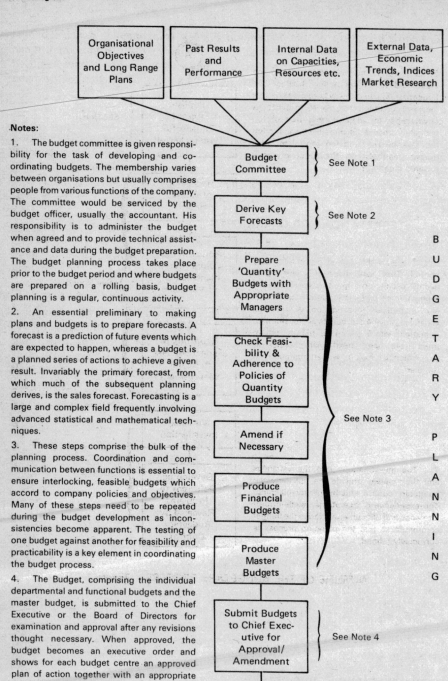

Notes:

1.   The budget committee is given responsibility for the task of developing and co-ordinating budgets. The membership varies between organisations but usually comprises people from various functions of the company. The committee would be serviced by the budget officer, usually the accountant. His responsibility is to administer the budget when agreed and to provide technical assistance and data during the budget preparation. The budget planning process takes place prior to the budget period and where budgets are prepared on a rolling basis, budget planning is a regular, continuous activity.

2.   An essential preliminary to making plans and budgets is to prepare forecasts. A forecast is a prediction of future events which are expected to happen, whereas a budget is a planned series of actions to achieve a given result. Invariably the primary forecast, from which much of the subsequent planning derives, is the sales forecast. Forecasting is a large and complex field frequently involving advanced statistical and mathematical techniques.

3.   These steps comprise the bulk of the planning process. Coordination and communication between functions is essential to ensure interlocking, feasible budgets which accord to company policies and objectives. Many of these steps need to be repeated during the budget development as inconsistencies become apparent. The testing of one budget against another for feasibility and practicability is a key element in coordinating the budget process.

4.   The Budget, comprising the individual departmental and functional budgets and the master budget, is submitted to the Chief Executive or the Board of Directors for examination and approval after any revisions thought necessary. When approved, the budget becomes an executive order and shows for each budget centre an approved plan of action together with an appropriate level of expenditure. (A budget centre is a section of the organisation so designated for budgetary purposes. It may be a cost centre, a group of cost centres or a department. It will be the responsibility of a designated person, the budget holder).

5.   The agreed budgets are published and distributed to all the budget holders and budget centres. In this way budgets serve as a means of communicating plans and objectives downwards. In addition, that part of the budgetary process concerned with monitoring results, known as budgetary control, provides upward feedback on the progress made towards meeting plans.

6.   These are the main stages in budgetary control. They take place after the actual events, usually on a monthly basis. Speedy production of budgetary control statements and immediate investigation of revealed variances provide the best basis for bringing operations into line with the plan or, where there have been substantial changes in circumstances, making agreed alterations to the plan.

7.   The investigations into the variances and their causes provide the link between budgetary control and budgetary planning. The experience of operations, levels of performance and difficulties are fed to the budget committee so that the planning process is continually refined.

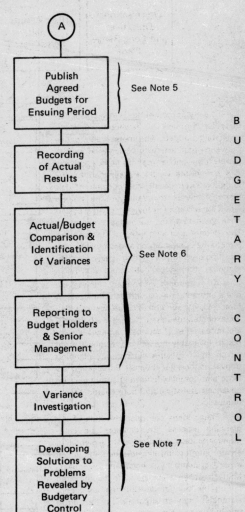

OUTLINE OF THE BUDGETARY PROCESS   Figure 1

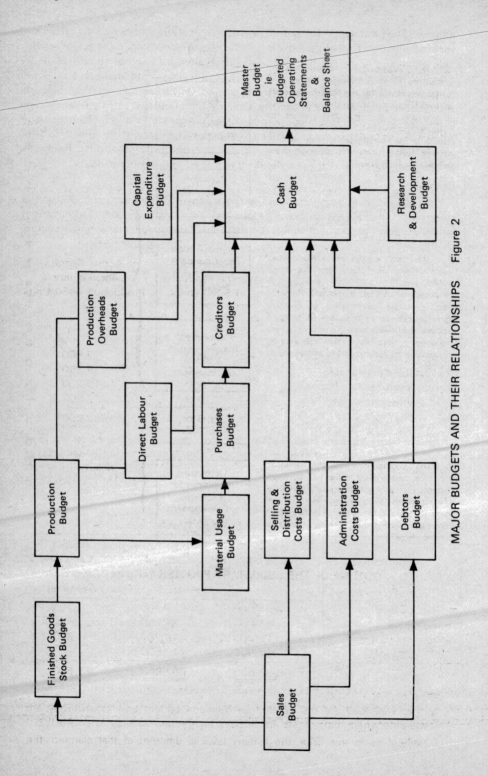

MAJOR BUDGETS AND THEIR RELATIONSHIPS   Figure 2

attained. The process by which this is done is by analysing costs into their fixed and variable elements so that the budget may be 'flexed' according to the actual activity. This procedure is exactly that previously described in Chapters 19 and 20 under marginal costing and in Chapter 21 under cost-volume-profit analysis. For control purposes it is vital that flexible budgeting is used. Only by comparing what the costs should have been with the expenditure incurred at the actual activity level can any control be exercised. The major purpose of a fixed budget is at the planning stage when it serves to define the broad objectives of the organisation. It is unlikely to be of any real value for control purposes except if the level of activity turned out to be exactly as planned. The following example illustrates fixed and flexible budgets.

Example 1

Ayres & Co. make a single product and have an average production of 5000 units a month although this varies widely. The following extract from the overhead statement for the extrusion department shows the make-up of the budget and a month's actual results.

	£	Budget for Average Production of 5000 Units £	Actual Results for January Production 4650 Units £
Indirect Labour			
Fixed	3000		
Variable £1/Unit	5000	8,000	7,900
Consumables (all variable)		15,000	14,250
Variable overheads		20,000	18,200
Fixed overheads		12,500	12,500
		£55,500	£52,850

Show two budgetary control statements for January, one based on the fixed budget for 5000 units and one based on a flexible budget for the actual level of production.

Solution:

Budgetary Control Statement 1
Fixed Budget c.f. Actual Results

Expense Type	Fixed Budget	Actual Results	Budget Variance Favourable (Adverse)
Indirect Labour	8,000	7,900	100
Consumables	15,000	14,250	750
Variable overheads	20,000	18,200	1,800
Fixed overheads	12,500	12,500	–
	£55,500	£52,850	£2,650

Notes:

a. The variances are the differences between budget and actual. They are favourable when actual costs are BELOW budget and adverse when ABOVE.

b. When, as in this case, the activity level is different to that planned, the comparison of actual results with a fixed budget shows little or no useful information. We see that total costs are lower than budget, but so is the activity level. What is required is the appropriate *budgeted expenditure* for the *actual production level*. This is shown below.

Budgetary Control Statement 2
Flexed Budget c.f. Actual Results

Expense Type	Flexed Budget for 4650 Units	Actual Results	Budget Variance Favourable (Adverse)
	£	£	£
Indirect Labour £			
Fixed 3000			
Variable £1/Unit 4650	7,650	7,900	(250)
Consumables @ £3 Unit	13,950	14,250	(300)
Variable overheads @ £4/Unit	18,600	18,200	400
Fixed overheads	12,500	12,500	–
	£52,700	£52,850	(150)

Notes:

a. Using a flexible budget the planned expenditure level for the actual activity can be compared with the actual expenditure so highlighting discrepancies.

b. A budget analysed to fixed and variable elements can be flexed to produce realistic budgeted expenditure for any given activity level, even where the activity changes month by month.

c. A word of caution. The expenditure levels obtained by flexing the budget are only as accurate as the initial analysis into fixed and variable elements. The difficulties inherent in that analysis have been dealt with in Chapter 18.

d. For control to be effective the actual expenditure must be compared with a *realistic* budget allowance.

HUMAN ASPECTS OF BUDGETING

15. The behavioural aspects of budgeting are of supreme importance but, as with many aspects of human behaviour, they are complex, often contradictory and imperfectly understood. Considerable research has been carried out on this aspect of budgeting, but broad generalisations are difficult to make. On one point there does seem to be agreement. That is, that budgeting is not considered by participants as a neutral, objective, purely technical process which is a view adopted by many accountants. The human, subjective aspects cannot be overemphasised and these are dealt with below under the following headings: participation, motivation, goal definition and communication.

PARTICIPATION

16. Budgets can be imposed by top management upon the budget holders or they may be evolved following participation of the budget holders in the budget preparation. Participation promotes common understanding regarding objectives and makes the acceptance of organisational goals by the individual much more likely. The control process is also assisted by participation of the budget holders into the investigation of solutions to the problems which arise. If people are genuinely involved they feel more a part of the team and become more highly motivated.

MOTIVATION

17. The whole process of budget preparation and subsequent performance evaluation by budgetary control needs to be carried out so as to motivate managers rather than create resentment and adverse reactions. If the process is designed to be participative, encourages initiative and responsibility, is not seen merely as a pressure device, then the motivation of individuals will be strengthened. An emphasis on impossible targets, over emphasis on the short run, imperfectly set and understood objectives will cause motivation to be stifled.

GOAL DEFINITION

18. In general people work more efficiently when they have clearly defined targets and objectives. In a perfect world personal goals would coincide with organisational goals so that individual motivation would be at its highest and targets would be totally accepted and completely defined. Such an ideal is unattainable, but the importance of goal definition and of ensuring that individual aspirations and goals are considered is an important part of enlightened budget preparation.

COMMUNICATION

19. The process of communication, between and across the layers in the organisation, is an important factor in all planning and control systems. If any control system, including budgetary control, is not accepted by the people who have to operate it they will hamper and obstruct the flow of information so that realistic planning and control decisions will be difficult to take. Research has shown that frequent, up to date feedback of information to a manager regarding his performance has a motivating effect. Undue delay, inaccurate data, reports containing details of items over which the manager has no control, all reduce motivation and severely restrict the usefulness of the information system.

SUMMARY

20. a. A budget is a quantitative expression of a plan and the full budgetary process includes planning and control.

b. Budgeting can bring a number of real advantages including coordination, clarification of responsibility, improved communication, increased control and the motivation of personnel.

c. The limiting factor (or key factor or principal budget factor) is the factor which limits the activities of the organisation. Typical limiting factors include: sales, shortage of materials or production capacity or skilled labour, lack of finance etc.

d. The budget is prepared by the budget committee having regard to the organisation's objectives and is submitted to the Board of Directors or the Chief Executive for approval. When approved it becomes an executive order.

e. When the budget is approved it is issued so that the budgetary control process can be carried out when actual results are to hand. The investigation of variances and the development of solutions to problems discovered is the key to controlling expenditure.

f. A fixed budget is a budget for a single level of activity whereas a flexible budget, because of the analysis of costs into fixed and variable elements, can be adjusted or flexed for various activity levels.

g. The attitude of the people who have to operate the budgetary system is of critical importance. Budgets are frequently seen as pressure systems imposed by top management.

h. To avoid adverse reactions from the people involved there should be full and meaningful participation, clear goal definition and good communications all of which will contribute to the budgetary process being a motivating rather than a disruptive force.

POINTS TO NOTE

21. a. A master budget is the summary of all other budgets and is expressed as a budgeted Profit and Loss account and Balance Sheet.

b. Too much attention is paid, particularly by accountants, to the mechanics of budgeting. Of far greater importance are the behavioural aspects, i.e. is the process acceptable to those who have to operate it? Does it motivate them? Do they feel threatened by it?

c. Remember it is the quantities/volumes/units etc which are budgeted and then converted into financial terms as a common measure. Money figures are not directly budgeted.

d. Budgets can be used for both planning and for control. Frequently too much attention is paid to the control aspects of budgeting and the positive planning and coordinating activities of budgetary planning are not given the attention they deserve.

e. The problems of budgetary slack are frequently encountered. This is the term used to describe the way some managers obtain a budget larger than strictly necessary so that they either can spend more liberally up to the budget or appear to be containing costs very efficiently by beating their budget. An attempt to overcome this and other problems, particularly in public sector organisations, is the concept of *zero-base budgeting*. The zero base refers to the idea of starting with a nil budget to which is added an agreed budget allowance for each planned activity. In this way it is hoped that tighter limits will be set and that there should not be a perpetuation of past anomalies and inefficiencies which occur when the budget amount is arrived at by adding a percentage to last year's amount. Unfortunately experience suggests that such a concept has at least as many problems as other methods and has as many subjective elements and is just as susceptible to political pressure.

SELF REVIEW QUESTIONS

1. *What is a budget?* *(2)*
2. *What are the benefits to be gained from budgeting?* *(4)*
3. *How does the budgetary process assist communication?* *(7)*
4. *What is the budget period?* *(10)*
5. *What is the principal budget factor?* *(11)*
6. *Describe the major steps in the budget process.* *(12)*
7. *What are the typical contents of a cash budget?* *(13)*
8. *Distinguish between fixed and flexible budgets.* *(14)*
9. *Why are the behavioural aspects of budgeting so important?* *(15)*

EXAMINATION QUESTIONS

1. R Limited manufactures three products: A, B and C. You are required:

    a. using the information given below, to prepare budgets for the month of January for:
        i.   sales in quantity and value, including total value;
        ii. production quantities;
        iii. material usage in quantities;
        iv. material purchases in quantity and value, including total value;
    (N.B. Particular attention should be paid to your layout of the budgets.)

    b. to explain the term principal budget factor and state what it was assumed to be in (a) of this question.

Data for preparation of January budgets

Sales:

Product	Quantity	Price each £
A	1,000	100
B	2,000	120
C	1,500	140

Materials used in the company's products are:

Material	M1	M2	M3
Unit cost	£4	£6	£9
Quantities used in:	units	units	units
Product: A	4	2	–
B	3	3	2
C	2	1	1

Finished stocks:

Product	A	B	C
Quantities			
1st January	1,000	1,500	500
31st January	1,100	1,650	550

Material stocks:	M1 units	M2 units	M3 units
1st January	26,000	20,000	12,000
31st January	31,200	24,000	14,400

(ICMA, Cost Accounting 1, November 1979).

2. Next year's preliminary budget workings for Scrunchie, a breakfast cereal, the only product manufactured by H. F. Ltd, are shown below.

H.F. Ltd
Budgeted Revenue Account for the Year ended 30 September 1980

		£
Sales (20,000 boxes, containing standard packets)		600,000

	£	£
Direct Materials	240,000	
Direct Labour	102,000	
Variable Overhead	70,000	
Fixed Overhead	122,200	534,200
Profit		£65,800

H.F. Ltd
Budgeted Net Assets as at 30 September 1980

		£
Fixed Assets (Net of Depreciation)		310,000
Working Capital:	£	
Debtors	50,000	
Stocks	65,000	
Creditors	(25,000)	90,000
Net Assets Employed		£400,000

The existing plant and equipment is considerably under-utilised and a proposal being considered is to extend sales to supermarkets, where the product would be sold under a different brand name.

Estimated effects of this proposal are:

1. Additional annual sales, to supermarkets, 8,000 boxes @ £25 per box.

2. Cost of direct materials will be reduced as a result of a 5% quantity discount on all purchases.

3. Extra supervisory and clerical staff will be required at a cost of £16,000 p.a.

4. Market research has indicated that sales to existing outlets will fall by approximately 10%, there will be no change in selling price to these customers.

5. Stocks and creditors will increase by £25,000 and £15,000 respectively and the credit period extended to supermarkets will be double that given to existing customers.

Required:

Present data to assist in the evaluation of the proposal.

Specifically you should:

a. Prepare a revised budgeted revenue account and statement of net assets employed incorporating the results of the proposal.

b. Calculate the effect on profit of each of the changes resulting from the proposal and reconcile the total of these with the difference in budgeted profits.

c. Advise management on the suitability of the proposal making any further calculations you consider necessary and adding any other comments or reservations you think relevant.

(ACCA, Costing, June 1979).

3. What are the behavioural aspects which should be borne in mind by those who are designing and operating standard costing and budgetary control systems? *(ICMA, Cost Accounting 2, May 1979)*.

4. Fancitoys Limited is preparing its budgets for the quarter beginning 1 July. Stock on hand at the end of June is expected to be £72,000 and the balance at bank £10,000. In view of the pressure on liquid resources the directors have decided to reduce the stock level at the end of each month to an amount sufficient to cover the following two months' sales. Purchases are paid for by the end of the following month; the amount payable for June's purchases is £36,000.

Budgeted sales (which provide a gross profit of 33⅓% on cost) are:

	£		£
July	40,000	October	48,000
August	42,000	November	52,000
September	46,000	December	44,000

Ten per cent of the sales are for cash and of the credit sales two-thirds are paid for during the month after the sale and the remainder during the following month. Credit sales during May amounted to £24,600 and during June £26,100.

The annual rental for the company's premises is £18,000 payable monthly. Other payments to be made are:

	July £	August £	September £
Salaries, wages and commission	4,800	5,100	5,500
Rates	800		
Other expenses	1,600	1,800	2,000

You are required to prepare the company's cash budget for the quarter beginning 1 July showing the balance at the end of each month.
(ACCA, Costing, June 1978).

5. ABC Limited manufactures three products from three basic raw materials in three departments. The company operates a budgetary control system and values its stock of finished goods on a marginal cost basis. From the data given below, you are required to produce for the month of June 1979 the following budgets:

a. production;

b. materials usage;

c. purchases;

d. profit and loss account for each product and in total.

Budgeted data, for June 1979:

Product:	A	B	C
Sales	£1,500,000	£1,080,000	£1,680,000
Stock of finished products at 1st June, 1979, in units	3,000	2,000	2,500

Department:	I	II	III
Fixed production overhead	£239,000	£201,300	£391,200
Direct labour hours	47,800	67,100	65,200
Direct material:	DM 11	DM 21	DM 31
Stock at 1st June, 1979, in units	24,500	20,500	17,500

The company is introducing a new system of inventory control which should reduce stocks. The forecast is that stocks at 30th June, 1979 will be reduced as follows: raw materials by 10% and finished products by 20%.

Fixed production overhead is absorbed on a direct labour hour basis. It is expected that there will be no work-in-progress at the beginning or end of the month.

Administration cost is absorbed by products at a rate of 20% of production cost and selling and distribution cost is absorbed by products at a rate of 40% of production cost.

Profit is budgeted as a percentage of total cost as follows: product A 25%; product B 12½% and product C 16⅔%.

Standard cost data, per unit of product:

Product:	Price per unit £	A units	B units	C units
Direct material				
DM 11	2.00	5	–	12
DM 21	4.00	–	10	9
DM 31	1.00	5	5	–

	Rate per hour £	A hours	B hours	C hours
Direct wages				
Department: I	2.50	4	2	2
II	2.00	6	2	3
III	1.50	2	4	6
		£	£	£
Other variable costs		10	20	15

(ICMA, Cost Accounting 2, May 1979).

6. BX Ltd manufactures two products, Plain and Fancy, using one basic raw material and one grade of labour. Shown below are the actual operating results achieved for the eleven months ended November 1979.

	£	£
Sales: Plain (£12.00 each)	48,000	
Fancy (£20.00 each)	40,000	88,000
Actual Cost of Sales: Direct Material	44,000	
Direct Labour	14,000	
Variable Overhead	6,000	
Fixed Overhead	10,000	74,000
Profit		£14,000

The company operates a standard costing system and during the above period, the actual material consumption was as specified in the standard, which for Plain is 3 kilos per unit, and for Fancy, 4 kilos per unit. The standard wage rate is £3 per hour. The standard labour cost of Plain is £1.50 per unit and Fancy £3 per unit. Labour achieved standard efficiency but, throughout the above period, the actual wage rate paid was higher than standard and consequently an adverse rate variance of £2,000 was incurred. Overheads were as specified in the standard, variable overheads varying directly with labour hours worked. There was no change in any stock levels during the period.

Budgeted production for 1980 is 6,000 units of Plain and 4,000 units of Fancy. Material stocks are budgeted to decrease by 2,000 kilos, there will be no change in any other stocks. The standard material consumption per unit will be as specified in 1979 and, after careful consideration, it has been agreed that the 1980 standard material price will be the actual average price paid during the eleven months ended November 1979.

The actual wage rate for 1979 will be increased by 70p per hour for 1980, 50p per hour of which is the result of a productivity agreement which will enable the company to reduce its standard time for each product by 20%. Budgeted overheads will be at the same rate as shown for 1979 and it may be assumed there are no wages included in overheads.

Required:

a. Calculate the material purchase budget and the wages budget, showing both quantities and values for the year ended December 1980.

b. Calculate the net cost-savings which the company should achieve during 1980 as a result of the productivity agreement, assuming that there is no restriction on the number of labour hours which could be made available, if required.

(ACCA, Costing, December 1979).

7. Mr Drinkall, a graduate chemist, is the recently appointed assistant works manager in a company manufacturing a range of glassware. During the absence of the works manager he has been asked to participate in the preparation of next year's production budgets, but he knows very little about either accounting or budgeting.

Required:

To assist Mr. Drinkall:

a. Explain the purpose of budgeting.

b. Explain briefly what you understand by the term 'Flexible Budget', outline its purpose, and identify any problems which may arise in the construction and operation of such a budget.

(ACCA, Costing, June 1980).

8. In addition to providing accommodation, food and services to its normal clientele, an hotel also provides facilities to a large industrial group in respect of the latter's conferences and training courses, its convalescent staff and its incentive holidays for staff.

The proportion of the hotel's total business that goes to the industrial group is quite sizable, and the group has agreed to pay the hotel on one of the following two bases:

Bases A:

In each department, the charges (at normal rates) for services to the group are expressed as a proportion of the total charges (at normal rates) for all services performed by that department.

These proportions are then applied to the agreed costs for the relevant department and the resulting sum, increased by 10%, is charged to the group.

Basis B:

    i.   for bedroom accommodation (department A) — the proportion of the cost that group guest/nights bears to total guest/nights is calculated and increased by 12½%.

    ii. For all other departments (B-F) — the combined total of charges (at normal rates) for services to the group are expressed as a proportion of the combined total charges (at normal rates) for all services provided by those departments.

This proportion is then applied to the total of agreed costs for these departments, and the resulting sum, increased by 10%, is charged to the group.

Data available for the year are as follows:

Departments	Charges at normal rates		Agreed costs
	To the group	To non-group guests	
	£	£	£
A. Bedroom accommodation	75,000	175,000	215,000
B. Restaurant	48,000	96,000	104,100
C. Snack bar/coffee shop	28,000	112,000	84,000
D. Conference facilities	24,000	12,000	29,100
E. Hydro/sports club facilities	10,000	80,000	83,700
F. Tour organisation facilities	3,000	39,000	15,050
Total guest/nights		50,000	
Group guest/nights		16,000 (included in total)	

You are required to:

    a. calculate the total charges that the hotel would make to the group under the agreement:

        i.   on basis A;

        ii. on basis B;

    b. on the assumption that the total charges to the group under either basis A or basis B, will be lower than they would be at normal rates, explain very briefly what additional cost data you would need to determine whether or not the group business was worthwhile to the hotel.

(ICMA, Cost Accounting 2, May 1977).

9.   The Victoria Hospital is located in a holiday resort which attracts visitors to such an extent that the population of the area is trebled for the summer months of June, July and August. From past experience this influx of visitors doubles the activity of the hospital during these months. The annual budget for the hospital's laundry department is broken down into four quarters, i.e. April/June, July/September,

October/December and January/March by dividing the annual budgeted figures by four. This budgeting work has been done for the current year by the secretary of the hospital using the previous year's figures and adding 16%. It is realised by the Hospital Authority that management information for control purposes needs to be improved and you have been recruited to help to introduce a system of responsibility accounting.

You are required, from the information given, to:

a. comment on the way in which the quarterly budgets have been prepared and to suggest improvements which could be introduced when preparing the budgets for 1979/80;

b. state what information you would like to flow from the actual against budget comparison (NB: calculated figures are NOT required);

c. state the amendments that would be needed to the current practice of budgeting and reporting to enable the report below to be used as a measure of the efficiency of the laundry manager.

<table>
<tr><td colspan="3" align="center">Victoria Hospital — Laundry Department
Report for quarter ended 30th September, 1978</td></tr>
<tr><td></td><td>Budget</td><td>Actual</td></tr>
<tr><td>Patient days</td><td>9,000</td><td>12,000</td></tr>
<tr><td>Weight processed, in lbs</td><td>180,000</td><td>240,000</td></tr>
<tr><td>Costs:</td><td>£</td><td>£</td></tr>
<tr><td>Wages</td><td>8,800</td><td>12,320</td></tr>
<tr><td>Overtime premium</td><td>1,400</td><td>2,100</td></tr>
<tr><td>Detergents and other supplies</td><td>1,800</td><td>2,700</td></tr>
<tr><td>Water, water softening and heating</td><td>2,000</td><td>2,500</td></tr>
<tr><td>Maintenance</td><td>1,000</td><td>1,500</td></tr>
<tr><td>Depreciation of plant</td><td>2,000</td><td>2,000</td></tr>
<tr><td>Manager's salary</td><td>1,250</td><td>1,500</td></tr>
<tr><td>Overhead, apportioned:</td><td></td><td></td></tr>
<tr><td>for Occupancy</td><td>4,000</td><td>4,250</td></tr>
<tr><td>for Administration</td><td>5,000</td><td>5,750</td></tr>
</table>

(ICMA, Cost Accounting 1, November 1978).

10. AEF Limited is a retail organisation which operates three sales departments and an administration department in a large supermarket complex. Each sales department has a manager responsible for its operation to the general manager and its own prescribed gross margin related to selling price.

Exceptionally, the general manager permits the departmental managers to reduce the selling price of a product by giving a quantity discount, a special price for a large order or for an item of out-dated stock.

The following data are given:

	Audio and video equipment	Electrical appliances	Furniture
Stock at 1st April:	£	£	£
Cost	120,000	80,000	200,000
At full sales value	200,000	110,000	280,000
Transactions during April:			
Purchases	150,000	40,000	160,000
Net sales	215,000	63,000	224,000
Price reductions approved	5,000	3,000	7,000

Expenditure incurred during April was:

Item	Amount £	Basis of apportionment to sales and administration departments
Rates	4,000	Area occupied
Light and heat	2,000	
Advertising	35,250	
Transport	25,850	Sales value for month before any reductions
Insurance	3,525	
Miscellaneous	1,175	
Canteen	4,125	Number of employees
Salaries and wages	24,910	See detailed information given below
Depreciation	3,750	
Administration	2,500	Direct

Other detailed information for April was:

Department	Salaries and wages £	Depreciation £	Number of employees	Area occupied sq. feet
Audio and video equipment	11,900	500	27	6,000
Electrical appliances	2,000	750	4	2,000
Furniture	6,000	1,000	15	5,000
Administration	5,010	1,500	9	3,000
Total	£24,910	£3,750	55	16,000

Each month the total costs of the administration department are apportioned to the three sales departments on the basis of the sales values for the month before any reductions.

You are required using the data given to:

a. calculate the value of stock at 30th April for balance sheet purposes;

b. prepare a tabulated profit and loss statement for each sales department for April;

c. discuss an alternative system of accounting which you consider would produce more realistic results to aid management.

(ICMA, Cost Accounting 2, May 1980).

11. A company manufactures a range of products which it sells through manufacturers' agents to whom it pays commission of 20% of the selling price of the products.

Its budgeted profit and loss statement for 1978 is as follows:

	£	£
Sales		225,000
Production costs:		
Prime costs and variable overhead	78,750	
Fixed overhead	36,250	
		115,000
		110,000
Selling costs:		
Commission to manufacturers' agents	45,000	
Sales office expenses (fixed)	2,000	
		47,000
		63,000
Administration costs (fixed)		30,000
Profit		£33,000

Subsequent to the preparation of the above budgeted profit and loss statement, the company is faced with a demand from its agents for an increase in their commission to 22% of selling price.

As a result, the company is considering whether it might achieve more favourable results if it were to discontinue the use of manufacturers' agents and, instead, to employ its own sales force.

The costs that this would involve are budgeted as follows:

	£
Sales manager (salary and expenses)	7,500
Salesmen's expenses (excluding travelling costs)	2,000
Sales office costs (additional to present costs)	5,000
Interest and depreciation on sales department cars	3,500

4 salesmen at a salary of £4,000 each plus commission of 5% on sales, plus car allowance of 10 pence per mile to cover all costs except interest and depreciation.

On the assumption that the company decides to employ its own sales force on the above terms, you are required to ascertain:

a. What is the maximum average mileage per annum that salesmen could travel if the company is to achieve the same budgeted profit as it would have obtained by retaining the manufacturers' agents and granting them the increased commission they had requested.
Assume that sales in each case would be as budgeted.

b. At what level of sales would the original budgeted profit be achieved if each salesman were to travel an average of 14,000 miles per annum.
Assume that all other assumptions inherent in the budgets were maintained.

c. What is the maximum level of commission on sales that the company could afford to pay if it wished to achieve a 16% increase in its original budgeted profit and expected a 16% increase in sales (at budgeted selling prices) and an average of 16,000 miles per annum to be travelled by each salesman. (Calculate your answer to one decimal place).

(ICMA, Cost Accounting 2, May 1977).

12. Describe how the cost accountant contributes to the process of overhead cost control in any large manufacturing or service organisation.

(ACCA, Costing, December 1979).

13. Betayet Ltd is a small company manufacturing one type of component in a single operation. The company employs 10 direct workers on a basic 40 hour week at £3 per hour with a guaranteed minimum weekly wage of £120 per operative. The maximum amount of overtime which may be worked, paid at time rate plus one third, is in total 200 hours per week. Additional direct workers cannot be recruited.

The average time for one operative to manufacture one component is 40 minutes.

Demand for the product varies considerably, the minimum weekly output is 450 units, but for a significant part of the year the company cannot satisfy total demand despite working the maximum overtime hours available. The nature of the component is such that stocks of work in progress or finished goods cannot be stored.

After appropriate studies have been made an incentive scheme has been proposed, based upon a standard operator time of 30 minutes per component, in which operatives will be paid £2 for each component produced. The guaranteed minimum wage would still apply, and if required, overtime would continue to be worked, up to the maximum shown above, and be paid at the previous time rate premium.

The selling price of the component is £9 per unit, material costs £2 per unit, variable overheads varying with hours worked £3 per labour hour, and fixed overheads £1,200 per week.

Required:

a. Produce columnar revenue accounts, comparing weekly profits at the following activity levels:

I Under the current wages scheme at,
  i. minimum weekly output
  ii. current maximum output

II Under the proposed incentive scheme, with labour achieving standard efficiency, at,
  i.   minimum weekly output
  ii. current maximum output
  iii. proposed maximum output

Briefly explain the reasons for the change in profit caused by the incentive scheme.

b. Assuming the incentive scheme is adopted and labour achieved standard efficiency, calculate the effect on company profits of a labour dispute in which 100 hours of direct operatives' time were lost, and not paid for, during a week in which demand was:

  i. 450 units
  ii. greater than the proposed maximum level of output

Carefully explain your calculations.

(ACCA, Costing, June 1980).

14. Your company is considering a trade union claim for an increase of 10% on the hourly wage rates of all direct workers. As an alternative the management would prefer to negotiate a productivity deal whereby a bonus to direct workers of £0.08 for every unit produced is paid. The work study department has estimated that production could be increased by 12½% without any additional hours being worked, if the productivity bonus were paid. The sales director is confident of selling the increased output if the price for all sales were to be reduced by £0.10 per unit.

Budgeted results for the forthcoming year, excluding the above possible wage or sales increases, are as follows:

	£000	£000
Sales, 1,200,000 units		2,400
Direct materials	480	
Direct wages	720	
Variable production overhead	108	
Fixed production overhead	200	
Variable selling cost (5% of sales value)	120	
Fixed selling cost	80	
Variable distribution cost	96	
Fixed distribution cost	74	
Fixed administration cost	202	
		2,080
Profit		320

You are required, in the form of a report to the managing director to:

a. set out the budgeted results for each alternative and recommend the course of action to be followed; and

b. indicate three of the uncertainties which have to be taken into consideration when making the decision.

(ICMA, Cost Accounting 1, November 1978).

23 Standard Costing – Introduction

INTRODUCTION

1. This chapter introduces standard costing and defines the main types of standard. The relationship between standards and budgets is explained and the way in which standards are set relating to materials, labour, and overheads is described. Standard revisions and the all important behavioural aspects of standard costing are discussed. Finally the advantages and disadvantages of standard costing are given.

STANDARD COSTING DEFINED

2. Standard costing is a technique which establishes predetermined estimates of the costs of products and services and then compares these predetermined costs with actual costs as they are incurred. The predetermined costs are known as STANDARD COSTS and the difference between the standard cost and actual cost is known as a VARIANCE. The process by which the total difference between actual cost and standard cost is broken down into its different elements is known as VARIANCE ANALYSIS. Standard costing in practice is a detailed process and requires considerable development work before it is a useful tool. It can be used in a variety of costing situations, batch and mass production, process manufacture, transport, certain aspects of repetitive clerical work and even in jobbing manufacture. Undoubtedly, however, the greatest benefit is gained when the manufacturing method involves a substantial degree of repetition. Its major application in practice is in organisations involved in mass production and/or repetitive assembly work.

STANDARD COST

3. Previously this has been simply defined as a 'predetermined cost'. More formally, a standard cost can be defined as, 'a predetermined cost calculated in relation to a prescribed set of working conditions, correlating technical specifications and scientific measurements of materials and labour to the prices and wage rates expected to apply during the period to which the standard cost is intended to relate, with an addition of an appropriate share of budgeted overheads. Its main purposes are to provide bases for control through variance accounting, for the valuation of stocks and work in progress, and, in exceptional cases, for fixing selling prices.' *Terminology*. This is a long, technical description, but close study of it shows that a standard cost is a target cost which should be attained. The build-up of a standard cost is based on sound technical and engineering studies, known production methods and layouts, work studies and work measurement, material specifications and wage and material price projections. A standard cost is not an average of previous costs. These are likely to contain the results of past inefficiencies and mistakes. Furthermore changes in methods, technology and costs make comparisons with the past of doubtful value for control purposes.

TYPES OF STANDARDS

4. There are three main types of standard; basic, ideal and expected.

a. **Basic standards**. These are long term standards which would remain unchanged over the years. Their sole use is to show trends over time for such items as material prices, labour rates and efficiency and the effect of changing methods. They cannot be used to highlight current efficiency or inefficiency and would not normally form part of the reporting system except as a background, statistical exercise.

b. **Ideal standards.** These are based on the best possible operating conditions, i.e. no breakdowns, no material wastage, no stoppages or idle time, in short, perfect efficiency. Ideal standards, if used, would be revised periodically to reflect improvements in methods, materials and technology. Clearly ideal standards would be unattainable in practice and accordingly are rarely used. However, their use could be considered worthwhile for investigative and development purposes, but not for normal day-to-day control activities.

c. **Expected standard.** This is by far the most frequently encountered standard. It is a currently attainable standard based on efficient (but not perfect) operating conditions. The standard would include allowances for normal material losses, realistic allowances for fatigue, machine breakdowns etc. It must be stressed however that an expected standard must be based on a high performance level so that its achievement is possible, but has to be worked for. Expected standards provide a tough, but realistic target and thus can provide motivation for management. They can be used for product costing, for cost control, for stock valuation and as a basis for budgeting. Expected standards would be revised periodically to reflect the conditions expected to prevail during the ensuing period when the standards would apply. Unless otherwise stated, all subsequent references in this manual to standards mean *expected standards*.

STANDARDS AND BUDGETS

5. Both standards and budgets are concerned with setting performance and cost levels for control purposes. They therefore are similar in principle although they differ in scope. Standards are a *unit* concept, i.e. they apply to particular products, to individual operations or processes. Budgets are concerned with *totals*; they lay down cost limits for functions and departments and for the firm as a whole. As an illustration the standard material cost of the various products in a firm could be as follows:

		Standard Material cost/unit	Planned Production	Total Material Cost
		£		£
Product	X321	3.50	5000 units	17,500
Product	Y592	7.25	1500 units	10,875
Product	Y728	1.50	2500 units	3,750
etc	etc	etc	etc	etc
etc	etc	etc	etc	etc

OVERALL TOTAL = MATERIALS = £275,000
BUDGET

In this way the detailed unit standards are used as the basis for developing meaningful budgets. This is particularly so for direct material and direct labour costs which are more amenable to close control through standard costing whereas overheads would normally be controlled by functional and departmental budgets. Further differences are that budgets would be revised on a periodic basis, frequently as an annual exercise, whereas standards are revised only when they are inappropriate for current operating conditions. Such revisions may take place more or less frequently than budget revisions. The accounting treatment of standards and budgets also differs. Budgets are memorandum figures and do not form part of the double entry accounting system whereas standards and the resulting variances are included. The double entry treatment of standards, variances and all costing data is explained in Chapter 26.

SETTING STANDARDS
6. Meaningful standards which can be used for control purposes rest on a foundation of properly organised, standardised methods and procedures and a comprehensive information system. It is little point trying to develop a standard cost for a product if the production method is not decided upon. A standard cost implies that a target or standard exists for every single element which contributes to the product; the types, usage and prices of materials and parts, the grades, rates of pay and times for the labour involved, the production methods and layouts, the tools and jigs and so on. Considerable effort is involved in establishing standard costs and keeping them up to date. Traditionally, the standard cost for each part or product is recorded on a standard cost card and an example is given later in this chapter. With the increased usage of computers for costing purposes frequently nowadays there is no physical standard cost card. When a computer is used, the standard costs are recorded on a magnetic disc or tape file and can be accessed and processed as required. Whether a computer or manual system is used, there are no differences in the principles of standard costing, although there are many differences in the method of day to day operation. The following paragraphs explain some of the detailed procedures involved in setting standards.

SETTING STANDARDS – MATERIALS
7. The materials content of a product; raw materials, sub-assemblies, piece parts, finishing materials etc. is derived from technical and engineering specifications, frequently in the form of a Bill of Materials. The standard quantities required include an allowance for normal and inevitable losses in production, that is, machining loss, evaporation, and expected levels of breakages and rejections. The process of analysis is valuable in itself because savings and alternative materials and ways of using materials are frequently discovered. The responsibility for providing material prices is that of the buying department. The prices used are not the past costs, but the forecast expected costs for the relevant budget period. The expected costs should take into account trends in material prices, anticipated changes in purchasing policies, quantity and cash discounts, carriage and packing charges and any other factor which will influence material costs.

SETTING STANDARDS – LABOUR
8. Without detailed operation and process specifications it would be impossible to establish standard labour times. The agreed methods of manufacture are the basis of setting the standard labour times. The techniques of work measurement are involved, frequently combined with work study projections based on elemental analysis when a part is not yet in production. The labour standards must specify the exact grades of labour to be used as well as the times involved. Planned labour times are expressed in standard hours (or standard minutes). The concept of a standard hour is important and can be defined as, "a hypothetical unit pre-established to represent the amount of work which should be performed in one hour at standard performance". *Terminology*. It will be noted that a standard hour represents a given work content. Indeed, production for a given period is frequently described as 'so many standard hours'

rather than a quantity of parts. Once the times and grades of labour have been established, a forecast can be made of the relevant wage rates for the appropriate future period. This is usually done by the Personnel Department.

Note:

A standard hour is a measure of the work content of a labour hour, not a measure of time.

SETTING STANDARDS – OVERHEADS

9. It will be recalled from Chapters 2, 3 and 10 how overhead absorption rates are established. These predetermined overhead absorption rates become the standards for overheads for each cost centre using the budgeted standard labour hours as the activity base. For realistic control, overheads must be analysed into their fixed and variable components and separate absorption rates calculated for both fixed and variable overheads thus:

$$\text{Standard Variable O.A.R.} = \frac{\text{Budgeted variable overheads for cost centre}}{\text{Budgeted standard labour hours for cost centre}}$$

$$\text{and Standard fixed O.A.R.} = \frac{\text{Budgeted fixed overheads for cost centre}}{\text{Budgeted standard labour hours for cost centre}}$$

The level of activity adopted, expressed in standard labour hours, is the budgeted expected annual activity level which is the basis of the Master Budget. For reporting and control purposes this would be classed as 100% capacity.

SETTING STANDARDS – SALES PRICE AND MARGIN

10. Fundamental to any form of standard costing, budgeting and profit planning is the anticipated selling price for the product. The setting of the selling price is frequently a top level decision and is based on a variety of factors including: the anticipated market demand, competing products, manufacturing costs, inflation estimates and so on. Finally, after discussion and investigation, a selling price is established at which it is planned to sell the product during the period concerned. This becomes the standard selling price. The standard sales margin is the difference between the standard cost and the standard selling price. Where a standard marginal costing system is used, the standard contribution is calculated following the normal marginal costing principles explained in Chapter 19.

Note:

Normally when 'standard cost' is mentioned it means total standard cost, i.e. total absorption cost principles are used incorporating fixed and variable costs. Standard marginal costing is also employed, but students should assume that total absorption cost principles are involved whenever the term standard cost is used without qualification. This nomenclature is adopted in this manual. When marginal costing principles are used the term *standard marginal cost* is employed.

RESPONSIBILITY FOR SETTING STANDARDS

11. The line managers who have to work with and accept the standards must be involved in establishing them. These managers and their superiors have the ultimate responsibility for setting the standards. Work study staff, accountants and other specialists provide technical support and information, but do not make the final decisions upon standards and performance levels.

THE STANDARD COST CARD

12. The process of setting standards results in the establishment of the standard cost for the product. The makeup of the standard cost is recorded on a standard cost card. In practice there may be numerous detail cards together with a summary card for a given product, or the standard cost details may be on a computer file. The principles, however, remain the same. A simple standard cost card is shown below:

Standard Cost Card

PART NO. *X291* DESCRIPTION *Stub Joint* BATCH QUANTITY *100*

TOOL REF. *T5983* WORK STUDY REF. *WS255* DRAWING NO. *D592/5*

REVISION DATE *3/12/80* REVISED BY *G.R.P.*

COST TYPE AND QUANTITY	STANDARD PRICE or RATE	DEPT 7	DEPT 19	DEPT 15	TOTAL
		£	£	£	£
Direct Materials					
2.5Kg P101	*£14.8kg*	*37.00*			*37.00*
1000 units A539	*£3.75 100*		*37.50*		*37.50*
					74.50
Direct Labour					
Machine					
Operation					
Grade 15					
4.8 hrs	*£2.5 hr*	*12.00*			*12.00*
9.2 hrs	*£2.5 hr*		*23.00*		*23.00*
Assembly					
Grade 8					
16.4 hrs	*£1.75 hr*			*28.70*	*28.70*
Production					*63.70*
Overhead					
Machine Hour					
Rate	*£11 hr*	*52.80*	*101.12*		*153.92*
Labour Hour					
Rate	*£6 hr*			*98.40*	*98.40*
		101.80	*161.62*	*127.10*	*252.32*

STANDARD COST SUMMARY

	£
DIRECT MATERIALS	*74.50*
DIRECT LABOUR	*63.70*
PRODUCTION OVERHEADS	*252.32*
STANDARD COST PER *100*	*£390.52*

STANDARD COST CARD   Figure 1

REVISION OF STANDARDS

13. To show trends and to be able to compare performance and costs between different periods, standards would be rarely changed. On the other hand, for day to day control and motivation purposes standards which reflect the most up to date position are required and consequently revisions would need to be made continually. The above positions reflect the extremes of the situation. There is no doubt that standards which are right up to date provide a better target and are more meaningful to the foremen and managers involved, but the extent and frequency of standard revision is a matter of judgement. Minor changes in rates, prices and usage are frequently ignored for a time, but their cumulative effect soon becomes significant and changes need to be made. Prior to computer maintained standard cost files, standard cost revisions were a time consuming chore as it was necessary to ensure that all the effects of a change were recorded. For example, a price change of a common raw material would necessitate alterations to

a. the standard cost cards of all products, parts and assemblies using the material;

b. any price lists, stock sheets and catalogues involving the material and products derived from the material.

Because of such factors, commonly all standard costs are revised together at regular, periodic intervals such as every six or twelve months, rather than on an individual, random basis.

BEHAVIOURAL ASPECTS OF STANDARDS

14. The points made in the previous chapter regarding the importance of the human aspects of budgeting apply equally to standard costing. Both techniques employ similar principles and both rely absolutely upon the people who have to work to the budgets and standards. Because of the detailed nature of standard costing and its involvement with foremen and production workers, communication becomes of even greater importance. Production workers frequently regard any form of performance evaluation with deep suspicion and if a cost-conscious, positive attitude is to be developed, close attention must be paid to the behavioural aspects of the system. Full participation, realistic standards, prompt and accurate reporting, no undue pressure or censure — all contribute to an acceptable system. Remember: if the system is not accepted by the people involved it will be unworkable.

ADVANTAGES OF STANDARD COSTING

15. a. Standard costing is an example of 'management by exception'. By studying the variances, management's attention is directed towards those items which are not proceeding according to plan. Management are able to delegate cost control through the standard costing system knowing that variances will be reported.

b. The process of setting, revising and monitoring standards encourages reappraisal of methods, materials and techniques so leading to cost reductions.

c. Standard costs represent what the parts and products should cost. They are not merely averages of past performances and consequently they are a better guide to pricing than historical costs. In addition, they provide a simpler basis of inventory valuation.

d. A properly developed standard costing system with full participation and involvement creates a positive, cost effective attitude through all levels of management right down to the shop floor.

DISADVANTAGES OF STANDARD COSTING

16. a. It may be expensive and time consuming to install and to keep up to date.

b. In volatile conditions with rapidly changing methods, rates and prices, standards quickly become out of date and thus lose their control and motivational effects. This can cause resentment and loss of goodwill.

c. There is research evidence to suggest that overly elaborate variances are imperfectly understood by line managers and thus they are ineffective for control purposes.

SUMMARY

17. a. Standard costing involves comparing actual costs with predetermined costs and analysing the differences, known as variances.

b. There are three main types of standard: Basic standards, ideal standards and expected standards.

c. Basic standards are long term standards which remain unchanged for long periods; ideal standards represent perfect working conditions and performances; expected standards are currently attainable standards based on high but not impossible performance levels. Expected standards are the most common.

d. Standards relate to individual items, processes and products; budgets relate to totals.

e. Setting standards is a detailed, lengthy process usually based on engineering and technical studies of times, materials and methods. Standards are set for each of the elements which make up the standard cost: labour, materials and overheads.

f. Accountants, work study engineers and other specialists provide technical advice and information, but do not set the standards. This is the responsibility of the line managers and their superiors.

g. The culmination of the standard setting process is the preparation of a standard cost card for the product showing the target cost for the following periods.

h. Difficulties arise with the too frequent revision of standards. Consequently it is common practice to revise them on a periodic basis, half yearly or yearly.

i. The behavioural aspects of standard costing, like budgeting, are all important. The system must be acceptable to the people who will have to operate it.

POINTS TO NOTE

18. a. A standard cost, like any cost, is made up from two basic components; the *usage* of materials, labour etc. and the *price* or *rate* of these elements. This cost makeup plays a significant part in variance analysis covered in the next chapter.

b. Standard costing and variance analysis are important examination topics. Because examiners are always seeking novel applications a thorough understanding of basis principles is vital for all students.

SELF REVIEW QUESTIONS

1. What is standard costing? *(2)*
2. Describe the three main types of standard. *(4)*
3. What is the relationship between standards and budgets? *(5)*

4. How are standards relating to materials set? (7)
5. What is a standard hour? (8)
6. How are overhead standards established? (9)
7. What is the standard sales margin? (10)
8. Who sets standards? (11)
9. What is a standard cost card? (12)
10. Why are the behavioural aspects of standard costing so important? (14)
11. What are the advantages and disadvantages of standard costing? (15 & 16)

EXAMINATION QUESTION

1. From the information given below you are required to:

    a. prepare a standard cost sheet for one unit and enter on the standard cost sheet the costs to show sub-totals for:
    i.   prime cost;
    ii. variable production cost;
    iii. total production cost;
    iv. total cost;

    b. calculate the selling price per unit allowing for a profit of 15% of the selling price.

The following data are given:

Budgeted output for the year   9,800 units

Standard details for one unit:

    Direct materials 40 square metres at £5.30 per square metre

    Direct wages:
    Bonding department   48 hours at £2.50 per hour
    Finishing department   30 hours at £1.90 per hour

Budgeted costs and hours per annum:

Variable overhead:	£	hours
Bonding department	375,000	500,000
Finishing department	150,000	300,000

Fixed overhead:	
Production	392,000
Selling and distribution	196,000
Administration	98,000

(ICMA, Cost Accounting 1, May 1980).

24 Standard Costing – Variance Analysis (Material, labour and overheads)

INTRODUCTION

1. This chapter defines variance analysis and discusses its purpose. A chart is provided showing the relationship between common variances. Each variance is defined and explained and a worked example provided. Basic variances relating to material and labour are dealt with first and then overhead and more advanced material variances are described.

VARIANCE ANALYSIS DEFINED

2. It will be recalled from the previous chapter that a variance is the difference between standard cost and actual cost. The term variance is rarely used on its own. Usually it is qualified in some way, for example; direct materials cost variance, direct labour efficiency variance and so on. The process by which the total difference between standard and actual costs is sub-divided is known as variance analysis which can be defined as: "That part of variance accounting which relates to the analysis into constituent parts of variances between planned and actual performance." *Terminology*. Variances arise from differences between standard and actual quantities and/or differences between standard and actual prices. These are the *causes* of variances; the *reasons* for the differences have to be established by management investigation.

Note:

Variances may be ADVERSE, i.e. where actual cost is greater than standard, or they may be FAVOURABLE i.e. where actual cost is less than standard. Alternatively they may be known as MINUS or PLUS variances respectively.

THE PURPOSE OF VARIANCE ANALYSIS

3. The only purpose of variance analysis is to provide practical pointers to the causes of off-standard performance so that management can improve operations, increase efficiency, utilise resources more effectively and reduce costs. It follows that overly elaborate variance analysis which is not understood, variances that are not acted upon and variances which are calculated too long after the event do not fulfill the central purpose of standard costing. The types of variances which are identified must be those which fulfill the needs of the organisation. The only criterion for the calculation of a variance is its usefulness – if it is not useful for management purposes, it should not be produced.

RESPONSIBIITY FOR VARIANCES

4. Ideally, variances should be detailed enough so that responsibility can be assigned to a particular individual for a specific variance. Cost control is made much more difficult if responsibility for a variance is spread over several managers. In such circumstances it is all too easy to 'pass the buck'. Because of the importance of this principle, standard costing and budgetary control are known in America as 'responsibility accounting'. A simple example of the process of calculating variances in accordance with responsibilities is the subdivision of the direct materials cost variance, that is, the total difference in material costs between actual and standard. This is composed of a usage component, which is usually the responsibility of a foreman, and a price component which is usually the responsibility of the buyer. Accordingly, a usage variance and a price variance need to be calculated to show how much of the total difference is attributable to either person. This example is at the most basic level; frequently more variances are calculated than those given above.

THE RELATIONSHIP OF VARIANCES

5. The overall objective of variance analysis is to subdivide the total difference between budgeted profit and actual profit for the period into the detailed differences (relating to material, labour, overheads and sales) which go to make up the total difference. The particular variances which are computed in any given organisation are those which are relevant to its operations and which will aid control. The chart overleaf shows typical variances which are generally found useful, but it must be emphasised that relevance and appropriateness to management are the only criteria, not the fact that a variance is mentioned in textbooks and on examination papers. The chart shows a hierarchy of frequently encountered variances and should be studied carefully together with the notes which follow:

Note:

a. Each variance and sub-variance is described in detail in the paragraphs which follow.

b. For simplicity the full title of each variance is not shown in each box. The full titles are easily derived from the chart. For example, under the Direct Materials Cost Variance is found the *Direct Materials* Price Variance, the *Direct Materials* Usage Variance and so on.

c. The chart is arithmetically consistent, i.e. the total of the linked variances equals the senior variance shown. For example,

Variable Overhead Expenditure Variance + Overhead Efficiency Variance

= Variable Overhead Variance

d. The price and quantity aspects of each variance are shown clearly on the chart and can be summarised as shown in the table below.

Cost Element	Price Variances	Quantity Variances
Direct Wages	Rate	Efficiency
Direct Materials	Price	Usage
Variable Overheads	Expenditure	Efficiency
Fixed Overheads	Expenditure	Volume

e. The 'OPERATING PROFIT' variance is the difference between budgeted and actual operating profit for a period. This variance can be calculated directly and it is the sum of all variances, i.e. cost variances and sales variances. The operating profit variance is not entered in a ledger account because budgeted profit does not appear therein. All other variances do appear in ledger accounts. The bookeeping entries for all forms of costing systems, including standard costing, are described in Chapter 26.

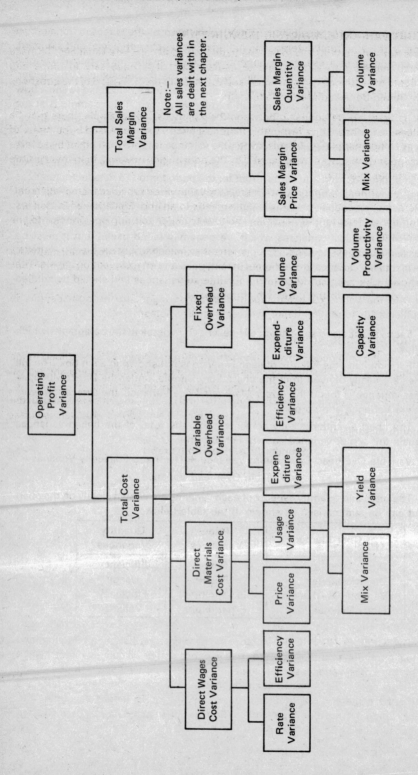

CHART OF COMMON VARIANCES   Figure 1

MAKING VARIANCE ANALYSIS MEANINGFUL

6. It is not sufficient merely to be able to describe and calculate variances. To make variance analysis into a useful aid to management it is necessary to probe and investigate the variances and the data used to calculate them. Typical of the questions which should be asked are the following:

a. Is there any relationship between the variances? For example, there may be pleasure in observing a favourable materials price variance caused by purchase of a job lot of material, but if this favourable variance is more than offset by adverse usage and labour variances caused by the poor quality material, then there is little cause for rejoicing.

b. Can further information than merely the variance be provided for management? Remember, variance analysis is but a means to an end. Management's task is to find the reasons for the variances and to take action to bring operations into line with the plan.

c. Is the variance significant and worth reporting? This is an important matter for both the accountant and the manager and the ways of assessing the significance of variances are dealt with in the next chapter.

d. Are the variances being reported quickly enough, to the right people, in sufficient or too much detail, with explanatory notes?

THE VARIANCES DESCRIBED

7. Each of the variances shown in the Variance Chart, Figure 1, is described in the following paragraphs. Each variance is defined and explained, a formula and typical causes of the variance are given together with a worked example.

The worked examples for the basic material and labour variances are based on the following abstract from the Standard Cost Card for Part No. 100X and actual results for the month of January.

Standard Cost Card (abstract)

Part No. 100X

	Standard Cost/Unit £
Raw Materials 50 lbs @ £2.50/Kg.	125
Direct Labour 14 hrs @ £2.75/hour	38.50
	£163.50

Actual Results for January

Production	150 units
Direct Material Purchases	7000 Kgs at a cost of £18,200
Opening Stock Direct Material	1300 Kgs
Closing Stock Direct Material	850 Kgs
Wages paid (2020 hrs)	£5,858

THE BASIC MATERIALS VARIANCES

8. This paragraph deals with the Direct Materials Cost Variance, the Direct Materials Price Variance and the Direct Materials Usage Variance. A particular problem arises with Materials variances in that materials can be charged to production at either actual prices or standard prices. This affects when the price variance is calculated, i.e. either at the time of purchase or at the time of usage. Although both these approaches are possible, the procedure where materials are charged to production at standard price has many advantages and will be adopted in this manual. This method means that variances are calculated as soon as they arise, (i.e. a price variance when the material is purchased) and that they are more easily related to an individual's responsibility (i.e. a price variance would be the buyer's responsibility). Accordingly for materials variances (and ALL other variances), price variances are calculated first and thereafter the material is at standard price. The individual material variances can now be considered:

Direct Materials Cost Variance — definition:

"The sum of the price and usage variances" *Terminology*

Direct Materials Price Variance — definition:

"That portion of the direct materials cost variance which is the difference between the standard price and the actual price paid for direct materials purchased during that period". *Terminology*.

Direct Materials Usage Variance — definition:

"That portion of the direct materials cost variance which is the difference between the standard quantity specified for the production achieved, whether completed or not, and the actual quantity used, both valued at standard prices". *Terminology*.

FORMULAE

Actual purchase quantity x Actual price
(i.e. Total Purchase Cost)

MINUS } PRICE VARIANCE

Actual purchase quantity x STANDARD PRICE

} TOTAL DIRECT MATERIAL COST VARIANCE

Actual quantity used for actual production x STANDARD PRICE

MINUS } USAGE VARIANCE

STANDARD QUANTITY FOR ACTUAL PRODUCTION x STANDARD PRICE

Example 1 (based on data from Para. 7)

		£		
	Total Purchase Price	18,200	Price VARIANCE	
MINUS	7000 Kgs @ £2.50	17,500	£700 ADVERSE	TOTAL MATERIALS VARIANCE £575 ADVERSE
	7450 Kgs @ £2.50	18,625	USAGE VARIANCE	
MINUS	(150 x 50) @ £2.50	18,750	£125 FAVOURABLE	

Notes:

a. Although rules can be given regarding the sequence of the formulae so that a minus variance is always adverse and a plus is favourable, it is easier and less error prone to determine the direction of the variance by common sense, i.e. if the price/usage is less than standard the variance is favourable, if more, then the variance is adverse.

b. The price variance is based on the actual quantity purchased and is extracted first. Thereafter the actual price is never used for variance calculations.

c. In the above example, the actual usage (7450 lbs) was calculated as follows:

Opening Stock + Purchases − Closing Stock = Usage

i.e. 1300 + 7000 − 850 = 7450 lbs

d. It follows from the above calculations that a price variance could arise even if there was no usage, provided that there were purchases during the period.

e. Students should note how the formulae develop from actual values (in lower case) progressively to STANDARD VALUES (in capitals). This layout is used throughout the manual.

Typical causes of material variances

Price variances

a. Paying higher or lower prices than planned.

b. Losing or gaining quantity discounts by buying in smaller or larger quantities than planned.

c. Buying lower or higher quality than planned.

d. Buying substitute material due to unavailability of planned material. (both (c) and (d) may affect usage variances).

Usage Variances

a. Greater or lower yield from material than planned.

b. Gains or losses due to use of substitute or higher/lower quality than planned.

c. Greater or lower rate of scrap than anticipated.

Note:

As can be seen from the variance chart, Figure 1, the usage variance can be further divided into mix and yield variances. This is only done when useful information can be thus provided. An example is given later in this chapter (Para. 16).

LABOUR VARIANCES

9. This paragraph deals with the Direct Wages Cost Variance, the Direct Wages Rate Variance (the 'price variance') and the Direct Labour Efficiency Variance (the 'usage' variance). These are defined below:

− Direct Wages Cost Variance − definition.

"The difference between the standard direct wages specified for the actual production, whether completed or not, and the actual direct wages incurred". *Terminology.*

− Direct Wages Rate Variance − definition.

"That portion of the direct wages cost variance which is the difference between the standard rates of pay specified and the actual rates paid". *Terminology.*

– Direct Labour Efficiency Variance – definition.

"That portion of the direct wages cost variance which is the difference between the standard direct wages cost for the production achieved, whether completed or not, and the actual hours at standard rates (plus incentive bonus, if any)." *Terminology*.

The formulae are given below and it should be noted that they follow a similar pattern to the material variances described in the previous paragraph.

FORMULAE

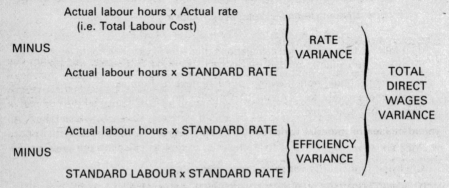

Actual labour hours x Actual rate
(i.e. Total Labour Cost)

MINUS

Actual labour hours x STANDARD RATE

} RATE VARIANCE

} TOTAL DIRECT WAGES VARIANCE

Actual labour hours x STANDARD RATE

MINUS

STANDARD LABOUR x STANDARD RATE

} EFFICIENCY VARIANCE

Notes:

a. It will be seen that the second line of the rate variance and the first line of the efficiency variance are identical.

b. As with the material variances the price (rate) variance is dealt with first; thereafter all calculations use the standard rate.

c. Where appropriate records exist, an idle time variance can be calculated by multiplying the hours of idle time by the standard rate. The variance so calculated, together with the efficiency variance, forms the labour usage variance. Where no idle time variance is calculated, as in the example above, the efficiency variance is equivalent to the labour usage variance. As with labour efficiency, the effect of idle time on variable and fixed overheads can also be calculated.

Example 2 (based on data from Para. 7)

Actual Wages paid	£5,858	} RATE VARIANCE £303 Adv.		
MINUS 2020 hrs @ £2.75	£5,555		}	TOTAL DIRECT WAGES VARIANCE
	£5,555	} EFFICIENCY VARIANCE £220 Fav.	}	£83 Adv.
MINUS (150 x 14) hrs @ £2.75	£5,775			

The total variance can be verified by calculating the difference between actual wages, £5858, and the standard labour cost of the actual production, £5775, i.e.

$$£5858 - £5775 = \underline{£83 \text{ ADV.}}$$

Typical causes of labour variances:
Rate

    a. Higher rates being paid than planned due to wage award.
    b. Higher or lower grade of worker being used than planned.
    c. Payment of unplanned overtime or bonus.

Efficiency

    a. Use of incorrect grade of labour.
    b. Poor workshop organisation or supervision.
    c. Incorrect materials and/or machine problems.

BASIC VARIANCE ANALYSIS

10. So far only the basic material and labour variances have been dealt with. The illustrations have been deliberately kept simple in order to emphasise the major principles of variance analysis. There is considerable similarity between the methods of calculating all types of variance and students are advised to master the first part of this chapter before proceeding to the overhead and other variances which follow. An important general principle which should be apparent at this stage is that actual prices or rates are never used in variance analysis, except to calculate the price or rate variance which is *always done first*.

INTRODUCTION TO OVERHEAD VARIANCE ANALYSIS

11. Before dealing with the individual variances it is necessary to recall some of the earlier material in the manual. Overheads are absorbed into costs by means of predetermined overhead absorption rates (OAR) which are calculated by dividing the budgeted overheads for the period by the activity level anticipated. The activity level can be expressed in various ways (units, weight, sales etc.), but by far the most useful concept is that of the Standard hour. It will be recalled that the 'Standard hour' is a unit measure of production and is the most commonly used measure of activity level. Thus:

    Total overhead absorbed = OAR x SHP

where SHP is the number of Standard Hours of Production.

    Where the Standard costing system uses total absorption costing principles (i.e. where both fixed and variable overheads are absorbed into production costs) the total overheads absorbed can be subdivided into Fixed Overhead Absorption Rates (FOAR) and Variable Overhead Absorption Rates (VOAR) thus:

FIXED OVERHEADS ABSORBED	= FOAR x SHP
VARIABLE OVERHEADS ABSORBED	= VOAR x SHP and
TOTAL OVERHEADS ABSORBED	= (FOAR + VOAR) x SHP.

    Where standard *marginal* costing is used, only variable overheads are absorbed into production costs and thus only variances relating to variable overheads arise; fixed overheads being dealt with by the budgetary control system. Thus it will be seen that overhead variance analysis is considerably simplified when standard marginal costing is employed.

    All the overhead variances are described and illustrated below and the following data will be used for the examples:

Budget for February Department No. 82

	£
Fixed overheads	11,480
Variable Overheads	13,120
Labour Hours	3280 hrs
Standard Hours of Production	3280 hrs

Actual results for February Department No. 82

	£
Fixed Overheads	12,100
Variable Overheads	13,930
Actual labour hours (i.e. clock hrs)	3,150
Standard hours produced	3,230

Based on the budgeted figures the predetermined overhead absorption rates can be calculated:

$$\text{F.O.A.R.} = \frac{\text{Budgeted fixed overheads}}{\text{Budgeted activity level}} = \frac{£11,480}{3280 \text{ Std. hrs}} = £3.5/\text{hour}$$

$$\text{V.O.A.R.} = \frac{\text{Budgeted variable overheads}}{\text{Budgeted activity level}} = \frac{£13,120}{3280 \text{ Std. hrs}} = £4/\text{hour}$$

Notes:

a. It will be seen that *budgeted* labour hours and the *budgeted* standard hours production are the same. This is the normal planning basis. If actual labour hours and the standard hours actually produced also were the same, then efficiency would be exactly as planned and no efficiency variances would arise. It will be seen from the data that this is not the case on this occasion.

b. It will be apparent that because absorption rates for fixed overheads have been calculated the examples will be based on total absorption costing principles.

c. The absorption base is the standard hours of production.

VARIABLE OVERHEAD VARIANCES

12. This paragraph describes the variable overhead variance, the variable overhead expenditure variance and the variable overhead efficiency variance.

– Variable overhead variance – definition.

The difference between the actual variable overheads incurred and the variable overheads absorbed.

(This variance is simply the over or under absorption of overheads)

– Variable overhead expenditure variance – definition.

The difference between the actual variable overheads incurred and the allowed variable overheads based on the actual hours worked.

– Variable overhead efficiency variance – definition.

The difference between the allowed variable overheads and the absorbed variable overhead.

FORMULAE

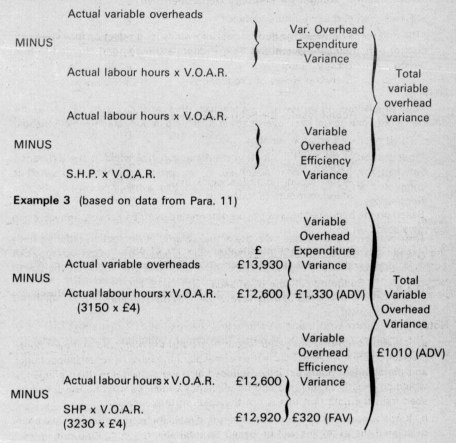

Example 3 (based on data from Para. 11)

Note:

The total variance can be confirmed by calculating the difference between what variable overheads actually cost and what the actual production absorbed in variable overheads.

£13,930 − £12,920 = £1010 (ADV).

FIXED OVERHEAD VARIANCES

13. This paragraph describes the fixed overhead variance, the fixed overhead expenditure variance, the fixed overhead volume variance and its sub-variances the capacity variance and the volume productivity variance.

Definitions

− Fixed overhead variance

"The difference between the standard cost of fixed overhead absorbed in the production achieved, whether completed or not, and the fixed overhead attributed and charged to that period". *Terminology.*

Note:

As with the variable overhead variance, the fixed overhead variance simply represents under or over absorption.

— Fixed overhead expenditure variance —

"The difference between the budget cost allowance for production for a specified control period and the actual fixed expenditure attributed and charged to that period." *Terminology.*

Note:

More simply, though somewhat less precisely, this variance can be defined as the difference between actual fixed overheads and allowed or budgeted fixed overheads.

— Fixed overhead volume variance

"That portion of the fixed production overhead variance which is the difference between the standard cost absorbed in the production achieved, whether completed or not, and the budget cost allowance for a specified control period." *Terminology.*

Note:

The volume variance arises from the actual volume of production differing from the planned volume. As shown in the variance chart, Figure 1. the volume variance can be subdivided because the total difference in the volume of production can be due to either

i. Labour efficiency being greater or less than planned (the efficiency variance).

ii. Hours of work being greater or less than planned (the capacity variance) or some combination of both. The formal definitions of these variances follow.

— Fixed overhead efficiency variance.

"That portion of the fixed production overhead volume variance which is the difference between the standard cost absorbed in the production achieved, whether completed or not, and the actual direct labour hours worked (valued at the standard hourly absorption rate)." *Terminology.*

— Fixed overhead capacity variance.

"That portion of the fixed production overhead volume variance which is due to working at higher or lower capacity than standard. Capacity is often expressed in terms of average direct labour hours per day, and the variance is the difference between the budget cost allowance and the actual direct labour hours worked (valued at the standard hourly absorption rate)." *Terminology.*

The formulae for these variances are given below:

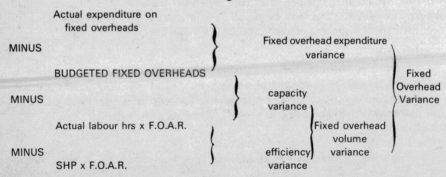

Example 4 (based on data from Para. 11)

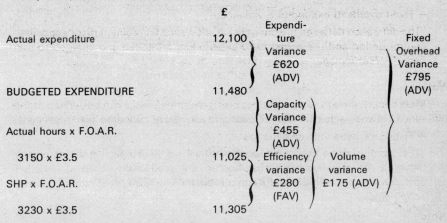

	£		
Actual expenditure	12,100	Expenditure Variance £620 (ADV)	Fixed Overhead Variance £795 (ADV)
BUDGETED EXPENDITURE	11,480		
Actual hours x F.O.A.R.		Capacity Variance £455 (ADV)	
3150 x £3.5	11,025	Efficiency variance £280 (FAV)	Volume variance £175 (ADV)
SHP x F.O.A.R.			
3230 x £3.5	11,305		

The overall variance can be verified by comparing the actual expenditure and the amount of fixed overheads absorbed by the actual production, i.e.

$$£12,100 - £11,305 = \underline{£795 \text{ (ADV)}}$$

REASONS FOR OVERHEAD VARIANCES

14. Overhead variances are somewhat more complex than basic labour and material variances, mainly because of the conventions of the overhead absorption process. Overhead absorption rates are calculated from estimates of expenditure and activity levels and variances arise from differences in both of these factors. In addition, because overheads are frequently absorbed into production by means of labour hours, overhead variances can also arise when labour efficiency is greater or less than planned. Typical reasons for each of the variances

a. **Expenditure variances.** These arise when the actual expenditure differs from the allowed overheads. This may arise due to cost increases of bought-in supplies and services, indirect labour wage increases, misuse of services and facilities etc.

b. **Efficiency variances.** These variances are merely extensions of the labour efficiency variances, described in Para. 9, so will arise for the reasons previously described.

c. **Volume variance.** This variance measures the difference between budgeted fixed overheads and the amount absorbed by the actual production. The amount of actual production is dependent on the efficiency of production, described in (b) above, and also the actual capacity differing from the planned capacity. Typical reasons for capacity variations are: variations in demand, strikes, absenteeism, material/labour shortages and breakdowns.

CONTROL RATIOS

15. The information used in calculating efficiency and volume variances – budgeted and actual labour hours and standard hours produced – can also be used to calculate various ratios which provide clear information on important aspects of the firm's operations. These ratios relate to Activity, Capacity and Efficiency and the formulae are as follows:

$$\text{ACTIVITY RATIO} \quad = \frac{\text{Standard hours produced}}{\text{Budgeted labour hours}} \times 100$$

$$\text{CAPACITY RATIO} \quad = \frac{\text{Actual labour hours worked}}{\text{Budgeted labour hours}} \times 100$$

$$\text{EFFICIENCY RATIO} \quad = \frac{\text{Standard hours produced}}{\text{Actual labour hours worked}} \times 100$$

Example

Using the data from Para. 11, reproduced below, calculate the three control ratios.

Data:	Budgeted labour hours	3280
	Actual labour hours	3150
	Standard hours produced	3230

Solution:

$$\text{Activity ratio} \quad = \frac{3230}{3280} \times 100 = \quad 98\%$$

$$\text{Capacity ratio} \quad = \frac{3150}{3280} \times 100 = \quad 96\%$$

$$\text{Efficiency ratio} \quad = \frac{3230}{3150} \times 100 = 102\%$$

The control ratios are directly related to variances and can provide a useful relative measure rather than the absolute measure provided by variances.

The Activity ratio is equivalent to the Fixed Overhead Volume variance.

The Capacity ratio is equivalent to the Fixed Overhead Capacity variance.

The Efficiency ratio is equivalent to the Fixed and Variable Overhead and Labour Efficiency variances.

FURTHER MATERIAL COST VARIANCES

16. It will be recalled from Para. 8 that the material usage variance can be further subdivided into the Direct Material Mix Variance and the Direct Material Yield Variance. The calculation of these variances is likely to be useful when the production process involves mixing various materials, e.g. in the production of fertilisers, building blocks and food products, and/or where a process loss could occur. It follows that where mix and yield variances can be calculated, the usage variance is the total of the two sub-variances.

Definitions:

— Direct Materials Mix Variance

"That portion of the direct materials usage variance which is the difference between the actual quantity of ingredients used in a mixture at standard price, and the total quantity of ingredients used at the weighted average per unit of ingredients as shown by the Standard Cost sheet". *Terminology*.

— Direct Materials Yield Variance

"That portion of the direct materials usage variance which is the difference between the standard cost of the production achieved, whether completed or not, and the cost of that production arrived at by multiplying the actual total quantity of ingredients used by the weighted average price per unit as shown by the standard cost sheet." *Terminology*.

Note:

These formal definitions are somewhat complex. More simply, they can be expressed as the variances which arise due to the actual direct materials mixture/yield differing from the standard mixture/yield. (In this context mixture means proportions).

FORMULAE

Direct Materials Mixture Variance = STANDARD COST of the *actual* quantity of the *actual* mixture minus STANDARD COST of the *actual* quantity of the STANDARD MIXTURE

Direct Materials Yield Variance = STANDARD COST of the *actual* quantity of the STANDARD MIXTURE minus STANDARD COST of the STANDARD QUANTITY of the STANDARD MIXTURE

Notes:

a. Because the price variance is always dealt with first, the mix and yield variances use only standard prices.

b. Note how the expressions move from *actual* to STANDARD values and that the second part of the mix variance is the same as the first in the yield variance.

c. The yield variance measures abnormal process losses.

Example 5

An industrial plastic is made by mixing and processing three chemicals, X, Y and Z. The standard cost data are as follows:

	Standard Proportions	Standard Cost
Chemical X	60%	£15 per tonne
Y	30%	£20 per tonne
Z	10%	£45 per tonne

A standard process loss of 10% is anticipated.
During a given week the output of plastic was 81 tonnes and the inputs were as follows

	ACTUAL CONSUMPTION	ACTUAL PRICE	ACTUAL COST £
Chemical X	56 tonnes	£14 per tonne	784
Y	32 tonnes	£22 per tonne	704
Z	12 tonnes	£41 per tonne	492
	100 tonnes		£1,980

Calculate all relevant material variances.

Solution

There are three variances to be calculated: Price, Mix and Yield, and they must be calculated in that order. (The usage variance is, of course, merely the total of the mix and yield variances).

The summary of the variance calculations is given below followed by explanatory notes.

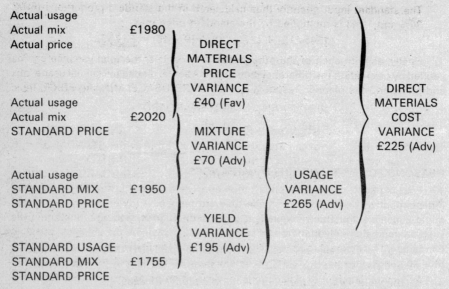

Actual usage
Actual mix   £1980
Actual price

         DIRECT
         MATERIALS
         PRICE
         VARIANCE   DIRECT

Actual usage   £40 (Fav)   MATERIALS
Actual mix   £2020   COST
STANDARD PRICE   MIXTURE   VARIANCE
         VARIANCE   £225 (Adv)
         £70 (Adv)

Actual usage   USAGE
STANDARD MIX   £1950   VARIANCE
STANDARD PRICE   £265 (Adv)
         YIELD
         VARIANCE
STANDARD USAGE   £195 (Adv)
STANDARD MIX   £1755
STANDARD PRICE

It will be seen how the factors involved, usage-mix-price, start all at *actual* and move stage by stage to become all at STANDARD. This is the key to remembering the method of calculation.

Notes:

a. Actual usage at actual mix at actual price is the total actual cost as given in the question, i.e.

$$£(56 \times 14) + (32 \times 22) + (12 \times 41) = £1980$$

b. The actual usage in the actual proportions is evaluated at the standard price for each chemical, thus —

$$£(56 \times 15) + (32 \times 20) + (12 \times 45) = £2020$$

c. The standard mix is obtained by putting the actual total input quantity (100 tonnes) into the standard proportions (60%, 30%, 10%) i.e.

Chemical X = 100 x 60% = 60 tonnes
Chemical Y = 100 x 30% = 30 tonnes
Chemical Z = 100 x 10% = 10 tonnes

and these standard proportions are evaluated at the standard prices, i.e.

$$£(60 \times 15) + (30 \times 20) + (10 \times 45) = £1950$$

d. The standard usage is obtained by working back from the actual output (81 tonnes) to determine what the standard total quantity of input should have been assuming that there was the normal process loss of 10%.

i.e. Standard output quantity $= \dfrac{9}{10} \times$ standard input quantity

$$\therefore \text{Standard input quantity} = \frac{10}{9} \times \text{actual output quantity}$$

$$= \frac{10}{9} \text{ (81 tonnes)}$$

$$= \underline{90} \text{ tons}$$

The standard input quantity thus calculated in the standard proportions (60%, 30% and 10%) is multiplied by the standard price thus

$$£(54 \times 15) + (27 \times 20) + (9 \times 45) = \underline{£1755}$$

Finally, as with each of the other types of variances, the total variance can be verified by calculating the difference between the actual results (i.e. actual usage, mix and price) and the planned results (i.e. STANDARD USAGE, MIX and PRICE) thus:

all at actual	all at STANDARD
£1980	− £1755
	= £225 (Adv)

REASONS FOR MIX AND YIELD VARIANCES

17. The material variances, price, mix and yield, should not be considered independently of each other because they are related. A lower quality of material might cause a favourable price variance, but with a corresponding reduction in the yield. In general the standard mix of standard qualities will be the cheapest possible combination having regard to the yield and technical qualities required of the output; thus an overall favourable variance is unlikely. Typical reasons for *mix variances* are

Accidental or intentional variations in standard proportions, unavailability of one or more ingredients.

Yield variances occur due to malfunctions in process or operator error,

use of non standard mix or materials,

and latent defects in materials.

SUMMARY

18. a. Variance analysis is the process of analysing the total difference between planned and actual performance into its constituent parts.

b. Variance analysis must be useful to management otherwise it is pointless.

c. Variances should be calculated in accordance with responsibilities.

d. Although there are different names, each type of variance, materials, wages and overheads has a PRICE element and a QUANTITY element.

e. The relationship between variances must be considered. Variances should not be considered in isolation.

f. The basic materials variances measure the differences between actual and standard price and actual and standard usage.

g. Price variances are ALWAYS extracted first. Thereafter all variance calculations use standard price.

h. The basic labour variances measure the difference between actual and standard wage rates and actual and standard labour efficiency.

i. An important factor in overhead absorption and overhead variance analysis is the activity level. Frequently this is measured in standard hours. A standard hour is a unit measure of production, not of time.

j. Using total absorption principles both fixed and variable overheads are absorbed into production, so variances relating to both fixed and variable overheads will arise. Using standard marginal costing only variable overheads are absorbed into production overheads so that fixed overhead variances cannot arise.

k. Variable overhead variances reflect differences in variable overhead expenditure and labour efficiency. Fixed overhead variances also reflect differences in expenditure and labour efficiency and in addition differences between the planned capacity (activity level) and actual capacity.

l. The basic materials usage variance can be subdivided into a mix variance and a yield variance. These variances measure differences due to mixing in non-standard proportions and to yields (i.e. process losses) being different to those planned.

m. The Total Cost Variance, shown in Figure 1, is merely the total of all the variances, i.e. the Direct Materials cost variance, the Direct Wages cost variance and the Variable and Fixed Overhead variances.

POINTS TO NOTE

19. a. Variances are related to responsibilities. It follows, therefore, that a manager should only be held responsible for a variance when he has control over the resource or cost element being considered.

b. It must be stressed that variance analysis merely directs attention to the cause of off-standard performances. It does not solve the problem, nor does it establish the reasons behind the variance. These are management tasks.

c. The variances described are ones commonly found, but many others exist. It would be impossible to describe or remember all the possible variances, but of far greater importance is to understand the principles underlying variance analysis; once this is done any given variance can be calculated easily.

d. The relationships between variances must always be considered. Rarely is a single variance of great significance. Is a favourable variance offset by a larger adverse one?

e. Although budgetary control and standard costing are techniques which use the **same** underlying principle, an important difference is that standard costs and variances form part of the double entry system (described in Chapter 26) whereas budgetary control is in memorandum form.

f. The overhead volume variances can be criticised because information which is intended for product costing purposes (i.e. absorption of fixed overheads into cost units) is used as a basis for control information. Fixed overheads are based more on time than activity so that it becomes very difficult to trace responsibility for an adverse volume variance. Because of this, the fixed overhead expenditure variance is probably the most relevant fixed overhead variance for control purposes.

SELF REVIEW QUESTIONS

1. What is variance analysis? (2)
2. What is its purpose? (3)
3. Should variances be related to responsibilities? Why? (4)
4. In what ways can variance analysis be made more useful for management? (6)

5. What are the main sub-divisions of the materials cost variance? (8)
6. Define the Direct Labour Efficiency Variance. (9)
7. What rôle does the number of standard hours produced have in overhead variance analysis? (11)
8. What is the Fixed Overhead Volume Variance? (13)
9. What are the main variable overhead variances? (12)
10. What are the formulae for the — Activity Ratio, Capacity Ratio, and Efficiency Ratio? (15)
11. Define simply the Direct Materials Mix and Yield Variances. (16)
12. What are typical reasons for the mix and yield variances arising? (17)

EXAMINATION QUESTIONS

1. For a product the following data are given:

Standards per unit of product:

Direct material   4 kilogrammes at £0.75 per kilogramme
Direct labour   2 hours at   £1.60 per hour

Actual details for given financial period:

Output produced in units	38,000
Direct materials::	£
purchased 180,000 kilogrammes for	126,000
issued to production 154,000 kilogrammes	
Direct labour 78,000 hours worked for	136,500

There was no work-in-progress at the beginning or end of the period.

You are required to:

a. calculate the following variances:
    i.   direct materials cost;
    ii. direct materials price, based on issues to production;
    iii. direct materials usage;
    iv. direct wages cost;
    v.   direct wages rate;
    vi. direct labour efficiency;

b. state whether in each of the following cases, the comment given and suggested as the possible reason for the variance, is consistent or inconsistent with the variance you have calculated in your answer to (a) above, supporting each of your conclusions with a brief explanatory comment.

Item in

a.
    ii. direct materials price variance: the procurement manager has ignored the economic order quantity and, by obtaining bulk quantities, has purchased material at less than the standard price;
    iii. direct materials usage variance: material losses in production were less than had been allowed for in the standard;
    v.   direct wages rate variance: the union negotiated wage increase was £0.15 per hour lower than expected;
    vi. direct labour efficiency variance: the efficiency of labour was commendable.

(ICMA, Cost Accounting 1, May 1980).

247

2. The Budget Manufacturing Co. Ltd. use standard costs as the basis for setting the selling price of one of their products and the following information is available for the four week period ended 28 April:—

Actual expenditure per unit of production £

	£
Wages	.60
Materials	.60
Variable O/H	.80
Fixed O/H	1.00

Sales for the period totalled £34,500 which included an actual profit margin of 15%.

Recorded Variances:—

	£
Wages — Efficiency	400F
— Idle Time	600A
Materials — Price	100A
Usage	150A
Variable Overhead — Expenditure	200A
Fixed Overhead — Expenditure	250A
— Efficiency	700F
— Capacity	800A

A = Adverse
F = Favourable

You are required to:

a. Prepare a statement for the period showing the standard net profit reconciled to the actual net profit.

b. Comment upon the wages variances and any effects they may have upon the overhead variances.

c. Comment upon the pricing policy of the company.

(CIPFA, Management Accounting, June 1979).

3. K Limited uses standard costs and flexible budgets for control purposes. The following information is given:

Standard and budgeted data:

● The standard material allowed per unit is 4 kilograms at a standard price of £0.75 per kilogram.

● Budgeted direct labour hours for a four-week period were 80,000 hours at a budgeted cost of £152,000.

● Budgeted variable production overhead for 80,000 hours was £96,000.

Details for four-week period ended 29th April, 1978 were:

● Incurred:	£
Direct wages	163,800

● Variances:

Direct wages rate, £0.20 per hour adverse.

Direct materials price (calculated on purchases at time of receipt at £0.05 per kilogram)	9,000	favourable
Direct materials usage	1,500	adverse
Variable production overhead	2,200	favourable
Variable production overhead efficiency	2,400	adverse

● Production, 38,000 units

There were no stocks at beginning of period, but there were 26,000 kilograms of direct materials in stock at 29th April, 1978.
You are required to state for the period:

a. the number of kilograms of direct material purchased;

b. the number of kilograms of direct material used above the standard allowed;

c. the variable production overhead expenditure variance;

d. the actual hours worked;

e. the number of standard hours allowed for the production achieved.

(ICMA, Cost Accounting 1, May 1978).

4. a. Explain, briefly, what is meant by each of the following terms:
    i.   standard hour;
    ii. productivity (or efficiency) ratio;
    iii. production volume ratio.

b. Using the information given below, you are required to calculate the productivity ratio and the production volume ratio for each of the two production departments X and Y.

Department X	Product D	Product G
Budgeted production, in units	18,000	4,000
Standard minutes required to produce one unit:	20	30
Actual units produced	15,000	10,000

Total actual hours worked on both products: 11,111.

Department Y	
Budgeted standard hours	10,000
Actual hours worked	9,000
Standard hours produced	9,450

(ICMA, Cost Accounting 1, May 1980).

5. Shown below is an extract from the April budget for the weaving shed of Textrex Ltd, a canvas manufacturer.

Canvas Grade	Economy	Super
Production Quantities (standard width)	40,000 metres	32,000 metres
Standard Prime Cost:	per metre	per metre
Direct Materials Yarn A (£3 per kilo)	0.2 kilos	0.2 kilos
Yarn B (£4 per kilo)	0.2 kilos	0.3 kilos
Direct Labour (£2 per hour)	12 mins	15 mins
Department Overheads Variable	Fixed	

	£		£
Power	8,000	Supervision	6,400
Indirect Labour	9,600	Heat and Light	2,500
Maintenance	6,400	Depreciation	6,300
		Rent and Rates	4,800
	£24,000		£20,000

Production overhead is absorbed on the basis of standard hours produced, and it should be assumed that variable overheads do vary directly with this measure of production.

During April the following actual results were achieved:

Production   35,000 metres of Economy; 34,000 metres of Super

Direct Materials consumed   Yarn A 13,000 kilos, cost £40,500

Yarn B 19,000 kilos, cost £72,000

Direct Labour 15,800 hours worked, cost £30,500

Department Overheads		£		£
	Power	8,250	Supervision	6,950
	Indirect Labour	9,000	Heat and Light	2,900
	Maintenance	7,500	Depreciation	6,200
			Rent and Rates	5,000
		£24,750		£21,050

Required:

Produce a working paper calculating and analysing the variances which you consider should be incorporated into the weaving shed's operating statement for April.

(ACCA, Costing, June 1979).

25 Standard Costing – Variance Analysis (Sales and Standard marginal costs)

INTRODUCTION

1. This chapter continues the study of variances by dealing with the Sales Margin variances. Standard marginal costing is also described and its relationship with standard costing systems using total absorption costing is explained. Finally to conclude the chapters on standard costing there is a discussion on the significance of variances and the use of variance control charts.

SALES MARGIN VARIANCES

2. The previous chapter described the various cost variances and it will be recalled that the objective of that analysis was to help management to control costs. To achieve planned profits management also wish to control sales, or more correctly, to control the profit (or margin) from sales. This is the overall objective of calculating sales margin variances. Because cost variance analysis extracts all the differences between planned and actual costs, the products *are treated at standard manufacturing cost for the purpose of sales margin variance analysis.* Part of Figure 1, Chapter 24, is given below to show the variances dealt with in this chapter.

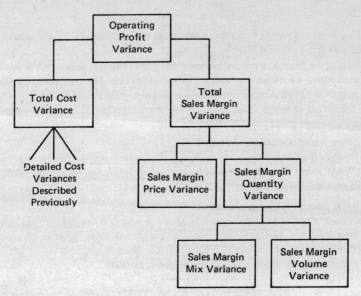

EXTRACT FROM Figure 1, Chapter 24

STANDARD SALES MARGIN

3. This is the difference between the standard selling price of a product and its standard cost and it is the same as the standard profit for the product.

Note:

The 'standard cost' referred to above is the 'total standard cost', i.e. it includes both fixed and variable costs. When fixed costs are excluded it becomes the standard marginal cost and the difference between standard selling price and standard marginal cost is known as the *standard sales contribution*.

SALES MARGIN VARIANCES – DEFINITIONS

4. – Total sales margin variance –

The difference between the budgeted margin from sales and the actual margin when the cost of sales is valued at the standard cost of production.

– Sales margin price variance –

That portion of the total sales margin variance which is the difference between the standard margin per unit and the actual margin per unit for the number of units sold in the period.

Note:

This is a normal price variance and could equally well be described as the 'sales turnover price variance'.

– Sales margin quantity variance –

That portion of the total sales margin variance which is the difference between the budgeted number of units sold and the actual number sold valued at the standard margin per unit.

Note:

This is a normal usage variance, analogous to the direct materials usage variance described in the previous chapter.

Where more than one product is sold, the Sales Margin Quantity Variance can be subdivided into a Mix Variance and a Volume Variance. The mix variance shows the effect on profits of variations from the planned sales mixture, and the volume variance shows the effect of the unit volume varying from standard. These sub-variances are defined below.

– Sales margin mixture variance –

That portion of the sales margin quantity variance which is the difference between the actual total number of units at the actual mix and the actual total number of units at standard mix valued at the standard margin per unit.

– Sales margin volume variance –

That portion of the sales margin quantity variance which is the difference between the actual total quantity of units sold and the budgeted total number of units at the standard mix valued at the standard margin per unit.

The formulae for these variances are given below.

Note:

There is considerable similarity in approach between these variances and the direct materials variances shown in Example 5 in the previous chapter.

Example 1

A company makes and sells three products, W, X and Y. During a period, budget and actual results were as follows:

Product	Budget					Actual				
	Total Sales	Unit			Budgeted Total Margin	Total Sales	Unit			Actual Total Margin
		Volume	Price	Margin			Volume	Price	Margin	
	£		£	£	£	£		£	£	£
W	5,000	500	10	2	1,000	5,500	550	10	2	1,100
X	4,500	300	15	3	900	4,000	250	16	4	1,000
Y	4,000	200	20	4	800	1,900	100	19	3	300
	£13,500	1000			£2,700	£11,400	900			£2,400

Calculate all relevant sales margin variances.

Solution:

The summary of the variance calculations is shown below followed by explanatory notes.

Note

Notes:

a. This is the actual total margin achieved as shown in the question, i.e.

$$£(550 \times 2) + (250 \times 4) + (100 \times 3) = £2,400$$

b. This is the actual units in the actual proportions, but at the budgeted margins i.e.

$$£(550 \times 2) + (250 \times 3) + (100 \times 4) = £2,250$$

c. This is the actual total number of units sold (900), but at the standard proportions, i.e. 50%, 30% and 20%, valued at standard.

$$£(450 \times 2) + (270 \times 3) + (180 \times 4) = £2,430$$

d. Finally the total budgeted margin is required. This is given in the question i.e.

$$£(500 \times 2) + (300 \times 3) + (200 \times 4) = £2,700$$

The total variance can be verified by comparing the budgeted position with the actual position i.e.

Total budgeted margin − Actual margin = Total sales margin variance

$$£2700 - 2400 = £300 \text{ Adv.}$$

By this stage the student should be totally familiar with the pattern of variance calculation and should be in a position to calculate an unfamiliar variance(s) from first principles. Get into the habit of cross-checking the detailed variances by calculating the total variance in the manner shown in each example in this manual.

LIMITATIONS OF SALES MARGIN VARIANCE ANALYSIS

5. The purpose of all variance analysis is to aid management control. To do this variances must be relevant and within a manager's control. Because there are so many external factors involved, the control of sales volume, sales margins and sales mix is extremely difficult and it is somewhat doubtful whether full variance analysis in this area is useful. In certain circumstances however, some of the variances may provide useful information; for example, where the sales price is under the control of the selling organisation and prices are stable, then the sales margin price variance could be useful, alternatively when a manager is responsible for two or more products which are substitutes for one another (different qualities of paint) then the mix variance would show the effect of changes in demand and therefore might be useful.

Note:

In the above example the standard proportions were based on the number of units. On occasions where there are substantial differences in the selling prices of the various products within a firm (e.g. bicycle tyres and tractor tyres) standardising on the number of units could product distortions. In such cases the proportions for the standard mix would be based on sales turnover, not units. This procedure would only alter the balance between the mix and volume variances. The overall quantity variance would remain unchanged.

SALES VARIANCE c.f. SALES MARGIN VARIANCES

6. Historically variance analysis in the sales area commenced with variances based on sales turnover, i.e. if actual sales were above budget there was a favourable sales variance even if profits fell, perhaps because the sales of low profit items had increased. Although information on variations in sales turnover is important, nowadays it is likely to be supplied by detailed sales analyses, not through variance analysis. Management need to have information about profit performance related to

budget and for this reason sales margin variances are generally of much greater importance and so have been described in the preceding paragraphs.

STANDARD MARGINAL COSTING

7. Most standard costing systems are based on total absorption cost principles and the standards and variances described in the last two chapters are typical of such systems. Standard costing can also incorporate marginal cost principles and is then termed standard marginal costing. It will be recalled that marginal costing involves the separation of costs into those which vary with activity, termed variable costs, and those which remain unaffected by activity changes, known as fixed costs. Fixed costs are not absorbed into individual units of production and are deducted in total from the contribution (sales – marginal cost) earned from units sold. Standard marginal costing incorporates these principles and has the following characteristics.

   a. Standards are developed in the normal manner and entered as usual on the standard cost card, except that fixed costs do not appear. The standard cost card includes

> Direct materials
> Direct labour
> Direct expenses
> Variable overheads
> i.e. no fixed costs

   b. A standard contribution is set for each product and added to the standard marginal cost. This sets the standard selling price. The standard contribution becomes the standard sales margin.

   c. A budgeted profit statement is prepared for the next period with budgeted levels of sales and fixed overheads. Typically this would appear as follows.

Budgeted Profit Statement for Period

		£
	Budgeted sales	XXX
	(Budgeted no. of units x standard selling price)	
less	Budgeted cost of sales	XXX
	(Budgeted no. of units x standard marginal cost per unit)	
=	Budgeted Contribution	XXX
less	Budgeted fixed costs	XXX
=	Budgeted profit	XXX

   d. Variance analysis is simplified because of the disappearance of the fixed overhead volume variance and its sub-variances, the capacity and volume productivity variances. All other variances are identical or very similar. The diffferent categories are listed below.

TYPES OF VARIANCE	CHARACTERISTICS OF STANDARD MARGINAL COST VARIANCES
DIRECT MATERIALS	IDENTICAL TO ABSORPTION STANDARD COST VARIANCES
DIRECT LABOUR	"
VARIABLE OVERHEADS	"
FIXED OVERHEADS	ONLY VARIANCE IS THE FIXED OVERHEAD EXPENDITURE VARIANCE. ALL OTHER FIXED OVERHEAD VARIANCES DISAPPEAR
SALES VARIANCES	WITH THE EXCEPTION THAT THE STANDARD SALES MARGIN IS NOW THE STANDARD CONTRIBUTION, THE VARIANCES ARE CALCULATED IN AN IDENTICAL MANNER. THE NEW TITLES ARE: — Sales contribution variance (was sales margin variance) — Sales contribution price variance (was sales margin price variance) — Sales contribution quantity variance (was sales margin quantity variance) — Sales contribution mixture variance (was sales margin mixture variance) — Sales contribution volume variance (was sales margin volume variance)

STANDARD MARGINAL COST EXAMPLE

7.

Example 1

The following data relate to the budget and actual results of a firm which makes and sells a single product and which employs standard marginal costing.

Budget			Actual		
PRODUCTION		10,000 units	PRODUCTION		10,600 units
SALES		10,000 units	SALES		10,600 units
		£			£
Sales		180,000	Sales		180,200
less			*less*		
Standard Marginal Cost			Actual Marginal Cost		
	£			£	
— Materials	10,000		— Materials	11,600	
— Labour	60,000		— Labour	63,000	
— Var. Overheads	80,000	150,000	— Var. Overheads	83,000	157,600
= Contribution		30,000	= Contribution		22,600
less			*less*		
Fixed Costs		15,000	Fixed Costs		15,600
= *Budgeted Profit*		£15,000	= *Actual Profit*		£7,000

The Standard cost card for the product is as follows:

		£
Materials	5 Kgs @ 20p/Kg.	1.00
Labour	4 hrs @ £1.50/hour	6.00
Var. Overheads	4 hrs @ £2/hour	8.00
= STANDARD MARGINAL COST		15.00
STANDARD CONTRIBUTION		3.00
STANDARD SELLING PRICE		£18.00

During the period material usage was 55,000 Kgs and 41,300 labour hours were worked.

Calculate all relevant variances.

Solution:

The total variance is the Operating Profit variance, i.e. the difference between budgeted and actual profit i.e.

$$£15,000 - £7,000 = \underline{£8000 \text{ Adv.}}$$

All other variances will in total equal the operating profit variance and will account for the difference between budgeted and actual profit.

The cost variances are as follows:

MATERIALS VARIANCES

Actual quantity Actual price	£11,600	Price variance £600 Adv.	Direct Materials £1000 (Adv.) Variance
Actual quantity STANDARD PRICE (55,000 x 20p)	£11,000	Usage variance £400 Adv.	
STANDARD PRICE STANDARD QUANTITY (53,000 x 20p)	£10,600		

LABOUR VARIANCES

Actual hours Actual rate	£63,000	Rate variance £1,050 (Adv.)	Direct Wages £600 (Fav.) Variance
Actual hours STANDARD RATE (41,300 x £1.50)	£61,950		
STANDARD HOURS STANDARD RATE (42,400 x £1.50)	£63,600	Efficiency variance £1,650 (Fav.)	

VARIABLE OVERHEAD VARIANCES

Actual variable overheads	£83,000	Expenditure Variance £400 (Adv.)		
Actual labour hours x V.O.A.R. (41,300 x £2)	£82,600		Variable Overhead Variance	£1,800 (Fav.)
S.H.P. (i.e. 4 per unit) x V.O.A.R. (10,600 x 4 x £2)	£84,800	Efficiency Variance £2,200 (Fav.)		

Note:

All the above variances are calculated exactly as described in the previous chapter.

FIXED OVERHEAD VARIANCE

$$\text{Actual fixed overheads } - \text{ Budgeted fixed overheads}$$
$$£15,600 - £15,000 = \underline{£600 \text{ (Adv.)}}$$

Note:

This is the fixed overhead expenditure variance and is the only variance for fixed overheads.

SUMMARY OF COST VARIANCES:

Direct materials	1,000 Adv.
Direct wages	600 Fav.
Variable overheads	1,800 Fav.
Fixed overheads	600 Adv.
∴ Total cost variance =	£800 Fav.

The sales variances are as follows:

Standard contribution = £3/unit and standard cost is £15/unit.

Actual contribution when sales are valued at standard cost (£180,200 − (10,600 x £15))	£21,200	Contribution Price Variance £10,600 (Adv.)		
Actual units @ STANDARD CONTRIBUTION (10,600 x £3)	£31,800		Sales Contribution Variance £8,800 (Adv.)	
BUDGETED UNITS @ STANDARD CONTRIBUTION (10,000 x £3)	£30,000	Contribution Quantity Variance £1,800 (Fav.)		

OVERALL VARIANCE SUMMARY

Total cost variance	£800 (Fav.)
Total sales variance	£8,800 (Adv.)
= Operating Profit Variance	£8,000 (Adv.)

The variances could be used to show the change from budgeted to actual profit, i.e.

		£	£
	Budgeted profit		15,000
less	Adverse variances	£	
	Contribution price variance	10,600	
	Direct materials variance	1,000	
	Fixed overheads variance	600	12,200
			2,800
plus	Favourable variances		
		£	
	Contribution quantity variance	1,800	
	Direct wages variance	600	
	Variable overhead variance	1,800	4,200
	ACTUAL PROFIT =		£7,000

THE SIGNIFICANCE OF VARIANCES

8. Standard costing is an example of management by exception. Hopefully, the majority of items will be according to plan (i.e. at standard or budget) and only a few will show significant variances. It is of importance to decide what is a 'significant variance' both to the accountant and the manager. From a practical viewpoint a variance can be considered significant when it is of such a magnitude, relative to the standard or budget, that it will influence management's actions and decisions. Variances may arise for a number of reasons of which the following three are the most important:

a. Failure to meet a correctly set and agreed standard.

b. An incorrectly set or out of date standard.

c. Random deviations.

Variances arising from reasons (a) and (b), if of sufficient magnitude, are variances which require further investigation and possibly management action. Random deviations, i.e. fluctuations which have arisen by chance are, by definition, uncontrollable. The problem remains of how to determine whether a variation from standard is attributable to chance and not significant or whether it is due to a controllable cause and therefore significant.

STANDARD COSTS AS A RANGE

9. Typically a standard cost is shown as a single figure, but more correctly it should be considered as a band or range of values with the standard cost as the central value. This is illustrated below by a graph representing the times taken for a number of batches of an assembly.

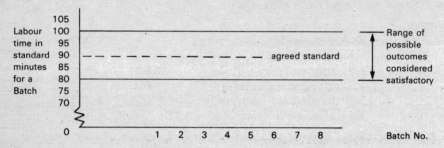

Standard Labour time for Assembly 100 X

If the actual result falls within the band it is considered satisfactory and the variance would not be deemed to be significant. If the actual result was outside this band it would be considered significant and would be reported and possibly a fuller investigation mounted. When used in this fashion, the range of values shown on the graph is known as a CONTROL BAND and the upper and lower limits known as CONTROL LIMITS.

SETTING CONTROL LIMITS

10. The control limits may be set by estimation or statistical analysis.

a. Estimation

This approach is the most commonly used and bases the control limits on judgement or experience. Typically a figure of ± 5% is used and variances within this range would be deemed insignificant. Although obviously lacking any statistical rigour, this approach is practical and implicitly uses the same concepts as more rigorous methods.

b. Statistical analysis

Up until now the term 'significant' has been used in a general sense. More precisely, a variance which is statistically significant is one which is of such a magnitude that it is unlikely to have arisen purely by chance. Statistical probability tests based on the properties of normal distributions can be used to determine whether differences from standard arise from chance (i.e. not significant) or from controllable causes (i.e. significant). To set control limits which can be used to determine statistical significance is dependent upon certain statistical assumptions regarding costs and upon being able to calculate or estimate the standard deviation of the costs. (The statistical techniques alluded to above are covered in most statistics textbooks and would form part of Foundation Level Studies for all accounting students). Based on the properties of the normal distribution, control limits at any level can be set, for example:

> 5% control limits are set at mean ± 1.96 standard deviations
> 2% control limits are set at mean ± 2.33 standard deviations
> 1% control limits are set at mean ± 2.57 standard deviations
> 0.2% control limits are set at mean ± 3.09 standard deviations

Example 2

The standard usage of a part is 120 per assembly and analysis of past usage indicates that the standard deviation of usage is 4 items.

a. What are the 2% control limits?

b. What is the meaning of such control limits?

c. Show the control limits graphically.

Solution:

a. 2% control limits are set at mean ± 2.33 s.d.

$$\text{i.e.} \quad 120 \pm 2.33 \, (4)$$
$$\text{i.e.} \quad 120 \pm 9.32$$

Upper control limit = 120 + 9.32 = <u>129.32</u>

Lower control limit = 120 − 9.32 = <u>110.68</u>

b. The meaning of these control limits is that if chance alone cause variations from standard, then 98% of variances should fall within the range of the mean (standard) ± 2.33 standard deviations. If a variance falls outside these limits i.e. above 129.32 or below 110.68, then the variance is said to be significant at the 2% level.

c.

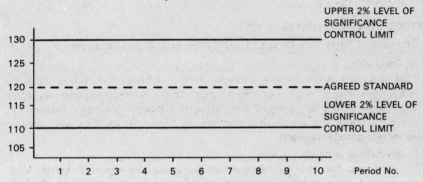

Graph of Control Limits

Note:

Although setting control limits by statistical means appears to be more rigorous, it must be pointed out that some of the necessary statistical assumptions regarding the cost distribution may be invalid in practice and also that the calculation or estimation of the standard deviation may be difficult.

VARIANCE CONTROL CHARTS

11. Whether the control limits are set by statistical analysis or by estimation, a variance control chart can be a useful device, particularly for the identification of trends in the variance. A series of increasing adverse variances, although still within the control limits, may point to a growing problem which perhaps may be rectified before it becomes significant. Not all variances which are significant, i.e. outside the control limits, require detailed investigations. Often the cause is already known or readily ascertainable. The likely benefits of a detailed investigation must be compared with the costs involved.

SUMMARY

12. a. Sales margin variances have the objective of helping to control the profit, i.e. margin, on sales.

b. The standard sales margin is the difference between the standard selling price and the standard cost of an item.

c. The total sales margin variance can be subdivided into Price and Quantity variances. Where more than one product is sold, the Quantity variance can be subdivided into mixture and volume variances.

d. The method of calculating the sales margin variances is very similar to the methods used for calculating materials variances.

e. Standard costing can employ marginal costing principles and becomes known as Standard marginal costing. Fixed costs are not absorbed into individual units of production.

f. A standard marginal cost is the total of all standard variable costs. A standard contribution is added to give a standard selling price.

g. Using standard marginal costing variance analysis is simplified because all fixed overhead variances disappear, except for the fixed overhead expenditure variance.

h. Material, labour and variable overhead variances are identical and, with the exception that the standard contribution becomes the sales margin, so are the sales variances.

i. Significant variances are those which are of such a magnitude that management action will be called for.

j. The determination of what is a significant variance can be done by comparison with control limits.

k. Control limits can be set by judgement, for example plus or minus 5%, or by statistical analysis based on the properties of the normal distribution.

SELF REVIEW QUESTIONS

1. *What product cost is used in sales margin variance analysis? (2)*
2. *What is the standard sales margin? (3)*
3. *What is the standard sales contribution? (3)*
4. *What are the sub divisions of the total sales margin variance? (4)*
5. *What drawbacks are there in sales margin variance analysis? (5)*
6. *Distinguish between sales variances and sales margin variances. (6)*
7. *What are the major differences between standard marginal costing and standard costing based on total absorption costing principles? (7)*
8. *What is a significant variance? (9)*
9. *What are control limits? (10)*
10. *In what ways can control limits be set? (11)*

EXAMINATION QUESTIONS

1. *a. Explain the difference between:*
   i. sales variances; and
   ii. sales margin variances.
   Which do you consider to be more useful to management and why?

   b. Some cost accounting textbooks refer to 'idle time variance' within the context of direct wages while others refer to idle time as an overhead cost item. Which view do you support and why?

(ICMA, Cost Accounting 1, May 1979).

2. You are required, as assistant management accountant of Ayebee Limited, to prepare a profit and loss statement for the month of April 1978. The format of the statement and the relevant data are given below:

Information taken from the standard costs and budgets for the company's two products are:

Per Article:		Price per unit £	Product Aye units	Product Bee units
Direct material:	W	4.3	4	–
	X	6.0	5	–
	Y	2.0	–	10
	Z	2.2	–	4
		Rate per hour £	hours	hours
Direct wages, grade:	I	2.2	8	4
	II	1.8	4	8

Budgeted:
Output per month, articles   320   400
Overhead for the month is £34,560,
    absorbed on an hourly rate basis.
Profit, 20% of selling price.

Actual data for April 1978 were as follows:

		units	price per unit £
Used, direct material:	W	1,280	4.2
	X	1,600	6.2
	Y	4,000	2.1
	Z	1,680	2.0

	Product Aye	Product Bee
Output, articles	315	390

	£
Overhead incurred	33,400

Direct wages paid:	Rate per hour £	hours
grade: I	2.0	3,960
II	1.7	4,260

There were no stocks at the beginning or end of the month.

Format of:

Profit and Loss Statement
for month ended 30th April, 1978

	Product Aye £	Product Bee £	Total £
Sales, actual quantity at standard price	_____	_____	_____
Standard cost of sales:			
Direct material			
Direct wages			
Overhead			
	_____	_____	_____
Total			
	_____	_____	_____
Standard profit on actual sales			
	_____	_____	_____
Variances:			
Direct materials: price			
usage			
			_____
cost			
			_____
Direct wages: rate			
efficiency			
			_____
cost			
			_____
Overhead: expenditure			
productivity			
capacity			
			_____
cost			
			_____
Total			
			_____
Actual profit			
			=========

(ICMA, Cost Accounting 2, May 1978).

3. *Merlon Ltd produces and sells a single perishable product to order, carrying no stocks of either materials or finished goods and no work-in-progress. Its last financial year ended on 31st October 1978.*

The company operates a system of standard costing. A "Statement of Variances" is prepared in respect of each of thirteen four-week accounting periods in each financial year, and is distributed to senior management for consideration at a "Variances Meeting" early in the following period.

The standards are revised annually with effect from the start of the financial year. A summary of the standards for 1977/78 and 1978/79 is shown below:

Standards per unit of output

	1977/78	£	1978/79	£
Materials:	40 lbs at 36p per lb	14.40	38 lbs at 44p per lb	16.72
Labour:	14 hrs at 60p per hr	8.40	12 hrs at 76p per hr	9.12
Variable overheads:		1.50		1.66
Fixed overheads:	based on budgeted output of 500 units in each period	1.30	based on budgeted output of 650 units in each period	1.20
		25.60		28.70
Selling price		30.00		33.00
Profit		4.40		4.30

By an astonishing coincidence the actual results for the last period of 1977/78 and the first period of 1978/79 were absolutely identical, and were as follows in each period:

Actual results, 1977/78 Period 13 and 1978/79 Period 1

	£	Quantity
Materials	8,932	22,330 lbs
Labour	5,510	7,250 hrs
Variable overheads	920	
Fixed overheads	720	
Total costs	16,082	
Sales	19,140	580 units
Profit	3,058	

The following Statement of Variances was presented in respect of 1977/78 Period 13 at the Variances Meeting early in November 1978:

Statement of Variances*, 1977/78 Period 13

	£	£
Materials: price	(893.2) ADV	
usage	313.2 FAV	
		(580.0) ADV
Labour: rate	(1,160.0) ADV	
efficiency	522.0 FAV	
		(638.0) ADV
Variable overheads		(50.0) ADV
Fixed overheads: budget	(70.0) ADV	
volume	104.0 FAV	
		34.0 FAV
Sales: price		1,740.0 FAV
Profit		506.0 FAV

* Note: ADV = adverse; FAV = favourable.

265

You are required:

    a. to calculate the Statement of Variances for 1978/79 Period 1, and

    b. to write a short report comparing the Statements of Variances for 1977/78 Period 13 and 1978/79 Period 1. Comment in particular on the significance of the variances calculated, by reference to the overall basis or bases on which you would infer that the revised standards have been set, and give your own views as to the overall basis or bases you would yourself recommend in setting standards for 1978/79.

(ICA, Management Accounting, December 1978).

26 Cost Accounting

INTRODUCTION

1. This chapter deals with the book-keeping entries required for costing systems. Integral accounts and interlocking accounts are described and illustrated. Where separate financial and costing accounting systems are maintained, the procedures for reconciliation are explained. The accounting entries for standard costing systems are also described.

ACCOUNTING SYSTEMS FOR COSTS

2. Because there are no statutory requirements to maintain detailed cost records, some small firms keep only traditional financial accounts and prepare cost information in an ad-hoc fashion. In all but the very smallest firm this approach is likely to be unsatisfactory and the majority of firms maintain cost accounts in some form or other. There is a vast range of systems in operation ranging from simple analysis systems to computer based accounting systems incorporating standards, variance analysis and the automatic production of control and operating statements. Invariably the systems are tailored to suit the particular firm and so will have unique features. Nevertheless there will be recognisably common aspects to most systems and the records will be maintained using proper double entry principles. Whatever system is adopted for recording costs, it will depend on accurate coding of source data, i.e. items such as invoices, job tickets, time sheets and requisitions. (The principles of coding have been dealt with in chapter 4). Despite the variety of cost accounting systems, two particular categories are frequently encountered. These are known as integrated cost accounts and interlocking cost accounts. Descriptions of these terms follow.

'Integrated cost accounts'.

This is a single, comprehensive accounting system with no division between financial and cost accounts. It follows therefore that the same bases for items such as stock valuation and depreciation will be used and that there is no need for reconciliation between cost profit and financial profit. Financial profit will be the cost profit adjusted by any non-cost items, e.g. income from investments, charitable donations etc.

'Interlocking cost accounts'

This system (of which there are many variants) uses separate cost accounts which periodically are reconciled with the financial accounts. Naturally the cost accounts use the same basic data (purchases, wages etc) as the financial accounts, but frequently adopt different bases for matters such as depreciation and stock valuation. The interlocking of the two systems is carried out by the use of control accounts in each set of accounts, i.e.

a cost ledger control account in the financial ledger and
a financial ledger control account in the cost ledger.

INTEGRATED COST ACCOUNTS

3. The following outline diagram shows the main flow of accounting entries in a typical integrated system. It has been kept free from the many complications and variations that occur in practice to show clearly the underlying principles. It should be studied in conjunction with the notes which follow.

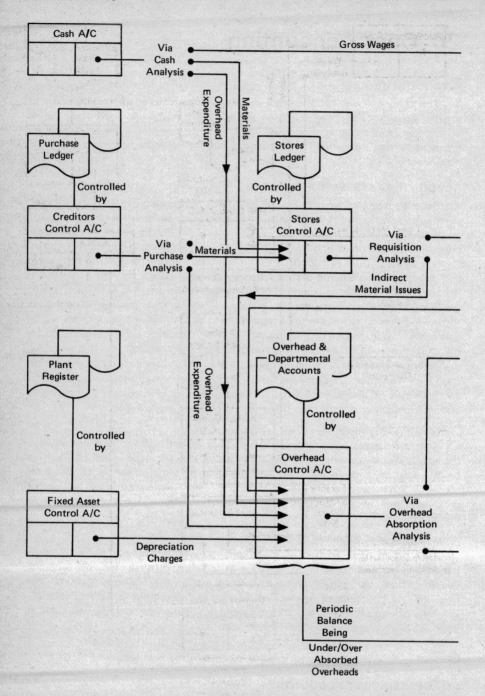

TYPICAL ACCOUNTING ENTRIES IN AN INTEGRATED COST ACCOUNTING SYSTEM

Figure 1

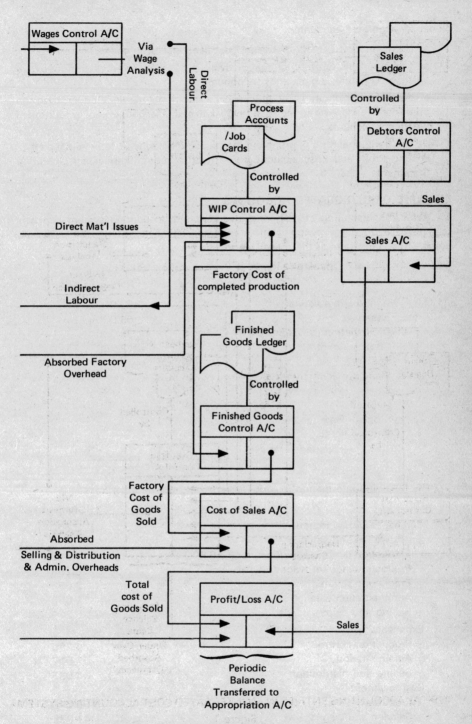

TYPICAL ACCOUNTING ENTRIES IN AN INTEGRATED
COST ACCOUNTING SYSTEM   Figure 1

Notes on integrated accounts

a. No distinction is made between 'cost accounts' and 'financial accounts'.

b. The emphasis is on functional analysis, e.g. selling overheads, rather than analysis by nature, e.g. salaries, telephone etc.

c. If analysis by nature is required, as in a traditional nominal ledger, then the prime data needs to be coded accordingly and natural accounts kept in addition to functional accounts.

d. The traditional form of profit and loss account disappears to be replaced by a costing Profit and Loss account or, as it is frequently known, an Operating Statement.

EXAMPLE OF INTEGRATED ACCOUNTS

4. Acme manufacturing Ltd. operate an integrated accounting system and it is required to record the following balances and transactions in the ledger accounts and prepare Final Accounts at the month's end.

Opening balance at the 1st June 19XX

	£	£
Issued share capital		250,000
Reserves		65,000
Depreciation provision (plant)		38,000
Creditors control		42,750
Buildings	80,000	
Plant & machinery (at cost)	146,500	
Bank	23,291	
Debtors	49,856	
Stocks — Raw materials	41,200	
— WIP	24,260	
— Finished Goods	30,643	
	395,750	395,750

The following information is supplied regarding the month's transactions.

	£
Purchases of raw materials	122,600
Gross wages and salaries	
Production direct wages (including £6,800 accrued)	24,910
Production indirect wages	6,253
Production salaries	2,985
Administration salaries	11,058
Selling and distr. salaries	6,219
Expenses	
Production control	4,286
Administration	7,017
Selling and distribution	4,935
Cash payments	
Creditors	155,296
Salaries and wages	41,025
Cash receipts — Debtors	185,473

	£
Discounts allowed	2,100
Discounts received	3,926
Overheads recovered	
Production	28,750
Administration	18,500
Selling and distribution	10,800
Provisions	
Depreciation on plant	9,520
Bad debts	4,100
Factory cost of completed production	155,000
Factory cost of goods sold	173,000
Sales	220,800
Material issues	
Production	83,621
Works maintenance	6,509

Stores Control

Balance	41,200	WIP	83,621
Purchases	122,600	Prod. Ohd.	6,509
		Bal c/f	73,670
	163,800		163,800
Balance	73,670		

W.I.P. Control

Balance	24,260	Fin Goods	155,000
Wages	24,910	Balance	6,541
Materials	83,621		
Prod. Ohds.	28,750		
	161,541		161,541
Balance	6,541		

Finished Goods Control

Balance	30,643	Goods Sold	173,000
Production	155,000	Balance c/f	12,643
	185,643		185,643
Balance	12,643		

Cost of Sales

Fin. Goods	173,000	P & L	202,300
Adm. Ohds.	18,500		
S & D Ohds.	10,800		
	202,300		202,300

Wages/Salary Control

Cash	41,025	WIP	24,910
Deductions	3,600	Prod. Ohd.	6,253
Accrued	6,800	Prod. Ohd.	2,985
		Adm. Ohd.	11,058
		S & D Ohd.	6,219
	51,425		51,425
		Balance	6,800

Prod'n. O'hd. Control

Wages	6,253	WIP	28,750
Salaries	2,985	Under Recov.	803
Expenses	4,286		
Depreciation	9,520		
Materials	6,509		
	29,553		29,553

Admin. O'hd. Control

Salaries	11,058	Cost of Sales	18,500
Expenses	7,017		
Over Recovery	475		
	18,500		18,500

S & D O'hd. Control

Salaries	6,219	Cost of Sales	10,800
Expenses	4,935	Under Recovery	354
	11,154		11,154

Share Capital

		Balance	250,000

Reserves

		Balance	65,000
		Profit	15,494
			80,494

Discount Allowed

Debtors	2,100	P & L	2,100

Discount Received

P & L	3,926	Creditors	3,926

Bank

Balance	23,291	Credits	155,296
Debits	185,473	Wages	41,025
		Balance c/f	12,443
	208,764		208,764
Balance	12,443		

Buildings

Balance	80,000		

Plant & Machinery

Balance	146,500		

Debtors Control

Balance	49,856	Cash		185,473
Sales	220,800	Discounts		2,100
		Balance		83,083
	270,656			270,656
Balance	83,083			

Creditors Control

Cash	155,296	Balance		42,750
Discounts	3,926	Purchases		122,600
Balance	22,366	Expenses		16,238
	181,588			181,588
		Balance		22,366

Bad Debts Provision

	P & L	4,100

Wage/Salaries Deductions

	Wages	3,600

Depreciation Prov. Plant

Balance c/f	47,520	Balance	38,000
		Prod. O'hd.	9,520
	47,520		47,520
		Balance	47,520

Overhead Adjustment A/c

Prod. Ohds.	803	Admin. Ohds.	425
S & D Ohds.	354	P & L	732
	1,157		1,157

Sales

P & L	220,800	Debtors	220,800

Profit and Loss

Cost of Sales	202,300	Sales	220,800
Overhead adjustment	732	Discount Received	3,296
Discounts allowed	2,100		
Bad Debts Prov.	4,100		
Transfer to Reserve	15,494		
	224,726		224,726

Balance Sheet

Share Capital		250,000	Buildings		80,000
Reserves		80,494	Plant	146,500	
			Less Deposit	47,520	98,980
					178,980
Current Liabilities			*Current Assets*		
Creditors	22,366		Cash	12,443	
Accrued Wages	6,800		Debtors 83,083		
Deductions	3,600	32,766	− B.D.P. 4,100	78,983	
			Stocks		
			Raw Matls	73,670	
			WIP	6,541	
			Fin. Goods	12,643	184,280
		£363,260			£363,260

INTERLOCKING COST ACCOUNTS

5. This system, with its many variants, is commonly encountered in practice. It involves separate cost accounting and financial accounting systems in which the basic accounting data are used in the normal manner in the financial accounts and then the data and documents passed to the cost department. There the source data on costs will be re-classified into the functional analysis necessary for costing purposes, using such supplementary information as labour and machine times, production statistics, material requisitions and scrap reports. The financial accounting system has the normal debit and credit entries within itself and in addition has a memorandum account frequently termed the Cost Ledger Control A/C. This account will have posted to it all items which are to be transferred to the cost accounting system.

In the cost ledger there will be the necessary accounts for costing purposes, e.g. Stores Control A/C, W-I-P Control A/C etc. and, in addition, an account which is equal and opposite to the memorandum financial account. The cost ledger account is termed the Cost Ledger Contra Account in the ICMA terminology, but to avoid confusion with the memorandum cost ledger control account in the financial accounts, it is frequently called the Financial (or General) Ledger Control A/C.

The Financial Ledger Control account is an essential element of the cost ledger because it forms part of the double entry system within the ledger. It also enables the financial and cost ledgers to be interlocked because it must agree with the memorandum Cost Ledger Control account in the financial ledger. A summary of the two ledgers is shown below.

FINANCIAL ACCOUNTS including all usual accounts found in a financial system e.g.		COST ACCOUNTS typically including:	
usual double entries made between accounts	Sales A/c Purchase A/c Cash A/c Fixed Asset A/cs Debtor's A/cs Creditor's A/cs etc.	Stores control A/c Wages control A/c Overhead A/cs W-I-P A/c Finished goods control A/c Cost of sales A/c Costing Profit + Loss A/c etc.	Double entries include the Fin. Ledger Control A/c
	PLUS	PLUS	
not part of double entry	the *memorandum* COST LEDGER CONTROL A/c	Financial ledger control A/c (or Cost ledger contra A/c)	

These two accounts
should be in
agreement.

n.b.

There is no double entry connection between the Financial accounts and the Cost accounts although the use of the memorandum control account in the financial ledger and the financial ledger control A/c in the cost ledger enables the two sets of accounts to be kept in agreement.

The diagram overleaf shows the main flows in an interlocking system and should be studied in conjunction with the notes.

Notes on Financial Ledger

a. Typical entries relating to items which will be transferred to the cost accounts, i.e. wages, purchases etc. are shown as M1, M2 etc. The normal double entries are given together with the entry in the memorandum Cost Ledger Control A/c.

b. Examples of two entries are given which do not affect the cost ledger (Purchase of a fixed asset and payment of dividends). It will be seen that for these items there is no memorandum entry.

c. Other items which appear in the financial accounts, but not in the cost accounts, include:

    i.   Financial charges such as stamp duty, interest on loans, issue expenses, loss on sale of capital assets and similar financial items.

    ii.   Financial income such as dividends received, interest received on loans and deposits and profits from the sales of fixed assets.

    iii.   Appropriations of profit such as dividends paid, transfers to reserve and taxation.

d. Although there are no double entries spanning the cost and financial ledgers, control must be maintained over the information and documents transferred. The cost ledger control account assists this process together with batch control totals, pre-lists and document counts.

FINANCIAL LEDGER

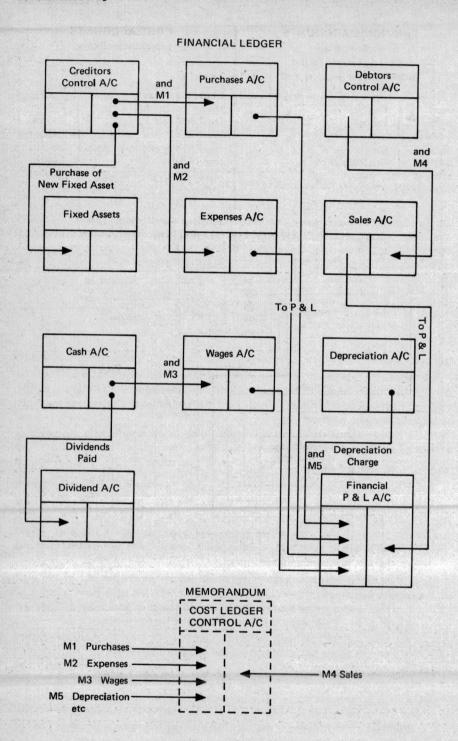

COST LEDGER

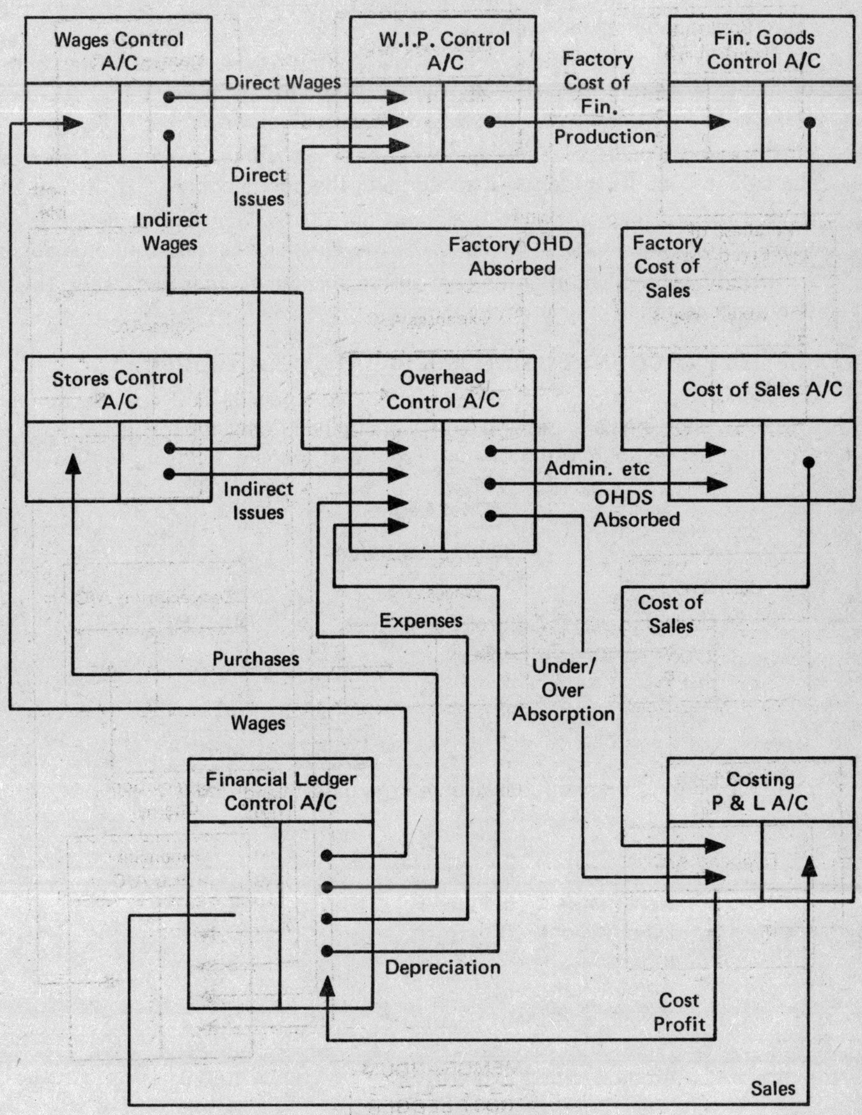

TYPICAL ACCOUNTING ENTRIES IN AN INTERLOCKING SYSTEM WITH
SEPARATE FINANCIAL & COST ACCOUNTS
Figure 2

Notes on the Cost Ledger

a. Comparison with Figure 1 will show a similar pattern of accounts in both integral and interlocking systems.

b. It will be seen that the Financial Ledger Control A/c is a necessary part of the double entry system within the cost ledger (alternative names for this account are General Ledger Control A/c or the Cost Ledger Contra A/c).

c. The balance on the Financial Ledger Control account represents the total of all the balances of the impersonal accounts in the cost ledger.

d. If work of a capital nature is carried out in the factory, this needs to be transferred to the financial accounts via the Financial Ledger Control account.

e. Periodic reconciliation of the cost and financial ledgers is necessary. This is dealt with in detail later in this chapter.

EXAMPLE OF ACCOUNTS USING A SEPARATE COST LEDGER

6. Jackson Assemblies Ltd. operate interlocking financial and cost accounting systems. The following balances and data relate to their Cost Ledger and it is required to record the entries, obtain the Costing Profit and prepare a closing trial balance.

Cost Ledger

Opening trial balance

	£	£
Financial ledger Control A/c		49,521
Stores Ledger Control A/c	8,951	
W-I-P Control A/c	26,367	
Finished Goods Control A/c	14,203	
	49,521	49,521

The following information is available regarding the period's operations.

	£
Raw material purchases	62,280
Direct wages	40,191
Indirect wages	6,280
Administration salaries	11,207
Selling and Distr. Salaries	6,817
Production expenses	9,380
Administration expenses	6,529
Selling and Distribution expenses	4,043
Stores issues – production	43,010
– Factory maintenance	2,005
Admin. maintenance	659
Production overheads absorbed	16,670
Admin overheads absorbed by finished goods	18,493
S + D overheads absorbed by sales	10,621
Factory cost of finished goods	111,032
Cost of Finished Goods sold	137,308
Sales	160,921

Accounting entries in Cost Ledger

Financial Ledger Control A/c

Sales	160,921	Bal.	49,521
Bal. c/f	47,183	Purchases	62,280
		Wages	46,471
		Salaries	18,024
		Prod. exs.	9,380
		Admin exc.	6,529
		S + D exs.	4,043
		Profit	11,856
	208,104		208,104
		Bal.	47,183

Stores Ledger Control A/c

Bal.	8,951	W.I.P.	43,010
F.L. control	62,280	Prod. Ohd.	2,005
		Admin Ohd.	659
		Bal c/f	25,557
	71,231		71,231
Bal.	25,557		

W.I.P. Control A/C

Bal.	26,367		
Issues	43,010	Fin. goods	111,032
Wages	40,191	Bal c/f	15,206
Prod. Ohds	16,670		
	126,238		126,238
Bal. c/f	15,206		

Finished Goods Control A/c

Bal.	14,203		
W.I.P.	111,032	Cost of Sales	137,308
Admin. Ohd.	18,493	Bal. c/f	6,420
	143,728		143,728
Bal c/f	6,420		

Production Overheads Control A/c

Wages	6,280	W.I.P.	16,670
Exps.	9,380	Ohd. adjustmt.	
Stores	2,005	(under recovery)	995
	17,665		17,665

Admin. overhead Control A/c

	£		£
Salaries	11,207		
Expenses	6,529	Fin. goods	18,493
Material	659		
Ohd. adj A/c	98		
	18,493		18,493

Selling + Distr. overhead Control A/c

	£		£
Salaries	6,817	Cost of sales	10,621
Expenses	4,043	Ohd. Adj. A/c	239
	10,860		10,860

Wages Control A/c

	£		£
F.L. Control A/c	46,471	W.I.P.	40,191
		Prod. Ohds.	6,280
	46,471		46,471

Salaries Control A/c

	£		£
F.L. Control A/c	18,024	Adm. Ohds.	11,207
		S + D Ohds	6,817
	18,024		18,024

Overhead Adjustment A/c

	£		£
Prod. Ohds.	995	Admin. Ohds.	98
S + D Ohds	239	P + L	1,136
	1,234		1,234

Cost of Sales A/c

	£		£
Fin. Goods	137,308	P + L	147,929
S + D Ohds.	10,621		
	147,929		147,929

Costing P & L A/c

	£		£
Cost of Sales	147,929	Sales	160,921
Ohd. Adj.	1,136		
Profit	11,856		
	160,921		160,921

Closing Trial Balance

	£	£
Financial ledger Control A/c		47,183
Stores ledger Control A/c	25,557	
W.I.P. Control A/c	15,206	
Finished Goods Control A/c	6,420	
	47,183	47,183

RECONCILIATION OF COST AND FINANCIAL ACCOUNTS

7. Differences can arise between the profits shown by the cost accounts and the financial accounts. Periodically these differences must be reconciled to ensure that there are no errors in either set of accounts.

Differences arise due to several factors:

a. Items appearing in financial accounts and not in cost accounts. Typical examples have been given earlier in the chapter.

b. Variations in the valuations given to stocks.

c. Items appearing only in the cost accounts. These are infrequent and usually relate to imputed charges for such matters as rent and interest.

d. Differences in the treatment of depreciation.

The reconciliation is carried out using a memorandum reconciliation account as shown in the following example.

Example

The profit shown in the financial accounts is £18,592 and for the same period the cost accounts showed a profit of £20,496.

Comparison of the two sets of accounts revealed the following:

Stock Valuations	Cost Accounts	Financial Accounts
Raw Materials	£	£
Opening Stock	6,821	7,259
Closing Stock	5,483	5,128
Finished Goods		
Opening Stock	13,291	12,905
Closing Stock	11,430	11,131

Dividends and interest received of £552 and a loss of £1,750 on the sale of a milling machine were not entered in the cost accounts.

Reconcile the profit figures.

Solution:

Memorandum Reconciliation A/c

	£		£
Profit as per Financial A/cs	18,592	Profit as per cost A/cs	20,496
Stock differences			
	£	Item not credited	
Raw material-opening 438		Dividends + interest recd.	552
closing 355		Stock difference	
Finished Goods closing 299	1,092	Finished Goods-Opening	386
Items not charged in cost accounts			
Loss on sale of machine	1,750		
	£21,434		£21,434

ACCOUNTING FOR STANDARD COSTING SYSTEMS

8. Standard costs and the resulting variances form part of the double entry accounting system. Whether the accounting system is an integrated one or separate financial and cost records are kept, there are common features in the way standard costing is normally dealt with in the accounts.

a. Variances are isolated as early as possible, i.e. as near as possible to the point of occurrence or when the element of cost is charged to production by being debited to the Work-in-Progress A/c.

b. Variance accounts are maintained for each type of variance. Each period these accounts are closed down and the balances transferred to the Costing P + L account.

c. Transfers between the Work-in-Progress, Finished Goods, and Cost of Sales accounts are at standard.

d. Stocks of W.I.P., Finished Goods, and Raw Materials are the balances on the respective accounts and are automatically valued at standard.

A diagram of typical entries in a standard costing system is shown overleaf.

Notes on Figure 3:

a. The general pattern is for the actual amount to be charged to the appropriate control account and the price (or expenditure) variance extracted at that point. The actual quantity (or hours) at the standard price (or rate) is then charged to W.I.P. where the remaining variances relating to efficiency and usage are extracted.

b. For simplicity, only the main entries have been shown on the chart. For example, issues of indirect materials would be charged to the Variable Overhead Control account at actual quantity times standard price.

c. The procedure shown on the chart means that the balances on all stock accounts, stores control, W.I.P. control and Finished Goods are at standard cost.

d. The accounting entries shown relate to unfavourable variances only. This is for clarity and obviously favourable variances do arise. The entries for favourable

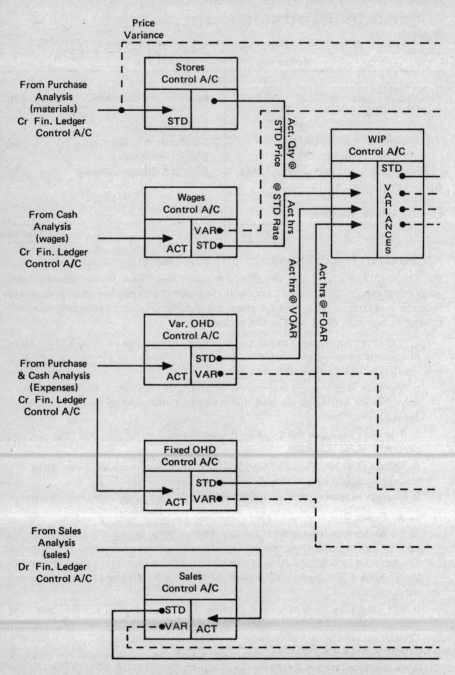

TYPICAL ACCOUNTING ENTRIES IN A STANDARD ABSORPTION COSTING SYSTEM

Figure 3

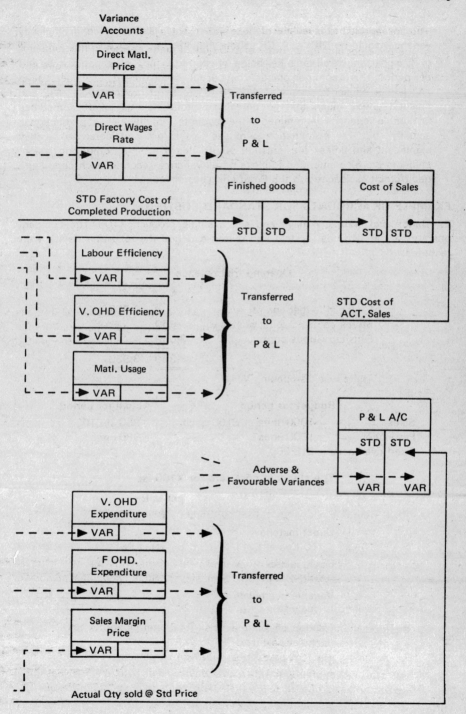

variances would be the reverse of those shown, e.g. a favourable labour efficiency variance would be DR W.I.P. CR Labour Efficiency Variance account.

e. The chart shows all variances being transferred to the P + L account at the end of a period. This is common practice, but because favourable material price, usage and labour efficiency variances relating to stocks of raw materials, WIP and finished goods mean that an unrealised profit may be taken, sometimes favourable variances are retained in the accounts until the relevant production is actually sold. For examination purposes this is not considered to be very significant and unless the question points clearly to some other conclusion, students are recommended to close off all variance accounts each period and debit/credit as required to the Profit and Loss account.

EXAMPLE OF ACCOUNTS FOR STANDARD COSTING

9. Dalton and company make and sell a single product, X100. The company operates a standard cost system and during a period the following details were recorded.

Opening trial balance

	£	£
Financial ledger control A/c		3,930
Stores control A/c (at standard)	850	
Finished Goods control A/c ,,	3,080	
	3,930	3,930

There was no opening W.I.P.

	Budget for period	Actual for period
Sales	1000 units at £100 each	950 at £103
Production	1000 units	980 units
Fixed overheads	£18,000	

The standard cost card for X100 is:

	per unit £
Direct materials (10 Kgs at £2)	20
Direct labour (6 hrs at £2.50)	15
Variable overheads (6 hrs at £4/hr)	24
Fixed overheads (6 hrs at £3/hr)	18
Total standard cost	77
Standard Profit	23
Standard Selling Price	100

During the period the following details were recorded:

	£
Purchases of materials (13,000 Kgs)	26,500
Direct wages (5600 hours)	14,560
Variable overheads	24,192
Fixed overheads	17,850
Material issues to production were 9810 Kgs	

Using the above information it is required to prepare all cost and variance accounts and a profit and loss account and a closing trial balance.

Solution:

The first stage is to calculate the variances.

Cost Variances

Material Price = (13000 x £2) – £26,500	=	£500 Adv.
Material Usage = (9810 – (980 x 10)) x £2	=	£20 Adv.
Labour Rate = (14560 – (5600 x £2.50))	=	£560 Adv.
Labour Efficiency = (5600 – (980 x 6)) x £2.50	=	£700 Fav.
Variable Overhead Expenditure (£24192 – (5600 x £4))	=	£1792 Adv.
Variable Overhead Efficiency (5600 – (980 x 6)) x £4	=	£1120 Fav.
Fixed Overhead Expenditure = £18000 – £17850	=	£150 Fav.
Fixed Overhead Volume = 20 units x £18	=	£360 Adv.

Sales Margin Variance

Standard sales margin = £23 and actual margin = £26

∴ Sales margin price variance
= (£26 – £23) x 950 = £2850 Fav.

Stores Control

Balance	850	WIP	19,620
F.L. control	26,000	Balance	7,230
	26,850		26,850
Balance	7,230		

Financial Ledger Control A/c

Sales	97,850	Balance	3,930
		Purch (std)	26,000 (a)
		Purch variance	500
		Wages	14,560
		Vari. Ohds.	24,192
Balance	12,620	Fixed Ohds.	17,850
		Profit	23,438
	110,470		110,470
		Balance	12,620

Wages Control

F.L. control	14,560	Labour Rate Var.	560
		WIP	14,000
	14,560		14,560

Finished Goods Control

Balance	3,080	Cost of Sales	73,150 (b)
WIP	75,460	Balance c/f	5,390
	78,540		78,540
Balance	5,390		

285

Variable Overhead Control

F.L. control	24,192	Expen. Var.	1,792
		WIP	22,400
	24,192		24,192

Fixed Overhead Control

F.L. control	17,850	Volume	360
Expen. Var.	150	WIP	17,640
	18,000		18,000

Sales Control

Marg Price Var	2,850	F.L. control	97,850
P + L	95,000		
	97,850		97,850

Cost of Sales

Fin. goods	73,150	P + L	73,150

WIP Control

Wages	14,000	Mat. usage var.	20
Lab. Eff. var	700	Fin. goods	75,460 (c)
Material	19,620		
Var. Ohd.	22,400		
Vr. Ohd. Eff. var	1,120		
Fixed Ohd.	17,640		
	75,480		75,480

Variance Accounts

Material Price

F.L. Control	500	P + L	500

Material Usage

WIP	20	P + L	20

Labour Rates

Wage control	560	P + L	560

Labour Efficiency

P + L	700	WIP	700

Variable Overhead Expenditure

Ohd. control	1,792	P + L	1,792

Variable Overhead Efficiency

P + L	1,120	WIP	1,120

Fixed Overhead Expenditure

P + L	150	Ohd. control	150

Fixed Overhead Volume

Ohd. control	360	P + L	360

Sales Margin Price

P + L	2,850	Sales Cont	2,850

Profit Statement

		£
	Sales (at standard)	95,000
Less	Cost of sales (at standard)	73,150
=	Standard Profit on actual sales	21,850
+	Sales margin price variance	2,850
		24,700
Add	Favourable cost variances	
	Fixed Overhead Expenditure	150
	Labour Efficiency	700
	Variable Ohd efficiency	1,120 1,970
		26,670

		£	
Less Unfavourable cost variances			
Materials price	500		
Labour rate	560		
Material usage	20		
Fixed overhead volume	360		
Variable Ohd efficiency	1,792	3,232	
		23,438	(to Fin. Ledg. Con)

Closing trial balance

	£	£
Financial ledger control		12,620
Stores Control	7,230	
Finished Goods Control	5,390	
	12,620	12,620

Notes on accounts:

a. Price variance segregated so all materials carried at standard.

b. This is standard cost of 950 sales.

c. This is standard cost of 980 production.

Note:

In addition to the accounts and profit statement shown above management would also require an explanation of the difference between the actual results and the original budget.

ACCOUNTING FOR STANDARD MARGINAL COSTING

10. This follows very similar lines to standard absorption costing as previously described. Because fixed overheads are not included in the production accounts (WIP, Finished Goods and Cost of Sales) the following differences are necessary.

a. No fixed overheads are charged to WIP, finished goods and cost of sales.

b. The valuations of all types of stock, WIP, finished goods etc. will be at standard marginal cost.

c. Budgeted fixed overheads will be transferred directly from fixed overhead control to P + L, i.e. Cr Fixed overhead control Dr P + L, whilst any balance on the Fixed overhead control in comparison to actual fixed overheads, represents the Fixed Overhead Expenditure variance.

d. The standard sales margin becomes the standard sales contribution.

SUMMARY

11. a. Integrated cost accounts are a single system of accounting with no divisions between financial and cost accounts.

b. Interlocking cost accounts are systems in which separate financial accounts and cost accounts are kept.

c. Separate accounts are frequently encountered and are controlled ('interlocked') by a memorandum Cost Ledger Control A/c in the financial ledger and a Financial Ledger Control account in the cost ledger. The Financial Ledger Control

A/c in the cost ledger forms part of the double entry system within the cost ledger.

d. Where separate cost and financial ledgers are maintained, periodic reconciliation is necessary.

e. When standard costing is employed, the resulting variances form part of the double entry system.

f. Typically variances are isolated as early as possible and the flows through the main accounts (WIP, finished goods etc.) are at standard cost.

POINTS TO NOTE

12. a. Whatever system is adopted, proper double entry standards should be maintained in the accounting system.

b. Even when the accounting system is computerised the principles shown regarding the accounting entries still apply.

SELF REVIEW QUESTIONS

1. What are integrated cost accounts? (2)

2. What are interlocking cost accounts? (2)

3. Using integrated cost accounts is the emphasis on functional analysis or analysis by nature of expense? (3)

4. Using interlocking cost accounts what is the 'Cost Ledger Control A/c' in the Financial ledger? (5)

5. Why do differences arise between the cost and financial accounts? (7)

6. What are the major features of accounting for standard costs? (8)

7. What accounting differences arise when standard marginal costing is used? (10)

EXAMINATION QUESTIONS

1. C. D. Ltd, a company engaged in the manufacture of specialist marine engines, operates an historic job cost accounting system which is not integrated with the financial accounts.

At the beginning of May 1980 the opening balances in the Cost Ledger were:

	£
Stores Ledger Control Account	85,400
Work in Progress Control Account	167,350
Finished Goods Control Account	49,250
Cost Ledger Control Account	302,000

During the month the following transactions took place:

	£
Materials: Purchases	42,700
Issues – to production	63,400
– to general maintenance	1,450
– to construction of manufacturing equipment	7,650
Factory Wages: Total gross wages paid	124,000

£12,500 of the above gross wages were incurred on the construction of manufacturing equipment, £35,750 were indirect wages and the balance were direct.

Production Overheads:

Actual amount incurrred, excluding items shown above, was £152,350; £30,000 was absorbed by the manufacturing equipment under construction and under absorbed overheads written off at the end of the month amounted to £7,550.

Royalty Payments:

One of the engines produced is manufactured under licence. £2,150 is the amount which will be paid to the inventor for the month's production of that particular engine.

Selling Overheads: £22,000

Sales: £410,000

The company's gross profit margin is 25% on factory cost.

At the end of May stocks of work in progress had increased by £12,000. The manufacturing equipment under construction was completed within the month, and transferred out of the cost ledger at the end of the month.

Required:

Prepare the relevant control accounts, costing profit and loss account, and any other accounts you consider necessary to record the above transactions in the cost ledger for May 1980.

(ACCA, Costing, June 1980).

2.   The following totals were extracted from a weekly payroll for 400 employees at a production unit.

	£	£
Gross pay		32,000
Deductions:		
Employees' national insurance contributions	1,460	
Superannuation contributions	1,760	
Income tax	4,800	
Trade union dues	60	
Social club	40	
Total		8,120
Net pay		£23,880
Total of employees' and employer's national insurance contributions		£4,600

The wages analysis gave the following summary breakdown of the gross pay.

	Direct workers £	Indirect workers £
Ordinary time	12,000	7,000
Overtime	3,200	2,000
Overtime premium	800	900
Shift allowance	1,600	800
Sick pay	800	200
Idle time	1,100	–
Capital items	1,600*	–

* This represents work on building a special purpose machine for the toolroom and the machine is not yet complete.

You are required to show journal entries (narrations are NOT required) to indicate clearly how each item is dealt with in the accounts.

(ICMA, Cost Accounting 1, May 1979).

3. B Limited operates an integrated accounting system and the following details given relate to one year.

You are required from the details given to:

a. enter in the appropriate ledger accounts the transactions for the year;

b. prepare a profit and loss account for the year; and

c. prepare a balance sheet as at the end of the year.

Trial balance at beginning of the year:

	£000's	£000's
Capital	–	1,000
Reserves	–	200
Creditors	–	150
Expense creditors	–	20
Freehold buildings, at cost	500	–
Plant and machinery, at cost	300	–
Provision for depreciation of plant and machinery	–	100
Stock of: raw materials	220	–
work-in-progress	40	–
finished goods	60	–
Debtors	200	–
Bank	150	–
	1,470	1,470

The following data for the year are given:

	£000's
Materials: purchased on credit	990
returned to suppliers	40
issued to production	850
Production: wages incurred	250
salaries	60
expenses incurred	320
Carriage inwards	45
Provision for depreciation of plant and machinery	50
Production: overhead absorbed	425
Production, at standard cost	1,600
Administration: salaries	100
expenses incurred	260
overhead absorbed in finished goods	380
Selling and distribution: salaries	80
expenses incurred	120
absorbed in cost of sales	210
Finished goods sold	2,000
Sales on credit	2,500
Sales returns	60
Variance: direct material: price (adverse)	35
usage (favourable)	20
direct wages rate (favourable)	15
direct labour efficiency (favourable)	30
production overhead: expenditure (adverse)	25
efficiency (favourable)	40
Abnormal loss of raw material stock, insurance claim agreed and cash received	60
New machinery purchased, paid by cheque	50
Paid: creditors	895
expense creditors	730
Cash discount received from trade creditors	25
Paid wages and salaries	425
Deduction from wages and salaries	50
Received cheques from debtors	2,350
Cash discount allowed	35
Bad debts written off	25

All 'price' variances (i.e. direct material price, direct wages rate, production overhead expenditure) are recorded in the relevant expenditure accounts; 'quantity' variances (i.e. direct material usage, direct labour efficiency, production overhead efficiency) are recorded in the work-in-progress account.

(ICMA, Cost Accounting 2, November 1977).

4.   You are required, using the information given below for the month of April 1980, in respect of D Manufacturing Company Limited to:

   a. write up the integrated accounts;

   b. prepare a trading profit and loss account for April, 1980;

   c. compile a trial balance as at 30th April, 1980.

1. List of balances as at 1st April, 1980:

	£000
Land and buildings	500
Plant, machinery and office equipment	800
Provision for depreciation, plant, machinery and office equipment	200
Material stores	80
Work-in-progress	40
Finished goods stock	20
Debtors	260
Creditors	100
Bank overdrawn	50
Share capital	1,100
Share premium	200
Profit and loss, appropriation: credit balance	35
Creditor for PAYE and national insurance	15

2. Transactions for the month of April 1980:

	£000
Cash received from debtors	190
Cash paid to creditors	70

	Gross wages £000	PAYE & national insurance £000	
Direct wages paid	40	10	30
Indirect wages paid	20	5	15
Administrative staff salaries paid	30	10	20
Selling staff salaries paid	20	5	15
Cash paid to creditor for PAYE and national insurance			30
Cash paid, expenses: production			20
administration			10
Depreciation: production plant and machinery			20
administrative office equipment			5
Employer's contribution, national insurance: production			5
administration			3
selling			2
Materials received and invoiced			50
Materials price variance, adverse: extracted as materials are received			5
Materials issued to production from stores			40
Materials issued to production maintenance			8
Transfers from work-in-progress to finished goods stock			110
Sales on credit			160
Production cost of goods sold			112

Production overhead is absorbed on the basis of 200% on direct wages.
Administration and selling costs are treated as period costs.

(ICMA, Cost Accounting 1, May 1980).

292

5. a. NIA Limited operates a non-integrated accounting system. At the end of April, the financial accountant has produced the final accounts shown below. Based on these accounts and data supplied by the cost accountant, a reconciliation statement has been prepared, also as shown below:

You are required to prepare the following accounts as they would appear in the cost ledger:

  i. raw material stores;
  ii. work-in-progress;
  iii. finished goods.

Manufacturing, Trading and Profit and Loss Account, for month of April 1979

	£	£		£
Raw materials:			Cost of goods	
Opening stock	60,500		manufactured,	
Purchases	320,000		carried down	602,000
	380,500			
Closing stock	65,000			
		315,500		
Direct wages		125,000		
Production over-head		160,000		
Work-in-progress:				
Opening stock	36,700			
Closing stock	35,200			
		1,500		
		£602,000		£602,000

	£	£		£
Finished goods:			Sales	1,000,000
Opening stock	45,600			
Goods manu-factured	602,000			
	647,600			
Closing stock	47,600			
		600,000		
Gross profit, carried down		400,000		
		£1,000,000		£1,000,000

	£		£
Administration expenses	110,000	Gross profit, brought down	400,000
Selling and distribution expenses	150,000	Discount re-received	30,000
Discount allowed	50,000		
Debenture interest	20,000		
Net profit	100,000		
	£430,000		£430,000

Statement reconciling the profit of Financial Accounts and
Cost Accounts

	£	£	£
Profit as per financial accounts			100,000
Differences in stock valuation:			
add: Raw materials: closing stock	750		
Work-in-progress: opening stock	900		
Finished goods: opening stock	1,300		
closing stock	500		
		3,450	
less: Raw materials: opening stock	1,100		
Work-in-progress: closing stock	500		
		1,600	
			1,850
Other items			
add: Discount allowed	50,000		
Debenture interest	20,000		
		70,000	
less: Discount received		30,000	
			40,000
			141,850
Production overhead, over-absorbed			2,000
Profit, as per cost accounts			£139,850

b. Explain briefly why you think that the balances of work-in-progress shown in the financial accounts above differ from those in the cost accounts.

(ICMA, Cost Accounting 2, May 1979).

6. The cost accounting profit and loss statement for SC Limited for the four working weeks ended 28th October, 1979 is given below together with other relevant data.

Using the information given and showing clearly your workings, you are required to:

a. Calculate the following:
 i. actual output in units;
 ii. quantity of material E used in production;
 iii. price per tonne of material E;
 iv. man hours worked;
 v. fixed overhead incurred;

b. calculate the fixed overhead:
 i. productivity variance;
 ii. capacity variance;

c. show the work-in-progress control account as it would appear in the cost ledger at 28th October, 1979. Direct materials price and direct wages rate variances are extracted before the prime cost items are charged to work-in-progress.

Profit and Loss Statement
for four weeks ended 28th October, 1979

	£	£	£
Sales			177,500
Standard cost of sales:			
direct materials		63,900	
direct wages		28,400	
fixed overhead		49,700	
			142,000
Standard profit on actual sales			35,500
Variances:			
Direct materials: price	1,440 (F)		
usage	900 (A)		
cost	———	540 (F)	
Direct wages: rate	1,375 (A)		
efficiency	900 (F)		
cost	———	475 (A)	
Fixed overhead: expenditure	150 (F)		
volume	700 (A)		
		550 (A)	
	———		485 (A)
Net profit			£35,015

Note: favourable variances indicated by (F) and adverse variances by (A).

Other relevant data given are as follows:

Details taken from the standard cost of the only product manufactured by SC Limited are as follows:

Direct materials E at £360 per tonne is used to produce 400 units of the product. The basic wage rate of each employee is £2 per hour and the standard time allowed to produce one unit of product is 12 minutes.

Information taken from the budget for the year is as follows:

Production, in units   900,000 per annum
Fixed overhead   £630,000 per annum

There are 50 working weeks in the year and in the production process it is planned that the 90 employees will work 40 hours each week.

(ICMA, Cost Accounting 2, November 1979).

7. The A.B. Engineering Co. Ltd. use a job costing system for batches of machined components, overheads being recovered for Department A by Machine Hour Rate and those for Department B by a percentage on Direct Wages.

The following information has been extracted for 1978.

	Department A		Department B	
	Budget	Actual	Budget	Actual
Direct Labour Hours	40,000	43,000	90,000	95,000
Machine Hours	120,000	122,000	180,000	193,000
Direct Labour Cost	£80,000	£87,000	£153,000	£166,000
Department Overhead	£300,000	£304,000	£267,750	£298,000

a. Calculate the pre-determined departmental rates for overheads which would have been used in 1978.

b. Write up the overhead control accounts for both departments showing clearly how you would deal with any balances remaining on these accounts.

c. Calculate the cost of Job No. X.123 for which the cost office has provided the following information.

	Department A	Department B
Direct Labour Hours	60	80
Machine Hours	148	170
Direct Materials	£900	£500
Direct Labour Cost	£120	£136

d. List briefly the benefits which you think the company could expect from replacing the existing system of costing individual jobs with a system of standard costing.

e. If a standard costing system had been in operation during 1978 show what information you would have supplied to the manager of Department 'A' concerning the under/over absorption of overhead in his department given that the budgeted overhead is 80% fixed and that the total output for the year was equivalent to 119,000 standard machine hours.

(CIFA, Management Accounting, November 1979).

8.   Shown below is one week's basic payroll data for the assembly department of Wooden Ltd, a manufacturer of a range of domestic furniture.

	Direct Workers	Indirect Workers
Total attendance time	800 hours	350 hours
Basic hourly rate of pay	£1.50	£1.00
Overtime hours worked	100 hours	40 hours
Shift Premium	£150	£50
Group Bonus	£160	£70
Employees' deductions:		
Income Tax	£250	£100
National Insurance	£75	£35
Employer's Contributions:		
National Insurance	£125	£55

Overtime, which is paid at basic time rate plus one-half, is used as a means of generally increasing the factory output. However, 20% of the overtime shown above, for both direct and indirect workers, was incurred at the specific request of a special customer who requires, and is paying for, a particular batch of coffee tables to be completed quickly.

Analysis of the direct workers' time from returned work tickets shows:

Productive Time		590 hours
Non Productive Time:	Machine Breakdown	50 ,,
	Waiting for Materials	40 ,,
	Waiting for Instructions	45 ,,
	Idle Time	75 ,,

Required:

a. Assuming the company operates an historical batch costing system, fully integrated with the financial accounts, write up the assembly department's wages, work in progress and production overhead control accounts, and other relevant accounts.

b. Explain the reasons for, and effect on product costs of, your treatment of the following items:
    i.   Employer's National Insurance Contributions
    ii. Group Bonus
    iii. Overtime Earnings.

(ACCA, Costing, June 1979).

27 Uniform Costing

INTRODUCTION

1. This chapter defines uniform costing and discusses its major objectives. The features necessary for a system to be classed as uniform are described and the advantages and disadvantages of uniform systems are given.

UNIFORM COSTING DEFINED

2. This can be defined as, "the use by several undertakings of the same costing systems, i.e. the same basic costing methods and superimposed principles and techniques". *Terminology*.

Uniform costing systems do not, in general, contain novel or advanced features. Rather they ensure that there are similar costing foundations and reports in a number of organisations. Uniform costing may be employed by members of the same group, various local authorities, or members of the same trade association. Examples of the application of uniform costing systems include: the printing, hotel and dairy industries, retail and wholesale groups with multiple outlets etc.

OBJECTIVES

3. The major objectives of uniform costing are,

a. To promote uniformity of costing methods so that valid cost comparisons can be made between organisations.

b. To serve as a basis for competitive but non-destructive bidding.

c. To eliminate inefficiencies and promote good practices revealed by the cost comparisons.

d. To serve as a basis for government subsidies or grants which need similar costing systems to ensure equitable distribution.

FEATURES OF UNIFORM COSTING SYSTEMS

4. There is no hard and fast rule which determines what is a uniform costing system. However, it would be generally accepted that systems which follow agreed guidelines in the areas given below would be classed as uniform systems.

a. **Cost statements and reports.**
These should be organised and laid out in a similar fashion so that each element of cost/revenue can be compared easily.

b. **Accounting periods.**
There must be agreement on whether calendar months or 4 week months will be used. Invariably there will be a standard accounting calendar.

c. **Cost classification.**
An agreed classification system must be used so that similar items will be classified in the same manner by all concerned. This will avoid an item being classified by some as indirect and others as direct.

d. **Valuation bases.**
There must be agreement of the methods of valuing stocks and W.I.P. and of the methods of charging stores issues e.g. will FIFO, LIFO etc be used.

e. **Asset valuation.**
There must be agreement on the basis for fixed asset valuations e.g. pure historical cost or revaluation at agreed periods.

f. **Depreciation.**
Both the method (reducing balance or straight line) and the actual rates for each type of asset must be agreed.

g. **Costing principles and techniques.**
There will need to be full agreement on the methods of cost build-up and whether marginal/absorption/standard costing will be used.

h. **Bases of apportionment and absorption.**
When the type of system (marginal, absorption) is agreed, then there will have to be agreement on the way costs are apportioned to cost centres and on the way overheads will be absorbed into products. For example, will overheads be absorbed on units of production, labour hours, machine hours? What will be the basis of apportioning service costs to production cost centres?

ADVANTAGES OF UNIFORM COSTING

5. a. **Cost comparability.**
This is the prime advantage. Because similar principles, bases and valuations are used, genuine cost comparisons can be made between different firms or organisations.

b. **Professional expertise.**
Frequently uniform costing systems are designed by consultants or senior, experienced accountants employed by an association. In this way the systems are soundly developed to high professional standards in a manner which would be too expensive for a single organisation, particularly one operating on a small scale.

c. **Basis for data processing.**
Uniform costing systems make it easier to computerise the accounting system of the various organisations. Similar cost classifications and report layouts considerably reduce the systems and programming effort required.

d. **Staffing costs and staff flexibility.**
Because of the similar nature of the costing systems it may be possible to use lower grade staff in the separate organisations with qualified, senior personnel at headquarters. Also transferability between organisations may be facilitated.

DISADVANTAGES OF UNIFORM COSTING

6. a. **Inappropriateness to the individual organisation.** Where members of a trade association use uniform costing, the chosen system may not suit every firm, particularly where there is a range of sizes and structures. Frequently a tailor made system would be better for particular organisations.

b. **Inflexibility.**
Uniform costing systems, like most centralised systems, are slow to adapt to changing conditions and demands upon them.

SUMMARY

7. a. Uniform costing is the use by a number of undertakings of the same costing methods, principles and techniques.

b. The major objectives are to enable cost comparisons to be made, to serve as a basis for competitive bidding and to eliminate inefficiencies.

c. The major features of uniform costing include: similar cost statements, standard accounting periods, agreed cost classifications and valuation bases and agreed costing principles and techniques.

d. The major advantages are: genuine cost comparability, high professional standards, possibly lower staff costs and greater staff interchangeability.

e. The disadvantages are: possible inappropriateness to particular organisations and possible inflexibility in relation to changing circumstances.

SELF REVIEW QUESTIONS

1. What is uniform costing? (2)
2. What are the objectives of uniform costing? (3)
3. What are the major features which determine whether a system can be classed as uniform? (4)
4. What are the advantages and disadvantages of uniform costing? (5 & 6)

EXAMINATION QUESTION

1. a. Write a brief note to show clearly the distinction between service (or operating) costing and uniform costing.

    b. As assistant to the accountant of a public passenger transport authority, you have been asked to:
    i.   prepare a statement showing the profitability of routes R1, R2 and R3 including the contribution per vehicle and contribution per mile after deducting all direct costs;
    ii.   comment on a proposal that route R3 be discontinued;
    iii. comment on a proposal to reduce the service on route R3 by half on the assumption that only 4 vehicles would be used, operating for a total of 100,000 miles per annum and that the estimated revenue from passengers would be reduced by £40,000 per annum. (You may assume that any surplus vehicles could be readily sold for their written down values.)

The latest information available for the last twelve months is as follows:

Routes	R1	R2	R3	Total
Number of vehicles used	12	16	8	36
Total mileage on each route in thousands	300	400	200	900
	£000	£000	£000	£000
Revenue from passengers	210	296	116	622
Direct costs – variable	150	200	100	450
Direct costs – fixed (specific to vehicles)	36	48	24	108
Fixed costs – apportioned (garage maintenance and administration)	24	32	16	72

(ICMA, Cost Accounting 1, May 1980).

Appendix of Examination Questions
without answers

For use in the Classroom situation or as *extra* revision when the manual is used for independent study.

1. Meklect Limited produce two types of lawnmower, a mechanical model, and an electric model. The company's trading summary for the year recently ended is as follows:

	£	£
Sales		550,000
Direct material and labour	389,000	
Factory Overhead	40,000	
Administration Overhead	30,000	
Marketing Overhead	16,500	
		475,500
Profit		£74,500

The directors consider the profit/sales ratio (13.54%) to be inadequate and have asked you to analyse the trading summary in order to determine the profitability of each of the two models.

Your investigation reveals:

1. Sales for the year were

	£
5,000 mechanical models	325,000
3,000 electric models	225,000

2. Opening stocks of raw material were £45,000 and closing stocks £54,000. Purchases during the year were £324,000.

3. £150,000 of material was used in the production of mechanical models and the remainder on the electric models.

4. The piecework labour rate is £10 for a mechanical model and £8 for an electric model.

5. Included in Factory Overhead are the following costs with indications of the directors' views of their apportionment:

	£	Mechanical	Electric
Indirect labour	15,000	one-third	two-thirds
Power	6,500	three-fifths	two-fifths
Depreciation	12,600	three-sevenths	four-sevenths

The remaining Factory Overhead is to be apportioned equally.

6. Administration Overhead includes a computer bureau's charge of £11,000 for producing sales invoices; this charge is to be apportioned according to invoiced sales value; the remaining Administration Overhead is to be apportioned equally to the two models.

7. Marketing Overhead is to be borne by the two models in proportion to invoiced sales values.

8. Finished Stocks and Work in Progress were the same at the end of the year as they were at the beginning.

You are required to produce statements to show:

a. the trading results for each model

b. The unit cost and profit of each model, analysing cost as follows:

Direct Material
Direct Labour
Factory Overhead
Administration Overhead
Marketing Overhead

and to add brief comments which you think may be helpful to the directors.
(ACCA, Costing, December 1977).

2. The Managing Director of your company has been looking at the company's last Balance Sheet and is concerned at the high level of stocks contained in the working capital. In particular he considers the control of raw material stocks is relatively inefficient and has asked you to report on the fixing of economic levels of stock holding.

The company is an engineering company manufacturing components for which there is a regular demand and raw material stocks comprise a large range of items of varying types and values.

Prepare a short report to the Managing Director and in doing so you should state:

a. The stock levels you would fix and the factors that would influence the fixing of these levels.

b. How these levels would operate.

c. The major advantages to be derived from such a system.

(CIPFA, Management Accounting, November 1977).

3. For the purpose of measuring business income it has been suggested that 'the use of LIFO and replacement cost depreciation will almost completely adjust for the misleading result obtained by applying the historical cost convention.'

You are required to:

a. explain what is meant by 'the misleading result obtained by applying the historical cost convention';

b. provide definitions of
i. LIFO
ii. replacement cost depreciation;

c. explain how the use of the principles referred to will 'almost completely adjust for the misleading result obtained by applying the historical cost convention'.

(ACCA, Costing, June 1977).

4. You have recently been appointed accountant to a general engineering firm engaged in the production of special purpose machines. Orders are obtained by the firm's technical representatives who, having ascertained customers' needs provide the necessary information to the Estimator who prepares and submits the required quotation.

Recent trading results have been unsatisfactory, and the management feel that a costing system would provide greater opportunity for control and would help to improve the firm's profitability.

You have been requested to install a suitable costing system. How would you proceed?

(ACCA, Costing, June 1977).

5. A company selling chemicals direct to farmers remunerates its field sales force on a commission and year end bonus basis. The commission is 20% of standard gross margin (planned selling price less the standard cost of goods sold on a full absorption cost basis), contingent only on the collection of the account. A customer's credit is approved by the company's credit department. Price concessions are granted on occasion by the top sales management, but sales commission is not reduced by the granting of such discounts. A year end bonus of 15% of commissions earned is paid to salesmen who equal or exceed their annual sales target or quota. The annual sales target is usually established by applying approximately a 5% increase to the previous year's sales.

You are required to state with reasons:

a. what features of this remuneration plan are likely to be effective in motivating the salesmen to help meet the company's goals of higher profits and return on investment, and

b. what features are likely to be counter effective.

(ICA, Management Accounting, December 1976).

6. A manufacturing company has two production departments, viz. Machining and Assembly, and two service departments, viz. Tooling and Maintenance.

The budgeted monthly activity level of the Machining Department is 400 machine hours and the budgeted overhead cost £16,000. The Assembly Department's overhead budget is £9,600 per month during which 2,400 direct labour hours are expected to be worked.

In determining the overhead budgets of the production departments, the expenses of the service departments were dealt with as follows:

Tooling	70% to Machining
	20% to Assembly
	10% to Maintenance
Maintenance	50% to Machining
	30% to Assembly
	20% to Tooling

During May 1978, the Machining Department booked 415 hours of machine time to production, and the Assembly Department booked 2,350 direct labour hours.

Overhead incurred during the month was as follows:

	Machining £	Assembly £	Tooling £	Maintenance £
Material	4,600	5,200	1,800	600
Labour	6,100	1,200	2,700	1,600
Miscellaneous	700	900	500	300

You are required to:

a. prepare the overhead account for each production department showing the

303

amount of any over/under absorption and its disposition;

b. identify the causes which gave rise to the over/under absorption in each department, and state the amount attributable to each cause.

(ACCA, Costing June 1978).

7. A.B. Limited has produced the following budget trading account for the year ending 31 March 1977:

	£	£
Sales value of production		1,200,000
Direct materials		300,000
Direct wages		360,000
		660,000
Indirect wages and supervision		
Department A	11,350	
Department B	30,000	
Assembly Department	27,000	
Stores	11,550	
Maintenance Department	10,100	90,000
Maintenance wages		
Department A	4,000	
Department B	12,000	
Assembly Department	6,000	
Stores	1,400	
Maintenance Department	600	24,000
Indirect materials (ex stores)		
Department A	5,000	
Department B	10,000	
Assembly Department	20,000	
Stores	3,000	
Maintenance Department	7,000	45,000
Power		24,000
Rent and Rates		30,000
Lighting and Heating		6,000
Insurance (plant and equipment)		3,000
Depreciation		78,000
Production overhead		300,000
Cost of production		960,000
Budget trading profit		240,000

The following information is also available:—

Department	Power Consumption Kw Hours	Area Occupied Sq Metres	Book Value of Plant & Equipment £	Normal Productive Capacity Direct Hours	Normal Productive Capacity Labour Cost	Normal Productive Capacity Machine Hours
Production:						
Dept. A	40	4,000	100,000	60,000	120,000	40,000
Dept. B	40	2,000	80,000	75,000	150,000	50,000
Assembly	10	6,000	160,000	62,000	90,000	
Service:						
Stores	–	1,000	20,000			
Maintenance	10	2,000	40,000			

You are required to:—

a. Prepare an overhead analysis for the year ended 31 March 1977 using, where necessary, the most appropriate basis of apportionment.

b. Apportion costs of each service department to the three production departments. Maintenance department costs to be apportioned on the basis of the maintenance wages budgeted for each production department.

(CIPFA, Management Accounting, November 1977).

8. Due to recession in its industry, which has caused a reduction in its sales, a manufacturing company is proposing to reduce by one-fifth its productive capacity, as measured in terms of the number of direct labour hours of its operators.

It is considering doing this by either:

a. putting some of its operators on short time; or

b. making a number of its operators redundant through dismissal.

You are required to compare and contrast in tabular form the effects that each course of action is likely to have on the composition and level of the company's total annual:

    i.   direct materials cost;

    ii. direct wages;

    iii. production overhead;

    iv. other (non-production) overhead.

(ICMA, Cost Accounting 2, May 1976).

9. a. Recent regulations affecting pay policies are causing many businesses to re-examine the use of incentive schemes as a method of remunerating employees. Discuss the general principles which should be applied to incentive schemes.

b. Certain organisations, for example car manufacturers, have abandoned premium bonus schemes and piece work schemes and substituted a 'high day rate' system. List the advantages and disadvantages expected from following such a policy.

(ICMA, Cost Accounting 1, November 1977).

10. a. In the context of the output from a factory or group of workers, define and distinguish 'production' and 'productivity'.

b. X Y and Z are the members of a team making metal brackets. The expected output of the team is 6,000 brackets per week, each member working a 40 hour week and being paid a basic rate of £1.75 for each hour worked. A bonus of 50% of the team's productivity index in excess of 100 is added as a percentage to the basic hourly rate.

During week No. 50, X worked 40 hours, Y 39 hours and Z 38 hours and the output for the week was 6,786 brackets.

You are required to calculate for week No. 50:

    i.   the team's productivity index

    ii. the effective hourly rate paid to the operatives

    iii. the wages rate and efficiency variances of the team

c. Name the type of bonus scheme under which the members of the team are remunerated and demonstrate your understanding of the characteristics of that scheme by reference to your answer to (b).

(ACCA, Costing, December 1977).

11. a. Define and illustrate by means of simple arithmetical examples:

    i.   contribution/sales ratio

    ii. margin of safety

b. Demonstrate the relationship between a firm's contribution/sales ratio, its percentage margin of safety, and its profit/sales ratio.

c. What is the significance of a firm's margin of safety?

d. The following details relate to product X

	£	£
Selling Price		120
Costs:		
Material	60	
Labour	15	
Variable Overhead	5	
Fixed Overhead	10	
	—	90
Profit		£30

During the forthcoming year it is expected that material costs will increase by 10%, wages by 33⅓% and other costs by 20%.

You are required to calculate the percentage increase in the selling price of X which would maintain the firm's contribution/sales ratio.

(ACCA, Costing, December 1977).

12. a. Explain briefly the distinction between joint products and by-products.

b. Discuss briefly the problems involved in calculating the cost of manufacture of joint products with particular reference to the apportionment of pre-separation point costs.

A common method of apportioning these pre-separation point costs is by physical measurement; outline two other methods.

c. In a process line of the JP Manufacturing Company Limited, three joint products are produced. For the month of October the following data were available:

Product:	X	Y	Z
Sales price per kilogram	£5	£10	£20
Post-separation point costs	£10,000	£5,000	£15,000
Output in kilograms	2,500	1,000	1,500

Pre-separation point costs amounted to £20,000.

The joint products are manufactured in one common process, after which they are separated and may undergo further individual processing. The pre-separation point costs are apportioned to joint products, according to weight.

You are required:

i. to prepare a statement showing the estimated profit or loss for each product and in total;

ii. as an alternative to the costing system used in (i) above, to present a statement which will determine the maximum profit from the production of these joint products.

The sales value of each product at separation point is as follows:

$$X = £3 \qquad Y = £4 \qquad Z = £6$$

(ICMA, Cost Accounting 2, November 1977).

13. a. The standard processing loss in refining certain basic materials into an industrial cleaning compound is 15%, this scrap being sold for 50p per kg.

At the beginning of Period 6, 8,000 kg of basic material was put into a process, the output of which was 7,000 kg of cleaning compound. The basic material cost 80p per kg, wages of process operators amounted to £1,200 and overhead applied to the process was £480.

Prepare the necessary accounts to show the results of the process.

b. The production of a product known as a Tojo requires the treatment of input units through three distinct processes at each of which refining material is added and labour and overhead costs are incurred.

Work in progress at the beginning of Period 9 consisted of 8,000 input units which had passed through the first process, the cost to that point being £96,000. During Period 9, refining material which cost £31,594 was put into the process and labour costs amounted to £23,940. Process Overhead is applied at the rate of 40% of process labour.

7,200 units were completed during the Period and transferred to Process 3. Of the remainder, the firm's Chief Chemist estimated that in respect of refining material, labour and overhead, half were 75% complete at the end of Period 9, and the other half, 40% complete.

You are required to write up Process 2 Account for Period 9 showing clearly the cost to be transferred to Process 3, and the value of the work in progress at the end of the period.

(ACCA, Costing, December 1977).

14. a. In process costing show how and why you would distinguish between joint products and by-products giving examples of each.

b. A chemical company produces products X, Y and Z and the following details relate to their production for the month of March 1979.

Product	X	Y	Z
Selling price per kilo	£12	£6	£1.50
Output in kilos	2,500	1,500	200
Further processing costs	£10,000	£1,500	£40
Pre-separation point costs:			
Materials	£13,040		
Labour	£9,480		
O/H	£3,740		
	£26,260		

It is the company's practice to apportion joint product costs on the basis of physical quantities. As the newly appointed accountant to this company, you are required to:

    i.   produce a statement of Profit and Loss for each of the joint products;

    ii.   Reconsider the company's treatment of joint costs and produce an alternative solution;

    iii. Discuss the Managing Director's contention that such statements are meaningless as a basis for decision making.

(CIPFA, Management Accounting, June 1979).

15. A company manufactures a variety of liquids which pass through a number of processes. One of these products, P, passes through processes 1, 2 and 4 before being transferred to the finished goods warehouse.

You are required, from the details given below, to prepare accounts for the month of October 1978 for:

    a. process 4;

    b. abnormal loss/gain;

    c. finished goods.

Data for process 4, October 1978:

	Cost £
Work in process, 1st October, 1978: 6,000 units	19,440
degree of completion:	
Direct materials added 60%	
Direct wages and production overhead 40%	
Transferred from process 2:	
48,000 units at £2.30 per unit	
Transferred to finished goods: 46,500 units	
Incurred: Direct materials added	27,180
Direct wages	18,240
Production overhead	36,480
Work in process, 31st October, 1978: 4,000 units	
degree of completion:	
Direct materials added 50%	
Direct wages and production overhead 30%	
Normal loss in process: 6% of units	
in opening stock plus transfers from process 2	
less closing stock	

At a certain stage in the process, it is convenient for the quality control inspector to examine the product and where necessary reject it. Rejected products are then sold for £0.80 per unit. During October 1978 an actual loss of 7% was incurred, with product P having reached the following stage of production:

               Direct materials added   80%

               Direct wages and production overhead   60%

(ICMA, Cost Accounting 2, November 1978).

16. A concentrated liquid fertilizer is manufactured by passing chemicals through two consecutive processes. Stores record cards for the chemical ingredients used exclusively by the first process show the following data for May 1979:

	Opening stock	4,000 litres	£10,800
	Closing stock	8,000 litres	£24,200
	Receipts into store	20,000 litres	£61,000

Other process data for May is tabulated below.

	Process 1	Process 2
Direct Labour	£4,880	£6,000
Direct Expenses	£4,270	–
Overhead Absorption Rates	250% of Direct Labour	100% of Direct Labour
Output	8,000 litres	7,500 litres
Opening stock of Work in Process	Nil	Nil
Closing stock of Work in Process	5,600 litres	Nil
Normal Yield	85% of input	90% of input
Scrap Value of Loss	Nil	Nil

In Process 1 the closing stock of work in process has just passed through inspection, which is at the stage where materials and conversion costs are 100% and 75% complete respectively.

In Process 2 inspection is the final operation.

Required:

a. Prepare the relevant accounts to show the results of the processes for May 1979 and present a detailed working paper showing your calculations and any assumptions in arriving at the data shown in those accounts.

b. If supplies of the required chemicals are severely restricted and all production can be sold immediately, briefly explain how you would calculate the total loss to the company if, at the beginning of June, 100 litres of the correct mix of chemicals were spilt on issue to Process 1.

(ACCA, Costing, June 1979).

17. What is meant by 'Differential Cost Analysis'?

A.B.C. Company Limited manufactures a single product which is sold only in the Home Market. A recent market survey undertaken on behalf of the company has revealed that the selling price for each unit of production should be fixed in accordance with the levels of output and their associated costs as follows:–

Expenditure Head	Fixed, Variable or Semi-Variable	Output ('000 Units)						
		10	20	30	40	50	60	70
		£	£	£	£	£	£	£
Materials	Variable	6,000	9,000	13,500	18,000	22,500	27,000	31,500
Labour	Variable	12,000	18,000	27,000	36,000	45,000	60,000	63,000
Overhead:								
Factory	Variable	2,000	3,000	4,500	6,000	7,500	9,000	10,500
Factory	Semi-Variable	4,000	4,000	5,000	5,000	5,000	5,000	5,500
Factory	Fixed	30,000	30,000	30,000	30,000	30,000	30,000	30,000
Selling	Semi-Variable	4,000	4,000	7,000	7,000	7,000	7,000	8,500
Selling	Fixed	12,000	12,000	12,000	12,000	12,000	12,000	12,000
Administra-tion	Fixed	8,000	8,000	8,000	8,000	8,000	8,000	8,000
Total Cost		78,000	88,000	107,000	122,000	137,000	158,000	169,000
Selling Price per Unit		£20	£18	£15	£12	£9	£6	£3

Prepare a Budget Statement which will indicate to Management the total unit cost, the net profit per unit and the total net profit at each level of output. Indicate the level of output that you are recommending.

(CIPFA, Management Accounting, November 1977).

18. JEN Ltd manufactures three products, J E and N which undergo similar production processes and use similar materials and types of labour. The company's forecasted profit Statement for the forthcoming year, as submitted to the Board, is as follows:

	Product J £	Product E £	Product N £	Total £
Sales	1,344,000	840,000	680,000	2,864,000
Direct Materials	336,000	294,000	374,000	1,004,000
Direct Labour	201,600	168,000	136,000	505,600
Variable Overhead	268,800	168,000	204,000	640,800
	806,400	630,000	714,000	2,150,400
Contribution	537,600	210,000	(34,000)	713,600
Fixed Overhead				113,600
Profit				£600,000

At a Board meeting, a decision was made to discontinue the production of Product N as demand was falling and there was no possibility of increasing the selling price. Prospects for the other two products, however, were bright and the company had, in the past, been unable to meet the demand. It was decided, therefore, that the labour force released should be used to increase production of Products J and E; 60% of the budgeted labour for Product N being transferred to J and the remainder to E. The increased production of J and E is not expected to change their cost/selling price relationships.

You are required to prepare the revised forecast Profit Statement and to comment briefly upon the effect of the Board's decision.

(ACCA, Costing, June 1977).

19. The summarised operating statements of Marcosts Limited for the years ended 31 October 1977 and 1978 are as follows:

	Year ended 31 October	
	1977	**1978**
	£	£
Sales	160,000	184,800
Factory variable cost of sales:		
Material	80,000	85,350
Labour	30,000	35,450
Factory Services	20,000	21,000
	130,000	141,800
Contribution	30,000	43,000
Administration and Marketing Costs	10,000	9,000
Net Profit	£20,000	£34,000

The following additional information is available:

1. There were no stocks of finished goods, raw material or work in progress at the beginning or end of either year.

2. Selling prices were 5% higher in 1977/78 than in 1976/77.

3. Suppliers of material granted a trade discount of 2% on the later year's purchases in consideration of purchase undertakings given.

4. The labour force were awarded an increase of 15% from 1 November 1977 in consideration of increased productivity undertakings.

5. Factory services were improved as a result of a consultant's investigation, but costs increased generally by 5%.

6. Administration and Marketing costs whilst regarded as not variable with activity level were influenced by the facts referred to in (7), (8) and (9) below.

7. An area of unused office space was sublet from 1 November 1977 for £3,400 per annum.

8. A non-routine market research exercise was undertaken in 1977/78 the cost being £2,000.

9. Office Salaries (£4,000 in 1976/77) were increased by 10% from 1 November 1977.

You are required to prepare a detailed statement of the factors which gave rise to the increase of £14,000 in the profit for 1977/78.

(ACCA, Costing, December 1978).

20. Ayeco Limited, with a central organisation in Ayetown, has three manufacturing units. One is in Beetown, the second in Ceetown and the third in Deetown. The company manufactures and sells an air-conditioner under the brand-name of Ayecool at a price of £200. It is unable to utilise fully its manufacturing capacity.

Summarised profit and loss statements for the year are shown below:

	Beetown	Ceetown	Deetown	Total
	£000	£000	£000	£000
Costs:				
Direct materials	200	800	400	1,400
Direct wages	200	900	350	1,450
Production overhead:				
variable	50	300	150	500
fixed	200	600	300	1,100
	650	2,600	1,200	4,450
Sub-total				
Selling overhead:				
variable	25	200	100	325
fixed	75	250	150	475
Administration				
overhead	100	450	200	750
Sub-total	850	3,500	1,650	6,000
Central organisation				
costs	50	200	100	350
Total	900	3,700	1,750	6,350
Profit	100	300	250	650
Sales	1,000	4,000	2,000	7,000

The management of the company has to decide whether, or not, to renew the lease of the property at Beetown, which expires next year. The company has been offered an extension to the lease at an additional cost of £50,000 per annum. This situation concerning the lease has been known for some time, so the accountant has collected relevant information to aid the decision. It is estimated that the cost of closing down Beetown would be offset by the surplus obtained by the sale of plant, machinery and stocks.

If Ayeco Limited does not renew the lease of the Beetown property it can:

1. accept an offer from Zeeco Limited, a competitor, to take over the manufacture and sales in the Beetown area and pay to Ayeco Limited a commission of £3 for each unit sold;

2. transfer the output at present made in Beetown to either Ceetown or Deetown. Each of these units has sufficient plant capacity to undertake the Beetown output but additional costs in supervision, salaries, storage and maintenance would be incurred. These additional costs are estimated as amounting yearly to £250,000 at Ceetown and to £200,000 at Deetown.

If the Beetown sales connections are transferred to either Ceetown or Deetown, it is estimated that additional transport costs would be incurred in delivering to customers in the region of Beetown, and that these would amount to £15 per unit and £20 per unit respectively.

You are required to:

a. present a statement to the board of directors of Ayeco Limited to show the estimated annual profit which would arise from:
   i.   continuing production at all three sites;
   ii. closing down production at Beetown and accepting the offer of the sales

312

commission from Zeeco Limited;

   iii. transferring Beetown sales to Ceetown;

   iv. transferring Beetown sales to Deetown;

b. comment on your statement, indicating any problems which may arise from the various decisions which the board may decide to take.

(ICMA, Cost Accounting 2, November 1978).

21. A company is asked to quote for a special order to be delivered ex works. Direct material costs per unit of output are:

£

For a total of: 100 : 18 each

               200 : 18 less 10% discount each

               400 : 18 less 20% discount each

The work would be done in two departments:

Department F   employs highly skilled operators paid at £2.50 per hour. Each unit of output requires 6 direct labour hours of work for the first 100 units. However, experience has shown that an 80% learning curve can be expected to operate.

Department G   employs skilled operators paid at £2.00 per hour. Each unit of output requires 3 direct labour hours of work for the first 100 units. Here, too an 80% learning curve is expected.

Overtime in either department is paid at time and a half. No premium for overtime is included in standard manufacturing overhead.

Standard manufacturing overhead per direct labour hour is as follows:

	Department F	Department G
	£	£
Variable	1.00	1.00
Fixed	3.50(a)	2.00(b)

a. based on a budgeted level of 3,000 direct labour hours per period;

b. based on a budgeted level of 2,000 direct labour hours per period;

The special order will require special tooling of £300 which is chargeable to the customer.

If the order received is for 100 or 200 units, the work will have to be done in period No. 8 which, for department F, is already loaded with 2,200 direct labour hours of work. Department G, however, will be working at only around 55% of capacity.

On special orders of this type, it is the company's practice to add the following margins on cost in arriving at selling prices:

	%
Department F	20
Department G	10
Direct materials	2
Sub-contractor's work	2
(when used)	

An outside sub-contractor has offered, irrespective of the size of the order, to do the work of department G on this order for a price of £8 per unit, including collection from and delivery to the works.

You are required to calculate:

a. the price per unit for an order of 100 units if made entirely in the company;

b. the price per unit for an order of 200 units if made entirely in the company;

c. a separate price per unit for an extra 200 units subsequent to the order for 200 in (b) above, thus bringing the total order to 400 units; (N.B. You are to assume that:

    i.   this additional order for the extra 200 units could be done when there are no capacity limitations in either department;

    ii.   the materials supplier would give the full discount for the 400 units.)

d. the change in unit selling price that would result from using the outside sub-contractor instead of department G for an order of:

    i.   100 units
    ii.   200 units
    iii. 400 units.

(ICMA, Management Accounting 1, November 1979).

22. A company manufactures plastic-covered steel fencing in two qualities: standard and heavy gauge. Both products pass through the same processes involving steel-forming and plastic-bonding.

The standard gauge sells at £15 a roll and the heavy gauge at £20 a roll. There is an unlimited market for the standard gauge but outlets for the heavy gauge are limited to 13,000 rolls per year. However, the factory operations of each process are limited to 2,400 hours each per year.

Other relevant data are given below:

Variable costs per roll:

Gauge	Direct material £	Direct wages £	Direct expense £
Standard	5	7	1
Heavy	7	8	2

Processing hours per 100 rolls:

Gauge	Steel-forming	Plastic-bonding
Standard	6	4
Heavy	8	12

Agreement has been reached on revised working methods that will increase output of all processes by 10%. This could be achieved without additional manpower or longer working hours.

You are required to calculate:

a. the production mix which will maximise total contribution:
    i.   at present output levels; and
    ii.   assuming the 10% production improvement is achieved;

b. the total amount of productivity bonus which will be paid to employees under (a) (ii) on the basis of their receiving 40% of the additional contribution.

(ICMA, Management Accounting 2, November 1979).

23. The following information is extracted from the budgets of two manufacturing companies:—

	Company A £'000s	Company B £'000s
Sales	800	1200
Manufacturing Costs:		
Materials	200	420
Direct Labour	80	180
Fixed Factory Expenses	120	60
Variable Factory Expenses	20	120
Fixed Administration Costs	80	60
Variable Administration Costs	40	120
Fixed Selling Costs	120	60
Variable Selling Costs	60	120
Total Cost	720	1140
Profit	80	60

Using the information stated above:—

a. Prepare a contribution sales graph for each company.

b. Compare and comment on significant conclusions which can be derived from the graphs.

c. Explain the possible effects for each company of a 25% reduction in the availability of materials used, clearly stating any assumptions made.

(CIPFA, Management Accounting, November 1979).

24. Machinings Limited is engaged solely on the production of four components, P, Q, R and S, for Producers Limited of which it is a subsidiary. The budgeted production and component unit costs for the three months commencing 1 January 1979 are as follows:

	P	Q	R	S
Budgeted production	3,000	5,000	2,500	4,500
Costs:	£	£	£	£
Direct material	74	54	50	90
Direct labour	8	6	16	30
Variable overhead	5	10	5	25
Fixed overhead	7	2	4	15

The variable overhead relates exclusively to machine utilisation which costs £5 per hour.

Two of the machines have been found to be defective and unsafe to use and as a result only 24,000 hours of machine time will be available for the forthcoming three month period. However, Producers Limited require the full quantities of components budgeted and to enable this obligation to be met, Machinings Limited has decided to buy in components to meet the shortfall in its own production. Quotations received for components of acceptable quality, subject to minimum orders of 100 are:

P £95;   Q £75;   R £65;   S £175

You have been invited to advise Machinings Limited on the most economical way in which it can fulfil its obligations to Producers Limited, and for this purpose you are required to prepare a statement comparing the budgeted costs for the three month period with the costs applicable to your proposal and to comment upon any matters which you consider ought to receive the attention of management.

(ACCA, Costing, December 1978).

25. AB Limited manufactures two products, P and Q, which are normally made in a standard grade of material.

On some occasions AB Limited receives orders for its products to be made in a much more expensive material, whilst on others customers place orders for the two products but require special material to be used that the customer provides as a free issue. Neither of these variations from the normal procedure alters the conversion cost of the products manufactured.

Data on AB Limited's products are as follows:

Products:	P	Q
Per unit of product:		
Direct materials, in yards	5	10
Direct labour, in man-hours	4	6
	£	£
Selling price:		
using standard material	28	47
using expensive material	68	127
using free issue material	18	27
Cost of material, per yard:	£	
standard	2	
expensive	10	

Rate of pay for direct labour, £1 per hour

Variable overhead is 50% of direct wages

Fixed overhead is absorbed at a rate of £2 per man-hour

Budgeted man-hours per period are 4,400

For each of three successive periods Nos 7, 8 and 9, AB Limited's total output in numbers of each product was identical, but the proportions of each produced in standard material, expensive material, and free issue material varied as shown below. Opening and closing stocks were the same for each period.

Number of units of product:	Period 7		Period 8		Period 9	
	P	Q	P	Q	P	Q
Made in:						
standard material	300	300	200	100	250	100
expensive material	100	50	300	250	50	50
free issue material	100	50	–	50	200	250
Total	500	400	500	400	500	400

AB Limited prepares periodic accounts, and the managing director views with special interest the ratio of profit as a percentage of sales.

You are required to:

a. calculate the percentage of profit to sales for each of periods 7, 8 and 9;

b. state whether or not you consider the ratio of profit to sales to be a satisfactory index of periodic performance for AB Limited; explain very briefly your views;

c. state what other indices of profit performance (that can be drawn from the data available in this question) the managing director of AB Limited could advantageously use. List their advantages over the percentage of profit to sales.

(ICMA, Cost Accounting 2, May 1976).

26. The trading results of Bloggs & Co, manufacturers of the 'Bloggett', for the two years ended 31 May 1976 and 1977 are set out below:

	Year ended 31 May			
	1976		**1977**	
	£'000		**£'000**	
Sales		880		1,188
Costs of Goods sold				
Direct Material	352		500	
Direct Labour	220		330	
		572		830
Gross profit		308		358
Marketing Costs	66		100	
Administration Costs	42		58	
		108		158
Net Profit		£200		£200

Your enquiries reveal the following:

a. the unit selling price of the Bloggett was 12½% higher in 1976-77 than in 1975-76;

b. there were no stocks or work-in-progress at the beginning or end of either year;

c. Marketing costs vary in relation to quantity sold;

d. Administration costs are 'fixed' in the sense that they do not vary in relation to activity levels.

Using the 1975-76 figures as a basis, you are required to explain with supporting calculations, why the increased turnover in 1976-77 did not result in an increase in net profit.

(ACCA, Costing, June 1977).

27. A company located in London acts as a distributor for a range of specialist products that it sells to retailers throughout the United Kingdom.

The products vary considerably, and orders from retailers consist typically of a mixture of the products in the range. All despatches are made to retailers by hired road transport.

Hitherto the company has sent goods to retailers without charging for delivery, but due to increases in carriage costs it now proposes to place a bottom limit on free delivery orders. The limit proposed is £20 per order.

Data on the company's products are as follows:

	Per pack		
Product	Selling price £	Direct cost £	Weight kilograms
A	1.50	0.75	1.0
B	7.50	5.50	6.0
C	6.50	4.20	13.5
D	15.00	8.50	12.0
E	16.00	11.60	16.0
F	4.50	3.50	4.0
G	3.50	3.00	5.0

Carriage costs per delivery, for an average distance of 150 miles, are:

Weight kilograms	Cost £
10 or less	1.3
over 10 but not above 15	1.5
over 15 but not above 20	1.8
over 20 but not above 25	2.0
over 25 but not above 30	2.2
over 30 but not above 35	2.4
over 35 but not above 40	2.7
over 40 but not above 45	2.9

The company is considering making all sales to retailers in the North (200 or more miles from London) through a sub-distributor who has his own sales force. The company would make bulk deliveries fortnightly to the sub-distributor, but would continue to collect payment of accounts from retailers.

You are required to:

a. show the percentage contribution to sales for each product and rank them in descending order;

b. calculate, to one decimal place, the profits that would result from each of seven free delivery orders (for an average distance of 150 miles), the first being for £20's worth of product A, the second for £20's worth of B, the third for £20's worth of C, and so on through to the seventh order for £20's worth of G; (NB: Assume that packs can be split to make a £20 order).

c. state for which products £20 would be a suitable limit for free delivery if the company's criterion is that carriage costs (for an average distance of 150 miles) should not exceed one-third of the contribution provided by that product;

d. list the costs that the company would need to consider if it wished to decide what commission it could afford to pay to the sub-distributor in the North.

(ICMA, Cost Accounting 2, May 1976).

28. IS Limited produces an industrial solvent by means of a process through which various ingredients are mixed and changed in form, the output being in containers of 50-litre volume which have a selling price of £15 per container.

The input ingredients cost £10 per 50-litre container; wages, which are regarded as fixed costs amount to £2,000 per week. The production rate is 60 containers per hour; theoretical production time 40 hours per week. For some time plant breakdowns have resulted in a loss of ten hours per week on average and the production manager has suggested that preventive maintenance would reduce this idle time and the consequent lost production. Two alternatives have been suggested, viz.:

a. to have preventive maintenance carried out by a team of engineers working in the evenings, the cost being £800 per week which it is expected would reduce breakdown time to 20% of its current level;

b. to contract out the preventive maintenance to a firm which would carry out the work on Saturday mornings for a weekly fee of £300. A saving of half the breakdown time could be expected to result from this arrangement.

You are required to:
    i.   prepare a statement which would assist management to decide whether

to continue as at present or to adopt one or other of the two alternatives suggested;

ii.   state any other considerations management would probably have in mind in making its decision.

(ACCA, Costing, June 1978).

29. a. What do you understand by the term "limiting factor" when considering production budgets?

b. A company manufactures three products A, B, and C with the following annual production budget:

	A	B	C
Unit of output	6000	3000	5000
Machine hours per output unit	3	4	2
	£	£	£
Direct materials	40,000	36,000	30,000
Direct labour	17,850	18,600	16,300
Direct expense	2,150	3,400	3,700
Variable Overhead	6,000	8,000	4,000
Unit setting price	17.50	32	16

Production is restricted by a shortage of materials common to all three products, this shortage is expected to last for a further two years and the factory is operating below full capacity.

Fixed overhead for the year is estimated at £42,000 and is apportioned to each product on the basis of machine hours used.

Prepare a statement showing, in terms of the limiting factor, the profitability of each product, and calculate the effect on contribution if production is concentrated on the product showing the highest profitability.

(CIPFA, Management Accounting, June 1979).

30. A manufacturing company has two production cost centres, A and B, and one general services cost centre, GS, to which all common costs are charged.

The following data concerning the standard costs of its four products and its annual budgets are available:

Product:	W	X	Y	Z
Per unit:	£	£	£	£
Prime cost	40	70	50	60
Selling price:				
first quality products	148	218	117	148
second quality products	30	36	35	30
Direct labour:	hours	hours	hours	hours
Production cost centre: A	12	14	6	8
B	16	24	8	8
Sales and production, per annum	units	units	units	units
	300	200	600	400

Fixed overhead, per annum:	£
Production cost centre: A	26,400
B	52,800
General services cost centre GS	15,400*

* excludes any loss from second quality products.

Overhead of cost centre GS is apportioned to production cost centres according to their direct labour hours. Overhead is absorbed into product costs by a direct labour hour rate.

The company budgets for 10% of its production as second quality products, which are sold at the prices shown above.

You are required:

a. on the assumption that there were no second quality products, to calculate:
   i.   the cost per unit of each product;
   ii. the total profit budgeted to be earned in the year;

b. on the assumption that second quality products are as budgeted and that loss on these is charged entirely to cost centre GS, to calculate:
   i.   the cost per unit of each product;
   ii. the total profit budgeted to be earned in the year;

c. on the assumption that second quality products are as budgeted but that the income from these is treated entirely as an addition to sales income,

to calculate the total profit budgeted to be earned in the year;

d. on the assumption that second quality products were as budgeted but that sales were only 85% of production in the year, to state whether you would charge against sales for the year the cost of:
   i.   all second quality products manufactured in the year; or
   ii. only those second quality products that had been sold in the year;

and to give very briefly reasons for your choice.

(ICMA, Cost Accounting 2, May 1976).

31. a. The Secure Locke Company operates a system of standard costing, which it uses amongst other things as the basis for calculating certain management bonuses.

In September 1979 the Company's production of 100,000 keys was in accordance with budget. The standard quantity of material used in each key is one unit; the standard price is £0.05 per unit. In September 105,000 units of material were used, at an actual purchase price of £45 per thousand units (which was also the replacement cost).

The materials buyer is given a bonus of 10% of any favourable materials price variance. The production manager is given a bonus of 10% of any favourable materials quantity variance.

You are required:
   i.   to calculate the materials cost variances for September 1979;
   ii. to record all relevant bookeeping entries in Journal form;
   iii. to evaluate the bonus system from the viewpoints of the buyer, the production manager, and the company.

b. In October 1979 there was an adverse materials quantity variance of £500. A decision has to be made as to whether to investigate the key-making process to determine whether it is out of control.

On the basis of past experience the cost of an investigation is estimated at £50. The cost of correcting the process if it is found to be out of control is estimated at £100. The probability that the process is out of control is estimated at .50.

You are required:
   i.   to calculate the minimum present value of the expected savings that

would have to be made in future months in order to justify making an investigation;

ii. to suggest why the monthly cost savings arising from a systematic investigation are unlikely to be as great as the adverse materials variance of £500 which was experienced in the month of October 1979;

iii. to calculate, if the expected present value of cost savings were *first* £600 and *second* £250, the respective levels of probability that the process was out of control, at which the management would be indifferent about whether to conduct an investigation.

(ICA, Management Accounting, December 1979).

32. The NWA Plastic Company decides to manufacture 2 products and to implement a system of standard costing in respect of them. The standard costs are based on the following information for a standard week:—

   i. Expected output – Product A 20,000 units Product B 10,000 units
  ii. Materials required Product A 800 kilos Product B 600 kilos
 iii. Price per kilo – both products £7.50
 iv. Wages – Product A 0.25 standard hours per unit
              Product B 0.50 standard hours per unit
  v. Total cost of labour is expected to be £20,000 and labour grades are identical
 vi. Variable overhead is recovered at 40% of direct labour on both products
vii. Fixed overhead is £10,000 allocated 60% to Product A and 40% to Product B
viii. At the end of a week's production the following information was available:—

    Actual output – Product A   20,500 units
                – Product B   9,800 units
    Materials used– Product A   860 kilos @ £8.00 per kilo
                – Product B   560 kilos @ £8.00 per kilo
    Labour used   – Product A   5,000 hours @ £1.90 per hour
                – Product B   5,000 hours @ £1.90 per hour

    Variable overheads were fully recovered and total overheads incurred amounted to £19,020.

Using the information stated above:—

a. Prepare a statement of standard cost per unit for each product.

b. Calculate the variances and present them in the form of a statement for production management.

c. Comment briefly on the variances you have calculated and suggest any remedial action required.

(CIPFA, Management Accounting, November 1979).

33. Monkshood Ltd builds decorative arbours in a limited range of standard designs in the gardens of clients. The company has been awarded a contract to build ten arbours to its most popular design in the Duke of Nomium's Famous Safari Park. Completion was due before the start of the summer season on 1st July 1978. A further contract for another ten arbours (to be constructed in the Autumn of 1978) may be awarded if the Duke is satisfied with the work on the first contract.

The bid for the initial contract was based on cost estimates which included the following provision for materials for all ten arbours (in standard units):

Material	No. of units	Unit price (£)	Total cost (£)
Stone	600	15	9,000
Timber	800	20	16,000
Thatch	1,000	25	25,000

The cost estimates were all based on what was thought to be technically achievable under perfect conditions and represented an optimal standard of performance. Due, it is suggested, to bad weather only nine arbours were built by the due date for completion of the contract, 30th June 1978. The Famous Safari Park management have sought to postpone the building of the remaining arbour, construction of which has not started, and Monkshood have acceded to this. The cost of materials used in construction so far has been as follows (in standard units):

Material	No. of units	Unit price (£)	Total cost (£)
Stone	640	17	10,880
Timber	950	18	17,100
Thatch	870	28	24,360

You are required to:

    a. calculate the following variances for materials in respect of the contract:
      i.   total cost variance,
      ii. total price variance, analysed into standard price variance and standard mix variance and
      iii. total usage variance, analysed into standard usage variance and yield variance.

    b. write a short report to Monkshood's contract manager explaining the significance of the variances in the context of the probable need to construct a further eleven arbours in the autumn.

(ICA, Management Accounting, July 1978).

34. A.B.C. Limited manufactures a single product and a system of Standard Costing is in use. The following information is available:—

	£
Standard Cost of Product	
Materials at £1 per kilo	5
Labour at £1.50 per hour	6
Overhead	7
Standard Cost per Unit	18

Standard output for 4 week period commencing 1 April	8,000 units
Estimated fixed overhead for the 4 week period	£32,000

At the end of the 4 week period the costing section provide the following information:—

Actual production was 7,600 units. Actual wages were £44,800 which includes payment for 1,000 hours abnormal idle time.

Materials consumed were 5½ kilos per unit at 95p per kilo. Total overheads incurred were £57,000 and the variable overhead was fully recovered.

You are required to:—

a. Prepare a statement showing variances for the use of production management.

b. Suggest possible reasons for any materials variances you have calculated and make appropriate observations.

(CIPFA, Management Accounting, November 1977).

35. On the basis of a production/sales level of 10,000 units a month, the standard unit cost of a carton of Gimmet which sells for £12 is:

		£
Material		
	12 Kg at 50p	6.00
Labour		
	1½ hours at £1.60	2.40
	Fixed Overhead	0.60

The Operating Statement for November 1977 was as follows:

	£	£	£
Budgeted Profit			30,000
Add favourable variances			
Sales volume margin	1,500		
Materials price	1,268		
Wages efficiency	240		
Fixed Overhead volume	300		
		3,308	
Less adverse variances			
Sales price	1,000		
Material usage	400		
Wages rates	780		
Fixed Overhead expenditure	200		
		2,380	
Net favourable variance			928
Actual Profit			£30,928

You are required to:

a. Produce an operating statement in conventional accounting form.

b. Explain what is meant by 'interdependence' of variances, illustrating your answer by references to the above statement.

(ACCA, Costing, December 1977).

36. Mr T. Oymaker is in business as a manufacturer of children's toys. His involvement with the manufacturing and marketing operations of his business leave him no time to maintain a proper set of business records. He is aware, however, of the need for accounting information and to enable a practising accountant friend to prepare periodic accounts for him, he complies with a set of 'rules' prescribed for this purpose; these include:

1. Production overhead is absorbed by reference to direct labour cost, the rate being 80%.

2. Finished stock is valued at direct cost plus production overhead;
3. The amount added to production cost to arrive at selling price is 25%.

From the information set out below, you are required to:

a. write up the accounts for
   i.   Work in progress,
   ii. Finished stock,
   iii. Raw materials stock; and
b. prepare
   i. Profit and Loss Account for the month of October 1978,
   ii. Balance Sheet at 31 October 1978.

	30 September 1978 £	31 October 1978 £
Work in Progress	9,600	7,200
Finished Stock	12,000	7,920
Raw Materials Stock	14,400	12,000
Debtors for Goods Sold	8,400	9,300
Creditors for raw materials	6,400	7,600
Fixed Assets	5,000	5,000

Summary of bank transactions for the month to 31 October 1978:—

	£
Balance at Bank 30 September	2,000
Receipts from debtors	28,800
Payments:	
Direct labour	3,600
Creditors for raw materials	7,200
Production Overhead	3,200
Marketing Costs	1,200
Administration Costs	800

N.B. — You are advised to submit details of your workings.

(ACCA, Costing, December 1978).

37. The following balances were extracted from the records of CFL Ltd for the month of May 1976:

	May 1 £	May 31 £
Finished Goods Stock	7,298	16,732
Work-in-Progress: Materials	28,480	21,360
Work-in-Progress: Labour	44,500	49,840
Work-in-Progress: Factory Overhead	11,125	12,460
Raw Materials Stock	146,138	114,098

During the month raw materials costing £85,440 were purchased and the direct labour payroll amounted to £149,520.

Included in the issues from Raw Materials Stock were items valued £10,680 which were used for the maintenance of factory premises and plant and machinery.

Factory Overhead is absorbed on the direct labour cost basis, the rate for May 1976 being 25%.

From the foregoing data you are required to write up the accounts referred to above and to show the cost of goods sold during the month.

(ACCA, Costing, June 1977).

Examination Technique

INTRODUCTION

If you are a genius and/or can calculate and reproduce facts and figures with the speed of a computer and/or know the examiner then there is no need for you to read this section. On the other hand if you do not fall into any of the above categories then you will stand more chance of passing your examinations first time if you study this section carefully and follow the simple rules.

WELL BEFORE THE EXAMINATION

No amount of examination room technique will enable you to pass unless you have prepared yourself thoroughly beforehand. The period of preparation may be years or months long. It is no use expecting to pass with a feverish last minute bout of swotting. Plan your study and preparation systematically. Allocate specific times for study and stick to them. At a minimum your pre-examination preparation should include the following:—

a. Obtain the official syllabus of the examination.

b. Systematically follow a course of study directed towards the examination.

c. Obtain past examination papers for say the last five years.

d. Make sure you can answer *every* question previously set.

e. Analyse the questions. Are some topics more popular than others?

f. Make sure you enter for the examination in good time and receive official confirmation.

IMMEDIATELY BEFORE THE EXAMINATION

a. Make sure you know exact time, date and location of examination.

b. Carefully check your travel arrangements. Leave yourself adequate time.

c. Check over your examination equipment:—
   Calculator? Spare Battery? Pens? Pencils? Slide Rule? Tables? Watch? Sweets? Cigarettes? etc, etc.

d. Check your examination number.

IN THE EXAMINATION ROOM

If you have followed the rules so far you are well prepared; you have all the equipment you need; you did not have to rush — YOU ARE CALM AND CONFIDENT. Before you start writing:

a. Carefully read the whole examination paper including the rubric.

b. Decide what questions you are going to answer.

c. Decide the sequence you will tackle the questions. Generally, answer the easiest question first.

d. Decide the time allocation for each question. In general the time allocation should be in direct proportion to the marks for each question.

e. Read the questions you have decided to answer again. Do you know *exactly* what the examiner is asking? Underline the key words in the question and keep these in your mind when answering.

Before you start writing:

a. Make sure you plan each question first. Make a note of the main points or principles involved. If you are unable to finish the question you will gain some marks from these points.

b. Attempt all questions required and each part of each question.

c. Do not let your answer ramble on. Be as brief as possible consistent with covering all the points you know.

d. Follow a logical sequence in your answers.

e. Write neatly, underline headings and if the question asks for a particular sequence of answer then follow that sequence.

f. If diagrams graphs or tables are required give them plenty of space, label them neatly and comprehensively, and give a key to symbols, lines etc used. A simple clear diagram showing the main points can often gain a good proportion of the marks for a question.

When you have finished writing:

a. Check that you have followed the examination regulations regarding examination title, examination number, candidates number and sequence of answer sheets.

b. Make sure you include *all* the sheets you require to be marked.

c. If you have time carefully read each and every part of each answer and check each calculation.

General points.

a. Concentrate on answering the questions set not some related topic which you happen to know something about.

b. Do *not* leave the examination room early. Use every minute for checking and rechecking or adding points to questions answered.

c. Always attempt every question set and every part of each question.

Solutions to Examination Questions Set at the end of Chapters

Solutions

Chapter 1

1.

Report No. CA1   Date ....

To: MANAGING DIRECTOR

From: COST ACCOUNTANT

Subject — PROPOSED COST ACCOUNTING SYSTEM

As requested I give below the major aims of the system and give examples of specific information which could be provided by the system when installed.

MAIN AIMS

a. In general to provide the basis of an internal financial information service to management which will be of assistance in planning, control and decision making.

b. To assist forward planning by providing cost information on such matters as the relative profitability of products and departments so that the level of production, mix of products and pricing strategies can be decided.

c. To aid control by regular reporting of product costs and profitability, the performance of the different types of labour, the departments and sections.

d. To aid decision making by regular and special cost reports on any facet of operations.

e. To provide motivation and to promote cost consciousness for all levels of staff by providing them with feedback on their performance in the form of cost reports, budget statements etc.

f. To provide a formal means of gathering detailed information on operations which is vital now that the firm is beyond the size where personal observation is sufficient.

Typical information which would be available includes:—

i.   Product costs per unit and in total.
ii.   Departmental operating statements showing performance, expenditure etc.
iii. Efficiency statements on labour, machine and material utilisation.
iv.   Analysis of cost trends particularly in relation to changing levels of activity.
v.   Product profitability and contribution statements.
vi.   Periodic stock valuations.
vii. Cash budgets.
viii. Scrap and rectification costs.
ix.   Special order costs.

2. There are several ways in which a cost accountant could contribute to the efficient and economic operation of the equipment. In general the contribution that can be made is by detailed reporting on costs, times, outputs and other data. To be effective the reports should:—

a. Be produced at regular, appropriate intervals which may be per shift, day, week or month depending on the nature of the item.

b. Show controllable matters only.

c. Show comparative figures against budget or standard and the resulting variances, both periodic and cumulatively.

d. Be produced promptly.

e. Should be in a format which is effective and agreed by the recipients.

Typical areas covered by the reports include:

Machine utilisation:

including Down Time suitably analysed to maintenance, breakdowns, idle time, set-up time.

Production performance per hour/shift etc. compared with targets, capacity projections covering the next budget period showing potential overloads/under utilisation.

Operating costs:

including details of direct and indirect labour costs, Waste/Scrap and reworks, Power and consumable material consumption, Direct Material Consumption.

Chapter 2

Report No.   Date ....

To: MANAGING DIRECTOR

From: A. N. OTHER, MANAGEMENT ACCOUNTANT

Subject — VALUE ADDED STATEMENT

Terms of reference: To outline the concept of value added and to consider the advantages of producing a value added statement as part of our Annual Report.

Value added definition: Value added is the difference between the revenue from Sales and the cost of bought-in-materials and services. It is a key measure of performance of the wealth creating abilities of the organisation. Conventional profit calculations deduct all costs, i.e. bought in materials and services, labour, depreciation, interest etc. from sales income so it will be seen that added value equals pretax profits plus labour, depreciation and interest.

Thus, value added can be defined as the wealth the organisation has created by its own and its employees efforts.

Objectives of a value added statement: The Corporate Report states that such a statement is, ... the simplest and most immediate way of putting profit into proper perspective vis-a-vis the whole enterprise as a collective effort by capital, management and the employees". Thus it will be seen that such a statement is part of the information service to employees and shareholders and hopefully should help to improve relationships.

Advantages of value added statements:

a. To show clearly the wealth creating ability of the organisation.

b. To show the way that the wealth created is divided between employees, shareholders and government.

e. To avoid undue emphasis on one aspect of performance namely profit.

d. To help to improve employee/company relations.

A typical format would be

Statement of Value Added

	19 x 0		19 x 1	
	£	%	£	%
REVENUE				
Less Bought-in-Materials and Services	___	__	___	__
= ADDED VALUE	___	__	___	__
Applied as follows:				
To EMPLOYERS (wages, salaries, pensions, etc)				
To SUPPLIERS OF CAPITAL Interest on loans Dividends				
To GOVERNMENT Corporation Tax				
To MAINTENANCE & EXPANSION OF ASSETS Depreciation Retained Profits	___	__	___	__
= ADDED VALUE	___	__	___	__

Chapter 3

a. See Overhead Analysis Sheet opposite.

b. O.A.R. based on direct labour hours
  i. Assembly department

$$= \frac{\text{Total overheads}}{\text{Direct labour hours}} = \frac{46,930}{32,000} = \underline{£1.47 \text{ per labour hour}}$$

  ii. For finishing department.

$$= \frac{£10,440}{4,000} = \underline{£2.61 \text{ per direct labour hours}}$$

Overhead Analysis Sheet Four weeks ending ....

Cost Item	Basis of apportionment	Total £	Machining Dept. £	Assembly Dept. £	Finishing Dept. £	Stores £	Occupancy £
Allocated costs							
Indirect wages		34,000	9,000	15,000	4,000	6,000	
Indirect materials		2,400	400	1,400	600		
Maintenance		2,100	1,400	600	100		
Power		2,200	1,600	400	200		
Rent		2,000					2,000
Rates		600					600
Insurance on building		200					200
Lighting and heating		400					400
Cleaning of factory		800					800
Apportioned costs							
Depreciation on plant and equipment	Plant and equipment cost	16,700	14,000	2,000	600	100	
Wage related costs	Total wages	28,200	8,320	16,440	2,240	1,200	
Factory administration and personnel	No. of employees	7,100	2,000	4,000	1,000	100	
Insurance on plant and equipment	Plant and equipment cost	1,670	1,400	200	60	10	
Occupancy costs	Area in sq. feet		1,200	1,800	800	200	(4,000)
Stores costs	No. requisitions		1,680	5,090	840	(7,610)	
		98,370	41,000	46,930	10,440	–	–

c. The objective of apportioning costs over several cost centres is to share out common costs in an equitable fashion. In so far as it can be done the apportionment should reflect the incidence of usage or demand on the particular cost. In this question the cost items were dealt with as below

Item of Cost	Basis of Apportionment	Comment
Occupancy Costs	Area occupied	The most realistic basis as most of these costs will vary with area.
Depreciation and Insurance on plant	Plant and equipment cost	From the information given the only reasonable basis. Probably a fair correlation with cost.
Wage related costs	Total wages	An accurate basis. Such costs will follow wages paid more closely than, say, number of employees.
Factory admin. and personnel	No. of employees	Personnel costs probably vary with no. of employees and because administration costs are grouped with personnel then these also would be spread on no. of employees. However this is probably a poor basis.
Stores Cost	Number of requisitions	A typical basis and is probably some reflection on the loading of the stores.

d. To improve the apportionments it would be necessary to have more details, split down to departments on values, times etc. Typical examples are given below.

Depreciation – either departmental analysis, machine by machine, or depreciation related to usage in which case records of utilisation would be required.

Plant insurance – departmental analysis based on insurance valuations.

Stores costs – where there are substantial variations in the times taken to handle requisitions then some form of activity analysis on a sample basis might be better than the number of requisitions.

Factory administration – always a difficult cost to apportion but probably a better basis would be activity in each department.

As all apportionments are merely conventions there is no way to prove what is more accurate so that a commonsense approach must be adopted. If to develop a more accurate method of apportioning costs it is necessary to incur significant expenditure then it is probably not worth while.

2. a. Predetermined overhead absorption rates (OAR) are almost invariably preferred to actual OAR for the following reasons:
   i. Delays in being able to calculate production costs, estimates and possibly delays in sending invoices until actual rates were known.
   ii. Fluctuations in activity and incidence of costs (e.g. rate bills twice a year, winter heating costs) would cause unacceptable variations in absorption rates if calculated on an actual basis.

iii. Consistency of costing treatment month to month.
iv. Predetermined OAR aid the normal processes of costing and in particular are essential when standard costing is used.

b. In general, inferences on the relative efficiency of firms are difficult to draw unless all of the aspects of a firm's operations are considered. Certainly to draw conclusions based on overhead absorption rate differences would almost certainly be misleading. Even though the question states that similar products are made and similar methods are used for calculating the OAR, differences may still arise due to

i. Different scale of operation. One firm may be substantially larger than the other with a consequent different structure.
ii. Different levels of activity.
iii. Different methods of production. One firm may use more mechanisation.
iv. Different treatment of particular items of cost e.g. works salaries, depreciation.
v. Different costing conventions used. For example in one firm depreciation may be calculated on replacement values and in the other on historical cost.

Without a great deal more detailed information no conclusion can be drawn from statement that the OAR's differ.

3. a. Accrued wages.
It will be known how many days wages are to be accrued. Furthermore, by the time monthly accounts are prepared various production statistics will be available e.g. number of units/assemblies, weight produced, number of workers and so on. Based on this data the average cost of wages for a similar day(s) can be established from past wages records adjusted by any known variations such as changes in wage rates. If standard costing is in operation more detailed information will be available so that a more accurate estimate can be made.

b. **Overheads in scrapped sub-assemblies**.
The treatment varies whether the scrap can be considered within the range of 'normal' scrap or if the amount is sufficient to be classed as abnormal.
'Normal' scrap. The cost of normal scrap is absorbed in the cost of good sub assemblies and any gain from the sale of the scrapped assembly being credited to the W-I-P account.
Abnormal scrap. Normally an abnormal Loss account would be opened which would be debited with the cost of material, labour and overhead incurred in the sub-assembly. The balance of this account being written off to costing Profit and Loss.

c. **Goods received but yet invoiced**.
In such circumstances it is necessary to accrue for the anticipated amounts of the invoices so that reasonably accurate forecasts can be made of costs incurred and stock valuations. In most cases the purchase order price can be used. When the actual invoice is received any minor adjustments can be made.

Chapter 4

1. A functional classification is one that relates to the functions or tasks that need to be done. Accordingly within the marketing area the following functions can be found and the costs associated with each of the functions would be coded accordingly.

Typical functions include:

    i.   *Sales Administration;* e.g. managerial and clerical salaries, head office and branch office costs, showroom costs.

    ii.   *Sales Representation;* Salaries, commission and bonus payments, travelling and car expenses, training costs.

    iii.   *Sales Promotion;* e.g. advertising, printing and sample costs, exhibitions and demonstrations.

    iv.   *Market Research;* salaries, survey costs and fees, expenses of canvassers, computer costs (for analysis purposes).

    v.   *Invoicing, credit control and debt collection;* e.g. salaries, fees, legal expenses, stationery.

Depending on the particular organisation other functions might also come under the control of marketing e.g. warehousing, delivery, storage.

It should be realised that the functional classifications referred to above (Sales Representation, Sales Promotion etc.) are the OBJECTIVE classifications and the examples given of costs (salaries, bonus etc.) are the SUBJECTIVE classifications.

b. **Analysis of marketing costs.**

The costs mentioned in part (a) could be analysed (where possible and economically feasible) according to:

    i.   Product and product group

    ii.   Type of sales outlet

    iii.   By area

    iv.   By representative

    v.   By order size

and similar sub-divisions.

The purpose of this analysis is to assist management control, to increase marketing effectiveness and to increase profitability. In all cases the analysis is enhanced by comparison of actual with budget or target.

2. (A)

Report No.   Date ....

To: STORES CONTROLLER

From: COST ACCOUNTANT

Subject: MATERIAL CLASSIFICATION AND CODING

Classification is the process of arranging items into groups according to their likeness and is a fundamental process in any form of stores control system. A materials classification system is an example of subjective classification i.e. classification according to the nature of the material or item.

The major principles in designing a materials coding system are:—

a. Uniqueness of code for each material.

b. Distinctiveness of appearance of code.

c. Uniformity of code length and construction.

d. Brevity. Codes should be as brief as possible.

e. Exhaustiveness. The coding structure should encompass the full range of existing and proposed materials.

f. No ambiguity.

g. Adaptable for automatic data processing.

The major advantages of a sound, well designed coding system for stores control are:

a. Coding will enable items to be uniquely identified.

b. Ambiguity arising from varying descriptions will be avoided.

c. The coding system will aid communication between stores, purchasing, production control, costing and all departments concerned with materials.

d. Identification of redundant or slow moving items will be facilitated.

(B)

It can be deduced from the examples given that the code is split into four parts, each of 2 digits i.e.

Digit No's.	1 2	3 4	5 6	7 8
	Type of material	Length	Thickness	Width

It is also apparent that

$$02 = \text{Brass and } 04 = \text{Stainless Steel}$$

(i.e. alphabetical order) and the length is in units of 6", thickness in units of $\frac{1}{16}''$ and width in units of ¼".

i. Accordingly the codes required are as follows:

	Aluminium –	6'6"	x	¼"	x	3½"
Code =	01	13		04		14
	Copper –	1'	x	³⁄₈"	x	4¼"
Code =	03	02		06		17

ii. Finally the bars defined by the given codes.

Code	03	11	29	03
	Copper	5½' x	1¹³⁄₁₆" x	¾"

Code	01	07	17	21
	Aluminium	3½' x	1¹⁄₁₆" x	5¼"

Chapter 5

1. a. Centralised or de-centralised stores.
    i. *Stock levels.* Because duplication can be avoided overall stock investment can be reduced by a central stores.
    ii. *Control.* A centralised stores facilitates control by safeguarding high value items, better security measures, higher quality staff etc.
    iii. *Recording.* Certain aspects of paper work can be reduced e.g. single stock records but other aspects may be increased e.g. requests from remote locations.
    iv. *Equipment.* A centralised stores is likely to be able to justify the use of mechanised handling equipment, video displays, moveable racking etc.
    v. *Space.* In general a centralised stores is more economical on space.
    vi. *Convenience.* Decentralised stores at the scene of operations are likely to be more convenient. A remote central stores can introduce delays which might be unacceptable.
    vii. *Staff.* Theoretically less staff will be required in a central store and higher quality staff may be justifiable. However this might be offset by a lack of local knowledge.

    b. **Continuous Stocktaking.**
    This is the process by which the stock of items is checked at regular intervals by trained staff and compared with the stock record which would be kept on the perpetual inventory basis. This process has the following advantages:
    i. Stocks would be checked more frequently than the conventional annual stock take. Discrepancies and problems will thus be discovered much earlier.
    ii. Higher quality, trained staff can be employed so there should be fewer errors than on annual stock takes where untrained staff are frequently used.
    iii. There is no disruption or cessation of production during stock takes.
    iv. Continuous stocktaking and the investigations carried out on discrepancies found may deter pilferage or discover it earlier and should encourage more accurate documentation and recording.
    v. Because stock records are checked more frequently they should be more accurate. This will assist the ordering functions and the management control aspects of inventory systems e.g. maximum and minimum levels.

    c. **The layout of stores.**
    This is a technical subject for which engineering and work study advice would be required. Typical factors to be considered include:
    i. access for deliveries and issues
    ii. Well organised gangways large enough for loaders, fork lift trucks etc.
    iii. Logical distribution of stocked items with the most frequently required items adjacent to issue points.
    iv. Sufficient horizontal and vertical space for pallets, containers and racks.
    v. Good security features e.g. external walls, ceilings, TV scanners etc.
    vi. Space for making up bulk orders and issues.

2. Although there are inumerable reasons for stock differences arising they can be grouped into categories i.e.

    a. Quantity errors e.g. miscounts during the stock take.

    b. Classification errors e.g. a stainless steel part classified as mild steel.

    c. Pricing errors e.g. a correctly counted and classified item might be priced at £56 for 1000 instead of £56 per 100.

    d. Recording errors e.g. an omission of the entry of a goods received note.

    e. System errors e.g. no adequate recording of returns to stores.

The steps to be taken for an investigation involve scrutiny and analysis within the categories given above.

Quantity errors.

Examine the stock taking instructions and procedures. Sample count/weigh items and, allowing for subsequent stock movements, reconcile these balances with original stock sheets. Sample check prices and extensions on stock sheets.

Classification errors.

Sample check classifications on stock sheets and stock ledgers. Check for compensating errors on raw material, W-I-P and Finished Goods. Analyse coding systems in use.

Pricing errors.

Sample check prices on stock sheets. Check materials, labour and overhead books and valuations for W-I-P pricing. If standard costing is used check that all variances have been dealt with correctly.

Recording errors.

Reconcile stock lists and stores ledger balances. If bin cards and stores records are kept reconcile the balances. Examine the prelisting or batch control system used for ledger posting. Check that recording is up to date; have all invoiced goods/returns/transfers from W-I-P to finished goods etc. been dealt with?

System errors.

Are all issues to W-I-P recorded? – and returns? Was a common cut-off date used for all type of stocks? Is the scrap recording system effective? Can despatches be made without invoices being raised?

3. Accountant's contribution to material cost control.

This is a very wide ranging question indeed because material cost control can cover inumerable factors ranging from the design and specification of the product, ordering and reception, storage and handling, production methods, scrap control, rectification and so on.

Assuming that the accountant would not be responsible for the design of systems such as purchasing, inspection and the like his major role would be in the preparation of comparative cost data on all aspects of; materials handling and usage, the audit of procedures and results, the preparation of budgets and standards for purchasing, production and scrap.

Typical areas of involvement include:

Material selection/product design. Although primarily a technical function cost estimates are involved.

Purchasing, ordering and materials reception.

A purchase budget would need to be prepared and cost comparisons made of buying patterns, order costs etc. Variance reports may be prepared where standard costing is used.

Inventory control procedures.

The monitoring of the effectiveness of inventory control procedures, EOQ calculations and provision of cost data on stock holding costs.

Storage and handling.

Apart from routine cost reports on storage and handling there should be periodic reports on stocks held, perhaps using ABC or Pareto analysis, stock movements and turnover, obsolescence, stock losses, costs of pilferage etc.

Production.

All aspects of material issues, pricing methods, material utilisation, scrap, rejects and reworked materials must be analysed and costed. Regular, detailed material cost reports produced for all levels of management from chargehands upwards help to promote an awareness of material costs.

Chapter 6

Report No. .... Date ....

To: MANAGING DIRECTOR

From: MANAGEMENT ACCOUNTANT

Subject: INVENTORY CONTROL

1. Terms of Reference:

To report on the contribution which can be made to the raw materials stock control system of the following:

a. ABC Inventory Analysis

b. Setting of stock levels

c. Economic order quantity.

a. **ABC inventory analysis.**

This is the name given to a simple but effective technique which is aimed at directing control activities to where they can be most effective.

All stock items are arranged in decreasing order of annual cost of usage. This is not the cost per item but the actual total cost of usage for the year.

Typically when this is done it will be found that a small number of items account for a large proportion of annual cost and so strict control and monitoring measures are likely to be cost effective. Further down the scale typically it will be found that a large number of items represent only a small proportion of cost so that undue control activity is unlikely to be cost effective.

The following table summarises a typical situation

Category	No. of Stock items %	Proportion of Annual Usage Cost %	Control Activity
A	Say 10	70	Strict control likely to be cost effective.
B	25	20	Average control activity.
C	65	10	Low level of control activity likely to be sufficient.

The whole purpose of ABC analysis is to concentrate attention upon the most significant matters rather than dissipating monitoring activities over all items.

ABC analysis is akin to the 80/20 or Pareto rule which has the same rationale and objective.

b. and c. These parts of the question are dealt with directly in the text, Para. Nos. 8 & 9.

2. a. The Economic Order Quantity (EOQ) is the order quantity which minimises the balance of cost between stock holding costs and reordering costs. The basic EOQ formula is,

$$EOQ = \sqrt{\frac{2.Co.D}{Cc}}$$

where Co = ordering cost per order

D = Demand per annum

Cc = Carrying cost per item p.a.

The EOQ is illustrated below

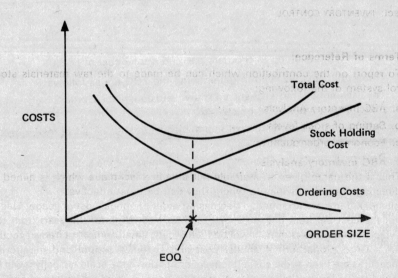

339

From the graph it will be seen that stock holding costs rise as the order size increases whilst total ordering costs fall as fewer orders of a larger quantity are placed during the year.

b. With a given annual usage (600 units) and from 1 to 6 orders being placed a year obviously the order size must vary.

i.e.

No of orders p.a.	1	2	3	4	5	6
Order Size	600	300	200	150	120	100

Where there is no buffer stock (as in this example) average stock is ½ reorder quantity.

Schedule of Costs for No. of Orders Placed

Line No.							
1	No. of Orders p.a.	1	2	3	4	5	6
2	Order Size	600	300	200	150	120	100
3	Average Stock $\frac{(Line\ 2)}{2}$	300	150	100	75	60	50
4	Av. Stock Value (Line 3 x £2.4)	£720	£360	£240	£180	£144	£120
5	Av. Holding Cost (Line 4 x 20%)	£144	£72	£48	£36	£28.8	£24
6	Order Costs p.a. (Line 1 x £6)	£6	£12	£18	£24	£30	£36
	Annual Cost (Line 5 + Line 6)	£150	£84	£66	£60	£58.8	£60

EOQ

∴ EOQ = 120 resulting in 5 orders p.a. and a total cost of £58.8.

c. Three problems involved in determining the EOQ are as follows:

a. The assumption that all costs are known and constant i.e. ordering costs, unit cost etc. This is unlikely to be so.

b. Determining the carrying cost is a subjective matter based on estimates of interest rates which may vary.

c. Demand forecasting. Again estimates are required of the anticipated usage or demand which are difficult to make particularly in volatile conditions.

3. The Lorenz curve for this question is shown below. It will be seen from the question that the conclusions and relevance of the data given are covered by the explanation of ABC analysis given in answer to Q1 of this chapter.

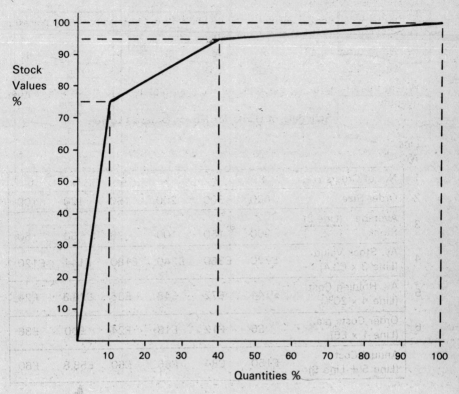

Lorenz Curve
(Relationship of quantities and stock values)

Note:

A Lorenz curve is simply the plotting of the cumulative values i.e.

10% of quantity totals   75% of stock value
40% of quantity totals   95% of stock value
100% of quantity totals 100% of stock value

4. This question can be answered largely from the text (Para 6) and from the answer given to 2(a) above.

In addition, the following factors should be considered:

a. Close liaison between production control, the Sales department and purchasing is essential.

b. A critical factor in all inventory control systems is the accuracy of the demand forecasts. If the material being considered is vital then considerable attention must be paid to the forecasting technique used and the way the forecasting system is monitored. Computer assisted forecasting may be of value.

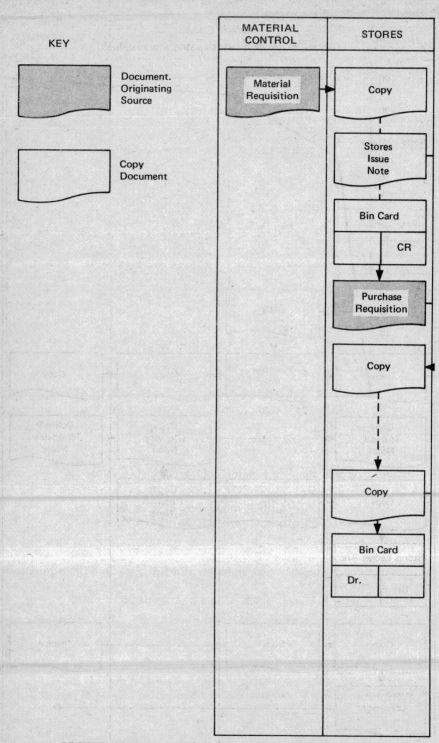

PROCEDURE & DOCUMENT FLOW OF MATERIALS CYCLE

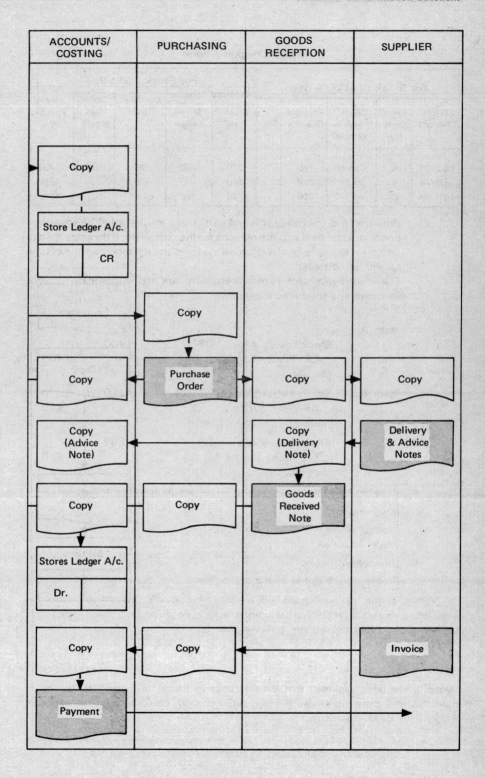

343

b. i.

Stock Checker's Form

For Stock Checker's Use					For Stock Audit Use				
					Recorded Balance		Cost per Unit	Stock Gain (Loss)	Journal Voucher No.
Date Checked	Item/ Code No.	Count/ Weigh or Estimate?	Physical Quantity	Sig.	Stock Card	Stores Ledger			
								£	
15/5/78	A	Count	180		200	200	£20	(400)	1293
15/5/78	B	✓	172		170	170	£5	10	1294
15/5/78	C	✓	700		740	760	£0.60	(36)	1295

ii. Wherever a discrepancy is found particularly if substantial, an investigation should be held into the reasons for the difference. If there are system errors, for example, goods returned to stores and not recorded, the system should be corrected.

The documents and entries necessary are the appropriate Journal vouchers and the following entries.

Item A.

      Stock Losses A/c   DR   £400

         CR Stores Ledger A/c (A)   £400

      (Reason: . . . . . .)

Item B.   Stores Ledger A/c (B)   DR   £10

         CR W-I-P A/c   £10

      (Reason: . . . . . .)

      C.   Stock Losses A/c   DR   £36

         CR Stores Ledger A/c (C)   £36

      (Reason: . . . . . .)

iii. Possible reasons for shortages. These are inumerable and include:—

a. miscounting

b. Storage errors

c. Theft

d. Unrecorded issues

e. Breakage/damage in stores and so on.

Whatever the reason established, management should attempt to correct the system to avoid occurrence. Typical actions include; better security, more stores staff, review of document procedures, palletisation etc.

5.

(**Note:** It has been assumed that the reference in Para 1 to 'gross lots' means 'in multiples of a gross' otherwise the only order quantity could be 1 gross which can hardly have been intended).

a.

Total annual cost of Purchasing and Stocking L186 motors

Line No.		1	2	3	4	5	6
1	Order Qty. (Gross)	1	2	3	4	5	6
2	Net Delivered Cost per Gross	£500	£500	£500	£500	£500	£500
3	Average Stock $\frac{(\text{Line 1})}{2}$ gross	½	1	1½	2	2½	3
4	Average Stock Value (Lines 2 x 3)	£250	£500	£750	£1000	£1250	£1500
5	Orders per year $\frac{(36)}{(\text{Line 1})}$	36	18	12	9	7.2	6
6	Annual Usage Cost (36 x Line 2)	£18000	£18000	£18000	£18000	£18000	£18000
7	Capital + Insurance (24% x Line 4)	60	120	180	240	300	360
8	Stock Room Cost (Line 1 x £12)	12	24	36	48	60	72
9	Order & Receiving (Line 5 x £30)	1080	540	360	270	216	180
	Total Purchase & Stocking Cost	£19152	£18684	£18576	£18558	£18576	£18612

It will be seen that a 4 gross order quantity has the lowest annual cost and is likely to be closest to the EOQ.

Notes:

   i.   It is apparent that there is little difference in cost between ordering 3, 4, 5 and 6 gross lots. This is fairly typical and means that the exact EOQ is not particularly important especially as many of the factors involved; demand, storage costs etc, are estimates which may vary.

   ii.   The Capital + Insurance value of 24% (Line 7) is the insurance charge of 4% and the cost of capital of 20%.

   iii. The delivered cost per gross is £800 less 40% discount + £20 freight = £500 (Line 2).

b. The stock reorder point should be calculated so that even if the maximum demand occurred each day of the lead time there should be just sufficient to avoid a stockout.

$$\text{Lead Time} = 20 \text{ days as given}$$

$$\text{Daily Maximum Demand} = \text{Average demand} + 8$$

$$= \frac{36 \text{ gross}}{250 \text{ working days}} + 8$$

$$= 28.74 \text{ motors}$$

$$\therefore \text{Reorder Point} = 20 \times 28.74 = \underline{575 \text{ motors}} \text{ (to nearest unit)}$$

Note that the safety stock is the (maximum − average demand) x lead time = 8 x 20 = 160 motors.

c. Safety stock costs compared to express service costs

The cost of holding the 160 safety stock is:–

$$24\% \text{ of stock value} + \pounds12 \text{ per gross stored}$$

$$= 24\% \ (\frac{160}{144} \times \pounds500) + (\frac{160}{144} \times \pounds12) = \underline{\pounds147} \text{ p.a.}$$

Express charges are £32 per gross extra and assuming that the loss of contribution during a stockout is not intended to be included and that express orders would not be placed until maximum demand has occurred repeatedly, the following steps can be followed.

If no safety stock is kept the reorder point is 415 motors. As stockouts can only occur during lead times they could occur 9 times per year.

If maximum demand exists a stock out could occur 14.4 days after reorder $(\frac{415}{28.74})$

$\therefore$ To be effective an express order must be placed after 9.4 days. A one gross order lasts 5 days at maximum demand (i.e. $\frac{144}{28.74}$).

$\therefore$ Express order placed day 9.4 arrives day 14.4 and lasts to day 19.4, i.e. just before the normal order would arrive on Day 20.

$\therefore$ There would be 9 express orders per annum at an extra cost of

$$9 \times \pounds32 = \pounds288 \text{ p.a.}$$

which should be compared with the £147 cost of the safety stock.

$\therefore$ based on the assumptions given above it would be preferable to keep the safety stock and avoid express orders.

Chapter 7

1.

Stores Ledger Records

Weighted Average Method

Date	Receipts Quantity	Receipts Price £	Issues Quantity	Issues Price £	Balance Quantity	Balance Price £	Stock Value £
Opening					100	39	3,900
May	100	41			200	40	8,000
June	200	50			400	45	18,000
July			250	45	150	45	6,750
August	400	51.875			550	50	27,500
September			350	50	200	50	10,000
October			100	50	100	50	5,000

F.I.F.O. Method

Date	Receipts Quantity	Receipts Price £	Issues Quantity	Issues Price £	Balance Quantity	Balance Price £	Stock Value £
Opening					100	39	3,900
May	100	41			{ 100 / 100	39 / 41	8,000
June	200	50			{ 100 / 100 / 200	39 / 41 / 50	18,000
July			250	{ 100 @ 39 / 100 @ 41 / 50 @ 50	150	50	7,500
August	400	51.875			{ 150 / 400	50 / 51.875	28,250
September			350	{ 150 @ 50 / 200 @ 51.875	200	51.875	10,375
October			100	51.875	100	51.875	5187.5

L.I.F.O. Method

Date	Receipts Quantity	Receipts Price £	Issues Quantity	Issues Price £	Balance Quantity	Balance Price £	Stock Value £
Opening					100	39	3,900
May	100	41			100	39	
					100	41	8,000
June	200	50			100	39	
					100	41	
					200	50	18,000
July			250	200 @ 50	100	39	
				50 @ 41			
					50	41	5,950
August	400	51.875			100	39	
					50	41	
					400	51.875	26,700
September			350	51.875	100	39	
					50	41	
					50	51.875	8,543.75
October			100	50 @ 51.875	100	39	3,900
				50 @ 41			

b.

Trading accounts for the period

Sales	Weighted Average £	FIFO £	LIFO £
Sales	47,900	47,900	47,900

	£			
Opening Stock	3,900			
+ Purchases	34,850	(38,750	(38,750	(38,750
− Closing Stock		5,000)	5,187.5)	3,900)
= Cost of Sales	33,750	33,562.5	34,850
= GROSS PROFIT	£14,150	£14,337.5	£13,050

c. In this example, with rising purchase prices, the most realistic profit will be found when the costs of material charged relate most closely to current prices. The method which does this is the LIFO system.

2. a. i.

Stores record of K using FIFO

Date	Receipts			Issues		Balance	
	Quantity	Price	Amount	Quantity	Price	Quantity	Price
		£	£		£		£
April	1,000	1.00	1,000			1,000	1.00
				500	1.00	500	1.00
May	500	1.20	600			{ 500	1.00
						500	1.20
				500	1.00		
				250	1.20	250	1.20
June	1,000	1.00	1,000			{ 250	1.20
						1,000	1.00
July				250	1.20		
				350	1.00	650	1.00
August	500	1.20	600			{ 650	1.00
						500	1.20
				650	1.00	500	1.20
September	500	1.30	650			{ 500	1.20
						500	1.30
				500	1.20		
				100	1.30	400	1.30

Stores record of L using LIFO

Date	Receipts			Issues		Balance	
	Quantity	Price	Amount	Quantity	Price	Quantity	Price
		£	£		£		£
April	1,000	1.00	1,000			1,000	1.00
				500	1.00	500	1.00
May	500	1.20	600			{ 500	1.00
						500	1.20
				500	1.20		
				250	1.00	250	1.00
June	1,000	1.00	1,000			1,250	1.00
July				600	1.00	650	1.00
August	500	1.20	600			{ 650	1.00
						500	1.20
				500	1.20		
				150	1.00	500	1.00
September	500	1.30	650			{ 500	1.00
						500	1.30
				500	1.30		
				100	1.00	400	1.00

Stores record of M using Six Months Weighted Average

Date	Quantity	Receipts Price	Amount	Issues Quantity	Balance Quantity
		£	£		
April	1,000	1.00	1,000	500	500
May	500	1.20	600	750	250
June	1,000	1.00	1,000		1,250
July				600	650
August	500	1.20	600	650	500
September	500	1.30	650	600	400
	3,500		3,850		

Weighted average price per sack = £3,850 ÷ 3,500 = £1.10

ii. From the stores records above it can be seen that the closing stock valuations are:

K   400 sacks @ £1.30 = £520
L   400 sacks @ £1.00 = £400
M   400 sacks @ £1.10 = £440

These figures can be used in the following statement:

Joint Venture profit Statement using alternative Stock Valuations

	FIFO		LIFO		Average	
	£		£		£	
Sales (3100 @ £1.50)	4,650		4,650		4,650	
	£		£		£	
Purchases	3,850		3,850		3,850	
Less Closing Stock	520	3,330	400	3,450	440	3,410
= Total Profit		£1,320		£1,200		£1,240
∴ Profit/Student		£440		£400		£413.33

iii. All three methods can be used for internal cost accounting purposes, as indeed can any method. However, only two of these methods, FIFO and weighted average, are acceptable to the Inland Revenue so only these two would be used in the financial accounts.

b. The sentence referred to is "such costs will include all related production overheads, even though these may accrue on a time basis". The costs which accrue on a time basis are fixed costs and SSAP 9 states clearly that stock valuations should include a proportion of fixed production overheads. It follows that a marginal cost valuation, although quite acceptable for cost accounting purposes, is not acceptable for financial accounting purposes. Using absorption costing a proportion of fixed overheads will automatically be included in stock.

3. a.

Stores Ledger A/C – Component X

Date	Details	Folio	Amount £	Date	Details	Folio	Amount £
1.11.79	Stock (440 @£5)		2,200	2.11.79	WIP (300 @ £5)		1,500
8.11.79	Creditors			9.11.79	Prod. O'hds. (50 @ £5)		250
	(400 @ £4.50)		1,800	13.11.79	WIP (90 @ £5,		
15.11.79	(400 @ £5.50)		2,200		210 @ £4.50)		1,395
21.11.79	W-I-P (40 @ £5.50)		220	16.11.79	WIP (190 @ £4.50,		
22.11.79	Accruals (400 @ £6)		2,400		310 @ £5.50)		2,560
				20.11.79	Capital (20 @ £5.50)		110
				28.11.79	Scrap (30 @ £5.50)		165
				30.11.79	P & L A/c – Stock loss		
					(40 @ £5.50)		220
				30.11.79	Closing Stock		
					(40 @ £5.50)		
					(400 @ £6.00)		2,620
	Units 1,680		£8,820		Units 1,680		£8,820

b. Comparison of LIFO and FIFO methods of pricing issues.

With stable prices — No difference between methods.

With rising prices — FIFO charges oldest prices (lowest) to production. LIFO charges newest (highest) prices to production.
FIFO values Stock at current valuations
LIFO values Stock at oldest valuations

With falling prices — FIFO charges highest prices to production and values stock at current lower valuations.
LIFO charges most current prices i.e. lowest to production and values stock at oldest valuations.

Acceptability — for internal purposes both acceptable
for external/taxation purposes only FIFO acceptable.

Chapter 8

1. a. Four factors leading to changes in the labour cost percentage
    i.   The increase in sales value may be due to selling price increases rather than the volume (no. of units) sold. If so the labour cost percentage is bound to fall.
    ii. Because fixed costs go to make up the sales value a variable cost such as direct labour would automatically become a smaller percentage.
    iii. The sales mix, and hence production mix, may be different in the two periods causing a change in the relative proportion of labour costs.
    iv. Although impossible to tell from the figures given there could be a genuine improvement in labour efficiency.

    b. The report is not an effective means of controlling labour costs. Specifically it lacks detail, and most importantly no comparison is shown between the actual labour cost for the actual production and what the labour cost should have been. Furthermore it is unsatisfactory to group all labour costs together and relate them to one factor such as sales value. Each type of labour cost should be considered separately and controlled individually. In general the most appropriate control measures would be:—

	Best controlled by:—
Direct labour	— Standard costs based on engineering and work study investigations. Control ratios.
Indirect labour	— Flexible budgets relating to the most appropriate measure of activity for each cost.

Note:

The latter part of this question uses some material covered later in the manual. The answer is given for completeness but, if desired, it can be ignored at this stage.

2. If indeed it is "common cost accounting practice to treat direct wages as an item of variable cost" then this is to be deprecated unless the analysis of actual wage costs compared with activity levels shows that direct wages *behave* as a variable cost. Any item of cost must be classified into variable, semi variable or fixed in accordance with its *observed behaviour* in the actual circumstances not in accordance with some traditional view of its nature.

Rarely, if ever, can wages be classed as a truly variable or truly fixed cost. The existence of guaranteed minimum wages, production bonuses and other specialised parts of wage agreements mitigates against simplistic categorisation.

The factors which should be considered when dealing with the classification of wages costs include:—

a. **The activity range.** The smaller the variation in activity the more likely the costs are to be of a fixed nature.

b. **The time period involved.** The shorter the period the more fixed the costs, the longer the period the more possibility of variability.

c. **The type and supply of labour.** Scarce and/or highly skilled labour will tend to be more safeguarded and protected by the company thus making their costs more of a fixed nature. Conversely unskilled or casual labour is likely to be more variable in nature.

d. The type of remuneration schemes and agreed bonuses/minimums built in the remuneration structure.

e. **The type of production method.** Highly mechanised factories will tend to have wages costs which have fixed characteristics.

Chapter 9

Remuneration of Employees

Employee	Hourly Rate		Basic Piece Rate		Bonus Scheme	
		£		£	Hourly £50 +	£
Salmon	40 hrs @ £1.25 =	50.00	270 @ £0.2 =	54.00	Bonus $\frac{1}{9}$ x £50 =	55.55
Roach	38 hrs @ £1.05 =	39.90	200 @ £0.25 =	50.00	Hourly £39.90 + Bonus $\frac{6}{25}$ x £39.90 = 49.48	
Pike	36 hrs @ £1.2 =	43.20	220 @ £0.24 =	52.80	Hourly £43.20 + Bonus $\frac{2}{11}$ x £43.20 = 51.06	

b. **Effectiveness of bonus scheme.**
Although such a bonus scheme has the theoretical advantage that time saved is shared between employer and employee it is likely to be unpopular to both. To the employer because it is more complicated to administer than straight piece work and to the employee because there is an inbuilt ceiling to earnings. Accordingly the normal piecework rate is likely to be preferred.

Chapter 10

1.

Calculation of Overhead Absorption Rates

	Machine Shop	Assembly Department	Canteen	Total
	£	£	£	£
Allocated overheads	68,000	39,000	16,000	123,000
Apportionment of canteen (on number of employees)	10,000	6,000	(16,000)	
= Total overheads	£78,000	£45,000	–	£123,000
Absorption Base	**Machine Hours**		**Labour Hours**	
Budgeted Hours (Note 1)	26,000		18,000	
∴ Budgeted absorption rate	£3 per machine hr.		£2.50 per labour hour	

Note 1. The budgeted hours are calculated as follows

Products	A	B	
Budgeted production (unit)	2,000	2,500	
Machine hours per unit	3	8	
. . Total machine hours	6,000	20,000	= 26,000 total
Labour hours per unit	4	4	
. . Total labour hours	8,000	10,000	= 18,000 total)

The absorption bases chosen. In general time based methods are superior and where overheads are likely to reflect machine costs a machine hour basis is preferable whereas where costs reflect the labour hours then a labour hour basis is probably more equitable.

b. Results if Sales and Production of A are 300 higher than budget.

Although it is stated that the company uses absorption costing it is fortunate that fixed and variable costs are separated in the figures supplied, thus:—

		£
Variable Cost per unit of A		
= Materials		8
Labour Machine Shop	15	
Assembly	8	23
(Note 1) Variable overheads:		
Machine Shop 3 hrs @ £1/hr	3	
Assembly 4 hrs @ £0.50/hr	2	5
= Total Variable Cost		£36
. . Contribution from additional 300		£
Sales = 300 x £60 =		18,000
Less Variable Cost 300 x £36 =		10,800
= Total extra contribution		£7,200

As the company is already operating over breakeven point the extra contribution becomes extra profit.

Note 1. The variable overhead absorption rates are:—

	Machine Shop	Assembly
	£	£
Variable Overheads	26,000	9,000
Absorption base	26,000 m/c hrs.	18,000 labour hours
. . VOAR	£1 per m/c hour	£0.50 per labour hour

2. The method of production overhead absorption given in the question is probably the worst that could be thought of in the circumstances described, (which is, no doubt, the reason it was selected by the Examiner!).

The main objections to it are as follows:

a. The units are not standard therefore overheads would not be shared equally.

b. No recognition is given to the differing nature of the production departments.

c. It makes no allowance for the differing demand the products make on the departments or the fact that some products do not pass through each department.

d. Product costs will be arbitrarily affected by the seasonal fluctuations.

e. Being calculated after the end of the period the advantages gained by the use of predetermined overheads will be lost.

The above objections include comments on the effect on product costs.

If the company bases its prices on costs then the absorption method used will influence prices in the following ways:

a. As costs are averaged, more complex and time consuming products will be under costed and thus under priced. This will mean that the company will tend to obtain more of this type of business to the detriment of profitability. The converse will apply to simpler and cheaper products.

b. Prices, if cost related, will be affected by the seasonable fluctuations resulting in higher prices when activity is low and lower prices when activity is high which is the exact opposite of a rational pricing policy.

c. There is also the real operational problem that if prices are cost related there will be delays in price fixing because predetermined O.A.R's are not used.

If prices are determined by market forces then the methods used in establishing costs will have no effect although the profitability shown for each of the products will have little basis in reality.

3. The first step is to calculate the budgeted O.A.R. for the two departments viz:

O.A.R. machining dept.

$$= \frac{\text{Budgeted overheads}}{\text{Budgeted absorption base}} = \frac{£9,000}{300 \text{ m/c hrs}} = \underline{\underline{£30/\text{hour}}}$$

O.A.R. Finishing dept.

$$= \frac{£7,500}{3000 \text{ labour hrs}} = \underline{\underline{£2.5/\text{hour}}}$$

Secondly an overhead schedule showing the allocations and apportionments is prepared.

	Machining	Finishing	Main-tenance	Materials Handling
	£	£	£	£
Materials	2,000	3,000	1,000	200
Labour	3,000	900	2,000	3,000
Other allocated costs	600	400	800	300
	5,600	4,300	3,800	3,500
Redistribution of Service Dept. costs				
Maintenance	2,280	1,140	-3,800	380
Materials Handling	1,164	1,940	776	-3,880
Maintenance	466	233	-776	77
Materials Handling	23	39	15	-77
Maintenance	10	5	-15	
Production Depts' Overhead incurred	£9,543	£7,657	—	—

Having dealt with these two essential preliminaries the question can be answered.

a. Overhead accounts.

Machining Department Overheads

Overheads incurred per Schedule	9,543	W.I.P. (absorbed)	8,760 (i)
		Under absorption – P & L A/c	783
	£9,543		£9543

Finishing Department Overheads

Overheads incurred per schedule	7,657	W.I.P. (absorbed)	7,750 (ii)
Over absorption – P & L A/C	93		
	£7,750		£7,750

Notes:
i. Overhead absorbed = actual hours x OAR
= 292 x £30 = £8,760
ii. = 3100 x £2.5 = £7,750

(b. and c.)
The only factors which can give rise to under/over absorption are:

Expenditure being greater/less than budget
and/or Activity being greater/less than budget

Thus, in the two departments given:

Machining Department

	Budget c/f	Actual	results in Under or Over Absorption (U or O)
Expenditure	£9,000	£9,543	£543 (U)
Activity	300 hrs	292 hrs	(8 hrs x £30) £240 (U)
			£783 (U)

Finishing Department

	Budget c/f	Actual	results in Under or Over Absorption (U or O)
Expenditure	£7,500	£7,657	£157 (U)
Activity	3,000 hrs	3,100 hrs	(100 x £2.5) £250 (O)
			£93 (O)

4. Part (a) Calculation of appropriate absorption rates

Dept.	Most Appropriate Base	Budgeted Overheads	Budgeted Absorption Base	Overhead Absorption Rate
Forming	Machine hours	£602,700	98,000	£6.15 per m/hr
Finishing	Labour Hours	£346,500	154,000	£2.25 per l/hr

The choice of absorption base has been dealt with in the text and in previous answers.

b. Based on cost criteria only it is worthwhile purchasing outside when the purchase price is below the marginal (ie variable only) cost of manufacture assuming the following:—

i. It is possible to isolate fixed and variable costs.

ii. That fixed overheads are period or time related costs and do not vary with activity.

iii. That variable costs vary linearly with activity.

Dealing with the specific figures given

	Component		
Marginal Cost of Manufacture	A	B	C
	£	£	£
Prime Cost	24.00	31.00	29.00
Variable Overheads* – forming	8.20	6.15	4.10
Finishing	2.25	7.50	1.50
= Marginal Cost/unit	£34.45	£44.65	£34.60
Purchase Price	£30	£65	£60

∴ based on cost criteria, Component A should be purchased and B & C manufactured.

* The variable overhead recovery rates and overhead absorbed are calculated as follows:

Forming $\frac{£200,900}{98,000}$ = £2.05 per machine hour

gives 4 x 2.05 = £8.20 Dept A
3 x 2.05 = £6.15 Dept B
2 x 2.05 = £4.10 Dept C

Finishing $\frac{£115,500}{£154,000}$ = £0.75 per labour hour

gives 3 x 0.75 = £2.25 Dept A
10 x 0.75 = £7.50 Dept B
2 x 0.75 = £1.50 Dept C

c. **Purpose of calculating production overhead absorption rates.**
The prime purpose is to obtain a product cost which can be used for Stock valuation, determining periodic profits, and as a basis for pricing and estimating. It must be remembered that the process of overhead absorption is an accounting convention with all the limitations that conventions imply. For purposes such as outlined above, if used consistently, production overhead absorption rates are useful and are an integral part of most costing systems. Absorption rates, which contain fixed and variable elements must be used with great caution for decision making purposes where activity levels may change because the fixed portion does not change whereas the variable proportion is influenced by the activity change.

5. a. See Overhead Analysis Sheet opposite.

c. Overheads absorbed by the two products

		Gamma		Delta
M/c Shop A	5 x £1.34	£6.70	3 x £1.34	£4.02
B	2 x £1.05	£2.10	7 x £1.05	£7.35
Assembly	7 x £0.07	£0.49	9 x £0.07	£0.63
= Absorbed O'heads		£9.29		£12.00

6. a.

	Production Cost Centres			Service Cost Centres	
	1	2	3	S	T
	£	£	£	£	£
Overheads Allocated	20,000	24,000	36,000	13,500	9,500
Apportionment of S	–	$\frac{(55)}{(90)}$ 8,250	$\frac{(35)}{(90)}$ 5,250	–13,500	
Apportionment of T	$\frac{(45)}{(95)}$ 4,500	$\frac{(35)}{(95)}$ 3,500	$\frac{(15)}{(95)}$ 1,500		–9,500
Chargeable overhead	£24,500	£35,750	£42,750	–	–

b.

	1	2	3	S	T
Overheads Allocated	20,000	24,000	36,000	13,500	9,500
Apportionment of T	$\frac{(45)}{(100)}$ 4,275	$\frac{(35)}{(100)}$ 3,325	$\frac{(15)}{(100)}$ 1,425	$\frac{(5)}{(100)}$ 475	–9,500
Apportionment of S		$\frac{(55)}{(90)}$ 8,540	$\frac{(35)}{(90)}$ 5,435	–13,975	
Chargeable Overhead	£24,275	£35,865	£42,860	–	–

c.

	1	2	3	S	T
Overheads Allocated	20,000	24,000	36,000	13,500	9,500
1st Apportionment of S	–	7,425	4,725	–13,500	1,350
1st Apportionment of T	4,883	3,798	1,627	542	–10,850
2nd Apportionment of S	–	298	190	–542	54
2nd Apportionment of T	24	19	8	3	–54
Final Apportionment of S	–	2	1	–3	
Chargeable Overhead	£24,907	£35,542	£42,551	–	–

a.

Overhead Analysis Sheet

	Bases	Machine shops A £	B £	Assembly £	Stores £	Engineering Service £	General Services £	TOTAL £
Indirect wages	—	23,260	20,670	8,110	4,100	2,670	3,760	62,570
Cons. supplies	—	6,300	9,100	2,100	1,400	2,100	1,600	22,600
Depreciation m/cy	Bk. value	8,800	6,600	2,200	880	2,640	880	22,000
Insurance of m/cy	Bk. value	1,600	1,200	400	160	480	160	4,000
Insurance of building	special	600	—	—	—	—	—	1,800
Insurance of building	Area	—	360	480	120	150	90	
Power	H.P.	1,800	1,200	150	—	450	—	3,600
Light and Heat	Area	600	720	960	240	300	180	3,000
Rent and Rates	Area	1,500	1,800	2,400	600	750	—	7,530
Rent and Rates	special	—	—	—	—	—	480	
		44,460	41,650	16,800	7,500	9,540	7,150	127,100
Transfers								
Stores	Cons. sppl.	2,700	3,900	900	(7,500)	—	—	—
Eng. services	m/c hours	4,240	5,300	—	—	(9,540)	—	—
Genl. service	lab. hours	2,200	1,650	3,300	—	—	(7,150)	—
		53,600	52,500	21,000	—	—	—	127,100

b.

	A	B	Assembly
Rate per machine hour	£1.34	£1.05	—
Rate per direct labour hour			£0.07

Chapter 12

1. Current overhead absorption rate –

   a. percentage of direct wages

   $$= \frac{\text{Budgeted production overhead}}{\text{Budgeted Direct Wages}} \times 100\% = \frac{£225,000}{£150,000} \times 100 = \underline{150\%}$$

   b. Production overhead – Production Cost and Gross Profit

   ### Cost of Job No. 657

	£
Direct Materials	190,000
Wages	170,000
= Prime Cost	360,000
Production Overhead	
(150% of 170,000)	255,000
= Total Production Cost	615,000
Gross Profit (⅓ of 615,000)	205,000
	£820,000

   c. i. A single overhead rate, as indicated in the first part of the question, is only likely to give accurate job costs when the incidence of overheads in each department is similar. From the data given it is apparent that this is not so. Department A with a quarter of the direct wages of B has four times the production overheads probably indicating a substantial amount of machinery related overheads. In such circumstances anomalies would arise between job costs because the rate used is an average of substantially different patterns of overheads.

   ii. **Departmental rates.**
   Department A. There are a considerable number of machine hours with a correspondingly high incidence of overheads. It is likely that a MACHINE HOUR RATE would be most appropriate i.e.

   $$\frac{\text{Budgeted overhead}}{\text{Budgeted Machine Hours}} = \frac{£120,000}{40,000} = \underline{£3 \text{ per machine hour}}$$

   Department B. In this department the large number of labour hours would indicate that a LABOUR HOUR RATE would be most appropriate i.e.

   $$\frac{\text{Budgeted Overhead}}{\text{Budgeted Labour Hours}} = \frac{£30,000}{50,000} = \underline{£0.6 \text{ per labour hour}}$$

   Department C. A machine hour rate cannot be considered because there are apparently no machine hours involved.
   Accordingly a labour hour rate would be appropriate or, as there appears to be only a single wage rate of £1 per hour, a percentage on direct wages. Both absorption bases would give the same result.

   Labour hour rate

   $$\frac{\text{Budgeted overheads}}{\text{Budgeted Labour Hours}} = \frac{£75,000}{25,000 \text{ hrs}} = \underline{£3 \text{ per labour hour}}$$

or **Direct Wages Percentage**

$$\frac{\text{Budgeted Overheads}}{\text{Budgeted Wages}} \times 100\% = \frac{£75,000}{£25,000} \times 100\% = \underline{300\%}$$

d. Production overhead using departmental rates

Job 657

Dept		£
A	40 machine hours x £3 per hour	120
B	40 labour hours x £0.6 per hour	24
C	10 labour hours x £3 per hour	30
		£174

This compares with the £255 shown in part (b) above.

e. Over or (under) absorption

i. Using single rate of 150% on wages

Dept	Absorbed £	Actual £	Over (under) Absorption £
A	45,000	130,000	(85,000)
B	120,000	28,000	92,000
C	45,000	80,000	(35,000)
	£210,000	£238,000	(£28,000)

ii. Using departmental rates

A	135,000	130,000	5,000
B	27,000	28,000	(1,000)
C	90,000	80,000	10,000
	£252,000	£238,000	£14,000

Chapter 13

1.

B Construction Ltd

Office Block Contract A/c

Contract No ....

Date Started 3/1/78

Target Completion 31/3/79

	£'000		£'000
Material issues	161	Material returns	14
Wages (+ accrued £2000)	70	Material on site c/f	24
Depreciation $\frac{10}{12} \times 12\frac{1}{2}\% \times 96,000$	10	Cost to date c/f	361
Plant hire	72		
Staff Direct	11		
Indirect	12		
Head Office charges	63		
	£399		£399
Cost to date b/d	361	Contractee A/c	
P & L A/c claimed profit	43	– Value of work certified	400
Profit in suspense c/f	36	Cost of work not yet	
		certified c/f	40
	£440		£440
1st November			
Material on site B/d	24	Profit in suspense b/d	36
Cost of work not yet certified	40	Accrued wages	2

Notes:

Calculation of profits	
Cost of work to date	£361,000
Less Cost of work not yet certified	40,000
= Net cost of work certified	321,000
Value of work certified	400,000
Calculated Profit	£79,000

The calculated profit is reduced by a contingency proportion (⅔) and again by the ratio of cash received to value of work certified i.e.

$$£79,000 \times \tfrac{2}{3} \times \frac{330,000}{400,000} = £43,450 \text{ rounded down to £43,000.}$$

b. The main reasons for the profit calculation shown above are:

a. **Prudence.** Many unforeseen contingencies may arise in construction work and this is an attempt to allow for this.

b. **Custom and practice in the construction industry.** Following normal practice in this way is consistent and allows some degree of comparability.

c. **Profit smoothing.** If no allowance was made for profit on uncompleted projects construction company accounts would alternate between heavy losses and substantial profits depending on the completion dates of contracts in relation to year end dates.

c. **Extracts from balance sheet at 31st October 1978.**

	£	£
Fixed Assets		
Plant at cost	96,000	
Depreciation to date	10,000	86,000
Current Assets		
Site materials		24,000
Work-in-progress		
costs to date	361,000	
plus Claimed profit	43,000	
	404,000	
less Cash receipts	330,000	74,000
Current Liabilities		
Accrued wages	-	2,000

Chapter 15

1. a. Differences between Job Costing and Process Costing.

(**Note:** In the examination room it would be essential to define Job and Process Costing before discussing the differences. The definitions are given in the text).

	Job Costing	**Process Costing**
COST UNIT	Is the Job. It is specific, usually unique and costs are collected using a Job Cost Card against a specific order number.	Is a standardised unit indistinguishable from other units. The cost per unit is an average of the costs and quantity produced over a period.
OVERHEADS	Are allocated and apportioned to cost centres then absorbed by Jobs in proportion to the time taken.	Because units pass through the same processes averaging is used thus making for simpler overhead procedures.
JOINT PRODUCTS/ BY PRODUCTS	Do not usually arise in jobbing work.	Frequently the process produces more than one product. When this occurs joint cost apportionment is necessary.

W-I-P Valuation	This is specific and is obtained from analysis of outstanding jobs.	Operating costs have to be spread over fully complete output and partially complete using the concept of equivalent units.
Standard Costing	Generally not suitable for jobbing work.	The standardised nature of the products and processing methods lends itself to the adoption of standard costing.

Any industry with standardised output which follows common processes could use process costing. Typical industries include:

Distilling and brewing.
Soap and detergent.
Paints and varnish.
Chemicals and plastics.

b. **Process Accounts, Abnormal Scrap and Packing Dept accounts**

Process 1 Account

	Kg	£		Kg	£
Material A	6,000	3,000	Normal Scrap –		
B	4,000	4,000	Cash A/C	500	80
Mixing labour			Abnormal Scrap		
(430 hrs)		860	(£1/Kg)	300	300
Mixing Overhead			Output to Process 2		
(at £4 per hour)		1,720	(£1/Kg)	9,200	9,200
	10,000	9,580		10,000	9,580

Process 2 Account

	Kg	£		Kg	£
Transfers from			Normal waste		
Process 1	9,200	9,200	(5% of 20,000)	1,000	–
Material C	6,600	8,250	Packing Dept		
D	4,200	3,150	(@ £1.22 Kg)	18,000	21,960
Flavouring		300	W-I-P c/f		
Labour (370 hrs)		740	– Mat'l (@ £1.10 Kg)	1,000	1,100
Overhead (£4 hour)		1,480	– Labour (500 Equiv. Units @ 4p)		20
			– Overhead (500 Equiv. Units @ 8p)		40
	20,000	23,120		20,000	23,120

Abnormal Scrap Account

	Kg	£		Kg	£
Process 1 (at £1 Kg)	300	300	Cash A/c (Sales @ 16p per Kg)	300	48
			Balance to P & L	–	252
	300	300		300	300

Packing Department Account

	Kg	£
Process 2 (Output @ £1.22 Kg)	18,000	21,960

Notes: On Process 1

a. Calculation of normal cost per unit used for abnormal scrap and output to Process 2.

Normal cost per unit

	£
Material A: 6000 Kg @ £0.50	3,000
B: 4000 Kg @ £1.00	4,000
Labour 430 hrs @ £2 hour	860
Overheads 430 hrs @ £4 hour	1,720
	9,580

Less Sale of normal scrap	
= 5% of 10,000 Kg @ £0.16 per Kg	80
∴ Normal output = 9500 Kgs costing	£9,500
	= £1 per Kg

Notes: on Process 2

Calculation of costs of output and W-I-P

	Material	Labour	Overhead	
Output units	18,000	18,000	18,000	
WIP equivalent UNITS	1,000	500	500	
Equivalent units of good O/P	19,000	18,500	18,500	
Equivalent units for cost calculations	19,000	18,500	18,500	
Costs £				
Materials Process 1 9,200				
Material C & D 11,400				
Flavouring 300	20,900			
Labour		740		
Overhead			1,480	
Total spread over net output of 19,000 units				23,120
Cost per equivalent unit	£1.10	£0.04	£0.08	£1.22

2. a. Characteristics and purpose of:–

    i.   Job Costing is used where work is undertaken to customers requirements. It is appropriate where the work is of relatively short duration and where costs can be identified to a particular job or batch as work progresses. It is equally applicable to product costing e.g. a special boiler or to service cost determination e.g. a software house writing a program for a customer. The major purpose is for cost determination.

ii. Process costing is used where quantities of a standardised good or service passes, more or less continuously, through a series of common operations. Costs are not identifiable with individual units but are charged to the processes and then averaged over the units produced. The major purpose is cost determination although, because of the standardised products and processes involved, cost control via cost comparison is feasible.

b. Material waste and process losses. Where loss or waste is unavoidable in the process of manufacture e.g. material loss when machining, the normal level of loss or waste forms part of the inherent cost of the product and would be included in the cost of manufacture and in inventory valuations. Where abnormal levels of waste occur, which could be considered as avoidable, the cost of the waste above normal level would not be included in normal production costs and inventory valuations but written off to Profit and Loss as they are incurred. For control purposes it is essential that waste and scrap levels are monitored and reported upon frequently.

Chapter 16

1. a. Cost apportionment based on weights at split-off point.

Dept 1 produces PA, PB and QA

	Cost per Batch
	£
Material 50 lbs P @ £0.8 =	40
70 lbs Q @ £0.6 =	42
30 lbs R @ £0.2 =	6
Conversion cost	32
= Cost per batch	£120

	PA	PB	QA
Output proportions	30	20	50
Proportions of £120 cost	£36	£24	£60

Dept 2

	Cost per Batch
Material 20 lbs PB	24
50 lbs S @ £0.30	15
Conversion Cost	10
= Cost of PX	49

	PA	PB	QA	PX
∴ Cost per Batch	£36	£24	£60	£49

b. Cost per lb of PAS

Dept 3

	Costs per batch
	£
30 lbs PA	36
20 lbs S @ £0.30	6
Conversion Cost	24
	£66

which would be spread over the main product i.e. 10 lbs of PAS

$\therefore$ Cost per lb of PAS $= \dfrac{£66}{10} = \underline{\underline{£6.6}}$

When net revenue from PAS reduces departmental costs.

$$\text{AZ Net revenue} = (£0.40 - £0.05) \times 40 \text{ lbs} = £14$$

$$\therefore \text{Cost per lb of PAS} = \dfrac{£66-14}{10} = \underline{\underline{£5.20 \text{ lb}}}$$

c. Total profit in Period 5

		£
Sales (Note 1)		27,564
Less Departmental Costs (Note 2)		
	£	
Dept 1	9,600	
Dept 2	2,000	
Dept 3	2,400	
Packing	128	
	14,128	
Less Closing Stocks (Note 3)	1,068	13,060
		14,504
Fixed costs		6,000
= Profit		£8,504

Note 1	Sales		£
PAS	80 batches x 10 lbs = 800 lbs @ £15	=	12,000
PX	80 batches x 50 lbs x 85% = 3400 lbs @ £1.1	=	3,740
AZ	80 batches x 40 lbs x 80% = 2560 @ £0.40	=	1,024
QA	80 batches x 50 lbs x 90% = 3600 lbs @ £3	=	10,800
			£27,564

Note 2

	Costs	
Dept 1	80 x £120 =	£9,600
Dept 2	(80 x 50 lbs x £0.30) + conversion (80 x £10) =	£2,000
Dept 3	(80 x 20 lbs x £0.30) + conversion (80 x £24) =	£2,400

Note 3

Closing Stocks

QA   10% of $(80 \times 50 \text{ lbs} \times \dfrac{£60}{50}) = £480$

PX   15% of $(80 \times 50 \text{ lbs} \times \dfrac{£49}{50}) = 588 = \underline{\underline{£1,068}}$

Net sales value per lb of PB

	£
Sales 50 lbs PX @ £1.10/lb	55
Less Dept 2 costs (Net of PB cost)	25
	£30

$\therefore$ net sales value of PB per lb $= \dfrac{£30}{20} = \underline{£1.50}$

Net sales value per batch

		£	%	Dept 1 costs pro rated £
PA	30 lbs @ £2	60	25	30
PB	(from above)	30	12.5	15
QA	50 lbs @ £3	150	62.5	75
		£240	100	£120

2.

Polimur Ltd
Process Operating Statement – October 1979

Sales		£	£
Product A 80,000 kilos x £5 =		400,000	
B 65,000 kilos x £4 =		260,000	
C 75,000 kilos x £9 =		675,000	1,335,000
Less Operating Costs		1,300,000	
*less Closing Stock**		200,000	1,100,000
= Profit			£235,000

* It is assumed that the phrase in the question, "Closing Stock is calculated by apportioning costs according to weight of output", means that closing stock is valued at average throughput cost per kilo regardless of the type of product

i.e. $\dfrac{\text{Total Cost}}{\text{Total Output}} = \dfrac{1,300,000}{260,000} = £5 \text{ per kilo}$

and as closing stock totalled 40,000 kilos the valuation is 40,000 x £5 = £200,000.

b. By establishing their own refining operation extra revenue per kilo can be obtained but additional variable and fixed costs would be incurred thus:–

Refining Proposal (all Products)

	Product A £	B £	C £	Total £
Additional Revenue/Kilo	12	10	11.50	
Variable costs/kilo	4	6	12.00	
Contribution/kilo	8	4	(0.50)	
Monthly Production/kilos	100,000	80,000	80,000	
	£	£	£	£
∴ Monthly Contribution	800,000	320,000	(40,000)	1,080,000
Less Specific Fixed Cost	–	360,000	–	360,000
	800,000	(40,000)	(40,000)	720,000
Less General Fixed Costs				700,000
= Profit				£20,000

Notes:

1. Under no circumstances would the refining of C be considered. If only A & B were refined the profit per month would be £20,000 + £40,000 = £60,000 whereas if only A was refined (and B & C sold unrefined) monthly profit would be £100,000 per month from the refining process.

2. If the volume of B could be increased by at least 10,000 kilos this could cause an increase in profit. However this perhaps could only be done by increasing the production of all three products which may cause sales difficulties.

3. The accuracy of all the estimates should be reviewed particularly for projected sales. Only a relatively small change in volume would cause the refining project to become unprofitable.

3.

Income Statement for June 1978
4 week period in which 220 loads were processed

	Marginal Cost per load $	Total Joint Costs $	Juice $	Rootmash $
Material Cost	600	132,000		
Washing – Variable	1	220		
– Fixed		5,000		
Crushing – Variable	10	2,200		
– Fixed		20,000		
		159,420		

Note 1

Joint Cost Apportionment		95,652	63,768
Cooking – Variable	20		4,400
– Fixed			15,000
Total Cost of Processing	631	95,652	83,168
Sales 88,000 litres @ $1.5 per litre		132,000	
88,000 kilos @ $1.00 per kilo			88,000
Less 10% Sales Tax		13,200	8,800
= Net Sales		$118,800	$79,200
Profit (loss)		$23,148	($3,968)

	Total
Profit b/d	$19,180

Less General Admin Costs	
4 x $ 6,140	24,560
= (LOSS)	$(5,380)

Note 1: The apportionment of joint costs has been done on the basis of net sales value per product per load i.e. $540 and $360

b. Breakeven no. of loads

Net Sales value per load =	$540 + $360
=	$900
Less Marginal cost per load	631
= Contribution per load	$269

. . No. of loads to break even given a total fixed cost per week of $16,140.

$$= \frac{\$16,140}{269} = \underline{60 \text{ loads}}$$

c. Revised working method and new breakeven point

1% extra yield would produce 1% of net sales value per load i.e. 1% x $900 = $9

. . Total contribution per load becomes $269 + 9 = $278

The new method will incur extra fixed costs of $1,636 of which the Government will pay half.

	$
. . Additional costs incurred = $\frac{1636}{2}$ =	818
but extra contribution on 60 loads = 60 x 9 =	540
. . Balance to be covered by extra loads =	$278

which equals 1 extra load

. . new breakeven point is 61 loads

4. The overhead absorption rate is

$$\frac{\text{Budgeted Overhead}}{\text{Direct Wages}} \times 100\% = \frac{£84,000}{21,000} = 400\%$$

The process accounts

Process I A/c

	Units	£		Units	£
Material introduced (£2 unit)	10,000	20,000	Normal loss (£1 unit)	1,000	1,000
Material added		6,000	Output to II (£6 unit)	8,800	52,800
Wages		5,000	Abnormal loss (£6 unit)	200	1,200
Expenses		4,000			
Production Overhead		20,000			
	£10,000	£55,000		£10,000	£55,000

Notes on Process I

Input 10,000 units cost £55,000

Normal loss 10% 1,000 Scrap value £1,000

∴ Normal output and cost = 9,000 units @ £54,000

∴ Normal cost/unit = £6 used for transfers and abnormal losses.

Process II A/c

	Units	£		Units	£
Material from Process I	8,800	52,800	Output to Process II (£12 unit)	8,400	100,800
Material added		12,640	Normal loss (£3 unit)	440	1,320
Wages		6,000			
Expenses		6,200			
Overhead		24,000			
Abnormal Gain (£12 per unit)	40	480			
	£8,840	102,120		£8,840	102,120

Notes on Process II

Input	8,800	units costing	£101,640
Normal loss	440	@ £3	1,320
Normal output	8,360		100,320

$$\therefore \text{Normal cost per unit} = \frac{100,320}{8,360} = £12$$

Process III A/c

	Units	£		Units	£
Material from Process II	8,400	100,800	Transfer to Fin. Goods (£24 unit)	7,000	168,000
Material added		23,200	BP9 Net Sales value (£6 unit)	420	2,520
Wages		10,000	Normal loss (£5 unit)	840	4,200
Expenses		4,080	Abnormal loss (£24 unit)	140	3,360
Overhead		40,000			
	8,400	178,080		8,400	178,080

371

Notes on Process III

Input	8,400 units @	£178,080
Less Normal loss	840 @ £5	4,200
Less BP9	420 Net Revenue	2,520
= Normal o/p	7,140 units at	£171,360 cost

$$\therefore \text{Normal cost per unit} = \frac{171,360}{7,140} = £24$$

BP9 Process A/c

	Units	£		Units	£
Transfers from III	420	2,560	Transfer to Fin. Goods	420	3,780
Process Cost (£2 unit)		840			
S & D Costs (£1 unit)		420			
	£420	£3,780		420	£3,780

Abnormal Loss A/c

	Units	£		Units	£
Process I	200	1,200	Scrap value (£1 unit)	200	200
II	140	3,360	(£5 unit)	140	700
			Bal. to P & L		3,660
	340	£4,560		340	£4,560

Abnormal Gain A/c

	Units	£		Units	£
Scrap value (£3 unit)	40	120	Process II	40	480
Bal. to P & L		360			
	40	£480		40	£480

5. a. The first stage is to calculate the individual weight proportions of the products to the total weight of 240 tonnes.

Products

	A	B	C
Weight proportion	$\frac{100}{240} = \underline{41.67\%}$	$\frac{60}{240} = \underline{25\%}$	$\frac{80}{240} = \underline{33.33\%}$

Profit Statement

	Products								
	A		B		C			Total	
	£		£		£			£	
Sales Revenue	50,000		48,000		48,000			146,000	
Less	£		£		£		£		
Pre-separation Costs in weight proportions	40,000		24,000		32,000		96,000		
Post separation costs	20,000	60,000	12,000	36,000	8,000	40,000	40,000	136,000	
=Profit (LOSS)	£(10,000)		12,000		8,000			10,000	

372

b. This part of the question involves comparing the extra revenue obtained from further processing after the separation point with the costs of that processing.

Financial effects of further processing

	Products		
	A	B	C
	£	£	£
Incremental Revenue from further processing.*	25,000	6,000	12,000
Less Post separation costs	20,000	12,000	8,000
= Incremental net revenue Profit (LOSS)	£5,000	(£6,000)	£4,000

The table shows that £6,000 additional profit would be gained if Product B was sold at separation point and was not further processed.

* The incremental revenue figures are obtained as follows:

Product A £500 – 250 = £250 tonne x 100 tonnes = £25,000
        B £800 – 700 = £100 tonne x 60 tonnes = £6,000
        C £600 – 450 = £150 tonne x 80 tonnes = £12,000

Chapter 18

1. a. i. Estimate of fixed and variable elements

High and Low points

	Machine hours (000's)	Fuel Oil ($)
High point – June 1979	48	680
Low point – Jan 1979	26	500
Range or difference	22	180

. ˙ . rate of change of variable cost (B)

$$= \frac{180}{22} = \$8.18 \text{ per 1000 machine hours}$$

Based on this value the fixed element (a) can be calculated by taking either the high or low point i.e.

Taking low point

$$500 = a + (8.18 \times 26)$$
$$\therefore \quad a = 500 - (8.18 \times 26)$$
$$= 287.32$$

Thus the full equation is

$$y = 287.32 + 8.18x$$

ii. Using the normal equations method the coefficients are calculated as follows

$$\Sigma y = a \, n + b\Sigma x \quad \ldots \ldots \text{ I}$$
$$\Sigma xy = a\Sigma x + b\Sigma x^2 \ldots \ldots \text{ II}$$

x	y	xy	x^2
34	640	21,760	1,156
30	620	18,600	900
34	620	21,080	1,156
39	590	23,010	1,521
42	500	21,000	1,764
32	530	16,960	1,024
26	500	13,000	676
26	500	13,000	676
31	530	16,430	961
35	550	19,250	1,225
43	580	24,940	1,849
48	680	32,640	2,304

$$\Sigma x = 420 \qquad \Sigma y = 6,840 \qquad \Sigma xy = 241,670 \qquad \Sigma x^2 = 15,212$$

Substituting in the equations we obtain

$$6840 = 12a + 420b \quad \ldots \ldots \text{ I}$$
$$241,670 = 420a + 15,212b \quad \ldots \ldots \text{ II}$$

and eliminating one equation in the normal manner thus

$$241,670 = 420a + 15,212b \quad \ldots \ldots \text{ II}$$
$$239,400 = 420a + 14,700b \quad \ldots \ldots \text{ I} \times 35$$
$$\overline{ \qquad \qquad \qquad}$$
$$2,270 = \qquad \qquad 512b$$
$$\therefore b = \underline{4.43}$$

and substituting in one of the equations the value of *a* can be obtained i.e.

$$6840 = 12a + (420 \times 4.43)$$
$$\therefore a = \underline{415}$$

Thus the least squares equation is

$$y = \underline{415 + 4.43x}$$

a. **Comparison of High/Low and Least Squares methods.**

The high/low method, being based on two extreme values only, is unreliable and statistically inefficient. No further tests relating to the coefficients can be made and therefore the high/low method is not recommended.

The least squares method takes account of all the data, is statistically sound, and further tests can be made based on the coefficients obtained.

c. **Coefficient of determination.**

This measure denoted by r^2 (because it is the square of the correlation coefficient) signifies what proportion of the variation of the actual values of y (Fuel oil expenses) may be predicted by changes in the values of x (machine hours). Thus, given that r^2 is 0.25 this means that only 25% of the values of fuel oil can be predicted by changes in the value of machine hours. The fuel oil cost is influenced by non-volume factors much more than by changes in volume.

2. a. The statement is correct in one sense and incorrect in another.
    It is correct in the sense that the fixed cost *per unit* falls as output increases. It is incorrect in that fixed costs in total do not fall as output increases. When the term fixed cost is used it invariably means a total cost such as rates, and as such the statement given is misleading.

    b. i.

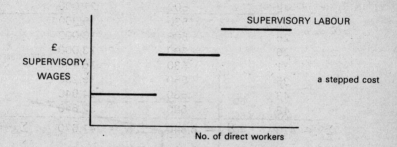

    ii.

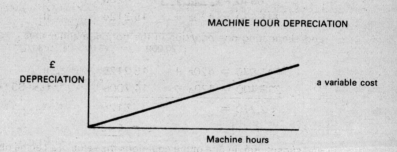

    iii.

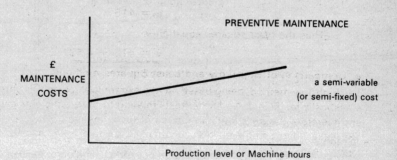

Note:

Depending on the incidence of unexpected maintenance there is no reason why the graph should not be curvi-linear;

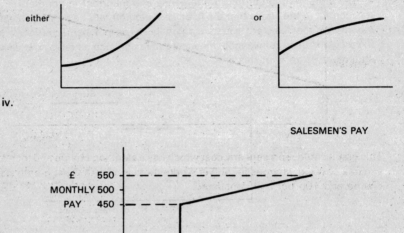

either   or

iv.

SALESMEN'S PAY

£   550 – – – – – – – – – – – – – – – –
MONTHLY 500 –
PAY   450 – – –

          250 –

          £20,000   £25,000   £30,000

          Previous month's sales

3. a. Overhead cost patterns

Reference No.	Cost Description	Graph Reference
1	Depreciation of equipment	C
2	Cost of a service	F
3	Royalty	B
4	Supervision	H
5	Machine hour depreciation	E
6	Cost of a service	K
7	Storage/carriage service	G
8	Outside finishing	D

b. Graphs not used A & J.

Graph A

Any cost which has a standing charge covering usage up to a given volume and thereafter has an additional charge per unit. e.g. Use of a photo copying machine with a standing charge of £500 which covers all copies up to 5,000. Above 5,000 copies would be charged at an additional cost of 10p per copy.

Graph J

Any scarce resource, with no standing charge, which has an increasing marginal cost e.g. engineer's service calls could be charged for the first 5 hours £10 per hour, from 5-15 hours £13 hour and so on.

c.

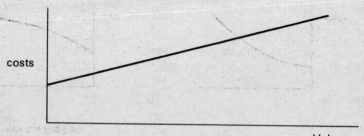

This graph could represent any cost which has a standing charge and then a linear variable cost e.g. charges for power where there is a £1,000 per month standing charge and 10p per unit consumed.

Chapter 19

1. a. i.

Budgeted profit/loss Statement based on absorption costing

	1981 Units	1981 £'000s	1982 Units	1982 £'000s
Sales	8,000	800	10,000	1,000
Production cost of sales				
Opening Stock	–	–	2,000*	150
+ Production Costs absorbed	10,000*	750	8,000*	600
– Closing Stock	2,000*	150		
= Net Production Cost	8,000 units	600	10,000 units	750
+ Overhead under absorbed		–	2,000 units**	40
+ Admin. overheads		100		100
+ Selling Overheads		50		50
= Total Cost of Sales		750		940
∴ Net Profit		£50		£60

* Valued at full production cost/unit of £75 i.e.

     Direct material + wages + Production overhead (Fixed and variable)

** Valued at the fixed overhead cost/unit of £20 which is the amount under absorbed by producing only 8,000 units.

ii.

Budgeted profit and loss statement based on marginal costing

	1981 Units	£'000s	1982 Units	£'000s
Sales	8,000	800	10,000	1,000
Less Marginal Cost of Sales				
Opening Stock *	–	–	2,000	110
+ Marginal Prod. Cost *	10,000	550	8,000	440
– Closing Stock *	2,000	110	–	–
	8,000	440	10,000	550
= CONTRIBUTION		360		450
Less Fixed Costs **		350		350
= Net Profit		£10		£100

* All valued at marginal cost/unit of £55 i.e.

Wages + materials + variable overheads

** Fixed costs include Production, Administration and Selling overheads.

b. The difference in profit between the two systems is entirely due to the differences in stock valuations. With the absorption system £40,000 of fixed overheads are carried forward from 1981 to 1982 whereas they are written off in the period they are incurred using marginal costing.

In general when production exceeds sales (1981) absorption costing shows the higher profit and when sales exceeds production (i.e. brought forward stocks are being sold) marginal costing shows the higher profit.

2. a. i. Stable sales, production and inventory – VARIABLE (or MARGINAL) COSTING

	t_1 £	t_2 £	t_3 £
Opening Stock *	1,200	1,200	1,200
+ Variable Costs of Production	12,000	12,000	12,000
	13,200	13,200	13,200
– Closing Stock *	1,200	1,200	1,200
= Production Cost of Sales	12,000	12,000	12,000
+ Variable Distribution Costs	1,000	1,000	1,000
= Total Variable Cost	13,000	13,000	13,000
Sales	25,000	25,000	25,000
∴ Contribution =	12,000	12,000	12,000
Less Fixed Costs	10,000	10,000	10,000
= Profit	£2,000	£2,000	£2,000 = £6,000 total

* Valued at variable cost of production i.e. £12/unit.

Stable Sales, production and inventory Absorption Costing

	£	£	£	
Opening Stock *	2,200	2,200	2,200	
+ Production Costs	22,000	22,000	22,000	
	24,200	24,200	24,200	
− Closing Stock *	2,200	2,200	2,200	
= Total Production Cost	22,000	22,000	22,000	
Sales	25,000	25,000	25,000	
Gross Profit	3,000	3,000	3,000	
Less Distribution Costs	1,000	1,000	1,000	
= Profit	£2,000	£2,000	£2,000	= £6,000 total

* Valued at total production cost of £22 per unit including fixed costs of £10 per unit based on normal level of 1,000 units.

a. ii.

Stable Sales fluctuating production and stock − Variable Costing

	t_1 £	t_2 £	t_3 £	
Opening Stock	1,200	7,200	4,800	
+ Variable Production Costs	18,000	9,600	8,400	
	19,200	16,800	13,200	
− Closing Stock	7,200	4,800	1,200	
= Production Cost of Sales	12,000	12,000	12,000	
+ Variable Distribution Cost	1,000	1,000	1,000	
= Total Variable Costs	13,000	13,000	13,000	
Sales	25,000	25,000	25,000	
= Contribution	12,000	12,000	12,000	
− Fixed Costs	10,000	10,000	10,000	
= Profit	2,000	2,000	2,000	= £6,000 total

Stable Sales, fluctuating production and stock – ABSORPTION COSTING

	£	£	£
Opening Stock	2,200	13,200	8,800
+ Total Production Costs	33,000	17,600	15,400
	35,200	30,800	24,200
– Closing Stock	13,200	8,800	2,200
	22,000	22,000	22,000
+ under recovery * – (over recovery)	(5,000)	2,000	3,000
= Cost of Sales	17,000	24,000	25,000
Sales	25,000	25,000	25,000
= Gross Profit	8,000	1,000	–
Less Distribution Costs	1,000	1,000	1,000
Profit (Loss)	7,000	–	(1,000)

Total £6,000

* This is the over or under recovery of the fixed element of cost e.g. in t_1 – Production is 1,500 so that 1500 x £10 of fixed costs recovered but only £10,000 incurred . . over-recovery of £5,000.

iii.

Stable production, fluctuating Sales and Stock – VARIABLE COSTING

	t_1 £	t_2 £	t_3 £
Opening Stock	1,200	7,200	4,800
+ Variable Production Cost	12,000	12,000	12,000
	13,200	19,200	16,800
– Closing Stock	7,200	4,800	1,200
= Production Var. Cost of Sales	6,000	14,400	15,600
+ Variable Distribution Costs	500	1,200	1,300
= Total Variable Cost	6,500	15,600	16,900
Sales	12,500	30,000	32,500
= Contribution	6,000	14,400	15,600
Less Fixed Costs	10,000	10,000	10,000
= Profit (LOSS)	£(4,000)	£4,400	£5,600

= £6,000 Total

Stable production, fluctuating Sales and Stock – ABSORPTION COSTING

	£	£	£
Opening Stock	2,200	13,200	8,800
+ Total Production Cost	22,000	22,000	22,000
	24,200	35,200	30,800
− Closing Stock	13,200	8,800	2,200
= Total Production Cost	11,000	26,400	28,600
Sales	12,500	30,000	32,500
Gross Profit	1,500	3,600	3,900
Less Distribution Costs	500	1,200	1,300
= Net Profit	1,000	2,400	2,600

= £6,000
total

b. Comparative evaluation of variable (marginal) and absorption costing.
Variable costing systems charge all fixed costs in the period they are incurred.
Stocks are valued at marginal cost only so that no portion of fixed costs gets
carried forward.

Absorption costing absorbs both fixed and variable costs into production so that
any stock remaining contains a proportion of one period's fixed costs which are
transferred to the next period.

All the variations in profit measurement arise from this difference. In the first part
of the question the opening stock and final closing stock were the same so that,
over the three year period, the total profit is the same under both systems.

For some purposes, e.g. profit planning, alterations in product mix, make or buy
decisions etc. information prepared on variable or marginal costing principles is
extremely useful whilst for external reporting purposes stock values based on
total cost (and the profits which result) are generally used.

It is important to select the type of costing system so that it will produce the most
relevant information, in the appropriate format, for the particular purpose
intended.

3.   a. Marginal costing/absorption costing features.

Note:
This is covered in detail in the text and in the answers to other questions.

b. i.   Fixed production overhead absorbed.

$$\text{F.O.A.R. per unit} = \frac{\text{Budgeted fixed overheads}}{\text{Budgeted production at 100\%}} =$$

$$= \frac{£200,000}{400,000 \text{ units}} = \underline{50\text{p per unit}}$$

. . amount absorbed

$$= 110,000 \times 50\text{p} = \underline{£55,000}$$

ii. Overabsorption

= amount absorbed − Budget for quarter

$$= £5,500 - \frac{£200,000}{4} = £5,000 \text{ over absorbed}$$

iii.

	£	£
Sales (80,000 x £5)		400,000
Less Costs	£	
Production - Variable (110,000 x £2)	220,000	
Production - Fixed (110,000 x 50p)	55,000	
Sales - Variable (80,000 x £1)	80,000	
Sales - Fixed (80,000 x 75p)	60,000	415,000
Less:		
Closing Stock (30,000 x £2.50)		75,000
		340,000
Over/under absorption of overheads		
Deduct		
Over Absorbed Production (10,000 x 50p)		5,000
Add		
Under Absorbed Sales (20,000 x 75p)	15,000	350,000
= PROFIT		50,000

iv. Marginal Costing. As above with the exception that the closing stock valuation is £2 not £2.50 which means that costs will be, 30,000 x 50p = £15,000 greater and profit will be £35,000.

Chapter 20

1. i. **Contribution and pricing.**
        Contribution is the difference between variable (or marginal) costs and Sales revenue. Fixed costs are deducted in total from contribution to arrive at profit. Accordingly in any decision, whether pricing or not, a firm must seek to maximise contribution, usually in relation to some limiting factor, so as to maximise profit.
        The circumstances to which the question alludes are probably those where a firm, with surplus capacity, is offered work at lower than normal selling prices yet which still produces some contribution. In such circumstances the work is likely to be worthwhile even though it is below full cost. Marginal cost pricing can be advantageous but care must be taken that overall a profit is earned.

Note:

Students should be aware that cost information is only one input into pricing decisions. Frequently selling prices are determined in relation to demand rather than product costs.

ii.

Contribution/unit	£20	£18	£16	£14	£12	£10	£8
Demand	2,000	2,400	3,000	3,800	4,800	6,000	7,500
Total Contribution	£40,000	£43,200	£48,000	£53,200	£57,600	£60,000	£60,000
Less Fixed costs	8,000	10,000	12,000	16,000	20,000	24,000	30,000
= Net Profit	£ 32,000	33,200	36,000	37,200	37,600	36,000	30,000

Optimal production and sales point
Selling Price £32

2.

Notes:

It should be apparent that there is a limiting factor involved in this question i.e. machine hours. Accordingly the key element is to gain the maximum amount of contribution from the machine hours saved by buying in components.

Report No.   Date ....

To: BOARD OF DIRECTORS

From: ACCOUNTANT

Subject: BUYING IN OF COMPONENTS

The present cost structure is as follows:

Profit Statement per 100 tools

		£
Selling Price		250
Less Marginal Costs	£	
Component A	26	
B	32	
C	32	
Less Assembly	52	142
= Contribution		108
Less Fixed Costs		76
= Profit		£32

383

The buying in of one component is being considered because machine capacity cannot be increased for the next 12 months and it is forecast that demand could be increased by 50% or 75% providing capacity was available.

The following table shows the immediate cost effects of buying in each component.

Component	Buying in Price	Marginal Cost Avoided	Increase in cost
	£	£	£
A	36	26	10
B	46	32	14
C	54	32	22

To offset the immediate cost effect there is the net contribution consequences of using the machine hours released to increase throughput by 50% and 75%. The following tables show the effect of using hours released for the production of the other components.

Table 1

50% increase in Production
Net effect of using machine hours released
(all figures per 100 tools)

Compon-ent to be bought in	Variable Cost Increase	Capacity Released	Hours Required for 50% increase	Production Increase Possible	Increase in Cost	Contribution from increased capacity	Net Effect
	£	Hours	Hours		£	£	£
A	10	10	18 [1]	27.7% [2]	12.77 [3]	29.92	17.15 gain
B	14	16	15	53.3% (ltd to 50%)	21	54	33 gain
C	22	20	13	76.9% (ltd to 50%)	33	54	21 gain

Notes on calculations:

[1] If A is bought in, B & C require a total of 36 hrs . . a 50% increase is 18 hours.

[2] The proportion that the hours saved (10) bears to hours required (36)

$$= \frac{10}{36} \times 100\% = 27.7\%$$

[3] Cost increase is £10 x 127.7% = £12.77.

In the same manner a table for the 75% increase in production can be prepared.

75% increase in production

Compon-ent to be bought in	Variable Cost increase	Capacity Released	Hours Required for 75% increase	Production increase possible	Increase in Cost	Contribution from increased capacity	Net Effect
	£.	Hours	Hours		£	£	£
A	10	10	27	27.7%	12.77	29.92	17.15
B	14	16	22.5	53.3%	21.46	57.56	36.10
C	22	20	19.5	76.9% (ltd to 75%)	38.5	81	42.5

Therefore based on the schedules shown above I would recommend

for 50% extra demand Component B is purchased

for 75% extra demand Component C is purchased

If these recommendations are followed the following costs and profits should apply:

Forecasted statements with bought in components

	50% Sales increase £		75% Sales increase £	
Sales	375		437.50	
	(i.e. 150 tools)		(i.e. 175 tools)	
Variable Costs	£		£	
Component A	39		45.5	
B*	69		56	
C	48		*94.5	
Assembly	78	234	91	287.00
= Contribution		141		150.50
Less Fixed Costs		76		76.00
		£65		£74.50

* Bought in component

In each case if the original profit of £32 is deducted the profit increase shown in Tables 1 and 2 is obtained.

b. The main assumptions underlying report are:

   a. That variable costs behave in a linear fashion

   b. That fixed costs remain unchanged

   c. That sales estimates are realised exactly and that prices do not have to be reduced to sell the extra production

   d. That buying in prices are firm for 12 months

   e. That the reliability of supplier with regard to delivery and quality is assured.

3. The overhead absorption rate totalling 200% on wages comprises

$$\frac{(£64,000)}{(\ 80,000\ )} \times 100 = \text{variable rate} = \qquad 80\%$$

$$\frac{(£96,000)}{(\ 80,000\ )} \times 100 = \text{Fixed rate} = \qquad 120\%$$

$$= \text{Total rate} \qquad \underline{200\%}$$

Problem 1 Special order

Marginal cost per unit =	Materials	£8
	Labour	£4
	Variable overheads	
	(80% x £4)	£3.20
		£15.20

. . . as special order price is £16, contribution of 80p per unit would be gained, which for 2000 units = 2000 x £0.80 = £1,600.

Assuming that fixed costs would remain unchanged the order would be worthwhile.

Problem 2   Buying in component

On the assumption that the recovery rates previously calculated would apply the marginal cost of manufacture can be calculated i.e.

	£	
Materials	4.00	per unit
Labour	8.00	per unit
Variable Overheads		
(80% x £8)	6.40	
	£18.40	

This cost can be compared with the buying in price of £20. Thus to buy in would cost an extra £1.60 and is not recommended.

b. The principle used in the above cost analyses is that of marginal costing. The characteristics, advantages etc. are given in the text and in the answers to other questions.

4.   a. **Objective function and constraints.**
The contributions and limitations must be calculated.

Contribution/unit	Product L £		Product P £	
Selling Price		200		240
	£		£	
Variable Costs				
Materials	45.00		50.00	
Wages Dept 1	16.00		20.00	
2	22.50		13.50	
3	10.00		30.00	
Variable Overhead	6.50	100	11.50	125
= CONTRIBUTION		£100		£115

Availability of Hours

= No. of employees x Weekly Hours   Dept 1 = 20 x 40 = 800
                                                              2 = 15 x 40 = 600
                                                              3 = 18 x 40 = 720

. . . formulation is as follows

maximise	$100L + 115P$	. . . . Objective function
Subject to	$8L + 10P \leqslant 800$	. . . . Dept 1 constraint
	$10L + 6P \leqslant 600$	. . . . Dept 2 constraint
	$4L + 12P \leqslant 720$	. . . . Dept 3 constraint

and the formal non-negativity constraints
$$L, P \geqslant 0$$

b. Graphing the problems

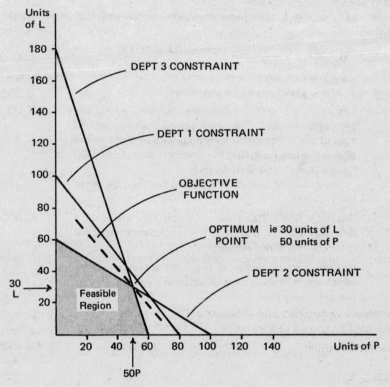

The solution is the point on the feasible region which is furthest to the right judging by the slope of the objective function i.e. 30L & 50P which gives a contribution of (30 x 100) + (50 x 115) = £8,750.

Note:

It will be seen from the graph that the Dept 1 constraint does not touch the feasible region. Technically this constraint is redundant and spare capacity exists i.e. 30L & 50P uses (30 x 8) + (10 x 50) Dept 1 hours i.e. 740 cf 800 available.

5. a. Characteristics of direct costs.
This can be taken directly from the text.

b. There are important principles involved in this part of the question. They apply whenever any form of decision making is being considered.
Only relevant costs and incomes should be considered and relevant costs and incomes are those which will alter in the future as a result of the decision. It follows that costs incurred in the past, sunk costs, cannot be altered and are not relevant. It also follows that where there is a choice between alternatives, the use of an asset in alternative A precludes its use in alternative B so that any benefit that would have been gained in B is lost. This is known as the opportunity cost. Based on these principles the relevant costs for the research project are:

		Relevant Costs £
1.	Cost already incurred of £150,000. Sunk cost . . not relevant	−
ii.	Materials. Cost already incurred of £60,000 . . not relevant. Disposal costs which can be avoided if used on project £5,000. This is a *gain* to the project	(5,000)
iii.	Labour. The £40,000 will be paid whether or not the project is initiated. The cost involved is an opportunity cost of the contribution which could be earned in the alternative use excluding the common cost of £40,000 i.e. Sales − (Prime Cost-Labour). The overhead absorbed is a fixed cost and therefore not relevant.	90,000
	Research Staff. This cost could be avoided so is a relevant cost for the project. The redundancy pay is un-avoidable so is not relevant	60,000
	General Building Services. This is an apportioned cost which are unlikely to be affected by this project . . they are not relevant.	
	. . Relevant project Costs	£145,000
	Project Proceeds	£300,000
	. . Return from continuation of project =	£155,000

Note:

   The timing differences in the project relating to redundancy payments have been ignored. Their impact is likely to be very slight.

6. a. i. **Opportunity Cost and Sunk Cost.**

Opportunity cost is the benefit foregone i.e. it is the sacrifice made when one option is taken and another is not. Opportunity cost is an important concept in decision making and can be quantified as the net cash inflow lost as a result of preferring one alternative rather than the next best one. Sunk costs are past costs. They are costs which have already been incurred and thus will be unaffected by whatever course of action is being considered. For decision making, only future costs (and revenues) are relevant so that sunk costs are irrelevant. Their only usefulness is that they might provide some guide to the level of future costs.

ii. **Fixed cost and controllable cost.**

A fixed cost, sometimes termed a period cost, is one which within a given range will not be affected by changes in activity.

Controllable cost is a cost which can be influenced by the person in control of the cost centre to which the cost is charged.

There is no relationship between these two definitions as they are used for quite distinct purposes. A fixed cost may be controllable or not and a controllable cost may or may not be fixed in relation to activity changes.

iii. **Direct and indirect cost.**
This can be answered directly from the text Paras 4 and 5.

b. It is, of course, a self evident truth that 'past events cannot be altered' but the implication that the past can be ignored is not true. The collection and analysis of past costs can help.

    a.   To plan future activities
    b.   To estimate future costs to aid current decisions
    c.   To help control costs particularly if similar operations, products and activities are to be carried out in the future
    d.   To assist in setting future targets, budgets and performance levels.

Note:

Although it is undoubtedly correct that sunk costs are irrelevant for decision making purposes the way the accounting system reports sunk costs might influence a manager. For example, if the sale of a fixed asset is being considered the original cost of the asset or its written down accounting value could influence the decision even though these two values are irrelevant to the particular decision being considered.

7. a. Increase in profit in 1979 = £1,350,000 − £1,000,000 = £350,000.

Analysis of profit increase

		£
Note 1.	Additional contribution from additional sales volume	700,000
Note 2.	+ Selling price increase	720,000
		1,420,000

		£	
	Less Cost increases		
Note 3.	Increase in material price	500,000	
Note 4.	Increase in material usage	100,000	
Note 5.	Increase in labour rate	150,000	
	Increase in Fixed overheads	200,000	
	Increase in variable overheads	120,000	1,070,000
	= Additional Profit		£350,000

$$\text{1978 Sales Volume} = \frac{\text{£6,000,000}}{\text{£6/unit}} = 1,000,000 \text{ units}$$

$$\text{1979 Sales Volume} = \frac{\text{£7,920,000}}{\text{£6.6/unit}} = 1,200,000 \text{ units}$$

$$= \text{Additional Sales volume} \qquad 200,000 \text{ units}$$

Notes:

1. Contribution per unit based on 1978 prices excluding the labour costs which are fixed.

		£
Selling Price		6.00 unit

Less Variable costs	£/unit	
Material	2.00	
Variable Overheads	0.50	2.50
∴ Contribution =		£3.50

∴ Contribution from extra volume = £3.50 x 200,000 = £700,000

Note 2

Selling price increase

$$= £0.60 \times 1,200,000 \text{ units} = £720,000$$

Note 3

Material Price increase

Purchases represent $\frac{120}{100}$ of purchases at 1978 prices

∴ Price increase represents ⅙ of total

i.e. ⅙ x £3,000,000 = £500,000

Note 4

Material usage increase.
This is the difference between cost of actual 1979 usage and actual usage in 1978 both priced in 1978 terms i.e.

$$1979 \text{ purchases at 1978 prices} = £3,000,000 \times \frac{100}{120} = £2,500,000$$

$$1979 \text{ usage at 1978 rate, all at 1978 prices} = £2,000,000 \times \frac{120}{100} = £2,400,000$$

∴ Amount attributable to extra usage is £2,500,000 − £2,400,000 = £100,000

Note 5.

Increase in labour rate.
As the number of workers is unaffected by volume all the labour cost difference is due to rate changes i.e. £1,150,000 − 1,000,000 = £150,000.

Note 6.

Variable overhead increase.

1978 Fixed overheads = Total overheads − Variable overheads
= £2,000,000 − (1,000,000 units @ £0.50) = £1,500,000

1979 Fixed overheads = £1,500,000 + 200,000 = 1,700,000

∴ 1979 Variable overheads = Total overheads − Fixed overheads
= 2,420,000 − 1,700,000 = £720,000

At 1978 rates variable overheads for 1979 would be

1,200,000 units x £0.50 = £600,000

∴ Increase in variable overheads = £720,000 − £600,000
= £120,000

Part (B)

Sales volume to achieve profit of £1,500,000

Total contribution required

		£
= Target profit		1,500,000
Fixed costs Labour		1,150,000
Overheads		1,700,000
		£4,350,000

1980 Contribution/unit

		£
Selling Price		6.10

	£	
Less Materials $\frac{(3,000,000)}{(1,200,000)}$	2.50	
Variable overheads	0.60	3.10
		£3.00

∴ Sales Volume to achieve target profit

$$= \frac{£4,350,000}{3} = 1,450,000 \text{ units}$$

8. a. Enquiry for an extra 1,000 gallons of each product

	Present Spare capacity Hours	Capacity Required for enquiry Hours	Shortfall (i.e. Limiting Factor)
Heating	6,000	5,000	OK
Blending	6,000	6,000	OK
Cooling	4,000	5,000	Shortfall

Thus the cooling capacity is the single limiting factor and the optimal plan is to produce the product which gives the highest contribution per unit of the limiting factor.

	ERIGERON	**STACHYS**
Contribution per hour of cooling	£1.5	£1.33

∴ concentrate upon Erigeron first:

Extra demand is 1,000 gallons of Erigeron which uses 1,000 x 2 cooling hours = 2,000 hours leaving 2,000 hours remaining for Stachys which can produce

$$\frac{2,000}{3} = 667 \text{ gallons}$$

∴ Optimal response to enquiry is 1,000 gallons of Erigeron and 667 gallons of Stachys assuming that a part delivery is acceptable.

b. When each process has a limit of 3,000 hours there are now 3 limiting factors so the simple decision rule of maximising contribution per unit of a single limiting factor will not suffice and Linear Programming (LP) must be used to produce a solution. Because there are only 2 unknowns (number of gallons of Erigeron and Stachys) a graphical solution method is possible. First the problem must be stated in the standard manner (E = Erigeron S = Stachys).

Maximise $3E + 4S$:— Objective function showing contribution per gallon.

Subject to

$$2E + 3S \leqslant 3000:— \text{ Cooling constraint}$$
$$4E + S \leqslant 3000:— \text{ Heating constraint}$$
$$E + 5S \leqslant 3000:— \text{ Blending constraint}$$
$$0 \leqslant E \leqslant 1000:— \text{ Demand Constraint Erigeron}$$
$$0 \leqslant S \leqslant 1000:— \text{ Demand Constraint Stachys}$$

The graphical solution:

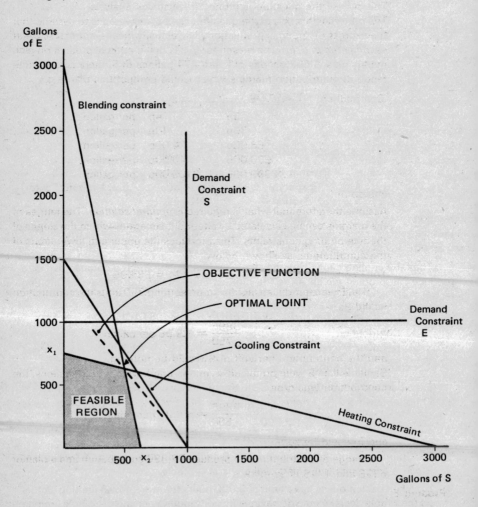

The optimal point shows a production mix of

  632 gallons of ERIGERON and
  474 gallons of Stachys

This can be checked by solving the simultaneous equations of the two binding constraints i.e.

$$E + 5S = 3000 \dots 1 \text{ (Blending Constraint)}$$
$$4E + S = 3000 \dots 2 \text{ (Heating Constraint)}$$

Thus $4E + 20S = 12000 \dots 1$ times 4
minus $4 + S = 3000 \dots 2$
gives $S = 474$
and substituting gives
    $E = 632$

ii. Range of contributions.

This part of the question is termed a sensitivity analysis.

The only way this part of the question can be answered is to assume that the expression 'optimal production plan' actually means *optimal solution as indicated in b. (i)'*. The reason for this is that if optimal production plan merely means 632 gallons of E and 474 gallons of S, there is an infinite range of contribution margins which could product this plan e.g.

Contribution	E	S	
	3p	4p	per gallon
	30p	40p	per gallon
	£3.00p	£4.00p	per gallon
	£30.00p	£40.00p	per gallon
	£300.00p	£400.00p	per gallon

and so on.

Assume therefore that what is required is *optimal solution*. The ranges of the margins can be calculated by altering the margins within the slopes of the two binding constraints. This produces the upper and lower limits of the contributions as shown below:

Total contribution = £4 x 632 + 3 x 474 = £3,896

. . if all E were produced, point x_1 representing 750 units the contribution would be

$$\frac{3896}{750} = \text{£5.06 per gallon}$$

and the contribution per unit of S would be nothing.

Similarly if all S were produced, x_2 on the graph which is 600 gallons, the contribution would be

$$\frac{3896}{600} = \text{£6.33 per gallon}$$

and E would be zero.

. . Range of contributions to produce £3,896 contribution and a plan of 632E and 474S is as follows.

Product E

Just above zero to just below £5.06 per gallon.

Product S

Just above zero to just below £6.33 per gallon.

9.

Products	A	B	C	
Demand (units)	12,000	20,000	16,000	
Machine Hours/unit	4	6	2	
Total machining requirement	48,000	120,000	32,000	= 200,000 hours

From the above table it is apparent that with the existing limit of 152,000 hours all the products cannot be made by the firm and some will need to be supplied on a sub-contract basis. The following table shows the contributions and contributions per unit of the limiting factors of the various products.

Products	A	B	C
	£	£	£
Selling Price/unit	45.00	40.00	35.00
Marginal Cost	30.00	28.00	24.00
= Contribution	15.00	12.00	11.00
. . Contributions per unit	£3.75	£2.00	£5.50

The firm should prefer to manufacture with the following priorities C-A-B thus

	Production Quantity	Hours	Cumulative Hours
Product C	16,000 units	32,000	32,000
Product A	12,000 units	48,000	80,000
Product B	12,000 units	72,000	152,000

leaving 8,000 units of B to be bought in at £34 per unit. This will produce the following profit

Profit Statement for 1979

Own Manufacture

Product	A	B	C	Bought in B	Total
	£	£	£	£	£
Sales	540,000	480,000	560,000	320,000	1,900,000
Marginal or bought in Cost	360,000	336,000	384,000	272,000	1,352,000
Contribution	180,000	144,000	176,000	48,000	548,000
Less Fixed costs					200,000
= Net Profit					£348,000

c. Products should always be bought in if the buying in price is less than the marginal cost of manufacture. This does not apply in this example but it is still worthwhile buying in when there is a limitation on some resource, in this case, machine hours, and there is unsatisfied demand. In these circumstances providing that the buying in price is less than the selling price it is worthwhile buying in. Whenever there is a limiting factor a firm should attempt to maximise contribution per unit of the limiting factor which is the reason why the manufacturing priority of C-A-B is specified above.

Chapter 21

1. The data given can be rearranged thus:

		£
Sales		600,000
Less Marginal Cost		350,000
=	Contribution	250,000
Less Fixed Cost		150,000
=	Profit	£100,000

The P/V graph is shown below

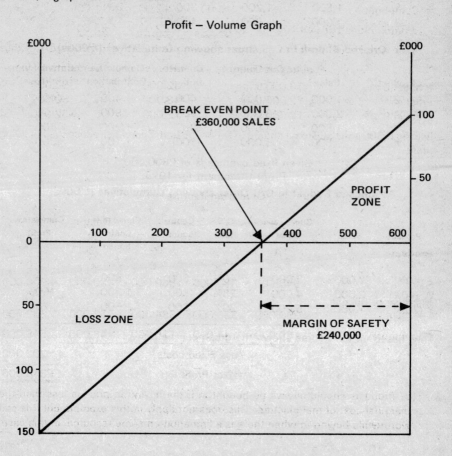

Profit – Volume Graph

b. A P/V graph plots the profit/loss line at an angle which depends on the contribution/sales ratio which, in the example above, is

$$\frac{250,000}{600,000} = 41.67\%$$

The limitations of P/V graphs are similar to break even charts and can be taken directly from the text.

2. To show the results of a multi-product company on a P/V graph it is necessary to rank the products in ascending order of their P/V or, using the more descriptive term their Contribution/Sales ratios and to show the cumulative effects of each product thus:

Original Budget in £'000s

Product	Sales	Variable Costs	Contribution	C/S Ratio %	Ranking Order
W	2,000	1,500	500	25	2
X	500	600	(100)	(20)	4
Y	1,500	1,200	300	20	3
Z	1,000	600	400	40	1

Original Budget in C/S Order showing Cumulatives (£'000s)

Product	Sales	Cumulative Sales	Contri-bution	Cumulative Contribution	Cumulative Profit (Loss)*
Z	1,000	1,000	400	400	(400)
W	2,000	3,000	500	900	100
Y	1,500	4,500	300	1,200	400
X	500	5,000	(100)	1,100	300

* Given fixed overheads of £800,000.

Proposed Budget in C/S Order showing Cumulatives (£'000s)

Product	Sales	Cumulative Sales	C/S Ratio	Contri-bution	Cumulative Contri-bution	Cumulative Profit
	£	£	£	£	£	£
Z (40%)	2,000	2,000	40%	800	800	–
W (40%)	2,000	4,000	25%	500	1,300	500
Y (20%)	1,000	5,000	20%	200	1,500	700

Thus based on the figures shown the graph can be drawn.

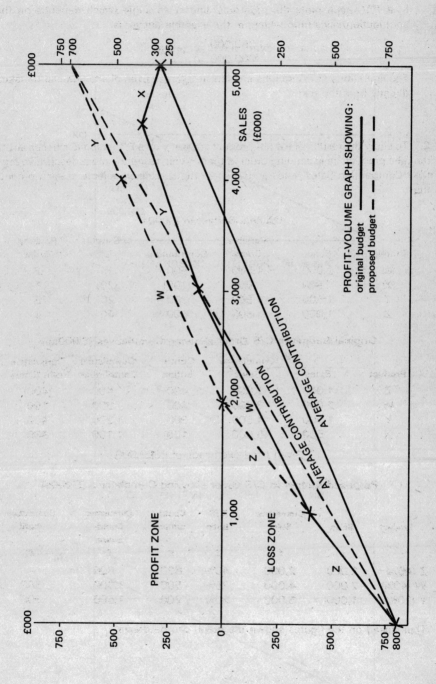

3.

Note:

The axes of all graphs are identical and represent £'000s.

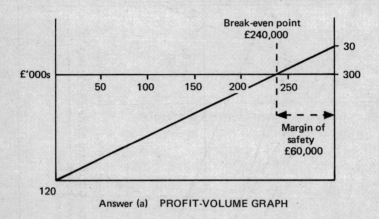

Answer (a)   PROFIT-VOLUME GRAPH

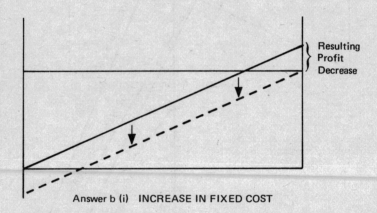

Answer b (i)   INCREASE IN FIXED COST

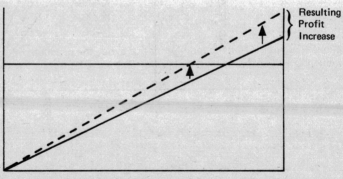

Answer b (ii)   DECREASE IN VARIABLE COST

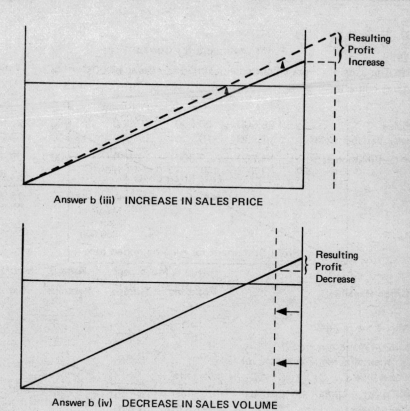

Answer b (iii)   INCREASE IN SALES PRICE

Answer b (iv)   DECREASE IN SALES VOLUME

4. Preliminary workings are as follows:

	Potatoes £	Turnips £	Parsnips £	Carrots £
Variable cost/acre	470	510	595	660
Tonnes/acre	10	8	9	12
Revenue/tonne	100	125	150	135
Revenue/acre	1,000	1,000	1,350	1,620
. . Contribution/acre	530	490	755	960

In general, providing that the requirements are met, the products would be ranked in the following order: Carrots — Parsnips — Potatoes — Turnips.

399

a. i.

Profit Statement for Current Year

	Potatoes	Turnips	Parsnips	Carrots	Total
Acres cultivated	25	20	30	25	100
	£	£	£	£	£
Sales	25,000	20,000	40,500	40,500	126,000
Less Variable Costs	11,750	10,200	17,850	16,500	56,300
= Contribution	13,250	9,800	22,650	24,000	69,700
Less Fixed Costs					54,000
= Profit					15,700

a. ii.

Profit Statement for recommended mix

	Area A (45 acres)		Area B (55 acres)	
Crops Possible	Potatoes ✓	Turnips	Parsnips	Carrots ✓
Min. Tons required	40	40	36	36
Min. Acreage required	4	5	4	3
Balance of acreage available for best crop	36	–	–	48
∴ Recommended mix (acres)	40	5	4	51
Contribution/acre	£530	£490	£755	£960
∴ Contribution/Crop =	£21,000	£2,450	£3,020	£48,960

	Total
Total Contribution	75,630
Less Fixed Costs	54,000
	21,630

b. i. With no market commitment, production should be concentrated upon the highest yielding crop i.e. carrots.

ii. Profit with total carrot crop:

$$= 100 \times 960 = 96,000 \text{ contribution}$$
$$\text{Less Fixed Costs} \quad 54,000$$
$$42,000$$

iii. Contribution to sales ratio of carrots

$$= \frac{£24,000}{40,500} \times 100 = 59.259\%$$

$$\therefore \text{Break even point} = \frac{\text{Fixed overheads}}{\text{C/S ratio}} = \frac{54,000}{59.259} \times 100 = £91,126$$

5. This is a straightforward question involving contribution and a limiting factor i.e. the identified 'critical shortage of labour in Dept 3.'

a.

Product Contribution Statement
(all figures per UNIT)

	Product					
	X		Y		Z	
	£		£		£	
Sales	136		140		165	
Less Variable						
Material A	9		15		9	
B	20		30		35	
Wages Dept 1	6		12		15	
2	21		7		14	
3	6		4		8	
4	18		27		9	
Variable Overheads	20	100	25	120	35	125
= Contribution/Unit		£36		£20		£40

b. The company should concentrate product on the product which gives the maximum contribution per unit of the limiting factor — labour hours in Dept 3.

Contribution per hour

	Product		
	X	Y	Z
Contribution per unit (from above)	£36	£20	£40
Dept 3 Labour hours per unit	3	2	4
. . contribution per labour hour	£12	£10	£10

Thus, assuming that there are no technical or marketing considerations, from a purely costing viewpoint production should be concentrated upon Product X resulting in the following total contribution being achieved.

$$\text{Dept 3 labour hours available} = \frac{£360,000}{£2/\text{hour}} = 180,000$$

As 3 hours are required per unit the total production of X possible is

$$\frac{180,000}{3} = 60,000 \text{ units}$$

. . Total contribution = 60,000 x £36 = £2,160,000

(Alternatively the total contribution could be obtained by multiplying the labour hours available (180,000) by the contribution per labour hour (£12) i.e.

$$180,000 \times £12 = £2,160,000).$$

c. Steps necessary to achieve production of 60,000 units of Product X.

 ˜ a. Analysis of effects on labour, machinery and factory schedules of exclusive production of X.

 b. Analysis of material requirements and availability.

   c.   Redeployment/retraining etc. necessary for labour.
   d.   Study of factory layout, tooling etc. necessary for exclusive production of X.

It must be pointed out that a simplistic solution such as the exclusive production of one product is unrealistic because it is hardly credible that a firm could change from a sales mix of three products to selling one product only. It is, of course, perfectly possible to produce all of one product but selling that production is an entirely different matter.

d. Profit when there is exclusive production of X.

		£
=	Contribution (from above)	2,160,000
	Less Fixed costs	1,000,000
=	Profit	£1,160,000

Assuming that the production could be sold at the prices given.

6.   a.   From the data given the overall and unit contribution and sales volume can be deduced.

	£
Expected profit	275,000
+ Fixed cost	85,000
= Current contribution	360,000

and as the unit contribution is £6 the base sales volume is

$$\frac{360,000}{6} = 60,000 \text{ drills}$$

The alternative strategies can be evaluated

Strategy	Selling Price/Unit £	Contribution/ Unit £	Sales Volume	Total Contribution £
1	9.50	5.50	66,000	363,000
2	9.30	5.30	72,000	381,600
3	9.00	5.00	75,000	375,000

Thus with fixed costs of £85,000, Strategy 2 is the most profitable giving:

$$£381,600 - £85,000 = £296,600 \text{ profit}$$

b. Other considerations include
   i.   Will the cost relationships, particularly the amount of fixed costs, remain as estimated?
   ii.   How accurate are the demand estimates? They suggest considerable demand elasticity. Is this reasonable?
   iii.   Could the underutilised capacity be used for more profitable work than for the standard power drill sold at a lower price?
   iv.   What will be the competitor's reaction to the projected price reduction?

Chapter 22

1.

Note:

Most of the budgets required are merely rearrangements of the data given.

a. i.

Sales Budget (Quantity & Value)

	Products			
	A	B	C	
Sales quantities (units)	1,000	2,000	1,500	
Selling price (per unit)	£100	£120	£140	Total
Sales Value	£100,000	£240,000	£210,000	£550,000

a. ii.

Production Budget (Quantities)

	Products		
	A	B	C
Sales (units) from Sales Budget	1,000	2,000	1,500
Add Closing Stock (units)	1,100	1,650	550
	2,100	3,650	2,050
Less Opening Stock (units)	1,000	1,500	500
= Required Production	1,100	2,150	1,550

a. iii.

Material usage budget (Quantities)

Production Budget (Units)	Materials					
	M1		M2		M3	
	Units per Product	Total	Units per Product	Total	Units per Product	Total
A 1,100	4	4,400	2	2,200	–	–
B 2,150	3	6,450	3	6,450	2	4,300
C 1,550	2	3,100	1	1,550	1	1,550
Material Usage		13,950		10,200		5,850

a. iv.

Material Purchases Budget (Quantities & Values)

	Materials			
	M1	**M2**	**M3**	
Usage from budget (units)	13,950	10,200	5,850	
Add Closing stock (units)	31,200	24,000	14,400	
	45,150	34,200	20,250	
Less Opening stock (units)	26,000	20,000	12,000	
= Required purchases (units)	19,150	14,200	8,250	
Unit Cost	£4	£6	£9	Total
= Value of purchases	76,600	85,200	74,250	£236,050

Part (b) Principal Budget Factor – the explanation of this can be taken directly from the Chapter (Para 11).

In this question, and wherever no specific principal budget factor is given, sales are assumed to be the limiting factor.

2. This question illustrates a common problem encountered in practice i.e. whether to utilise spare capacity for less than full price sales.

To prepare a revised budget certain preliminary calculations are necessary.

Proposed Sales

	£
18,000 x £30	540,000
8,000 x £25	200,000
	740,000

Variable Costs

As existing cost per box x 26,000 less 5% for materials.

			Per box £		Total £
Materials					
	$\frac{£240,000}{20,000}$	−5% =	11.40	x 26,000 =	296,400
Labour					
	$\frac{102,000}{20,000}$	=	5.1	x 26,000 =	132,600
Variable overheads					
	$\frac{70,000}{20,000}$	=	3.5	x 26,000 =	91,000
			£20.00		£520,000

Revised Budget Revenue Account

		£
Sales		740,000
Less Variable Costs	£	
Material	296,400	
Labour	132,600	
Variable Overheads	91,000	520,000
= Contribution		220,000
Less Fixed costs (122,200 + 16,000)		138,200
= Profit		£81,800

Revised Budgeted Net Assets as at 30.9.80

		£
Fixed Assets		310,000
Working Capital	£	
(Note 1) Debtors	78,333	
Stocks	90,000	
Creditors	(40,000)	128,333
= Net assets employed		438,333

Note 1

$$\text{Current debtors period} = \frac{50,000}{600,000} = 1 \text{ month}$$

	£
∴ Debtors on proposed normal sales	
= 1/12 x 540,000	45,000
Debtors on Supermarket sales	
= 1/6 x £200,000	33,333
	£78,333

b.

Profit Reconciliation

		£
Profit difference	Existing	65,800
	Proposed	81,800
	Profit Gain	16,000

Made up from

GAINS

	£
Extra contribution from Supermarket sales	
= £(25 − 20) x 5,000 boxes	40,000
Material quantity discounts 18,000 x £0.60	10,800
= Total Gains	50,800

LOSSES

		£	
Extra Supervisory Staff		16,000	
(Note 1) Loss of contribution caused by			
10% sales loss = 2,000 boxes x £9.4		18,800	34,800
= Profit Gain			16,000

Note 1

Contribution per box in existing budget	
= Selling Price	30.00
Less Variable Costs	20.60
=	£9.40

c. The proposal increases profit by 24% and is probably worthwhile but before a final decision is made consideration should be given to the following points:

   i.   Can the spare capacity be utilised for full price sales?

   ii. Are all the estimates made realistic particularly the projected 10% drop in normal sales volume?

  iii. Will the given cost structures hold in the proposed circumstances? For example, can we be sure that there will only be a £16,000 increase in fixed costs?

  iv. How will the proposed increase in capital employed be financed? If on overdraft at say 20% p.a. the financing of the increase will take approximately half the calculated profit increase. Is this worthwhile?

   v. What is the contractual position vis-a-vis the supermarket? What is the position about possible price changes due to inflation?

If satisfactory answers can be obtained to the above enquiries then the proposal should be recommended.

3. This question can be answered largely from the text (Para 15) Particular points of importance include

a. Full participation in establishing budgets and standards.

b. Full consultation at all stages.

c. Regular and full feedback of results.

d. Realistic achievement levels should be incorporated into standards and budgets.

4.

Fancitoys Ltd
Cash Budget July-September

	July		August		September	
	£	£	£	£	£	£
Receipts						
Cash Sales (1)		4,000		4,200		4,600
	8,200		8,700		12,000	
Credit Sales (2)	17,400	25,600	24,000	32,700	25,200	37,200
		£29,600		£36,900		£41,800
		£		£		£
Payments						
Purchases (3)		36,000		24,000		36,000
Rent		1,500		1,500		1,500
Salaries, Wages and Commission		4,800		5,100		5,500
Rates		800				
Other Expenses		1,600		1,800		2,000
		£44,700		£32,400		£45,000
		£		£		£
Summary						
Balance b/fwd.		10,000		(5,100)		(600)
Receipts		29,600		36,900		41,800
		39,600		31,800		41,200
Payments		44,700		32,400		45,000
Balance c/fwd.		(£5,100)		(£600)		(£3,800)

Detailed Workings		(1)		(2)		
	Sales	Cash Sales	Credit Sales	Credit Sale Month 1	Receipts Month 2	Cost of Sales
	£	£	£	£	£	£
July	40,000	4,000	36,000	24,000	12,000	30,000
August	42,000	4,200	37,800	25,200	12,600	31,500
September	46,000	4,600	41,400	27,600	13,800	34,500
October	48,000	4,800	43,200	28,800	14,400	36,000
November	52,000	5,200	46,800	31,200	15,600	39,000
December	44,000	4,400	39,600	26,400	13,200	33,000

	July £	August £	September £
Cost of Sales	30,000	31,500	34,500
Stock c/d.	66,000	70,500	75,000
	96,000	102,000	109,500
Stock b/fwd.	72,000	66,000	70,500
(3) Purchases	£24,000	£36,000	£39,000

5. Comment. A key element, which is not given directly, is the budgeted sales quantities for each product. This can be derived by calculating the standard selling price per product (i.e. Total cost + profit percentage) and using this to calculate the budgeted quantities from the budgeted sales revenues given.

Cost and selling price Statement

		A £		B £		C £
Direct Materials						
	£		£		£	
DM 11	10		–		24	
DM 21	–		40		36	
DM 31	5	15	5	45	–	60
Direct Wages						
Dept I	10		5		5	
Dept II	12		4		6	
Dept III	3	25	6	15	9	20
Other Variable Costs		10		20		15
Total Variable Costs		50		80		95
Fixed Production Overheads						
Dept I @ $\frac{£239,000}{47,800}$ hr = £5 hr.	20		10		10	
Dept II @ $\frac{£201,300}{67,100}$ hr = £3 hr.	18		6		9	
Dept III @ $\frac{£391,200}{65,200}$ hr = £6 hr.	12	50	24	40	36	55
Total Production Cost		100		120		150
Admin. Costs + 20%		20		24		30
Selling Costs + 40%		40		48		60
= Total Cost		160		192		240
+ Standard profit	(25%)	40	(12½%)	24	(16⅔%)	40
= SELLING PRICE		£200		£216		£280

	Products		
	A	B	C
Budgeted Sales Revenue	£1,500,000	£1,080,000	£1,680,000
Budgeted Sales Quantities	7,500	5,000	6,000 units

These calculated quantities are used to calculate the various budgets.

a.

Production Budget (in Units)

	Product		
	A	B	C
Sales quantities	7,500	5,000	6,000
plus Closing Stock			
(80% of opening stock)	2,400	1,600	2,000
	9,900	6,600	8,000
less Opening stock	3,000	2,000	2,500
= Production Required	6,900	4,600	5,500

b.

Materials Usage Budget

	DM 11	DM 21	DM 31
Budgeted Production			
A (6900)	34,500	–	34,500
B (4600)	–	46,000	23,000
C (5500)	66,000	49,500	–
= Total Material Req.	100,500	95,500	57,500

c.

Purchasing Budget

	DM 11	DM 21	DM 31	Total
Material requirements for production	100,500	95,500	57,500	
add Closing Stock	22,050	18,450	15,750	
	122,550	113,950	73,250	
less Opening stock	24,500	20,500	17,500	
= Req. Purchases (units)	98,050	93,450	55,750	
Target price per unit	£2	£4	£1	Total
= Req. Purchase (value)	£196,100	£373,800	£55,750	£625,650

d. It can be inferred from the statement in the question that finished goods are valued at marginal cost that a profit and loss budget on marginal cost lines is required.

Budgeted Profit and Loss Statement

	A £	B £	C £	Total £
Sales	1,500,000	1,080,000	1,680,000	4,260,000
less Marginal Cost of Sales	375,000	400,000	570,000	1,345,000
= Contribution	1,125,000	680,000	1,110,000	2,915,000

	£	
less Fixed Costs		
Production	831,500	
* Administration	450,000	
* Selling	900,000	2,181,500
Profit		£733,500

* The assumption has been made that all administration and selling overheads are fixed. This is probably not true but without further information no analysis is possible.

The figures for these overheads are obtained from the amount per unit in the various products multiplied by the sales budget i.e.

Administration

$$= £(20 \times 7500) + (24 \times 5000) + (30 \times 6000) = \underline{£450,000}$$

Selling

$$= £(40 \times 7500) + (48 \times 5000) + (60 \times 6000) = \underline{£900,000}$$

6.

Materials Purchases Budget for 1980

	Plain	Fancy	
Budgeted sales (units)	6,000	4,000	
Material usage per unit	3 kilos	4 kilos	**Total**
∴ Budgeted consumption (kilos)	18,000	16,000	34,000

Less Planned stock decrease	2,000
= Budgeted Purchases	32,000 kilos
Budgeted Purchases Price* =	£2.20 per kilo
∴ Budgeted Purchases Value =	£70,400

* Purchase price can be calculated from the 1979 figures given i.e.

Plain 4000 x 3 kilos =	12,000 kilos
Fancy 2000 x 4 kilos =	8,000 kilos
	20,000 kilos

and as total cost was £44,000, average price per kilo

$$= \frac{44,000}{20,000} = \underline{£2.20}$$

Wages budget for 1980

| | | Note 1 | | Note 2 | |
Product	Budgeted Sales	Standard Time/unit	Budgeted Standard Hours	Wage Rate	Budgeted Wages
Plain	6000 units	24 mins	2400	£4.20/hr	£10,080
Fancy	4000 units	48 mins	3200	£4.20/hr	£13,440
				Total	£23,520

Note 1

Standard Time/Unit

	Plain	Fancy
1979 Standards	30 mins	60 mins
Less 20% Productivity	6 mins	12 mins
= 1980 Standard	24 mins	48 mins

Note 2

Wage rate/hour

$$1979 \text{ Actual Rate} = 1979 \text{ Standard Rate} + \frac{\text{Rate Variance}}{\text{Hours Worked}}$$

$$= £3 + \frac{£2,000}{4,000 \text{ hrs}} = £3.50 \text{ per hour}$$

$$\therefore 1980 \text{ Wage Rate} = £3.50 + 70p = \underline{£4.20/hr}$$

b. Net cost savings resulting from productivity.

This involves a comparison of the wages cost (+ variable overhead recovery) for the 1980 budget with and without the productivity implications.
The 1980 budget is 5,600 standard hours.

Without Productivity Deal

To produce 5,600 standard hours at 1979 efficiency would involve working 5,600 hours which would cost per hour: Wages Rate £3.70 (i.e. excluding the productivity element) + Variable Overhead Absorption Rate of £1.50 per hour, a total of £5.20 per hour.

$$\therefore 5,600 \times £5.20 = \underline{£29,120}$$

With Productivity Deal

The 5,600 standard hours would take

$$5600 \times \frac{80}{100} = 4480 \text{ hours}$$

at a cost of

$$£4.20 \text{ wages} + £1.50 \text{ VOAR} = \underline{£5.70} \text{ hour}$$

$$\therefore \text{cost} = 4480 \times £5.70 = \underline{£25,536}$$

$$\therefore \text{Net cost savings with the productivity deal}$$

$$= £29,120 - 25536 = \underline{£3,584}$$

Note:

The VOAR is £6,000 ÷ 4000 hrs (1979 production) = $\underline{£1.50 \text{ per hour.}}$

7. a. Purpose of budgeting.

A budget is a financial or quantitative statement of the policy to be followed during a forthcoming period in order to achieve given objectives.

Budgeting is thus part of the formal planning procedures of an organisation. It helps in the process of reviewing resources and capabilities and because budgets are prepared for all aspects of operations, budgeting plays a key rôle in coordinating all facets of the business. This helps to avoid sub-optimality and to achieve the organisations dominant objectives. The budgetary process involves discussion and liaison so it is a means of communication.

Provided that there is proper participation in all stages of budgeting there can be beneficial behavioural effects and managers may be motivated by the processes of budget preparation, target setting and the achievement of these targets.

In addition to the planning aspects of budgeting, the regular comparison of actual results with budgets, termed budgetary control, can promote a cost effective attitude and is a classic example of management by exception.

b. **Flexible budget.**

A flexible budget is one which is designed so that a meaningful budget can easily be prepared whatever the actual activity level achieved. For comparative purposes it is of little point in relating a budget prepared for an anticipated 80% activity level to the actual expenditure when the activity level turns out to be 105%. To prepare a flexible budget it is necessary to establish the fixed and variable characteristics of costs so that, when the actual activity is known, a meaningful budget allowance can be readily calculated and compared with actual expenditure.

The particular problems which arise in flexible budgeting are:

- a. Establishing what are fixed and variable costs.
- b. Dealing with semi fixed or semi variable costs.
- c. Relating variable costs to a relevant indicator of volume or activity. Different costs, although variable, may vary in relation to different factors. One cost may vary with machine hours worked, one may vary with orders handled, another with sales, volume and so on. Because no one indicator of activity is likely to be all embracing the flexing of the budget may be a complex task or, if simplified too much, the budget produced may be inaccurate.

The above points are in addition to the general problems encountered in all budgeting systems e.g. difficulties of prediction, changing cost characteristics, budgetary slack, inflation and general uncertainty.

8. Part (a) of this question involves merely simple arithmetic once the charging rules are understood.

a. i.

Charges at normal rates (£'000s)

Dept	Group	%	Non Group	%	Total (100%)	Agreed Costs	Group % x agreed costs + 10%
	£		£		£	£	£
A	75	30	175	70	250	215,000	70,950
B	48	33⅓	96	66⅔	144	104,100	38,170
C	28	20	112	80	140	84,000	18,480
D	24	66⅔	12	33⅓	36	29,100	21,340
E	10	11	80	89	90	83,700	10,230
F	3	7	39	93	42	15,050	1,182
	188		514		702		£160,352

a. ii.

$$£$$

Dept A $\dfrac{16,000}{50,000}$ x £215,000 x 1.125 = 77,400

Depts B-F	Sub Totals	Group Charges	£113,000
		Non-Group Charges	339,000
			£452,000
		Agreed Costs	£315,950

$\therefore$ B-F charges $\dfrac{£113,000}{£452,000}$ x £315,950 x 1.1   86,886

Total group charges   £164,286

b. The additional cost data that would be required would be a breakdown of costs into variable and fixed so that the various alternative possibilities could be assessed. These possibilities include the following extremes:

    a. Replacing group business by normal rate business up to capacity or

    b. Having the capacity vacated by the group remain unused.

When the fixed/variable analysis had been made the viability of either of the two extremes, or any intermediate position could more easily be assessed.

9. a. Comments on the ways the quarterly budgets have been prepared.

    i. Budgets should be related to the activity level expected in a given quarter and should not be simply a quarter of the annual budget.

    ii. Budget periods should be reconsidered. Preferably monthly budgets should be prepared but, if quarterly budgets are desired, the quarters should be altered so that the high activity months (June, July and August) are treated as a quarter on their own.

    iii. Flexible budgeting should be adopted. This would mean separation of the costs into fixed and variable which would allow a realistic flexed budget to be compared with actual.

    iv. Inflation allowance. An overall blanket increase for all costs is likely to be inaccurate. Each cost must be considered separately and its own characteristics studied.

b. (**Note.** It is assumed that the 'budget' mentioned in this part of the question refers to the type of budget recommended in (a) i.e. a flexible budget and not the budget illustrated).

Information flow

    i. Realistic cost control data based on a flexed budget.

    ii. Performance data relating to Patient days, Weight processed and costs related to a meaningful unit.

    iii. Proper basis for future budget preparation.

    iv. Variance reports on controllable items.

c. Amendments to current practice of budgeting and reporting.
  i.   Proper breakdown of costs into fixed and variable.
  ii. Monthly and cumulative budgets to be prepared having regard to the activity anticipated month by month.
  iii. Full participation by laundry manager in the budget process and agreement by him of the amounts for the controllable items.
  iv. Flexible budgets to be prepared at month ends showing allowed expenditure, actual expenditure and variances for all controllable items.
  v.   Significant variances should be highlighted and investigated.

10. a. Value of Stock at 30th April for Balance Sheet

	Audio	Electrical	Furniture	Total
	£	£	£	£
Opening Stock (at cost)	120,000	80,000	200,000	400,000
+ Purchases	150,000	40,000	160,000	350,000
	270,000	120,000	360,000	750,000
Less Cost of Sales*	132,000	48,000	165,000	345,000
= Value of Stock	£138,000	£72,000	£195,000	£405,000

* Cost of Sales calculation. This involves establishing the 'prescribed gross margin' and using this on the gross sales value of actual sales.

	Audio	Electrical	Furniture
Cost/Sales Ratio			
(1st April Stock at Cost +	$\dfrac{120,000}{200,000}$	$\dfrac{80,000}{110,000}$	$\dfrac{200,000}{280,000}$
Full Sales value)	= 60%	= 72.72%	= 71.4286%
Actual Sales at full value	£220,000	£66,000	£231,000
∴ Cost of Sales			
(Ratio x Full value Sales)	£132,000	£48,000	£165,000

b.

Tabulated Profit & Loss Statement for April

	Audio £	Electrical £	Furniture £	Total £
Gross Sales	220,000	66,000	231,000	517,000
less Price reductions	5,000	3,000	7,000	15,000
= Net Sales	215,000	63,000	224,000	502,000
less Cost of Sales	132,000	48,000	165,000	345,000
= GROSS PROFIT	83,000	15,000	59,000	157,000
less Expenses*				
Rates	1,500	500	1,250	
Light & Heat	750	250	625	
Advertising	15,000	4,500	15,750	
Transport	11,000	3,300	11,550	
Insurance	1,500	450	1,575	
Miscellaneous	500	150	525	
Canteen	2,025	300	1,125	
Salaries	11,900	2,000	6,000	
Depreciation	500	750	1,000	
Admin.	4,600	1,380	4,830	
	49,275	13,580	44,230	107,085
= Net Profit	£33,725	£1,420	£14,770	£49,915

* The expense apportionments and allocations are shown below:—

Overhead Allocations & Apportionments

Item	Basis	Total £	Audio £	Elec. £	Furn. £	Admin. £
Rates	Area	4,000	1,500	500	1,250	750
Light and heat	Area	2,000	750	250	625	375
Advertising	Gross sales value	35,250	15,000	4,500	15,750	
Transport	Gross sales value	25,850	11,000	3,300	11,550	
Insurance	Gross sales value	3,525	1,500	450	1,575	
Miscellaneous	Gross sales value	1,175	500	150	525	
Canteen	No. employees	4,125	2,025	300	1,125	675
Salaries and wages	Allocated	24,910	11,900	2,000	6,000	5,010
Depreciation	Allocated	3,750	500	750	1,000	1,500
Administration	Allocated	2,500				2,500
Administration	Gross sales value	—	4,600	1,380	4,830	(10,810)
		107,085	49,275	13,580	44,230	—
Area	Sq. ft.	16,000	6,000	2,000	5,000	3,000
	%	100	37.5	12.5	31.25	18.75
Gross sales	£000	517	220	66	231	
	%	100	42.554	12.766	44.680	
Employees	No.	55	27	4	15	9
	%	100	49	7	27	16

c. It will be seen from the earlier statements that a number of the expenses have had to be apportioned over the departments on some conventional basis. This apportionment process may obscure the picture of departmental profitability. If only directly identifiable expenses (salaries, wages etc) are charged to departments the contribution that each department made could be seen more clearly. This would be a form of marginal costing and is likely to be more meaningful for management purposes.

11. a. Maximum average mileage p.a.

		£
Projected cost of agency		
22% commission on £225,000		49,500

Less Cost of own sales force (excluding mileage)	£	
Sales Manager	7,500	
Salesmen's expenses	2,000	
Sales Office Costs	5,000	
Interest & depreciation	3,500	
Salesmen's salary	16,000	
5% Commission on £225,000	11,250	45,250
Surplus to cover 10p/mile cost	=	£4,250

$\therefore$ mileage possible = 42,500 miles

b. Level of sales for 14,000 miles p.a.

It is necessary to calculate the amount of contribution to cover the original and extra costs and the budgeted profit. When this is done the sales required can be calculated using the P/V ratio i.e. the contribution/sales proportion.

		£
Required Contribution		
Budgeted profit		33,000
Original fixed costs (36,250 + 2,000 + 30,000)		68,250
Additional costs	£	
Sales Manager	7,500	
Salesmen's expenses	2,000	
Sales Office	5,000	
Interest & Depreciation	3,500	
Salesmen's salary	16,000	
56,000 miles @ 10p	5,600	39,600
		£140,850

		£
New contribution/Sales ratio		
Budgeted Sales	£	225,000
Variable production costs	78,750	
5% commission	11,250	90,000
= contribution		135,000

$$\therefore \text{C/S ratio} = \frac{135,000}{225,000} \times 100 = \underline{60\%}$$

. . . Sales to achieve original budgeted profit of £33,000

$$= \frac{£140,850}{.6} = \underline{£234,750}$$

c. Maximum level of commission

Required profit $= 33,000 \times 116\% =$ £38,280
Required Sales $= 225,000 \times 116\% =$ £261,000
Mileage Cost $= 4 \times 16,000 \times 10p =$ £6,400

	£	£
Sales		261,000
Less Required Contribution		
Profit	38,280	
Original fixed costs	68,250	
Sales manager	7,500	
Sales expenses	2,000	
Sales office	5,000	
Interest etc.	3,500	
Salesmen's salary	16,000	
Mileage	6,400	146,930
= Amount to cover all variable costs		114,070
Less Variable production costs (35% x £261,000)		91,350
Balance available to pay commission		£22,720

. . . Commission percentage $= \frac{22,720}{261,000} \times 100 = \underline{8.7\%}$

12. Before cost control can be carried out it is necessary to ensure that there is a comprehensive, well designed system of accounting for costs. The main elements of this being:—

a. Appropriate cost classification and coding systems.

b. Proper certification of expense authorisation.

c. Clearly defined cost centres with designated responsibilities.

d. Regular, detailed reporting of all overhead cost elements.

e. Agreed and consistent costing principles to be applied.

When an appropriate basic costing system is available the more specific aids to cost control can be implemented. The main ones being:—

a. Introduction of flexible budgetary control with regular reporting of planned and actual expenditure.

b. Involvement of all budget holders in setting and reviewing budgets and performance levels.

c. Frequent reporting of comparative figures on an exception basis where appropriate.

d. Special, in depth, investigations of particular overhead costs and discussing the results produced with budget holders.

e. In conjunction with the relevant managers conduct reviews of departmental operations, expenditure, manning levels etc. with a view to improving efficiency.

f. Where possible, to develop forms of output budgeting so that overhead costs can be related to some measurable output.

It must be recognised that many overhead costs are of a fixed, long term nature, for example, staff salaries. Such costs are not amenable to short term changes but this is no excuse for not monitoring costs and showing detailed comparisons with budget and activity levels. The mere act of reporting does not reduce costs but it may lead to management actions which help to control the tendency of overhead costs to increase inexorably. The regular monitoring and reporting of costs and budgets, helps to promote a cost effective attitude.

13. Revenue Accounts Showing Weekly Profits at various Output Levels

	(Note 1)	Minimum Output 450 Units		Current Maximum Output 900 Units		Proposed Maximum Output 1200 Units	
With Current Wages Scheme			£		£		£
	Sales		4,050		8,100		
	Less Costs	£		£		Not Possible	
	Materials	900		1,800		with current	
	Wages (Note 2)	1,200		2,000		Wages	
	Var. O'hds (Note 3)	900		1,800		Scheme	
	Fixed Overhead	1,200	4,200	1,200	6,800		
	Weekly Profit (Loss)		£(150)		£1,300		
With Incentive Scheme			£		£		£
	Sales		4,050		8,100		10,800
	Less Costs	£		£		£	
	Materials	900		1,800		2,400	
	Wages (Note 4)	1,200		1,850		2,600	
	Variable Overhead	675		1,350		1,800	
	Fixed Overhead	1,200	3,975	1,200	6,200	1,200	8,000
	Weekly Profit		£75		£1,900		£2,800
	Profit Change		£225		£600		£2,800

Reasons for profit changes:

at 450 units

25% Increase in labour efficiency causing a reduction in variable overhead costs of 25% i.e. £900 x 25% = £225.

at 900 units

25% saving of variable overheads − 25% of 1800 =   450
saving of overtime premium (see Note 4 below) =   150
   £600

Note 1   Output levels.   Minimum – given = 450 units

$$\text{Current maximum} = 600 \text{ hrs} \div 40 \text{ mins} = 900 \text{ units}$$
$$\text{Proposed maximum} = 600 \text{ hrs} \div 30 \text{ mins} = 1200 \text{ units}$$

Note 2   Wages at 450 and 900 level

at 450 level.   Hours $= \dfrac{450 \times 40}{60} = 300$ so guaranteed minimum of £1200 applies

at 900 level.   Hours = 600

so wages are 400 x £3 + overtime rates i.e. 200 x £4 = £2000 total

Note 3   Variable overhead is £3 per hour

∴ at 450 level.   300 hrs x £3 =   £900

∴ at 900 level.   600 hrs x £3 = £1800

Note 4   Labour cost with incentive scheme.

∴ at 450 level.   450 x £2 = £900 so minimum applies i.e. £1200

∴ at 900 level.   900 x £2 = £1800 *plus* overtime premium

on $(900 \times \dfrac{30}{60})$ – 400 hrs = 50 hrs at premium only i.e. £50,

making a total of £1,850.

at 1200 level.   1200 x £2 = £2400 + overtime premium

on 200 hrs i.e. £200 making a total of £2600

b. **Effect on profits of labour dispute**
   i.   When demand is 450 units the time taken should be

450 x 30 mins/unit =   225 hours.

Accordingly the minimum wage would normally be paid and operatives would be idle for (400-225) i.e. 175 hours per week. When 100 hours are lost, and assuming normal operations and efficiency during the rest of the week, these hours would be in the expected idle time and thus the operatives would not be paid as the guaranteed minimum wage will not apply to the 100 lost hours. Accordingly the company will save £(100 x 3) = £300.

   ii. When demand is greater than the proposed maximum, then production will be lost. The loss resulting will be the contribution on the output possible in 100 hours which, assuming that the 100 hours were overtime hours, would be:–

Loss to company

= 100 hrs x 2 units per hour x £3 per unit
= £600

The contribution of £3 per unit is calculated as follows:

		£
Sales price		9
Less Material	£2	
Wages	£2.5	
Variable o'hds	£1.5	6
		£3 per unit

The wages per unit are £2 per unit + ½ hour at the overtime premium rate of £1 per hour.

Note: The above contribution calculation is only applicable when the assumption is that the 100 hours are lost from overtime hours. If the hours were lost from normal time and the full 200 hours overtime were worked, the loss would be greater.

14.

Report No.　　　　　Date ....

To:　MANAGING DIRECTOR

From:　COST ACCOUNTANT

Subject: COMPARISON OF THE COST EFFECTS OF A 10% WAGE RATE INCREASE AND A PRODUCTIVITY BONUS OF 8p PER UNIT PRODUCED.

As requested I have set out below budgeted results for the coming year in the following comparative manner:

Original budget – Budget with 10% wage increase – Budget with productivity bonus of 8p per unit, 12½% increase in production and the selling price reduced by 10p per unit.

	Original Budget	Budget with 10% increase	Changes to original Budget	Budget with productivity deal
Sales qty (units)	1,200,000	1,200,000	+ 12½%	1,350,000
Sales at £2 per unit	£2,400,000	£2,400,000	Sales @ £1.90	£2,565,000
Variable Costs				
Direct Materials	480,000	480,000	+ 12½ increase	540,000
Direct wages	720,000	792,000	£720,000 + (8p x 1,350,000)	828,000
Production Overhead	108,000	108,000	+ 12½% increase	121,500
Selling Cost	120,000	120,000	5% of £2,565,000	128,250
Distribution Cost	96,000	96,000	+ 12½ increase	108,000
Total Variable Cost	1,524,000	1,596,000		1,725,750
. . Contribution =	876,000	804,000		839,250
Less Fixed costs	556,000	556,000		556,000
= Profit	£320,000	£248,000		£283,250

Therefore, based on the estimates provided the productivity deal is recommended.

b. There are numerous uncertainties in any extrapolation such as this.
   i. Uncertainty regarding the estimates of both the sales director and the work study department.
   ii. Uncertainty about the reaction of the production workers. Will they actually produce more or might they settle for the original production level and the bonus which would give them more than the 10% wage rate rise (i.e. £96,000 c.f. £72,000)?

iii. Uncertainty about the reactions of other types of staff to the increased wages of production workers and their increased work load. If they also demand increases then the cost relationships shown will be incorrect.

iv. General uncertainty regarding the behaviour of costs in the future. Are the variable costs truly variable? — Will the fixed costs remain the same?

Chapter 23

1 a.

Standard Cost Sheet
(Per Unit)

	£	£
Direct materials 40 M² @ £5.30 per M²		212
Direct wages:		
Bonding dept. 48 hours @ £2.50 per hour	120	
Finishing dept. 30 hours @ £1.90 per hour	57	
		177
		389

i.	PRIME COST		
	Variable overhead:		
	Bonding dept. 48 hours @ £0.75 per hour	36	
	Finishing dept. 30 hours @ £0.50 per hour	15	
			51
ii.	VARIABLE PRODUCTION COST		440
	Fixed production overhead		40
iii.	TOTAL PRODUCTION COST		480
	Selling and distribution cost	20	
	Administration cost	10	
			30
iv.	TOTAL COST		510

Profit 15% of selling price $= \dfrac{15}{(100-15)} \times 100$ of cost 90

b. SELLING PRICE PER UNIT £600

Workings

Variable overhead rates per hour

Bonding dept. $= \dfrac{£375,000}{500,000}$ hours   Finishing dept. $= \dfrac{£150,000}{300,000}$ hours

$= £0.75$ $= £0.50$

Rates per unit

Fixed production overhead $\dfrac{£392,000}{9,800 \text{ units}} = £40$

Selling and distribution cost $\dfrac{£196,000}{9,800 \text{ units}} = £20$

Administration cost $\dfrac{£98,000}{9,800 \text{ units}} = £10$

Note:

The fixed overheads have been recovered on a unit basis and considering the round figures that result from this method, there is little doubt that the examiner intended this basis to be used. However, strictly speaking this is incorrect. It will be noted that the budgeted output is 9800 units. Using the labour hours given the total labour hours are:–

Bonding 470,400 hrs but budget 500,000 hrs
Finishing 294,000 hrs but budget 300,000 hrs

Unless the discrepancy was unintended this can only mean that some other product(s) are being made, in which case they should bear their proportion of fixed overheads whereas *all* the fixed overheads are recovered on the 9800 units in the question. If there are other products then fixed overheads could be recovered on the total number of hours (800,000) resulting in the following overhead recoveries instead of the round figures previously obtained i.e. £40, £20 and £10.

Overhead Recovery

Fixed production overhead $= \dfrac{392,000}{800,000} = £0.49$ per hour x 78 = <u>£38.22</u>

Selling & Distribution overhead $= \dfrac{196,000}{800,000} = £0.245$ per hour x 78 = <u>£19.11</u>

Administration $= \dfrac{98,000}{800,000} = £0.1225$ per hour x 78 = <u>£9.55</u>

Chapter 24

1. a. Variance Calculations.

Material Variances

Actual cost for actual issues:—   £107,800

$(\frac{£126,000}{£180,000} \times 154,000)$

Direct Material Price Variance £7,700 (FAV)

STANDARD COST for actual issues
:—   £115,500

(154,000 x £0.75 per Kg)

Direct Material Usage Variance £1,500 (ADV)

STANDARD COST for STANDARD QUANTITY   :—   £114,000
(£0.75 x 38,000 x 4 Kg)

Direct Materials Cost Variance = £6,200 (FAV)

Labour Variances

Actual rates for actual hours:—   £136,500

Direct Labour Rate Variance £11,700 (ADV)

STANDARD RATES for actual hours:—   £124,800
(£1.60 hr x 78,000)

Direct Labour Efficiency Variance £3,200 (ADV)

STANDARD RATES for STANDARD HOURS:—   £121,600
(£1.60 x 38,000 x 2)

Direct Wages Cost Variance £14,900 (ADV)

b. ii.   Direct materials price variance, comments. *Consistent* because actual purchase price is lower than standard and quantities purchased are substantially higher than usage.

iii.   Direct materials usage variance, comments. *Inconsistent* because material usage was 2,000 Kg above standard.

v.   Direct wages rate variance, comments. *Inconsistent* because actual rate is 15p higher than standard.

vi.   Direct labour efficiency variance, comments. *Inconsistent* because only 76,000 hours should have been required for the actual production of 38,000 units and 78,000 hours were taken.

2.

Budget Manufacturing Company Ltd.

Sales are £34,500 including a 15% profit margin

$$\therefore \text{Total Costs} = £34,500 \frac{100}{115} = £30,000$$

$$\text{No. of units} = \frac{£30,000}{£3} = 10,000 \text{ units}$$

Total Cost Variance is the sum of all the variances given in the question i.e.

F £	A £
400	600
700	100
	150
	200
	250
	800
1100 (F)	2100 (A)

$$\therefore \text{Total variance} = £1000 \text{ ADV}$$

$$\therefore \text{Standard cost of the sales is } £30,000 - 1000 = £29,000$$

Operating Statement for 4 weeks ending 28th April

		£
Sales		34,500
Less Standard Cost of Sales		29,000
= Standard Profit		5,500
Plus Favourable variances		
	£	
Labour efficiency	400	
Fixed overhead efficiency	700	1,100
		6,600
Less Adverse Variances		
	£	
Idle Time Variance	600	
Materials Price	100	
Materials Usage	150	
Variable Overhead Expenditure	200	
Fixed Overhead Expenditure	250	
Fixed Overhead Capacity	800	2,100
= Actual Profit		£4,500

b. The wages variances show that labour produced at greater than the planned efficiency and that there was some idle time which was valued at the standard labour cost per hour.

Because overheads are recovered on labour hours in this example, a favourable labour efficiency variance will naturally cause favourable overhead efficiency variances which are valued at the overhead absorption rate. The capacity variance shows the effect on overhead recovery of working at a different level to that planned. It is likely that the capacity variance reflects the idle time variance in this example but it does not always follow that an adverse capacity variance means that there was idle time.

c. The pricing policy of the company is based on the standard cost of the product. As can be seen the standard cost is a total standard cost, including both fixed and variable costs. This may be a suitable pricing policy if,

   i.   Market forces play little part in determining selling prices.

   ii. Activity levels are reasonably constant.

   iii. Actual costs are close to standard.

   iv. There is little or no surplus capacity.

To base selling prices on full standard costs makes any form of marginal pricing more difficult to apply and is only likely to be completely satisfactory in strictly defined circumstances.

3. a. No. of kilos of direct material purchased

The amount purchased is standard quantity ± usage variance ± stock difference. Thus

Standard quantity = 38,000 units x 4	=	152,000 kilos
Add adverse usage variance $\frac{£1,500}{£0.75}$	=	2,000 kilos
Add increase in stock	=	26,000
= Purchases		180,000 kilos

b. Number of kilos used above standard

This is the adverse usage variance calculated above   2,000 kilos

c. Variable overhead expenditure variance

The variable production overhead variance given (£2,200 FAV) is the sum of the expenditure variance and the efficiency variance given (£2,400 ADV) thus

Total production Overhead Variance (2,200 FAV) =

      Efficiency, variance (2,400 ADV) + Expenditure variance

       ∴ Expenditure variance = £4,600 (FAV)

d. Actual hours worked.

This is calculated by dividing the actual wages paid by the actual rate per hour. The actual rate is the standard rate ± wage rate variance.

$$\text{Actual rate} = \frac{£152,000}{80,000} + £0.20$$

$$= £2.10$$

$$∴ \text{Actual hours worked} = \frac{£163,800}{2.10} = 78,000 \text{ hrs}$$

e. Standard hours allowed for actual production.

Assuming that variable overheads are recovered on labour hours the number of hours above standard can be calculated by analysing the variable overhead efficiency variance of £2,400 adverse. The hours above standard can then be deducted from the actual hours worked of 78,000 calculated above.

$$\text{Excess hours contained in Overhead efficiency variance} = \frac{\text{amount of variance}}{\text{V.O.A.R.}}$$

$$= \frac{2,400}{£1.20} = \underline{2000} \text{ hrs}$$

$$\therefore \text{Standard hours} = 78,000 - 2,000 = \underline{76,000} \text{ hours}$$

Note: The VOAR is $\frac{£96,000}{80,000} = \underline{£1.20}$ per hour

4. a. i. **Standard hour.**
   The definition given in Terminology is "A hypothetical unit pre-established to represent the amount of work which should be performed in one hour at Standard performance".
   In essence a standard hour is a measure of work content.
   ii. **Productivity (or efficiency) ratio.**
   The definition given in Terminology is "The standard hours equivalent to the production achieved, whether completed or not divided by (or expressed as a percentage of) the actual number of direct working hours".
   The ratio is a useful measure of labour and departmental efficiency.
   iii. **Production volume ratio.**
   The definition given in Terminology is "The number of standard hours equivalent to the production achieved, whether completed or not, divided by (or expressed as a percentage of) the budgeted number of standard hours.

   b. The first step is to calculate the budgeted standard hours and standard hours produced for Dept X (Dept Y's figures are given)

Dept X

Production in Standard hours	Budgeted standard hours
Product D	
$15,000 \times \frac{20}{60} = 5,000$	$18,000 \times \frac{20}{60} = 6,000$
Product G	
$10,000 \times \frac{30}{60} = 5,000$	$4,000 \times \frac{30}{60} = 2,000$
$\underline{10,000}$	$\underline{8,000}$

The ratios can now be calculated.

Productivity Ratio

Dept X	$\frac{10,000}{11,111} \times 100 =$	90%
Dept Y	$\frac{9,450}{9,000} \times 100 =$	105%

426

Production Volume Ratio

Dept X $\quad \dfrac{10,000}{8,000} \times 100 = 125\%$

Dept Y $\quad \dfrac{9,450}{10,000} \times 100 = 94.5\%$

5. Working Paper on Variances to be included in the weaving shed's Operating Statement.

Materials Variances

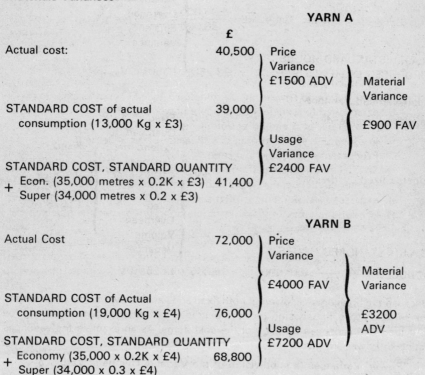

YARN A

	£		
Actual cost:	40,500	Price Variance £1500 ADV	Material Variance
STANDARD COST of actual consumption (13,000 Kg x £3)	39,000		£900 FAV
		Usage Variance £2400 FAV	
STANDARD COST, STANDARD QUANTITY + Econ. (35,000 metres x 0.2K x £3) Super (34,000 metres x 0.2 x £3)	41,400		

YARN B

	£		
Actual Cost	72,000	Price Variance £4000 FAV	Material Variance
STANDARD COST of Actual consumption (19,000 Kg x £4)	76,000		£3200 ADV
		Usage £7200 ADV	
STANDARD COST, STANDARD QUANTITY + Economy (35,000 x 0.2K x £4) Super (34,000 x 0.3 x £4)	68,800		

If required the total price variance, usage variance and material variance can be obtained by adding the Yarn A and Yarn B variances together.

Labour Variances

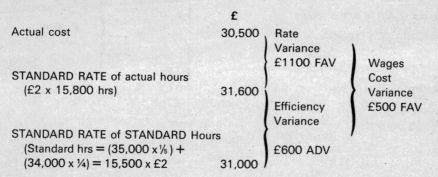

	£		
Actual cost	30,500	Rate Variance £1100 FAV	Wages Cost Variance
STANDARD RATE of actual hours (£2 x 15,800 hrs)	31,600		£500 FAV
		Efficiency Variance £600 ADV	
STANDARD RATE of STANDARD Hours (Standard hrs = (35,000 x ⅕) + (34,000 x ¼) = 15,500 x £2	31,000		

Variable Overhead Variances*

Actual overheads	24,750	Variable Overhead Expenditure Variance £1050 ADV	Variable Overhead Variance = £1500 ADV
V.O.A.R. x Actual hours $= \dfrac{£24,000}{16,000}$ x 15,800	23,700		
		Variable Overhead Efficiency Variance	
V.O.A.R. x STANDARD HOURS PRODUCED £1.50 x 15,500	23,250	£450 ADV	

Fixed Overhead Variances*

Actual fixed overheads	21,050	Fixed Overhead Expenditure Variance £1050 ADV	Fixed Overhead Variance
Budgeted fixed overheads	20,000		£1675 ADV
		Fixed Overhead Volume Variance	
F.O.A.R. x STANDARD HOURS PRODUCED $\dfrac{£20,000}{16,000}$ x 15,500	19,375	£625 ADV	

* Because the breakdown is given of both fixed and variable overheads into separate cost items (Power, Supervision etc) the overhead variances shown above can be subdivided into variances for each of the cost items. As an example the variances relating to Power are given.

'Power' Variances (a subdivision of the Variable Overhead Variance)

	£		
Actual expenditure	8,250	'Power' Expenditure Variance £350 ADV	Total 'Power' Cost Variance £500 ADV
Power O.A.R. x Actual hours $= \dfrac{£8,000}{16,000}$ x 15,800	7,900		
		'Power' Efficiency Variance	
Power O.A.R. x SHP £0.50 x 15,500	7,750	£150 ADV	

All other items can be treated in a similar manner.

Chapter 25

1. a. **Sales and Sales Margin Variances.**

   i. Sales variances deal with sales revenue and do not consider the margin or profit earned.

   ii. Sales margin variances are concerned with the margin earned between sales and costs. Where the costs include fixed elements the margin is profit; where only variable costs are included the margin is contribution. In most circumstances management are more concerned with what sales produce in terms of the margin rather than the simple amount of revenue. Sales margin variances, which include sub variances relating to volume and mix, enable management to probe the reasons for differences between budgeted and actual profit.

   Sales variances relating to the amount of sales revenue can also be subdivided and, used with care, could produce some useful information to marketing management. However it is likely that detailed sales analyses would be of greater value.

   b. **Idle Time Variance.**

   This variance is not defined in Terminology but is taken to mean the variance which results from the actual hours worked differing from what should have been worked, excluding the efficiency element. The idle time hours could be valued at

   either — the standard hourly labour rate

   or — the standard fixed overhead absorption rate per hour.

   Clearly idle time does result in a loss and it is a matter of judgement what it should be valued at.

   In a labour intensive factory with low fixed overheads possibly the standard wage rate could be used. Conversely where there are heavy fixed overheads, perhaps caused by substantial mechanisation, the F.O.A.R. would be appropriate.

   The real answer lies in the objectives to be fulfilled by variance analysis. It is what *management wish to know* that determines the nature of all variances, including idle time variances.

2. The format of the Profit Statement is provided but the standard sales price and all the variances need to be calculated first before the statement can be prepared.

   Standard sales price is standard cost $\times \frac{5}{4}$ i.e. including 20% profit on selling price.

	Standard Costs per Unit			
	£	£	£	£
Direct Material W (£4.3 x 4)	17.2			
X (£6 x 5)	30			
Y (£2 x 10)			20	
Z (£2.2 x 4)		47.2	8.8	28.8
Direct Wages				
I (£2.2 x 8) & (£2.2 x 4)	17.6		8.8	
II (£1.8 x 4) & (£1.8 x 8)	7.2	24.8	14.4	23.2
Overheads* £4 x 12 hrs		48		48
= Standard Total Cost		120		100
Standard Profit = Cost x $\frac{5}{4}$		30		25
= St. Selling Price		£150		£125

* Overhead absorption rate

$$= \frac{\text{Total overheads}}{\text{Total hours}} = \frac{£34,560}{(320 \times 12) + (400 \times 12)} = £4 \text{ per hr.}$$

Based on the details of the standard cost per unit and the actual results the variances can be calculated.

Materials variances

Actual price of actual usage
= £(1280 x 4.2) + (1600 x 6.2) + (4000 x 2.1)
+ (1580 x 2.0)   :— 26,856   Price Variance

£276 ADV   Total Material Variance £756 ADV

STANDARD PRICE of actual usage
£(1280 x 4.3) + (1600 x 6.0) + (4000 x 2.0)
+ (1580 x 2.2)   :— 26,580

Usage Variance

STANDARD PRICE of STANDARD
USAGE i.e. Standard cost from
previous calculations £(315 x 47.2)
+ (390 x 28.8)   :— 26,100   £480 ADV

Wage Variances

Actual rate x actual hours
£(3960 x 2) + (4260 x 1.7)   :— £15,162   Rate Variance

£1218 FAV   Total Wages Variance

STANDARD RATE x actual hours
£(3960 x 2.2) + (4260 x 1.8)   :— £16,380   £1,698 FAV

Efficiency Variance £480 FAV

STANDARD RATE x STANDARD
HOURS i.e. standard cost
£(315 x 24.8) + (390 x 23.2)   :— 16,860

Overhead Variances

Actual overheads	:—	33,400	Expenditure Variance £1,160 FAV
BUDGETED OVERHEADS	:—	34,560	Total Overhead Variance
			Capacity Variance £1680 ADV
STANDARD O.A.R. x Actual hours £4 x 8220	:—	32,880	£440 FAV
			Productivity Variance £960 FAV
STANDARD COST £(315 x 48) + (390 x 48)	:—	33,840	

Based on the above calculations the statement can be completed.

Profit and Loss Statement
for month ended 30th April, 1978

	Product Aye £	Product Bee £	Total £	
Sales, actual quantity at standard price	47,250	48,750	96,000	
Standard cost of sales:				
Direct material	14,868	11,232	26,100	
Direct wages	7,812	9,048	16,860	
Overhead	15,120	18,720	33,840	
Total	37,800	39,000	76,800	
Standard profit on actual sales	9,450	9,750	19,200	
Variances:				
Direct materials: price			276	ADV
usage			480	ADV
cost			756	ADV
Direct wages: rate			1,218	FAV
efficiency			480	FAV
cost			1,698	FAV
Overhead: expenditure			1,160	FAV
productivity			960	FAV
capacity			1,680	ADV
cost			440	FAV
Total			1,382	FAV
Actual profit			20,582	

3. a. Statement of variances for 1978/79 Period 1

		ADV £	FAV £

Materials: Price

	£		
Std 22330 lbs @ 44p/lb	9825.20		
Actual	8932		893.20

     : Usage

Std (580 x 38 lbs) = 22040 lbs

Actual	22330 lbs 290 lbs @ 44p	127.60	

Labour : Rate

Std 7250 hrs @ 76p =	5510		
Actual	5510	–	–

     : Efficiency

Std (580 x 12 hrs) = 6960 hrs

Actual	7250 hrs 290 hrs @ 76p	220.40	

Variable Overhead: Expenditure

Std 580 @ £1.66 = £962.8

Actual	920		42.80

Fixed Overhead : Budget (i.e. Expenditure)

Std 650 x £1.2 = £780

Actual	720		60.00

     : Volume

Budget 650 units

Actual 580	= 70 units @ £1.20	84	

Sales Margin: Price

Std 580 @ £33 £19140

Actual	19140	–	–
		£432	£996

     .˙. Net Favourable Variance = £564

This can be verified as follows

Profit Variance	£
Standard 580 @ £4.30	2,494
Actual	3,058
	£564 FAV

b. Comparison of variances for 1977/78, Period 13 and 1978/79 Period 1.

Study of the variances given in the question for Period 13 and of the new standards for 1978/79 indicate that standards have been immediately adjusted in line with the most recent variances.

Examples include;

Material usage – a favourable variance in Period 13 results in a 2 lb reduction in the standard quantity.

Labour Rate – an adverse variance in Period 13 results in a 16p per hour increase and so on.

Standards should be set with regard to what is expected in the future and not adjusted according to variances from one period to another. This process makes comparison difficult and could render the motivation aspects of budgeting meaningless. If managers know that a favourable variance one period will automatically cause a raising of the required performance level they are unlikely to react in a cooperative, positive fashion.

Chapter 26

1. Comment.

The question states that separate accounting systems are maintained and that the balances given are from the Cost Ledger. Accordingly, the account termed 'Cost Ledger Control Account' is the account in the cost ledger which in this manual has been termed the 'Financial Ledger Control A/c' or the 'Cost Ledger Contra A/c'.

The accounting entries are as follows:

Cost Ledger Control A/c

1st May		1st May	
		Balance	302,000
Sales	410,000	Stores Control (Purchases)	42,700
Capital work in progress	50,150	Wages Control	124,000
		Prod. overhead control	152,350
31st May		Direct expense control	2,150
Balance c/f	237,500	Selling overhead control	22,000
		Costing profit	52,450
	697,650		697,650
		1st June	
		Balance	237,500

Stores Control A/c

1st May			
Balance	85,400	W-I-P (Issues)	63,400
Cost ledger control	42,700	Production overhead	1,450
		Capital work (issues)	7,650
		31st May	
		Balance c/f	55,600
	128,100		128,100
1st June			
Balance	55,600		

Production Overhead Control A/c

Stores control (issues)	1,450	Capital work	30,000
Wages control	35,750	WIP (bal. charged to WIP)	152,000
Cost ledger control	152,350	Costing P & L (under absorption)	7,550
	189,550		189,550

Wages Control

Cost ledger control	124,000	Capital work	12,500
		Production overhead	35,750
		W-I-P	75,750
	124,000		124,000

Selling overhead control

Cost ledger control	22,000	Costing P & L	22,000

W-I-P control

1st May			
Balance	167,350		
Stores ledger control	63,400	Finished goods control	281,300
Wages control	75,750		
Production overhead	152,000	**31st May**	
Direct express control	2,150	Balance c/f (Note 1)	179,350
	330,650		330,650
1st June			
Balance	179,350		

Finished Goods Control A/c

1st May			
Balance	49,250	Cost of sales (Note 2)	328,000
W-I-P	281,300	**31st May**	
		Balance c/f	2,550
	330,550		330,550
1st June			
Balance	2,550		

Capital Work in Progress A/c

Stores control	7,650		
Wages Control	12,500	Cost Ledger Control	50,150
Production O/head	30,000		
	50,150		50,150

Direct Expenses Control

Cost ledger control	2,150	WIP	2,150

Sales account

Costing P & L A/c	410,000	Cost ledger control	410,000

Cost of Sales A/c

Finished Goods Control	328,000	Costing P & L A/c	328,000

Costing Profit & Loss A/c

Cost of Sales	328,000	Sales	410,000
Production o'hd underabsorbed	7,550		
Selling overhead	22,000		
Profit-Cost Ledger Control	52,450		
	410,000		410,000

(not asked for in question)

Closing trial balance

	£	£
Cost Ledger Control		237,500
Stores Control	55,600	
W-I-P Control	179,350	
Finished goods control	2,550	
	£237,500	£237,500

Notes 1. The WIP closing balance is opening balance of £167,350 + £12,000 increase = £179,350. Given this figure the transfer to finished goods is the balance on the account.

2. In the absence of further information and on the assumption the gross profit margin has been exactly achieved, the cost of sales transfer can be calculated thus

$$£410,000 \times \frac{100}{125} = \underline{£328,000}$$

2.

Journal Entries

	£	£
Wages Control A/c	32,000	
National Insurance A/c		1,460
Superannuation Contributions A/c		1,760
Income Tax A/c		4,800
Trade Union dues A/c		60
Social Club A/c		40
Bank A/c		23,880
Overhead Control A/c	3,140	
National Insurance A/c		3,140
W-I-P control	15,200	
Overhead Control	15,200	
Capital Work in progress	1,600	
Wages Control A/c		32,000

Notes:

a. N.I. to overhead control is employer's contribution i.e. £4,600 − 1460.

b. Charges from Wages Control to WIP and Overheads are made up as follows:

	W-I-P	Overhead
	£	£
Ordinary time	12,000	7,000
Overtime	3,200	2,000
Overtime premium		1,700
Shift allowance		2,400
Sick pay		1,000
Idle time		1,100
	£15,200	£15,200

3. a. The ledger accounts follow. All accounts are in £'000s.

Capital

		Balance b/d	1,000

Freehold Building (Cost)

Balance b/d	500		

Reserves

		Balance b/d	200

Plant & Machinery (Cost)

Balance b/d	500		
Bank	50		

Creditors

Returns	40	Balance b/d	150
Bank	895	Raw Materials	990
Discount Rec'd	25		
Balance c/f	180		
	1140		1140
		Balance	180

Expense Creditors

Bank	730	Balance b/d	20
Balance c/f	35	Prod'n Expenses	320
		Carriage inwards	45
		Admin. expenses	260
		Selling expenses	120
	765		765
		Balance	35

Raw Material Control

Balance b/d	220	Returns	40
Creditors	990	W-I-P	850
		Price Variance	35
		Bank (ins. claim)	60
		Balance c/f	225
	1210		1210
Balance	225		

W-I-P Control

Balance b/d	40		
Raw Material	850	Finished Goods	1,600
Salaries & Wages	250	Balance c/f	55
Prod. O'head	425		
Mat'l Usage Var.	20		
Labour Eff. Var.	30		
O'head Eff. Var.	40		
	1655		1655
Balance	55		

Finished Goods Control

Balance b/d	60	Cost of Sales	2000
W-I-P	1,600	Balance c/f	40
Adm. O'head	380		
	2040		2040
Balance	40		

Depreciation Provision Plant & M/c

		Balance b/d	100
		Prod'n Overhead	50
			150

Debtors Control

Balance b/d	200	Returns	60
Sales	2,500	Bank	2,350
		Cash Discount	35
		Bad Debts	25
		Balance c/f	230
	2700		2700
Balance	230		

Production O'Head Control

Salaries & Wages	60	W-I-P	425
Expense CRS	320	Expenditure Var.	25
Carriage	45	Overhead Adj.	25
Depreciation	50	(under absorbed o'hd)	
	475		475

Bank

Balance b/d	150	Plant & Mach.	50
Mat'l (Ins. claim)	60	Creditors	895
Debtors	2350	Expense Crs.	730
		Salaries & Wages	425
		Balance c/f	460
	2560		2560
Balance	460		

Salaries & Wages Control

Wage Rate Var.	15	W-I-P	250
Bank	425	Prod'n o/h	60
Deductions	50	Admin. o/h	100
		S & D	80
	490		490

Administration Overhead Control

Salaries & Wages	100	Finished Goods	380
Expense crs.	260		
Over absorbed o/h	20		
	380		380

Selling & Dist. Overhead Control

Salaries & Wages	80		
Expense creditors	120	Cost of sales	210
Over absorbed o/h	10		
	210		210

Cost of Sales

S & Dist.	210	P & L	2210
Fin. goods	2000		
	2210		2210

Sales

Returns	60	Debtors	2500
P & L	2440		
	2500		2500

Material Price Variance

Materials	35	P & L	35

Material Usage Variance

P & L	20	W-I-P	20

Wage Rate Variance

P & L	15	Salaries & Wages	15

Labour Efficiency Variance

P & L	30	W-I-P	30

Production O'head Efficiency Variance

P & L	40	W-I-P	40

Production O'head Expenditure Var.

Overheads	25	P & L	25

Salaries & Wages Deductions

		Salaries & Wages	50

Discount Allowed

Debtors	35	P & L	35

Discount Received

P & L	25	Creditors	25

Bad Debts

Debtors	25	P & L	25

Overhead Adjustment A/c

Prod'n Overhead	25	Admin. overhead	20
P & L	5	S & D overhead	10
	30		30

Profit and Loss A/c for year

		£
Sales		2,440,000
Less Cost of Sales		2,210,000
		230,000

Add Favourable Variances	£	
Material usage	20,000	
Wage Rate	15,000	
Labour Efficiency	30,000	
Overhead Efficiency	40,000	105,000
		335,000

Less Adverse Variances		
Material Price	35,000	
Overhead Expenditure	25,000	60,000
		275,000
Add Over absorbed overheads		5,000
		280,000

Less Net Discounts	10,000	
Bad Debts	25,000	35,000
= Net Profit		£245,000

Balance Sheet

		£			£
Capital		1,000,000	Fixed Assets		
Reserves	200,000		Freehold buildings at cost		500,000
Unappropriated p'fit	245,000	445,000	Plant & mach. cost £350,000		
			Less Depreciation £150,000		200,000
		1,445,000			700,000
Current Liabilities			Current Assets	£	
Creditors	215,000		Stocks-M'tls	225,000	
Deductions	50,000	265,000	W-I-P	55,000	
			Fin. Gds	40,000	
			Debtors	230,000	
			Bank	460,000	1,010,000
		£1,710,000			£1,710,000

4. a.

Integrated accounts for D. Manufacturing Co. Ltd.
for April 1980
All figures in £'000s

Land & Buildings		Plant, Machinery etc.	
April 1 Bal	500	April 1 Bal	800

Provision for Depreciation

	April 1 Bal.	200
	30 Prod. Ohd.	20
	Admin.	5
		225

Material Stores

April 1 Bal.	80	April 30 W-I-P	40
30 Creditors	45	Prod. Ohd.	8
(Std cost)		Bal c/f	77
	125		125
Balance	77		

W-I-P

April 1 Bal.	40	Fin. gds. trfs.	110
30 Wages	40	Balance c/f	90
Stores	40		
Prod. Ohd.	80		
	200		200
Balance	90		

Finished Goods

April 1 Bal.	20	Apr. 30 Cost of s'ls	112
30 W-I-P	110	Balance c/f	18
	130		130
Balance	18		

Debtors

April 1 Bal.	260	April 30 Bank	190
30 Sales	160	Balance c/f	230
	420		420
Balance	230		

Creditors

April 30 Bank	70	April 1 Bal.	100
Balance c/f	80	30 Materials	50
	150		150
		Balance	80

Share Capital

	April 1 Bal.	1100

Share Premium

	April 1 Bal.	200

Bank

April 30 Debtors	190	April 1 Bal.	50
Balance c/f	70	30 Creditors	70
		Wages & Sals.	80
		PAYE & NI	30
		Prod. exps.	20
		Admin. exps.	10
	260		260
		Balance	70

Production overhead

April 30			
Wages & Sals.	20	April 30	
Bank	20	W-I-P	80
Depreciation	20		
PAYE & NI	5		
Materials	8		
Over Rec. to P & L	7		
	80		80

P & L Appropriation A/c

April 30 P & L	20	April 1 Bal.	35
Balance c/f	15		
	35		35
		Balance	15

PAYE & NI Control

April 30 Bank	30	April 1 Bal.	15
Balance c/f	25	30 Wages & Sal.	30
		Prod. ohd.	5
		Admin. ohd	3
		Selling ohd	2
	55		55
		Balance	25

Wages & Salaries Control

April 30 Bank	80	April 30 W-I-P	40
PAYE & NI	30	Prod. ohd.	20
		Admin. ohd.	30
		Selling ohd.	20
	110		110

Admin. Overhead

April 30		April 30	
Wages & Sals.	30	P & L	48
Bank	10		
Depreciation	5		
PAYE & NI	3		
	48		48

Selling overheads			Materials Price Variance A/c		
April 30 Wages & Sals.	20	April 30 P & L 22	April 30 Creditors 5		April 30 P & L 5
PAYE & NI	2				
	22	22			

Sales			Cost of Sales		
April 30 Trading A/c 160		April 30 Debtors 160	April 30 Fin. goods 112		April 30 Trading A/c 112

Trading & Profit and Loss

April 30 Cost of Sales	112	April 30 Sales	160
Gross Profit c/f	48		
	160		160
Admin. overheads	48	Gross Profit	48
Selling overheads	22	Prod'n overheads (over absorbed)	7
Material Price variance	5	Net loss	20
	75		75

Trial Balance at 30/4/80

Land & Buildings	500	Provision for depreciation	225
Plant etc.	800	Creditors	80
Material Stores	77	Bank	70
W-I-P	90	Share Capital	1,100
Debtors	230	Share Premium	200
Finished Goods	18	P & L appropriation	15
		PAYE & NI control	25
	£1,715		£1,715

5. **Comment:** Although this appears a long, involved question it can be answered readily by taking the six stock valuations in the financial account given (i.e. opening and closing stocks for raw material, W-I-P, and finished goods) and adjusting these six values by the stock valuation differences shown in the Reconciliation Statement. The adjustments need to be made in the following directions.

Stock	Valuation in Cost A/cs	Costing Profit	Direction of Adjustment in Reconciliation Statement
Opening Balance	Higher	Lower	Deducted
	Lower	Higher	Added
Closing Balance	Higher	Higher	Added*
	Lower	Lower	Deducted

* As an example of the use of this table consider the closing stock of raw materials.

The adjustment in the reconciliation statement is ADDED to the financial profit because the costing profit is HIGHER because the closing balance valuation in the Cost A/cs is HIGHER. Thus, given the Financial valuation of £65,000 and reconciliation adjustment of ADD £750 the cost valuation of raw materials closing stock is £65,000 + £750 = £65,750.

The various stock valuations are given below

	Financial Valuation	Reconciliation Difference		Adjustment (From Table)	=	Cost Valuation
	£	£				£
Opening Stock Raw Material	60,500	Less	1,100	Higher		61,600
Closing Stock Raw Material	65,000	Add	750	Higher		65,750
Opening Stock W-I-P	36,700	Add	900	Lower		35,800
Closing Stock W-I-P	35,200	Less	500	Lower		34,700
Opening Stock Finished Goods	45,600	Add	1300	Lower		44,300
Closing Stock Finished Goods	47,600	Add	500	Higher		48,100

The various cost ledger accounts can now be entered.

Raw Materials Stores Account

Opening Stock	61,600	W-I-P	315,850
Purchases	320,000	Closing Stock c/f	65,750
	£381,600		£381,600
Balance	65,750		

W-I-P Account

Opening Stock	35,800		
Raw Materials	315,850	Finished Goods	603,950
Direct Wages	125,000	Closing Stock	34,700
*Production Overhead	162,000		
	£638,650		£638,650
Balance	34,700		

Finished Goods

Opening Stock	44,300	Cost of Sales	600,150
W-I-P	603,950	Closing Stock	48,100
	£648,250		£648,250
Balance	48,100		

* In the reconciliation there was a £2,000 adjustment relating to Production overheads overabsorbed.

. . production overheads to be charged are ACTUAL + £2,000 = £162,000.

b. Work in progress stocks in the cost ledger are valued at lower figures than the financial accounts. Various reasons are possible

i. The cost ledger valuations may be at marginal cost whilst the financial valuations may include elements of fixed cost.

ii. Regardless of whether absorption or marginal costing is used there may be additional costs included in the financial accounts not in the cost accounts e.g. head office costs.

iii. The valuations in the cost accounts may be a standard cost whereas the financial valuations may be at actual cost.

6. a. i. Actual output in units

$$= \frac{\text{Total Standard cost of direct materials}}{\text{Unit Standard cost of direct materials}}$$

$$= £63,900 \div \frac{£360}{400} = \underline{71,000} \text{ units}$$

ii. Quantity of material E used in production

Standard cost of actual tonnes used is standard cost of output + adverse usage variance

i.e. £63,900 + £900 = £64,800

which divided by standard cost per ton gives quantity used

i.e. £64,800 ÷ £360 = <u>180</u> tonnes

iii. Price per tonne of material E

To find this it is necessary to calculate the total actual cost of material used i.e.

	£
Standard cost	63,900
+ Adverse usage variance	+ 900
− Favourable price variance	− 1,440
= Actual cost of material	£63,360

$$\therefore \text{Price per tonne} = \frac{\text{Actual cost}}{\text{Quantity used}} = \frac{63,360}{180} = \underline{\underline{£352}}$$

iv. Man hours worked

This answer can be found by calculating the standard cost of the hours worked divided by the standard wage rate per hour:

	£
Standard direct wages	28,400
Less Favourable efficiency variance	900
= Standard cost of actual hours	£27,500

$$\therefore \text{Actual hours} = \frac{£27,500}{£2} = \underline{13,750} \text{ hours}$$

v. Fixed overhead incurred. This is the budgeted fixed overhead for a four week period less the favourable fixed overhead expenditure variance

$$\text{Budgeted fixed overhead} = \frac{£630,000}{50 \text{ weeks}} \times 4 \text{ weeks} = 50,400$$

	£
Less Favourable expenditure variance	150
= Fixed overhead incurred	£50,250

b. i. Fixed overhead productivity variance.

This is the fixed overhead absorption rate (FOAR) for the number of labour hours saved compared with standard. It is the equivalent of the labour efficiency variance.

$$\text{No of labour hours saved} = \frac{\text{Labour efficiency variance}}{\text{Wage rate per hour}} = \frac{£900}{£2} = \underline{450} \text{ hrs}$$

$$\text{Fixed overhead absorption rate/hour} = \frac{£630,000}{900,000 \text{ units}} \times 5 \text{ units/hour}$$

$$= \underline{£3.50}$$

∴ Fixed overhead productivity variance = 450 x £3.50 = £1,575 FAV

ii. The fixed overhead capacity variance is the difference between actual hours at the FOAR and the budgeted fixed overhead.

	£
Standard cost of actual hours = 13,750 x £3.50 =	48,125
Budget for period	50,400
∴ Fixed Overhead capacity variance =	£2,275 ADV

(Note that the two variances calculated above equal the volume variance shown in the question i.e. 1,575 (FAV) + £2,275 ADV = £700 ADV).

c.

Work-in-Progress Control A/c

Direct material	64,800	Finished Goods	142,000*
Direct wages	27,500		
Fixed overhead	50,400		
Favourable variances		Adverse variances	
Labour efficiency	900	Materials Usage	900
Fixed overhead productivity	1,575	Fixed overhead capacity	2,275
	£145,175		£145,175

* This is the standard cost of the units manufactured i.e. 71,000 x £2.

Note: It is assumed that the overhead expenditure variance is extracted before fixed overheads are charged to W-I-P in a similar fashion to the materials price and wage rate variances.

7. a. Departmental overhead rates.

Dept A

$$\text{Overheads/machine hour} = \frac{£300,000}{120,000}$$

$$= \underline{£2.5}$$

Dept B

$$\text{Percentage on direct labour} = \frac{£267,750}{153,000} \times 100\%$$

$$= \underline{175\%}$$

b.

Department A Overhead Control A/c

	£		£
Actual overheads	304,000	W-I-P	305,000
		(122,000 @ £2.5)	
Over-recovery (P & L)	1,000		
	£305,000		£305,000

Department B Overhead Control A/c

	£		£
Actual overheads	298,000	W-I-P	290,500
		(£166,000 x 175%)	
		Under-Recovery P & L	7,500
	£298,000		£298,000

c.

Cost of Job No X123

	£	£
Direct Materials (900 + 500)		1,400
Direct Labour (120 + 136)		256
Prime Cost		1,656
Overheads		
Dept A (148 hrs @ £2.5)	370	
Dept B (£136 x 175%)	238	608
= Total Cost		£2,264

d. Assuming that there is sufficient similarity between the jobs and/or processes involved to make the installation of standard costing worthwhile the following benefits might be achieved.

    a. Greater cost control from detailed variance analysis.

    b. Simpler basis for estimating which can be developed from predetermined standards.

    c. Increase in management information on which to plan and control production.

    d. Possible improvements in methods and procedures following the standard setting process.

e. More consistent stock valuation.

The management information would be the overhead variance analysis which is given below.

(**Note:** The question does not provide sufficient information for a full overhead variance analysis. In particular the actual overheads are not separated into fixed and variable components. Accordingly it is assumed that the actual expenditure on fixed overheads is as budgeted i.e. 80% of £300,000 = £240,000).

Budget   120,000 machine hours
                     £240,000 Fixed overheads
                     £60,000 Variable overheads

$$\therefore \text{Fixed O.A.R.} = \frac{£240,000}{120,000} = £2 \text{ per hour}$$

$$\text{Variable O.A.R.} = \frac{60,000}{120,000} = £0.5 \text{ per hour}$$

Actual

                     122,000 Machine hours
                     119,000 Standard machine hours produced
                     £240,000 Fixed overheads (assumed)
                     £64,000 Variable overheads

The total overhead variance is the difference between the actual overheads and the overheads absorbed by the actual production.

= £304,000 − (119,000 x £2.5) = £6,500 ADV

This can be analysed as follows:

Variable overheads

Actual overheads	£64,000	Variable Overhead Expenditure Variance £3000 ADV	Variable Overhead Variance £4500 ADV
V.O.A.R. x Actual hours (£0.50 x 122,000)	61,000	Variable Overhead Efficiency Variance £1500 ADV	
V.O.A.R. x SHP (£0.50 x 119,000)	59,500		

Fixed overheads

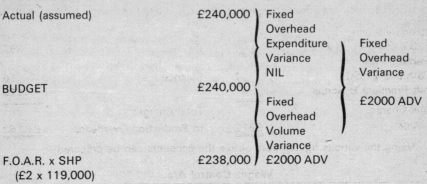

Actual (assumed)	£240,000	Fixed Overhead Expenditure Variance NIL	Fixed Overhead Variance
BUDGET	£240,000	Fixed Overhead Volume Variance	£2000 ADV
F.O.A.R. x SHP (£2 x 119,000)	£238,000	£2000 ADV	

8. Assembly department's Control A/cs.

Before the entries can be made in the accounts it is necessary to calculate and analyse the wages.

Wages Calculations

	Direct £		Indirect £
Attendance payments (800 x £1.50)	1,200	(350 x 1.00)	350
Overtime premium (100 x £0.75)	75	(40 x £0.50)	20
Shift Premium	150		50
Bonus	160		70
= Gross Wage	1,585		490
Deductions			
Income Tax	250		100
NI	75 325		35 135
= Net Wages	£1,260		£355

Analysis of Direct workers Gross Wages

	Direct (charged to WIP) £		Indirect (charged to Overheads) £
Productive time (590 x £1.50)	885	Balance	315
Overtime Premium (20 x £0.75)	15	Balance	60
Shift Premium & Bonus	–		310
	900		685

Analysis of Indirect Gross Wages

	£		£
Attendance time			
20% of 40 hours @ £1	8	Balance	342
Overtime Premium			
8 hrs @ £0.50	4	Balance	16
Shift Premium & Bonus	–		120
Total Charge:		Total Charge:	
to WIP	£912	to Production Overheads	£1,163

Using the various figures from above the accounts can be prepared.

Wages Control A/c

	£		£
Cash (Net direct Wages)	1,260	W-I-P	912
Cash (Net indirect Wages)	355	Production Overheads	1,163
Income Tax A/c (250 + 100)	350		
NI A/c (75 + 35)	110		
	2,075		2,075

W-I-P Control

Wages Control	912		

Production Overhead Control A/c

Wages Control	1,163		
NI A/c (Employers cont.)	180		

Bank A/c

		Wages Control	1,260
		Wages Control	355

Income Tax A/c

		Wages Control	350

NI A/c

		Wages Control	110
		Production Overheads	180
			290

b. **Treatment of various costs.**

It is preferable to charge costs as directly as possible where this can be done without excessive administration and where direct charging to a product or batch does not cause anomalies.

    i. **Employers NI Contribution.** This is not readily attributable to particular products or batches and so is normally charged to Production Overheads where it will be absorbed into products via the absorption rate.

    ii. **Group Bonus.** Frequently a bonus can be identified with a particular batch and, if so, it should be classified as direct and charged to W-I-P. However there is insufficient information given in this question for this to be done and so it is charged to Production Overheads for eventual absorption into all products.

Overtime earnings. There are two elements which make up total overtime earnings, basic rate and overtime premium. The basic rate is readily identifiable to a product or batch and should be charged direct. The overtime premium is also readily identifiable to a batch but it is generally accepted that the premium should be charged to overheads and thus spread over all batches. The reason for this is that it is usually fortuitous which particular batch is actually dealt with during the overtime hours so it would create anomalies by charging the premium direct to that batch. The exception to this rule would be where, as in this question, there is a special reason such as a request from a customer for a batch to be produced during overtime. In such cases the premium could legitimately be charged direct.

Chapter 27

1. a. Service (or operating) costing is a method of costing used where standardised (or nearly standardised) services are provided either by an undertaking or by a service cost centre within an organisation. Costs are averaged for a period over all the units of service provided. Typical examples of services where service costing is likely to be appropriate are; transport, gas, electricity, catering, steam generation etc.

   Uniform costing is not a costing method. It is the adoption by a number of undertakings of the same costing systems, principles, classifications and methods of reporting to aid cost comparability and to promote efficiency.

   Thus an organisation such as a transport undertaking may use service costing as their basic costing method whilst at the same time operating uniform costing in collaboration with other organisations.

   b. i.

Profitability Statement

Route	R1 £'000s	R2 £'000s	R3 £'000s	Total £'000s
Revenue	210	296	116	622
Less Direct Costs (variable)	150	200	100	450
= Contribution (A)	60	96	16	172
Less Direct costs (specific)	36	48	24	108
= Contribution (B)	24	48	(8)	64
Less Fixed Costs	24	32	16	72
Profit/(Loss)	–	16	(24)	(8)

Cost Analysis – Mileage & Vehicles

	R1 £	R2 £	R3 £
Revenue per mile	0.70	0.74	0.58
Contribution (A) per mile	0.20	0.24	0.08
Contribution (B) per mile	0.08	0.12	(0.04)
Contribution (B) per Vehicle	£2000	£3000	(£1000)

ii. **Proposal that R3 be discontinued.**

From a purely costing viewpoint R3 should be discontinued. It would have the following effects;

£16000 Contribution (A) lost but

£24000 costs specific to vehicles saved.

. . overall saving £8000 which is sufficient to offset the existing total loss of £8000 and cause the overall operation to break even. In addition the vehicles saved could be sold.

However, there may be other considerations, for example.

a.   Interdependence of routes – will cessation of R3 affect revenue from other routes?

b.   Loss of public service may cause adverse local reaction.

c.   Effect on cessation of R3 on future licensing applications.

An alternative to cessation is to consider raising the revenue per mile of R3, which is the lowest, up to say 70p per mile, which would bring in approximately £24,000 extra contribution, assuming the same rate of usage as at present.

iii. **Proposal to reduce R3 by a half.**

The differential effects of this are shown below.

		Existing operation		½ scale		Difference
No of vehicles		8		4		– 4
Mileage		200,000		100,000		– 100,000
Revenue		£116,000		£76,000		– £40,000
Less Costs Variable	100,000		50,000		– 50,000	
Costs specific	24,000	124,000	12,000	62,000	– 12,000	– 62,000
Contribution		(8)		14		+ 22

This means that the increase in contribution by the R3 reduction would change the overall position from £8,000 loss to a profit of £14,000 thus

Contributions	£
R1 (as previously)	24,000
R2 (as previously)	48,000
R3 (half scale)	14,000
	86,000
Less apportioned fixed cost	72,000
Overall profit	£14,000

Reciprocal Services –
An example using a computer

By Richard Sydenham M.Soc.Sc., F.C.A.
Principal Lecturer in Accounting, Leicester Polytechnic

The Service Department Cost Reallocation program was written and tested on a 3016 Commodore PET microcomputer. The program can be used with a cassette, floppy disc or time sharing system and can be easily modified to run on other micro-computers. The program includes introductory remarks and is self explanatory when 'run'. Results are displayed on the screen and, optionally within the program, on a printer.

The case material has been exposed to the criticism of colleagues and to student use in the classroom. The author would like to thank people concerned for their helpful suggestions, many of which have been incorporated into the final product.

CASE MATERIAL

Bases for the apportionment of service department costs have been established for the Zepatazat Engineering Company. The service relationships are expected to remain stable for some time and are given in the following table:—

To: From: Service Department	Service Departments					Production Departments		
	1	2	3	4	5	1	2	3
1	–	.1	.1	.1	.1	.2	.2	.2
2	.2	–	.1	.1	.1	.3	.1	.1
3	.1	.3	–	.1	.1	Ø	.2	.2
4	.1	.1	.1	–	.2	.1	.1	.3
5	.1	Ø	.2	.2	–	Ø	Ø	.5
Period Costs								
1	£10 000	8 000	12 000	3 000	15 000	£40 000	80 000	75 000
2	£ 5 000	7 000	15 000	4 000	12 000	£60 000	70 000	65 000
3	£ 8 000	9 500	12 700	5 500	13 500	£55 000	81 500	114 500

For each of the three periods, you are required to:—

1. allocate service department costs to production departments without regard for one service department's allocation to another;

2. allocate service department costs to all departments in order of the service department with the most cost to be allocated;

3. allocate service department costs using the algebraic approach implemented on the micro-computer; and

4. discuss which solution you believe best and why?

Solution

Zepatazat Engineering Company

Service department cost allocation for period 1.

1. Service department costs are allocated on the simplifying assumption that services are provided only to non-service departments (Chapter 10, paragraph 5).

	Production Departments					
	1		2		3	
	Proportion	£	Proportion	£	Proportion	£
Service Department						
1	$\frac{.2}{.6}$	3,333	$\frac{.2}{.6}$	3,333	$\frac{.2}{.6}$	3,334
2	$\frac{.3}{.5}$	4,800	$\frac{.1}{.5}$	1,600	$\frac{.1}{.5}$	1,600
3			$\frac{.2}{.4}$	6,000	$\frac{.2}{.4}$	6,000
4	$\frac{.1}{.5}$	600	$\frac{.1}{.5}$	600	$\frac{.3}{.5}$	1,800
5					$\frac{.5}{.5}$	15,000
		8,733		11,533		27,734
Production Cost		40,000		80,000		75,000
Total Cost		£48,733		£91,533		£102,734

2. Service department costs are allocated using the elimination method (Chapter 10, paragraph 9). The service department with the largest amount is eliminated first and so on until all service department costs have been allocated.

	Service Departments					Production Departments		
	1	2	3	4	5	1	2	3
Period 1 Cost	10,000	8,000	12,000	3,000	15,000			
Order for elimination	3	4	2	5	1			
Proportions								
S.D.5	$\frac{.1}{1.0}$	$\frac{\emptyset}{1.0}$	$\frac{.2}{1.0}$	$\frac{.2}{1.0}$		$\frac{\emptyset}{1.0}$	$\frac{\emptyset}{1.0}$	$\frac{.5}{1.0}$
S.D.3	$\frac{.1}{.9}$	$\frac{.3}{.9}$		$\frac{.1}{.9}$		$\frac{\emptyset}{.9}$	$\frac{.2}{.9}$	$\frac{.2}{.9}$
S.D.1		$\frac{.1}{.8}$		$\frac{.1}{.8}$		$\frac{.2}{.8}$	$\frac{.2}{.8}$	$\frac{.2}{.8}$
S.D.2				$\frac{.1}{.6}$		$\frac{.3}{.6}$	$\frac{.1}{.6}$	$\frac{.1}{.6}$
S.D.4						$\frac{.1}{.5}$	$\frac{.1}{.5}$	$\frac{.3}{.5}$

Cost Allocation

S.D.5	1,500	Ø	3,000	3,000	−15,000	Ø	Ø	7,500
S.D.3	1,667	5,000	−15,000	1,667		Ø	3,333	3,333
S.D.1	−13,167	1,646		1,646		3,292	3,292	3,291
S.D.2		−14,646		2,441		7,323	2,441	2,441
S.D.4				−11,754		2,351	2,351	7,052
						12,966	11,417	23,617
Production Cost						40,000	80,000	75,000
Total Cost						52,966	91,417	98,617

3. The algebraic method is used to allocate service department costs (described in Chapter 10, paragraph 10). The computer program enables the complex example to be solved with efficiency. Data is requested to allow the assembly of linear equations. If X, is taken to represent total overhead cost for service department one after all other service department costs have been allotted and similarly for the other four service departments then the following equations would be obtained:—

$$
\begin{aligned}
X_1 - .2X_2 - .1X_3 - .1X_4 - .1X_5 &= 10,000 \\
-.1X_1 + X_2 - .3X_3 - .1X_4 &= 8,000 \\
-.1X_1 - .1X_2 + X_3 - .1X_4 - .2X_5 &= 12,000 \\
-.1X_1 - .1X_2 - .1X_3 + X_4 - .2X_5 &= 3,000 \\
-.1X_1 - .1X_2 - .1X_3 - .2X_4 + X_5 &= 15,000
\end{aligned}
$$

The program uses matrix algebra to approach the solution in an orderly fashion. First the inverse for the left hand side of the five equations is determined and displayed. Then the right hand side values are multiplied with the inverse to give the values for the variables X_1 to X_5. This result is displayed. Next the values of the variables are allotted to production departments by applying the relevant proportions. The program shows the result in the final table which is given below.

	Production Departments		
	1 £	2 £	3 £
Service Department			
1	3,897	3,897	3,897
2	5,359	1,786	1,786
3	Ø	4,366	4,366
4	1,365	1,365	4,094
5	Ø	Ø	11,823
	10,620	11,414	25,966
Production Cost	40,000	80,000	75,000
Total Cost	50,620	91,414	100,966

4. Procedures of absorption and apportionment are conventions and therefore one cannot be said to be more *accurate* than another (see Chapter 10, paragraph 9, Note 4) *except* that the first two methods may be adopted by companies without computer facilities in order to make the calculations easier. Thus, should the third method be preferred as a convention it can be seen that, using a computer, it becomes the *easiest* method to use. As can be seen from the tables, the results from using each method vary considerably one from another. In relation to the algebraic (computer solution) the first method understates the allotment to production department one by 18% and the elimination method results in an over allotment to production department one by 22%. The user may wish to explore the example for periods two and three. If he does so, another feature of the algebraic solution becomes apparent. Once the inverse has been obtained for the left hand side of the linear equations the result may be used in conjunction with any service department cost values.

Where 'Costs' are changing (e.g. varying forecasts) or proportions are variable (e.g. changing amounts of work from service departments to production departments) then the impact on apportionments can quickly be assessed using a computer.

PROGRAM LISTING

```
1 REM COPYRIGHT  R. W. SYDENHAM  1982
2 REM LEICESTER POLTECHNIC , P. O. BOX 143 , LEICESTER  LEI 9BH.
3 A1$="   SERVICE DEPARTMENT COST REALLOCATION"
4 A2$="                                        "
5 A3$="              WRITTEN  BY"
6 A4$="         RICHARD  W.  SYDENHAM"
7 PRINT"⊐"
8 A5$="    _____  _____  _____  _____"
9 A6$="RATIO FOR ALLOCATION TO :-"
10 A7$="SERVICE   DEPARTMENT "
11 A8$="PRODUCTION DEPARTMENT"
12 A9$="                     "
13 A$="YOU ARE REQUIRED TO ENTER VALUES FOR THE VARIABLES"
14 B$="YOU HAVE ENTERED THESE VALUES FOR  THE   VARIABLES"
15 C$="ARE YOU SATISFIED WITH THESE VALUES ?"
16 D$="DO YOU WISH TO CHANGE ANY VALUES ?"
17 E$="ENTER  Y  FOR YES  AND  N  FOR NO "
18 B1$="              PERIOD"
19 PRINT"XXXXXX"A1$
20 PRINTA2$
21 PRINT"XXXXX"A3$
22 PRINT"XXXXXX"A4$
23 FORI=1TO1000:NEXTI
24 PRINT"⊐"
25 POKE59468,14
26 PRINT"THE PROGRAM PREPARES A STATEMENT ON THE"
27 PRINT"BASIS OF THE ALGEBRAIC  METHOD  FOR THE"
28 PRINT"REALLOCATION OF SERVICE DEPARTMENT COST"
29 PRINT"TO PRODUCTION DEPARTMENTS . YOU WILL BE"
30 PRINT"ASKED TO ENTER  THE  RATIOS REQUIRED TO"
31 PRINT"ALLOCATE  SERVICE  DEPARTMENT  COST  TO"
32 PRINT"OTHER SERVICE  DEPARTMENTS & PRODUCTION"
33 PRINT"DEPARTMENTS. THE RATIOS ARE USED AS THE"
34 PRINT"COEFFICIENTS IN LINEAR  EQUATIONS WHICH"
35 PRINT"GIVE TOTAL SERVICE  DEPARTMENT  COST TO"
36 PRINT"BE  REALLOCATED TO OTHER  DEPARTMENTS ."
37 PRINT"THE ALLOCATION OF THAT PORTION OF TOTAL"
38 PRINT"SERVICE   DEPARTMENT   COST  WHICH  IS"
39 PRINT"ALLOCATED TO PRODUCTION  DEPARTMENTS IS"
40 PRINT"SHOWN IN THE FINAL TABLE  OF  RESULTS ."
41 PRINT
42 PRINT"NOTE:THE PROGRAM DOES NOT ALLOCATE COST"
43 PRINT"TO  END  PRODUCT ."
44 PRINT:PRINT:PRINT:PRINT
45 GOSUB273
46 POKE59468,12
47 PRINTA$:PRINT
48 PRINT"THE NUMBER OF SERVICE DEPARTMENTS"
49 INPUT"( FROM 2 TO 10 )";A
50 A=INT(A):PRINT
51 IFA<2ORA>10THENPRINT"NUMBER OUTSIDE RANGE !":PRINT:GOTO48
```

```
52 PRINT"THE NUMBER OF PRODUCTION DEPARTMENTS"
53 INPUT"( FROM 2 TO 4 )";B
54 B=INT(B):PRINT
55 IFB<2ORB>4THENPRINT"NUMBER OUTSIDE RANGE !":PRINT:GOTO52
56 PRINT"⊐"
57 PRINTB$:PRINT
58 PRINTA"SERVICE DEPARTMENTS AND"B"PRODUCTION"
59 PRINT"DEPARTMENTS"
60 GOSUB277
61 IFZZ$="N"THENPRINT"⊐":GOTO47
62 A=A-1:B=B-1
63 DIMB(0,A),C(A,B),D(0,B),E(A,A+1)
64 DIMF(A+1,A),G(0,A),H(0,B)
65 PRINT"ENTER  THE  RATIOS  TO  BE  USED IN THE"
66 PRINT"ALLOCATION OF EACH SERVICE DEPARTMENT'S"
67 PRINT"COST TO THE OTHER"A"SERVICE DEPARTMENTS"
68 PRINT"AND THE"B+1"PRODUCTION DEPARTMENTS ."
69 PRINT
70 PRINT"ENTER EACH RATIO AS A PART OF ONE . FOR"
71 PRINT"EXAMPLE  0.3 ."
72 PRINT
73 FORI=0TOA
74 PRINTA7$I+1
75 PRINT"─────────────────────────"
76 PRINT:PRINTA6$:PRINT
77 Y=0
78 FORJ=0TOA
79 F(I,J)=1-ABS(SGN(I-J))
80 IFJ=ITHENE(I,J)=1:GOTO86
81 PRINTA7$J+1;
82 INPUTE(I,J)
83 IFE(I,J)>>1ORE(I,J)<0THENPRINT:GOTO81
84 Y=Y+E(I,J)
85 E(I,J)=-E(I,J)
86 NEXTJ
87 PRINT
88 FORK=0TOB
89 PRINTA8$K+1;
90 INPUTC(I,K)
91 IFC(I,K)>>1ORC(I,K)<0THENPRINT:GOTO89
92 Y=Y+C(I,K)
93 NEXTK
94 PRINT
95 IFINT(Y+.00001)<>1THENPRINT"YOUR RATIOS DO NOT SUM TO ONE !":PRINT:GOTO74
96 IFINT(Y+.99999)<>1THENPRINT"YOUR RATIOS DO NOT SUM TO ONE !":PRINT:GOTO74
97 PRINT"⊐":PRINTB$:PRINT
98 FORJ=0TOA
99 IFJ=ITHEN102
100 X=-1*E(I,J)
101 PRINTA7$J+1;X
102 NEXTJ
103 FORK=0TOB
104 PRINTA8$K+1;C(I,K)
105 NEXTK
106 GOSUB277
107 IFZZ$="N"THEN74
108 NEXTI
109 IFT>4THENPRINT"CHECK  YOUR  SERVICE  RELATIONSHIPS ARE UNCHANGED !":PRINT
110 PRINTA$:PRINT
111 FORI=0TOA
112 PRINTA7$I+1"COST",
113 INPUTB(0,I)
114 NEXTI
115 PRINT
116 FORI=0TOB
117 PRINTA8$I+1"COST",
118 INPUTD(0,I)
119 NEXTI
120 PRINT"⊐"
121 PRINTB$:PRINT
122 PRINT"SERVICE DEPARTMENT COSTS"
123 PRINT
124 FORI=0TOA
```

454

```
125 PRINTB(0,I);
126 NEXTI
127 PRINT:PRINT
128 PRINT"PRODUCTION DEPARTMENT COSTS"
129 PRINT
130 FORI=0TOB
131 PRINTD(0,I);
132 NEXTI
133 PRINT
134 GOSUB277
135 IFO=1THENPRINT:PRINT:PRINT:GOTO153
136 IFZZ$="N"THEN109
137 IFT>1THEN227
138 T=1
139 GOTO210
140 PRINTB1$;T
141 PRINTA9$:PRINT
142 PRINT"TOTAL SERVICE DEPARTMENT COSTS PRIOR TO"
143 PRINT"           ALLOCATION"
144 PRINT
145 FORI=0TOA
146 M=INT(G(0,I)+.5)
147 GOSUB255
148 PRINTA7$I+1,:PRINT"$"M$
149 NEXTI
150 PRINT
151 IFO=1THENPRINT:PRINT:PRINT:PRINT:GOTO153
152 GOSUB273
153 PRINTB1$;T
154 PRINTA9$
155 PRINT" ALLOCATION OF SERVICE  DEPARTMENT COST"
156 PRINT"     TO   PRODUCTION  DEPARTMENTS"
157 PRINT
158 PRINT"        PRODUCTION    DEPARTMENTS"
159 PRINT"      _____"
160 PRINT"      1      2      3      4"
161 PRINT"      _____"
162 FORI=0TOA
163 PRINT"S.D."I+1;
164 FORJ=0TOB
165 M=INT(G(0,I)*C(I,J)+.5)
166 GOSUB255
167 PRINTM$;
168 NEXTJ
169 PRINT
170 NEXTI
171 PRINTA5$
172 PRINT"          ";
173 FORI=0TOB
174 M=INT(H(0,I)+.5)
175 GOSUB255
176 PRINTM$;
177 NEXTI
178 PRINT
179 PRINT"PRODUCTION"
180 PRINT"   COST ";
181 FORI=0TOB
182 M=INT(D(0,I)+.5)
183 GOSUB255
184 PRINTM$;
185 NEXTI
186 PRINT:PRINTA5$
187 PRINT"TOTAL   ";
188 FORI=0TOB
189 M=INT(H(0,I)+D(0,I)+.5)
190 GOSUB255
191 PRINTM$;
192 NEXTI
193 PRINT:PRINTA5$:PRINT
194 IFO=1THENPRINT:PRINT:PRINT:PRINT:PRINT#1:CLOSE1:O=0:GOTO198
195 GOSUB273
196 IFO=0THENGOSUB265
197 IFO=1GOTO140
```

```
198 PRINT"DO  YOU  WISH  TO  REALLOCATE    SERVICE"
199 PRINT"DEPARTMENT  COSTS ON THE SAME BASIS FOR"
200 PRINT"A FURTHER PERIOD ?"
201 PRINT:PRINTE$;
202 INPUTZZ$
203 PRINT"]"
204 IF ZZ$="Y"THEN T=T+1:GOTO109
205 PRINT:PRINTD$:PRINTE$;
206 INPUTZZ$
207 PRINT"]"
208 IFZZ$="Y"THEN T=0:GOTO65
209 FORI=1TO1000:PRINT"END       ";:NEXTI:END
210 FORI=0TO(A-1)
211 FORJ=(I+1)TOA
212 X=E(J,I)/E(I,I)
213 FORK=0TOA
214 E(J,K)=E(J,K)-X*E(I,K)
215 F(J,K)=F(J,K)-X*F(I,K)
216 NEXTK
217 NEXTJ
218 NEXTI
219 FORI=ATO0STEP-1
220 FORK=0TOA
221 FORJ=(I+1)TOA
222 F(I,K)=F(I,K)-E(I,J)*F(J,K)
223 NEXTJ
224 F(I,K)=F(I,K)/E(I,I)
225 NEXTK
226 NEXTI
227 PRINT"INVERSE OF SERVICE DEPARTMENT COST"
228 PRINT"     REALLOCATION MATRIX"
229 PRINT
230 FORJ=0TOA
231 G(0,J)=0
232 FORK=0TOA
233 M=INT(F(J,K)*1000+.5)/1000
234 GOSUB252
235 PRINTM$;
236 G(0,J)=G(0,J)+F(K,J)*B(0,K)
237 NEXTK
238 PRINT
239 NEXTJ
240 PRINT:PRINT
241 IFO=0THENGOSUB273
242 IFO=1THENPRINT:PRINT:PRINT:PRINT:PRINT#1:CLOSE1:O=0:GOTO245
243 IFO=0THENGOSUB265
244 IFO=1GOTO227
245 FORJ=0TOB
246 H(0,J)=0
247 FORK=0TOA
248 H(0,J)=H(0,J)+C(K,J)*G(0,K)
249 NEXTK
250 NEXTJ
251 GOTO140
252 Z=6
253 GOSUB256
254 RETURN
255 Z=8
256 H$=""
257 M$=STR$(M)
258 N=LEN(M$)
259 FORL=1TOZ-N
260 H$=H$+" "
261 NEXTL
262 M$=H$+M$
263 M$=RIGHT$(M$,Z)
264 RETURN
265 PRINT"DO YOU WISH TO PRINT OUT THE DISPLAY ?"
266 PRINTE$;
267 INPUTZZ$
268 PRINT"]"
269 IFZZ$="N"THENRETURN
270 OPEN1,4:CMD1
271 O=1:PRINT:PRINT:PRINT:PRINT
```

```
272 RETURN
273 PRINT"PRESS RETURN TO CONTINUE"
274 GETY$:IFY$<>CHR$(13)THEN274
275 PRINT"⬛"
276 RETURN
277 PRINT:PRINTC$:PRINTE$;
278 INPUTZZ$
279 PRINT"⬛"
280 RETURN
```

Index

About DP Publications

The company specialises in books for business and accountancy students and has built up a considerable reputation for HIGH QUALITY manuals at LOW COST. Literally tens of thousands have been sold and they will be found in use in nearly all Polytechnics and Colleges.

DATA PROCESSING now in its 5th edition is a 'Best Seller' in its particular field and was the first manual published under the DPP label. Our other manuals are proving to be just as popular.

It goes without saying that the majority have found their way on to the Recommended Reading lists of the appropriate examination bodies.

Read what people have said about our manuals.

"Excellent sellers — the proof of the pudding is that we keep on and on reordering" — *Gee & Co.* "Sell themselves" — *Foyles.*

Lecturers

"An attractive layout and a refreshing approach"

"This is a very good course book, the type I have been looking for for a very long time.

Students

"Concise, lucid and no waffle approach"; "Excellent value"

"I appreciated the presence of actual examination questions and answers"

"Easy to read"; "At its price it's unique"

Aims of the Manuals

To give *comprehensive* coverage of specific examination syllabuses in a *simplified* manner and at an economic price i.e. one which most students would be willing to pay either as a main text book or as supplementary study material.

Types of Manuals

There are two types of manuals:

1. *Instructional manuals* — little, or no knowledge on the part of the student is assumed. The basic principles of the subject are presented in an easily assimilated form — manageable study areas with introductions and summaries. The *many questions* at the end of study areas *(answers at the back of the manual)* can be used for classroom confirmation of understanding or as a basis for discussion. Ideal for releasing valuable classroom time for concentration on *practice* of principles and teaching the more difficult areas. Perfect for *self study* where students have missed classes due to starting late, sickness etc. and for *revision purposes.* The tabular layout is designed to eliminate the need for note taking.

2. *Practice manuals* — knowledge of the basic principles is assumed. Using specially selected past examination questions from the *main examination areas*, fully worked solutions show the student *how to tackle* the particular question and guides him through the answer in such a way as to enable the student to pinpoint his problem areas — and thus to overcome them. Ideal for *confirmation* of understanding of each study area prior to going on to new fields, as well as *practice* before progress tests and the examination.

Notes

Notes

Financial Accounting

A.R. Jennings

NEW '82

These manuals are, together, aimed at providing in an instructional manner, the information needed by students to approach with confidence the professional level examinations of the ACCA and ICMA. There is also substantial coverage of the ICA examination requirements and the financial accounting content of relevant degree courses.

A vast number of books have been written on Financial Accounting but they tend to teach principles only without relating those principles to the specific requirements of professional level examinations.

These manuals *instruct* the student to be able to answer the questions that are *actually set* at professional level.

"This book is a credit to its author and publisher; without doubt it achieves its objective of providing the student with a well organised explanation of a wide range of topics, some of which are traditionally hard to master . . . the book is intended to enable students to pass examinations – and this it should well do".   *AUTA*

Manual 1 Contents

Bills of Exchange
Consignments
Joint Ventures
Royalties
Branches
Hire Purchase
Long Term Contracts
Investments
Partnerships
Issue and Redemption of Shares and
  Debentures
Taxation in Accounts

Preparation of Final Accounts of Limited
  Companies for Publication
Statements of Source and Application of
  Funds
Appendices:
  Summary of main disclosure requirements
  of Companies Acts 1948 to 1980
  Statements of Standard Accounting Practice
  (SSAPs) – printed in full
  Answers to section Examination Questions
  Examination Questions with Answers
  Examination Questions without Answers
  Annual Report Example

Manual 2 Contents

Value Added Statements
Financial Statement Analysis and
  Interpretation
Group Profit and Loss Accounts
Group Balance Sheets
Group Statements of Source and
  Application of Funds

Company Amalgamations and Absorptions
Company Reorganisation and Reconstructions
Accounting for Overseas Operations
Accounting for Changing Price Levels
Accounting Standards Committee (Current
  programme)
Stock Exchange Disclosure Requirements
Appendices
Final Accounts of a major and public national company
Companies Act 1981
Answers to Examination Questions
Examination Questions with Answers
Examination Questions without Answers

The author is Senior Lecturer in Accounting, Department of Accounting and Finance, Trent Polytechnic.

Note to Lecturers: Answer Supplement available – see inside front cover of catalogue.

1. 600 pages: 1981: ISBN 0 905435 19 2
2. 500 pages (approx): May 1982: ISBN 0 905435 23 0

Financial Management
R.B. Brockington 2nd Edition

This manual, on the recommended reading list of the ICMA, is intended for students who are preparing to take an examination in Financial Management at final professional level and it will provide them with the knowledge *and the skill in applying it*; both of which they will need to provide a safe pass.

First edition comments:
"Written in note format, the style is very clear and the development logical. There are many worked examples, together with questions and answers from the professional papers. Of great advantage to the professional student is the explanation of approach given clearly in the answers. Few students should be in any doubt as to how the answer was arrived at. In summary, this is a text which is without competitors for the student who is revising for the professional examinations in the subject, and may even prove to be a worthwhile main course text in this context"

Review extract AUTA

"A very strongly recommended text for easy convenient use", "it is liked by students", "explains matters simply and directly"

Lecturers comments

"Makes easy reading and understanding of such an involved subject", "it helped me to pass my examination with an 'A' — it is simple to understand, concise and well presented"

Students comments

Contents

The author is a Lecturer in Finance and Accounting, University of Bath.

Note to Lecturers: Answer Supplement available (see inside front cover of catalogue).

304 pages: 1981: ISBN 0 905435 16 8

Quantitative Techniques

T. Lucey 2nd Edition

NEW '82

This manual is designed to provide a sound understanding of Quantitative Techniques. It is particularly suited to students preparing themselves for the examinations of ICA, ACCA, ICMA and CIPFA (it is prescribed reading for ACCA and ICMA) but is also suitable for students on BEC Higher Level Courses and undergraduates reading Business Studies and allied subjects.

"The book is written in the form of a self-study course with plenty of examples and test exercises. Solutions to the exercises are given at the end of the book. One of the best characteristics of the approach is the use of flowcharts to illustrate the procedural steps for each method, and the whole book has a clarity and a sequential development that are highly desirable in a technical workbook"
review extract British Book News

Contents

The author is Head of the School of Business and Management, Wolverhampton Polytechnic.

Note: 2nd EDITION due for publication in July 1982 has been extensively revised and enlarged to meet the requirements of the Professional Bodies. It includes a major section on appropriate statistical concepts including: Probability, frequency distributions, significance tests, correlation, chi-square and calculus. Many more questions have been included from the Professional Examinations together with fully worked answers. Also, a selection of questions without answers for use by lecturers as assignments (see inside front cover of catalogue).

1st Edition: 352 pages: 1979: ISBN 0 905435 09 5
2nd Edition: 440 pages (approx): July 1982: ISBN 0 905435 27 3

Business Law

K. Abbott   N. Pendlebury

NEW '82

This manual is intended to provide students with a simplified approach to the understanding of Business Law. It covers the examination requirements of the students sitting the following examinations:

ACCA Level 1	— Law
ICMA Foundation	— Business Law
ICSA Part 1	— General Principles of English Law
ICSA Part 2	— Business Law
ICSA Part 3	— Industrial Law

It is also relevant to any other students taking an introductory law course e.g. Legal Executives, IAS and BEC.

Contents

Keith Abbott is a Senior Lecturer in Law at Luton College of Higher Education.
Norman Pendlebury has lectured for many years on Law.

Note to Lecturers: Answer Supplement available (see inside front cover of catalogue).

400 pages (approx): May 1982: ISBN 0 905435 22 2

Company Law

K. Abbott

NEW '82

This manual is designed to provide the knowledge required by, primarily, students sitting the ACCA and ICMA examinations in Company Law. Because there are only minor differences between syllabuses, it is also ideally suited to any other student of Company Law, whether at University level or for other professional bodies (e.g. The Law Society, The Institute of Chartered Secretaries and the Institute of Bankers).

Contents

Keith Abbott is a Senior Lecturer in Law at Luton College of Higher Education.

Note to Lecturers: Answer Supplement available (see inside front cover of catalogue).

350 pages (approx): June 1982: ISBN 0 905435 28 1

Management: Theory and Practice   G.A. Cole

This manual aims to provide, in one concise volume, the principal ideas and developments in the theory and practice of management as required by business and accountancy students.

It is thus principally aimed at providing a course textbook for students sitting ACCA, ICMA, ICSA and IOB. It will also be useful to students taking management topics in the examination of the IOM, IIM and IAM.

Relatively few books on management are written specifically for business and accountancy students and those that are on the market do not usually develop the links between the subject matter and the examinations set by the professional bodies. This manual aims to fill that gap.

Contents

Introduction to Management Theory
Background Developments
Definitions and Interpretations
Classical Theories
Henri Fayol
F.W. Taylor and the Scientific Management School
The Contribution of Urwick & Brech
The Concept of Bureaucracy
Human Relations Theories
Motivation and Assumptions about People
The Impact of Elton Mayo
Major Theories of Human Motivation
Systems Approaches to Management Theory
Organisations as Systems
Socio-technical Systems/Developments in Systems Theories
Contingency Approaches to Management
Management in Practice: Introduction
The Process of Management
Policy, Planning and Decision-making
Decision-making
Organization Objectives and Corporate Planning
Management by Objectives
Man-Power Planning

Organizing and Communicating
The Process of Organizing
Organization Structures
Line and Staff Relationships
Organization Development Techniques
The Role of External Consultants
Formal Communication in Organizations
Committees
Leadership and Delegation
Types of Leadership
Management Styles
Delegation and the Span of Control
Control in Management
Common Methods of Control
Techniques for Control
Functional Management: Introduction
Specialist Functions in Management
Marketing Management
The Marketing Concept
Marketing Research
Marketing and Sales Management
Production Management
Types of Production
Basic Elements of Production
Organization of a Production Department
Personnel Management
The Role of the Personnel Function
Recruitment and Selection
Training and Development
Job Evaluation
Employee Relations, Trade Unions and Collective Bargaining
Legal Aspects of Employment

Appendices
Outline Answers to Examination Questions
Commentary and Fuller Answers to Further Examination Questions
Guide to Examination Technique
Glossary of Management Terms
Selected Examination Questions without Answers

Gerald Cole is Senior Lecturer in Management Studies, Department of Management and Organizational Studies, Luton College of Higher Education.
Note to Lecturers: Answer Supplement available (see inside front cover of catalogue).

450 pages (approx): June 1982: ISBN 0 905435 26 5

Economic Analysis

D. Lockwood

The manual provides a comprehensive and in-depth coverage of the work required by students preparing for the following examinations:—

    ACCA Section 2   —   Managerial Economics
    ICMA Professional Stage 1 — Economic Analysis
    ICSA Part 4   —   Economic Policies and Problems

It may also be useful for those studying economics as part of a non-economics degree course and as secondary reading for 'A' level and Part 1 Economics degree students.

Contents

Introduction to Economic Analysis

Part A. Microeconomics: The Consumer and the Firm:
Allocating Scarce Resources; The Analysis of Demand; The Analysis of Costs; The Conventional Theory of the Firm; The Theory of the Firm; Some Related Issues; The Analysis of Market Power; The Analysis of Oligopoly; The Theory of the Firm Reconsidered; The Growth of Firms; Small Firms; Location of Industry and the Regional Problem; Capital and Investment; Nationalised Industries; Cost Benefit Analysis.

Part B. Macroeconomics: The Economy in General:
The Rise and Fall of Keynesian Economics; The Keynesian Model; The Accelerator; Money, Banking and all that; Stabilising the Economy; Inflation; Policies for Inflation; Unemployment; International Trade I: Why do we Trade with other Countries; International Trade II: The Balance of Payments Accounts; International Trade III: Government Policy; International Trade IV: The Exchange Rate; Planning and Growth; Developing Countries.

Part C. Current Economic Issues:
Are we getting value for the welfare state; The Economic Analysis of Alternatives to the Welfare State; The Taxation Debate; The Eltis/Bacon Thesis; The Economic Analysis of Trade Unions; The Economic Analysis of Marketing; North Sea Oil; The Economic Effects of Micro Technology; Membership of the E.E.C.

Appendices:
Economic Analysis in an examination situation; Outline answers to questions; Questions and Case Studies without Answers.

David Lockwood is Senior Lecturer, Department of Business Studies, West Bromwich College of Commerce and Technology.

Note to Lecturers: Answer Supplement available (see inside front cover of catalogue).

450 pages (approx): June 1982: ISBN 0 905435 29 X   £4.75

Management Information Systems

T. Lucey   4th Edition

This manual, dealing with the underlying principles of systems is a companion volume to Data Processing by Oliver & Chapman. It is prescribed reading for ICMA, ACCA and CIPFA students.

"The Author covers a lot of ground in a short space. He puts over the somewhat abstract concepts of systems theory, system objectives, control mechanisms, behavioural aspects and their importance to management, information and corporate planning in an admirably clear style. The simplicity of writing makes the book refreshingly easy to read. Not only is a clear summary of each topic given but each concept is firmly related to and illuminates the reality of business management.

The book is highly recommended to students, to accountants and to business managers who want a simple guide to modern systems theory. "   *Extract from Management Accounting Review.*

"Recommended as a book which summarises the main points". "I certainly recommend the students to purchase it". "At its price it is unique".   *Lecturers Comments*

"I appreciated the presence of actual examination questions and answers", "easy to read", "struck a perfect balance between a normal 'wordy' book and revision notes", "truly excellent value", "very concise".   *Students Comments*

Contents

What is Management? Introduction; Definitions of Management; Functions of Management; Size of Business; Levels of Management; Decision Making; Summary; Points to Note.

Management and Information. Introduction; Management Information Systems; Factors Governing Outputs of an M.I.S.; Management by Exception; M.I.S. Examples; Summary; Points to Note.

General System Concepts. Introduction; Definition of Systems; Ubiquity; System Classifications; Relationships with the Environment; System Elements; Scale of Systems; Inter Connections; Decoupling; Summary; Points to note; Questions.

System Objectives. Introduction; Company Objectives; Conflicting Objectives; Sub-system Objectives; Sub-optimisation; Summary; Points to note; Questions.

Control of Systems. Introduction; Information Equivalents; Control of Systems; Feedback Loops; Negative Feedback; Positive Feedback; Timing of Control Actions; Types of Control Systems; Feedback and Control Examples; Summary; Points to note; Questions.

Information and Communication. Introduction; Data and Information; Characteristics of Information; Urgency and Information; Handling Delays; Volume and Detail; Value of Information; Communication Theory; Summary; Points to note; Questions.

Models and Simulation. Introduction; Model Construction; Reasons for using models; Simulation; Optimization; Sensitivity; Summary; Points to note; Questions.

Behavioural Aspects of M.I.S. Introduction; Reaction to change, Dysfunctional Behaviour, Ways to Minimise Dysfunctional Behaviour; Summary; Points to note; Questions.

Corporate Planning and M.I.S. Introduction; CP Definition; CP Process-Assessment, Objectives, Evaluation; CP Implementation; Summary; Points to note; Questions.

Appendices. Suggested answers to questions at end of chapters. Progress Test Questions and answers. Examination Questions without answers.

The author is Head of the School of Business and Management, Wolverhampton Polytechnic.

Note to Lecturers: Answer Supplement available (see inside front cover of catalogue).

128 pages: 1981: ISBN 0 905435 20 6

Data Processing

E.C. Oliver and R.J. Chapman, (revised by J. Allen) 5th Edition

This manual presents a simplified instructional approach to the understanding of data processing principles. It is extensively used as a Course Textbook on full and part time courses in Polytechnics and Colleges. Prescribed reading for ACCA, ICMA, CIPFA, IAS, SCCA and IDPM students.

"All are to be congratulated on producing an easy to understand manual. They have placed great emphasis on the questions and answers which are split into three types. There are questions with outline answers only, which are intended to test the understanding of points arising out of a particular chapter. There are also examination questions, with comprehensive answers, inserted at the stage where it is considered the student will be best able to give a reasonable answer. Finally, there are progress tests comprising over 60 past examination questions, with answers ranging from mere chapter and section references to comprehensively worked solutions. Many students will find the authors notes on effective study and examination technique helpful . . . . This manual is highly recommended for all those whom it is intended to serve." *Review extract The Accountant.*

"Snappy and no waffle" — *Lecturers comment.*

Contents

E.C. Oliver and R.J. Chapman are partners in DP Publications. J. Allen is Principal Lecturer in Management Information Systems and Data Processing at South West London College.

Note to Lecturers: Answer Supplement available (see inside front cover of catalogue).

336 pages: 1981: ISBN 0 905435 15 X

Auditing
A.H. Millichamp 2nd Edition

The manual is designed to provide a simplified but thorough approach to the understanding of modern auditing theory and practice. It is particularly suited to students preparing themselves for the examinations of ICA, ACCA and IAS (it is prescribed reading for ACCA) but is also suitable for those studying Auditing as part of a Higher National Diploma or Certificate course in business studies.

"Mr. Millichamp certainly has a commendable command of the subject matter which he is able to convey in the course of his book . . . . it was interesting to note the effect of block capital headings at each relevant stage so that the student is not confused by the task of trying to assimilate unrelated points under the same heading. The chapters lead the student both into the subject matter and, at the right stage, the details related to the subject matter. This aspect is important in answering examination questions . . . . . . the author has adopted an informal and chatty style of addressing the reader, but such informality does not detract from the precision in the layout of the information and instruction to be imparted . . . . the questions and answers and appendices should leave a student in no doubt as to the need for precise language in reports and other forms of communication . . . . . the author has quite rightly assumed that when a candidate studies the subject matter of auditing he will bring to bear such knowledge on accounting procedures and law which will have been learned in separate courses of study. The book has no frills; it is packed with essential and relevant information set out in an easily assimilated manner and is designed to assist a student in presenting a good paper at his examination"
Review extract Certified Accountants Students Newsletter

"An excellent book", "Well presented and gives great assistance through the course and during revision"
Lecturers comments

"Without doubt the best text for examination preparation I have read"
Students comment

Contents

Introduction to Auditing
The Conduct of the Audit
Asset and Liability Verification
The Auditors Report
Holding Companies and Group Accounts
Specialised Audits
Audit Evidence
Auditors and the Law
EDP and the Auditor
Control of Audits
Audit Statements other than the P & L A/C
and Balance Sheet

Internal and Management Auditing
Investigations
Appendices:
Detail omitted from the text in the interests
of clarity
Outline Answers to Questions set at Chapter
Ends
Comprehensive Answers to Questions set
at Chapter Ends
Comprehensive Answers to Progress Tests
Notes on How to Study, Effective Study
and Examination Technique
Auditing standards, Guidelines, Case Studies,
Questions without answers

The author is Senior lecturer in Accounting at the Polytechnic, Wolverhampton.

Note to Lecturers: Answer Supplement available (see inside front cover of catalogue).

480 pages: 1981: ISBN 0 905435 21 4